Emergence and Change in Early Urban Societies

FUNDAMENTAL ISSUES IN ARCHAEOLOGY

Series Editors: Gary M. Feinman and T. Douglas Price
Department of Anthropology
University of Wisconsin–Madison

Editorial Board: Ofer Bar-Yosef, *Harvard University* • Christine Hastorf, *University of California–Berkeley* • Jeffrey Hantman, *University of Virginia* • Patty Jo Watson, *Washington University* • Linda Manzanilla, *Universidad Nacional Autónoma de México* • John Parkington, *University of Capetown* • Klavs Randsborg, *University of Copenhagen* • Olga Soffer, *University of Illinois* • Matthew Spriggs, *Australian National University* • John Yellen, *National Science Foundation*

EMERGENCE AND CHANGE IN EARLY URBAN SOCIETIES
Edited by Linda Manzanilla

FOUNDATIONS OF SOCIAL INEQUALITY
Edited by T. Douglas Price and Gary M. Feinman

A Continuation Order Plan is available for this series. A continuation order will bring delivery of each new volume immediately upon publication. Volumes are billed only upon actual shipment. For further information please contact the publisher.

Emergence and Change in Early Urban Societies

Edited by

LINDA MANZANILLA
Universidad Nacional Autónoma de México
Mexico City, Mexico

PLENUM PRESS • NEW YORK AND LONDON

Library of Congress Cataloging in Publication Data

Emergence and change in early urban societies / edited by Linda Manzanilla.
   p. cm.—(Fundamental issues in archaeology)
   Includes bibliographical references and index.
   ISBN 0-306-45494-7
   1. Cities and towns, Ancient. 2. Urbanization—History. 3. Extinct cities. I. Manzanilla, Linda. II. Series.
HT114.E44 1997
307.76′09′01—dc20
                                                        96-41911
                                                            CIP

ISBN 0-306-45494-7

© 1997 Plenum Press, New York
A Division of Plenum Publishing Corporation
233 Spring Street, New York, N. Y. 10013

10 9 8 7 6 5 4 3 2 1

All rights reserved

No part of this book may be reproduced, stored in a retrieval system, or transmitted in any form or by any means, electronic, mechanical, photocopying, microfilming, recording, or otherwise, without written permission from the Publisher

Printed in the United States of America

To Víctor Manzanilla

Contributors

Kathryn A. Bard • Department of Archaeology, Boston University, 675 Commonwealth Avenue, Boston, Massachusetts 02215, U.S.A.

David L. Browman • Department of Anthropology, Washington University in St. Louis, Campus Box 1114, One Brookings Drive, St. Louis, Missouri 63130-4899, U.S.A.

Marcella Frangipane • Dipartimento di Scienze Storiche, Archeologiche e Antropologiche dell'Antichità, Università di Roma "La Sapienza," Via Palestro 63, 00185 Roma, Italy

William H. Isbell • Department of Anthropology, State University of New York at Binghamton, Binghamton, New York 13902-6000, U.S.A.

Arthur A. Joyce • American Museum of Natural History, Central Park West at 79th Street, New York, New York 10024-5192, U.S.A.

Linda Manzanilla • Instituto de Investigaciones Antropológicas, Universidad Nacional Autónoma de México, UNAM-Cd. Universitaria, 04510 México D.F., México

James Edward Mathews • Field Museum of Natural History, Roosevelt Road at Lake Shore Drive, Chicago, Illinois 60605, U.S.A.

Miguel Rivera Dorado • Departamento de Antropología y Etnología de América, Facultad de Geografía e Historia, Universidad Complutense, Ciudad Universitaria, Madrid 28040, España

Walburga Wiesheu • Escuela Nacional de Antropología e Historia, Periférico y Zapote s/n, Delegación Tlalpan, México D.F. 14030

Preface

This book gives an overview of different factors involved in the emergence and change in early urban societies in fourth-millennium Mesopotamia and Egypt; pre-Shang China; Classic horizon Central Mexico, Oaxaca, and the Maya Area; and Middle Horizon societies in the Andean Region.

These factors range from centralized storage and redistributive economies, agromanagerial models, mercantile network control, conflict and conquest, conversion of military commanders into administrators, political power through monumental cosmic reproduction, and elite power through ideological change. It discusses specific archaeological data useful in theoretical construction.

In the Introduction, a discussion of different developmental processes of urban societies is made. The Eastern Anatolian example emphasizes the role played by interregional exchange networks linking the Mesopotamian plains with the Syro-Anatolian regions. The emergence of an elite is related with the control of the movement of craft goods and raw materials, more than with the appropriation of subsistence goods. The Chinese example stresses the importance of conflict provoked by demographic pressures on resources.

The Mesoamerican cases relate to vast urban developments and manufacturing centers, ideological importance of monumental planning, and changing behavior of elites.

The Andean cases are related either to the transformation of theocratic leadership into military administrators or to the agricultural intensification model.

These papers were presented in a preliminary version in a symposium entitled "Emergence and Change in Early Urban Societies" at the XIII International Congress of Anthropological and Ethnological Sciences in Mexico City, July–August 1993. The different cases were selected to give a full vision of different models and sets of data. Students and scholars interested in comparative studies of early urban societies will be attracted to debate these examples.

I thank the participants and audience of this symposium, as well as all of the contributors of this volume for the requested revisions. Finally, I also thank the editors of the series *Fundamental Issues in Archaeology*, Gary Feinman and T. Douglas Price, as well as the editor at Plenum, Eliot Werner, for their enthusiasm and support.

Contents

PART I. INTRODUCTION

Chapter 1 • Early Urban Societies: Challenges and Perspectives 3

Linda Manzanilla

An Apology for Redistributive Society in Mesopotamia 5
The Egyptian Case 15
The Andean Region 17
The Basin of Mexico 21
References 27

PART II. OLD WORLD

Chapter 2 • Arslantepe-Malatya: External Factors and Local Components in the Development of an Early State Society 43

Marcella Frangipane

Introduction 43
Arslantepe in Eastern Anatolia 46
    Monumental Architecture 47
    Administrative System 49
    Pottery Production 54
Conclusions 55
References 57

Chapter 3 • Urbanism and the Rise of Complex Society and the Early State in Egypt 59

Kathryn A. Bard

Introduction 59
Urbanism in Dynastic Egypt 61
Archaeological Evidence of Predynastic Settlements 63
    Upper Egypt 63
    Middle Egypt 70
    Lower Egypt, Cairo Region 71
    Lower Egypt, the Delta 74
Discussion 76
References 79

Chapter 4 • China's First Cities: The Walled Site of Wangchenggang in the Central Plain Region of North China 87

Walburga Wiesheu

Introduction 87
The Site of Wangchenggang 91
Other Henan Longshan Sites 96
Conclusions 101
References 104

PART III. NEW WORLD

Chapter 5 • Teotihuacan: Urban Archetype, Cosmic Model 109

Linda Manzanilla

Introduction 109
Teotihuacan 110
    Strategic Site 110
    A Great Demographic Concentration 110
    Monumentality 111
    Urban Planning 113
    Manufacturing Center 120
    Redistributive Center 121
    Political Capital 121
    Sacred Capital 122

A Diachronic View 125
References 127

Chapter 6 • Ideology, Power, and State Formation in the Valley of Oaxaca 133

Arthur A. Joyce

Introduction 133
Theoretical Background 135
   An Actor-Based Approach to Social Change 136
   Ideology, Power, and Inequality 138
Late/Terminal Formative Period Social Change in the
   Valley of Oaxaca 140
   Inequality 140
   Heterogeneity 145
The Consolidation of Power at Monte Albán 148
   Reciprocal Power 148
   Coercive Power 149
   Ritual and Ideological Power 150
   Militarism and Ideological Power 153
   Ideology and Power at Monte Albán 157
Conclusions 158
References 160

Chapter 7 • Clues to the System of Power in the City of Oxkintok 169

Miguel Rivera Dorado

Introduction 169
The Site of Oxkintok 175
Conclusions 178
References 179

Chapter 8 • Reconstructing Huari: A Cultural Chronology for the Capital City 181

William H. Isbell

Introduction 181
The Huari Site 186
   Churucana Phase 189
   Vista Alegre Phase 191

Quebrada de Ocros Phase................................ 194
Moraduchayuq Phase 199
Royac Perja Phase 208
Provincial Huari Architecture 209
Conclusion 214
Postscript.. 216
Appendix: Outline of Architectural Changes at Huari, by Phase..... 217
References... 221

Chapter 9 • Political Institutional Factors Contributing to the Integration of the Tiwanaku State 229

David L. Browman

Introduction 229
Cochabamba Valley, Bolivia.................................. 231
Oruro, Central Altiplano, Bolivia 232
Sillumocco, South Puno, Peru 233
San Pedro de Atacama, North Chile Region II 233
Azapa, North Chile Region I................................. 234
Moquegua, Peru 236
Tiwanaku Core 237
Summary Remarks 239
References... 241

Chapter 10 • Population and Agriculture in the Emergence of Complex Society in the Bolivian *Altiplano*: The Case of Tiwanaku........................ 245

James Edward Mathews

Introduction 245
The Tiwanaku Valley: Environment and Ecology................ 247
Results and Discussion 249
Summary of Field Data..................................... 249
   The Formative Period: 1350 B.C.–A.D. 100 249
   Formative Tiwanaku 253
   Tiwanaku IV: A.D. 375–750............................... 255
   Tiwanaku V: A.D. 750–1000 257
   The Post-Tiwanaku Period................................ 259
Testing the Models 263
   The Vertical Archipelago................................. 263
   The *Altiplano* Model of Production 263
   Agricultural Production.................................. 264

The Archipelago Model 264
The *Altiplano* Model 265
The Autochthonous Model 266
Summary 267
References 268

PART IV. CONCLUSION

Chapter 11 • Recapitulation and Concluding Remarks 275
Linda Manzanilla

Index 287

Part I

Introduction

Chapter **1**

Early Urban Societies
Challenges and Perspectives

LINDA MANZANILLA

Many pages have been written on the topic of the emergence of urban organizations, complex societies, and early states (*i.e.* Adams 1960, 1966, 1973; Armillas 1968; Athens 1977; Blanton 1976; Braidwood and Willey 1962; Carneiro 1970; Childe 1971, 1973; Claessen 1984a, 1984b, 1989; Claessen and Skalník 1978; Cohen and Service 1978; Doxiadis 1968; Flannery 1972; Fried 1967, 1974; Friedman 1975; Gledhill and Larsen 1982; Hardoy 1964; Hourani 1970; Jones and Kautz 1981; Kowalewski 1990; Krader 1968, 1975, 1979; Kraeling and Adams 1960; Kroeber 1953; Marcus 1983; Mumford 1970; Price 1979; Renfrew 1975, 1977; Ribeiro 1976; Rowlands 1989; Sanders and Webster 1978; Schädel 1968; Service 1975; Sjoberg 1973; Steward 1955, 1972; Terray 1975; Trigger 1972; Webster 1975, 1976; Wheatley 1971; Whitehouse 1977; Wittfogel 1970, 1974, 1976; Wolf 1990; Wright 1977a, 1977b, etc.).

Archaeological research is only beginning to properly analyze change in these societies. This book attempts to address these issues in the light of particular early examples of urban formations. In reviewing some aspects of organizational types leading to complex societies, we would like to point out some issues that can be relevant to the subject of this book. Redistributive organizations, particularly for facing productive disturbances and hazards, will be emphasized.

LINDA MANZANILLA • Instituto de Investigaciones Antropológicas, Universidad Nacional Autónoma de México, Cd. Universitaria, Circuito Exterior, México D.F. 04510, México.
Emergence and Change in Early Urban Societies, edited by Linda Manzanilla. Plenum Press, New York, 1997.

We are aware that there are many processes towards complex societies that do not involve chiefdom organizations, as Sanders and Webster (1978) pointed out. Yet the examples we will review in this book have issues that may promote revision on this orgnizational form.

Neale (1957:223) studied the case of the Oudh in XVIIIth century India, a society that is reciprocal in services and redistributive in agricultural production. Each villager (*i.e.*, in the Gonda village) participates in the division of the grain mounds. Due to the fact that Gonda was a only a part of a vast kingdom, this kind of village redistribution was the lowest in a hierarchy of redistributive centers, in which the storehouses of the governors and those of the king were placed in the highest levels (Neale 1957:227). Thus, the social pattern of redistribution is characterized by centrality: peripheric points are all connected with the center, and the redistribution of grain constitutes the foundation of political authority.

Renfrew (1974) proposed two types of chiefdoms: the individualizing chiefdom (investment in status defining elements) and the group-oriented chiefdom (investment in corporate labor). This division is useful for distinguishing between a hierarchical society, where a chief occupies the highest point in a hierarchy of lineages due to his nearness to the common godlike ancestor, and thus the head of the *aristoi*, as Kirchhoff (1955:6-9) stated for the "conical clan", from an organization derived perhaps from "lineage societies" (Meillassoux 1974; Rey 1975), where a group of elders represents the authority in the community (Manzanilla 1983:6). In both cases, redistributive activites may be found.

For example, the Gouro elders centralize foodstuff, such as rice, or those derived from hunting and gathering, and store them in storehouses under their control. In collective meals, these products are redistributed to the members of the community, to some kin in neighboring villages, and occasionally to people passing by. Only a small fraction is exchanged (Meillassoux 1974:188-189).

A variant is represented by the Sonjo, also in Africa (Gray 1974). Gray has observed that the hereditary elders' council obtains goats, honey or grain from the members of the community in exchange for irrigation water rights. What is stored is devoted to ritual or to redistribution (Gray 1974:236-237).

A further case would be complex chiefdoms in Hawaii where, following Earle (1977:218, 225), the redistributive hierarchy was directed to finance political activities of the elite. In these cases, redistribution does not emerge from economic specialization of communities, as Service stated, but rather from the massive mobilization of goods, and periodic ceremonial concentrations, directed by the elite. I would argue this example would fit our concept of asymmetrical redistribution (Manzanilla 1983) that will be developed further on.

Another element that should be taken into consideration is Dalton's (1977:194) statement that in clans corporate descent groups are religious units centered in common ancestors, heroic founders or divine spirits, to which the group thanks abundance, victory or health through seasonal offerings or sacrifices in times of crisis. This corporate units are visible in cases where group-oriented chiefdoms or collective political leaderships occur. For example, we agree with Maisel (1990:112, 114) in the idea that Chalcolithic societies in Mesopotamia could have been the origin of augmented corporate households, called *é* in Sumerian, recognizable in T-shaped multiroom structures since the Samarra culture. I would add that they could also have been religious units, that would further on become the center of the so-called "temple communities", when the elders' council was converted into institucionalized priesthood. In Classic Teotihuacan, central Mexico, a similar process could be mentioned (Manzanilla 1993a).

Without coming into the polemic of the non-universality of redistributive economies in certain levels of integration of society (see Earle 1991; Blanton, Kowalewski, Feinman, and Finsten 1993:19), we would like to argument in favor of an archaeological example where the different stages of redistributive organization are present.

AN APOLOGY FOR REDISTRIBUTIVE SOCIETY IN MESOPOTAMIA

Elsewhere (Manzanilla 1983, 1985a, 1986a, 1987a, 1987b, 1991a, 1993a) have I proposed that one of the main characteristics of the Mesopotamian process of early urban formation is the existence of a redistributive and complex administrative system centered in the temple organization. This first type of organization would be responsible for the development of organized centralization of economic surplus in storage facilities, the presence of full-time specialists (particularly in the manufacturing sector), the auspice of a long-distance exchange network undertaken by temple emissaries, and the appearance of complex administrative systems.

I consider an urban society as one with complex division of labor, that is, the existence of specialists in activities different from the production of subsistence goods; with institutions that coordinate economic processes; and finally, with specialists in decision-making that live in an urban center providing specific services to the surrounding region, such as the distribution of a large variety of goods. During the Ubaid and Uruk phases of

Mesopotamian prehistory, we see the emergence of these demographic centers around ceremonial cores.

Another consideration is that urban developments and states are not always coterminous and contemporaneous processes. A territorial tributary state is an entity with relatively precise demarcation of frontiers, conquest as a form of territorial appropriation, coercive institutions to maintain the tributary organization, and the first clear indications of accumulation of wealth in the palace organization (Manzanilla 1987a).

In Mesopotamia we have a clear example of the historicity of these two organizational forms. I will briefly review the different stages of the process.

Childe (1964:29-31; 1968; 1973:48) stated that with the "Urban Revolution", irrigation agriculture allowed the extraction of a vast social surplus by the temple or the king, and that after its storage, it was channeled to the maintenance of a number of resident specialists, detached from food production, as well as to foreign raw materials procurement. Hole (1974) stated that occupational specialization in subsistence activities in the Near East was related to the uneven distribution of resources; redistribution would be en efficient way to diversify diet.

Redistributive organizations seem to be present since the Neolithic horizon (sixth and fifth millennia B.C.) in northern Mesopotamia, where we find settlements (such as Umm Dabaghiyah, Hassuna, or Yarim Tepé) with central sectors occupied by rows of small rooms that served as storehouses for meat and grain (Kirkbride 1973:207, Plate I; Oates 1972; Merpert and Munchaev 1969). Due to the fact that there is no control institution yet detected, we have pointed out the possibility that a situation similar to present "lineage societies" occurred (Meillassoux 1974; Rey 1975:65-67): the elders' council would have been the organism devoted to communal tasks such as the organization of irrigation works and the redistribution of the communal produce stored in the center of the village to all members that contributed to it, in what we call a "circular redistributional circuit" (Manzanilla 1983:7, 1987a:278).

When the temple appears in Ubaid times, it seems to inherit and expand the above-mentioned network, and by Uruk times it is converted into an asymmetrical flow, deviating some of the stored production for the maintenance of craftsmen and bureaucrats, and also for long-distance exchange (Manzanilla 1983, 1987a). Thus, it was possible for Mesopotamian temple administrators to obtain all the raw materials (rocks, minerals, and metals) nonexistent in their territory but necessary for the production of the most essential tools, as well as for sumptuary goods.

Algaze (1993:2-4) has pointed out that periods of centralization in the alluvium were preceded by an increase in resource procurement, and were followed by expansion processes to control critical trade routes. He further points out that asymmetrical exchange relationships with the Mesopotamian periphery would have unleashed pressures leading toward new orders in peri-Mesopotamian regions, allowing for improved storage and distribution facilities, for for more complex administrative structures, and for ritual displays to validate changes in social relationships. We nevertheless believe that redistributive modules in Uruk times were efficient cellules of economic organization that were transposed to periferical areas, such as Eastern Anatolia as we shall see further on, processes that should not only be considered as pressures on peripherical societies.

In this respect we should evoke Redman's (1978:335) positive feedbacks:population growth within a circumscribed productive region, specialized food production by different units within society, and foreign raw materials needed for utilitarian purposes. Redman agrees that the new integrating mechanisms needed to cope with social tension created by demographic nucleation in early cities was fulfilled by the administrative elite associated with the temple and promoted through redistribution, rituals and social sanctions (Redman 1978:337-338).

Thus in regions with homogeneous and relatively limited resources, such as the Mesopotamian or the Maya Lowlands, asymmetrical redistribution would serve as a means to supply nonexistent raw materials. Flannery and Coe (1972) have also proposed that in the Maya Lowlands, maize produced by peasants was channeled to the regional center, to be redistributed to those lineages supplying services: bureaucrats, artisans, lapidaries, stone-cutters, and so forth.

In the fifth and fouth millennia B.C., Lowland Mesopotamia is the scene of the appearance of temple buildings in the largest settlements. These are characterized by a tripartite plan, consisting of a central sanctuary, surrounded by lines of storage rooms. They are particularly notable in the site of Uruk-Warka during the Late Uruk-Jemdet Nasr Period (3200-2900 B.C.)(Nissen 1972:794).

In bordering areas, such as Eastern Anatolia—rich in raw materials (such as metals and obsidian)(Palmieri 1989; Frangipane and Palmieri 1987, 1988/1989; Frangipane 1990-91, 1993)—we also see the appearance of administrative elites centered in temple complexes, which through a redistributive organization involving the flow of food rations from the temple storerooms, and the accounting of storage vessel contents as well as storehouse door openings by temple bureaucrats. The first appearance of complex metallurgy as part of the temple redistributive organization is an indicator of the consecuent auspice of craftsmen. This is also patent in pottery production, with the appearance of fast-wheeled mass-produced bowls to serve as containers for food rations in the redistributive system (Espinosa and Manzanilla 1985, Manzanilla 1986a, 1987b).

During the Early Dynastic at Sumer, the temple gradually collapses as the economic axis of society and this fact is contemporary with the appearance of the palace as a rival economic institution, concerning land, cattle, products, and centralization. The palace acquired the administrative functions of the temple, and although the goods in storage did not reach common people, as in the former sphere, they did form part of a closed circuit. The two institutions coexisted, but in the following Akkadian Period, a new kind of organization becomes clearly outlined, with the palace as the axis: the expansive and tributary state (Manzanilla 1979).

The main characteristics of this last organization are:

1. Tribute substitutes redistribution as the form of centralization of surplus production. Conquest assures the continuous flow of goods to the palace.

2. Another consequence of conquest is the emergence of the concept of wealth accumulation, in the form of war spoils, and in the adscription of marginal land. It can be said that, even though there are some cases of land lords rewarded with land, the basic property cell is the community (*calpulli, ayllu, nome*) which is the one that assigns land and tasks to its members. Then, this step marks the beginning of class societies and territorial tributary states.

3. A third element, in close relationship with the palace and its organization, is the market and the emergence of the independent merchant. Markets are institutions that come late in the process; they are created in close articulation with palace interests, as has been pointed out by Carrasco (1983). Since the Early Dynastic II in Mesopotamia, merchant groups associated with the palace stimulated popular demand for bronze weapons and luxury items (Adams 1973). In the Basin of Mexico, the *pochteca* substitute the older temple emmisaries.

4. As a consequence of the appearance of the market, in addition to the temple and palace craftsmen, one can also observe independent craftsmen, generally grouped in wards, exchanging their production freely.

Examples such as the Akkadian and the successive Babylonian and Assyrian empires belong to the same type of organization.

Polanyi (1957:250, 254) stated that redistribution designates movements toward a center and out of it again, and it is dependent upon the presence of some measure of centricity in the group. It occurs on all civilizational levels, from the hunting bands to vast storage system such as Egypt, Sumer, or Peru. It is "...apt to integrate groups at all levels and all degrees of permanence from the state itself to units of a transitory character" (Polanyi 1957:254).

To detect archaeological indicators of redistributive organizations we have proposed six analytical levels (Manzanilla 1987b):

1. *Centralized storage*, that is, the location of storage facilities beyond family needs, either in the center of a settlement, in or around a temple or inside a palace.

2. *The redistributive institution*. We have formerly proposed a transformation from elders' councils in lineage societies, to temple organizations particularly evident in Mesopotamia, and probably elsewhere, with a transformation of circular redistribution into an asymmetrical flow.

3. Types of goods redistributed. An analysis of warehouses and storage vessels could give us hints of what is flowing. Generally it is foodstuff (grain, bread, vegetables, fruit, grease and oil, fish, salted meat, etc.), but there are also mentions of fuel, whool, foreign raw materials, instruments, etc. For the temple at Khafajah, in central Mesopotamia, Frankfort (1951a:67) cites the storage of grain, sesame, onions, dates, beer, wine, salted or dried fish, grease, wool, skins.

4. *Who takes profit of the system*. In circular redistribution all who have participated in the collective concentration of goods receive their part. In asymmetrical redistribution during Uruk times, some of the people attending the sanctuary could receive foodstuff, but these stored items are destined also to the maintenance of bureaucrats, artisans, and servants of the temple, and some is also channeled to long-distance exchange.

For the Early Dynastic Period (*c.* 2900-2340 B.C.), there are tablets that enlist temple food rations consisting of bread and grain for different people (Frankfort (1951a:67; Wright 1969:42): persons who were participating in communal work, priests and other officials, and artisans. Some of the stored grain was kept for future agricultural cycles; another part went to feed temple flocks; another was channeled to the temple's brewery, bakery, and kitchen; and yet another was used for long-distance exchange of raw materials which were nonexistent in Mesopotamia (Frankfort 1951a:68, 72, 74). in Uruk times (but surely also during the Ubaid period) the temple was then the center of a redistributive circuit, that assured the maintenance of the temple officials as well as full-time artisans (particularly potters developing for the first time fast-wheel techniques to deal with the mass-production required by the redistribution of food rations, but surely also metallurgists).

5. *Forms of redistribution*. There are two main forms: the communal meals and the rationing system. The first one is represented archaeologically at Huánuco Pampa in Peru (Morris 1978), and the second is very well attested in Mesopotamian and Eastern Anatolian sites from the Late Uruk period onwards.

6. *Frequency*. Only with the concourse of written sources have we been able to know that in the first Sumerian cities there were daily rations of beer and bread, annual rations of whool and grease, and extraordinary

rations of dates, other fruit and legumes. For the Inca, state organized redistribution of foodstuff in the capital took place each four days.

An example will clarify all the issues involved in the analysis of mass-produced pottery as containers for redistributive purposes. As part of the Rome University Archaeological Mission at Arslantepé, my role was to excavate some of the storage buildings and to statistically analyze the volumes of the first coarse mass-produced bowls found related to centralized storage (Espinosa and Manzanilla 1995). These were produced by the first appearance of the fast-wheel in the Near East, and cutting the bottom with a string.

Two hypotheses were contrasted:

1. The first considers that the massive production of troncoconical bowls was directed to satisfy the needs of retribution and redistribution of central institutions. Thus, if the bowls are concentrated in discrete cathegories of volumes, they could perhaps represent rationing or measuring units for solid or liquid foodstuff, mainly grains.

2. The second one was proposed by Beale (1973) as part of a research on bevelled-rim bowls of the Late Uruk Period at Khuzistan. This author relates the bowls to the presentation of offerings to the temple institutions. He further states that they also indicate a change of offering items, from fish in the Ubaid Period, to grain during the Uruk Period, which can more easily be stored. They could thus show not standard capacities, but a variation spectrum with limits due to the process of production.

Using partition and hierarchical statistical methods, we began the analysis of the capacity of the first 52 bowls from the Early Bronze Age Uruk-like temple at Arslantepé. Four clear groups emerged:

1. Small bowls of 240 to 285 cubic centimeters.
2. Bowls with a broader range (from 360 to 550 cm^3).
3. Bowls up to 715 cm^3.
4. Large bowls with more than 2000 cm^3.

The variables which could have played a role in this variation would be:

a. Type of foodstuff offered or rationed and whether it was solid or liquid. Sargonic and Ur III texts of later date mention the rationing of liquids such as oil or beer in *sila* units of 840 cm.^{3}.

b. The social condition of he who received the ration or of who presents the offering
 – either sex and age, as mentioned by Neo-Babylonic texts,
 – or the social position of the person,

– or even the horizontal differentiation of society due to economic specialization.

c. A further variable would be the form in which the ration is measured. There would be two alternatives: either use the bowl as a measuring unit several times, or use it depending on its capacity, only once (Espinosa and Manzanilla 1985).

We also noted that the storerooms of the temple and the sanctuary itself (see Palmieri 1973) had examples of bowls belonging to groups 1, 2, and 3, but in different proportions.

The two windows that communicate the storerooms to the sanctuary, had three bowls belonging to groups 2 and 3. The largest ones could have housed bread, for example. According to the Neo-Babylonian ration system, group 1 would come close to a small-child's ration. Group 3 would be close to the ration for male sons. There is also the possibility that groups 2 and 3 were used several times to complete an adult's ration.

Making a correspondence between capacity units and weight of cereal in grain, of the four systems of the Near East—the Fenitian, the Egyptian, the Anatolian, and the Mesopotamian—only the Mesopotamian gets close to the groups we obtained for Arslantepé with statistical analysis.

We also analyzed bowl capacities from the other monumental buildings of Late Chalcolithic and Early Bronze Age times. The differences were that the Late Chalcolithic bowls were larger, with no presence of small bowls, as if fish could have been the main item redistributed. Then came a clear separation of two groups: the small ones and the large ones. And afterwards, the appearance of medium-sized bowls.

As we formerly stated, the repetition of the same redistributive and administrative system throughout Mesopotamia and also in peripheric resource-rich areas is a fact that underlines the importance of redistributive organizations in areas with uneven resource distribution, but also in regions where catastrophical events affecting production occurred. This fact will be followed in different examples outlined afterwards.

We want to fully stress that in Mesopotamia, the advantages of redistribution at a local scale were: to have a stored stock to face future harvests and eventualities in the agricultural cycle; to constitute a deposit of diversified goods coming from sectors specialized productively; to serve as a feeding basis for specialists not devoted to the production of foodstuff; and to constitute a material stock for long-distance exchange (Manzanilla 1985a).

At a vaster scale, Isbell (1978:306-307) would propose that in those areas where energetic perturbations were common, there were two alternatives: either to decrease the demographic or the organizational level of society, or to select in favor of progressively larger redistributive spheres. This latter alternative would have been chosen in the Central Andean region, and probably also in Classic Central Mexico. Fried (1974:30-31) adds that the advantages of redistribution would also lie not only in security in the face of adversities of food production, but also in the diversification of diet.

In the social realm, the greater the surplus, the greater the degree of stratification, as Hole (1974) stated. Thus, all the basic components of early urban life—surplus concentration, complex division of labor, long-distance exchange networks, and social stratification—could be explained through the analysis of the redistributive organization.

The Mesopotamian example is certainly one in which centralized storage is important to face energetic perturbations and climatic hazards. As Earle and Ericson (1977:10) pointed out, redistributive hierarchies as the dominant forms of regional organization may function as security mechanisms against natural and human hazards. So we will devote a part of this introduction to this relationship.

The first proto-Sumerian cities of the Lower Mesopotamian plain grew on ancient settlements near the great rivers, elevating their living sites more and more to protect them from floods. The Tigris and Euphrates regimes are erratic; changes in their courses provoked massive abandonment of settlements; catastrophic floods—one of which ravaged Baghdad in 1954 (Buringh 1957:37)—destroyed demographic clusters constructed with mudbricks. Flood strata observed in Kish, Shurrupak, and Ur (Raikes 1966:61-2) can be explained by meteorological and hydrological factors, as well as tectonics. Changes in exchange routes, so vital for Mesopotamia with respect to the supply of raw materials, also caused site abandonment.

These factors strongly affected the mentality of the inhabitants of Mesopotamia who, unlike the Egyptians, saw nature as a domain of constant and menacing changes. Furthermore the inhabitants of Mesopotamia could only occupy the southern portion of Iraq thanks to the use of irrigation techniques. The cultivated areas were located in the flood basins on both sides of the riverbanks. Yet, shifting channels created dendritic systems on their back slopes that cut minor depressions, inhibiting superficial drainage. This provoked a high level of salty phreatic water and the precipitation of salts on the surface. A part of these salts was brought by rivers and irrigation waters from sedimentary rocks in the mountainous, northern watershed. Another portion of the salts came from marine transgressions or was transported by aeolian agents from the Persian Gulf. When this water evaporated, calcium and magnesium were precipitated in form of carbonates, predominantly sodium. This tends to be absorbed by colloidal clay, resulting in a structureless soil, nearly impermeable to water. Salinization of soils was inevitable.

Three salinization phases have been monitored; the earliest from 2400 to 1700 B.C., which provoked the shift of the major centers of power from the south to the center of Iraq. The consequences of salinization led to the decline of wheat cultivation in the southern plain as this is least resistant to sodium. For a shorter time, barley, a more resistant crop, was the main plant grown, but even this declined and vast areas suffered desertification (Jacobsen and Adams 1958). The history of Sumer thus came to an end; a history so much based on urban life as a hallmark of civilization. The later history of the region is characterized by a new stage, a dimorphic state including both nomads and sedentary people (Rowton 1973).

From the viewpoint of climatic change, other factors were added to these anthropogenic and sociopolitical transformations. Recently a group of scholars, who have worked throughout the Near East, have assessed major climatic changes in the region. By the end of the third millennium B.C., a catastrophic collapse of Early Bronze Age societies from Turkey to India coincided with a severe shift towards a drier climatic era. Volcanic eruptions have also been detected in some regions. Lamentations of famine and drought characterize this epoch. Almost all the cities and towns in western Palestine were deserted (Rosen 1993). The decreased frequency and amount of rainfall changed the hydrological regime, eliminating the buffering effect of floodwater farming. Primary data for the study of this climatic change comes from pollen, paleolimnology, oxygen isotopes, and geomorphology (Rosen 1993). Evaporation and increased salt deposition, decline of oak pollen, *wadi* incision, and flooding of valley bottoms are some of the phenomena related to this change.

The main issue is why societies failed to adapt to the new situation. In the Near East, there are great fluctuations in precipitation, stream flow, and crop yield from year to year. Rosen (1993) cites some of the predictable measures: diversification of crops and herd animals, food storage, retention and distribution of information on famine foods, transformation of surplus food into non-perishable items of value that can be traded for food in times of stress, and extension of the social network to allow access to food resources from other regions. Rosen notes several factors that may explain why the agricultural sectors of Early Bronze III society failed to respond successfully to the climatic desiccation at the end of the period:

1. state control over surplus production,
2. non-diversification of subsistence crops,
3. loss of floodwater farming as a buffer; and
4. a slow response time on the part of elite managers.

The abrupt aridification of northern Mesopotamia between 2200 and 1900 B.C. has been well documented by Weiss (1993; Weiss *et al.* 1993) at Tell Leilan. The effects can be traced in the disruption of pastoral transhumance, a large scale population movement into southern Mesopotamia, and the peculiar military activities of the Third Dynasty of Ur. Weiss *et al.* (1993) argue that at 2200 B.C a considerable increase in aridity and wind circulation, subsequent to a volcanic eruption, induced degradation of land-use conditions: decreasing *per capita* yields, displacements of sedentary pastoralists from the Khabur region, the collapse of the Akkadian dry farming, further Akkadian imperial collapse in the south, the invasion of the Guti and Amorrites into southern Mesopotamia, and finally, collapse of Ur III intensive agriculture also in the south. Desertion of various sites was inevitable.

Archaeological indicators of aeolian deflation under drier conditions have also been registered by Courty (1993), who shows that sequential pedostratigraphic deposits from archaeological sites in northern Mesopotamia, dated by ceramic chronology and radiometry, provide micromorphological evidence for abrupt wind, temperature, and humidity changes coincident with the abandonment of sedentary urban settlements. Furthermore, the climatic shift, documented about 2000 B.C., has also been detected in the Rajakhstan lake pollen sequences, near the heartland of the Indus civilization in Pakistan, and related to salinization and the collapse of the Harappan civilization (Possehl 1993). In the Aegean region, the rise of Minoan palaces apparently coincided with climatic and geomorphological changes, as well as with soil erosion and the cultural dislocation of late third-millennium societies B.C. (Manning 1993).

Redistributive organizations were effective in coping with productive contingencies in the first phases of temple-based centralized organizations. As we have seen, in later periods the inexistence of buffer productions, the over-emphasis in monocrops, as well as slowness in managerial response led to an increasing vulnerability.

There are other areas of the world with more diversified resources that the Mesopotamian lowlands, where there are two options for Formative communities:

a) The "economic symbiosis" model (proposed by Sanders 1968:100), where communities located in different altitudinal positions specialize productively and cooperate intercommunally, having a distribution center where all the surplus is exchanged—a model that could be applied to Formative Basin of Mexico and Oaxaca Valley.

b) The "vertical archipelago" model of ecological complementarity, proposed by Murra (1975, 1985a, 1985b) for the Andean Region, where each "ethnic group made an effort to control a maximum of floors and ecological niches" maintaining "permanent colonies situated in the periphery in order to control distant resources". The relations between center and periphery "were those that are called reciprocity and redistribution in economic anthropology" (Murra 1985b:15-16). We will review further on these two last.

With respect to redistributive organizations, we may say that in later organizations we find relicts of these centralized movements. For example, Carrasco (1982) and Broda (1976) have written about different cases in which the Aztec *tlatoani* opened his warehouses to give foodstuff to common people or insignia to the warriors. The degree to which centralized storage was incorporated to Aztec palace economy has been recently reviewed by Rojas (1987). The *Huey tlatoani* had warehouses not only in Tenochtitlan, but also in each provincial capital (Rojas 1987:31), as was the case in the Inca and Akkadian states. The historical sources also cite openings of the imperial storehouses to face catastrophes, such as the ones under Motecuhzoma, Nezahualcoyotl, and Totoquihuatzin (Rojas 1987:36).

Another example is that of the Inca State, where we can better study the relicts of redistribution in palace organizations. Scholars such as Morris (1978), Earle and D'Altroy (1982) and other have described storehouses in different Peruvian centers, particularly in the region of the provincial capital of Huánuco Pampa and in the Mantaro Basin. These warehouses, that Murra (1975) mentions are vital when there are frosts or drought, served also to maintain state personnel, the army, and all the people that participated in state activities. The deposits were located either inside the settlements or on mountain slopes, depending on the permanent or temporal character of the population (Earle and D'Altroy 1982). On the other hand, Morris (1978) mentions the fact that at Huánuco Pampa, the two open sectors or plazas were devoted to the elaboration and redistribution of chicha and other foodstuff.

Due to the persistence of the basic elements of the former redistributive stage, we could consider the Inca case as a transitional or complex example. An element that would support this idea is the lack of importance of markets and merchants inside the Inca Empire.

We will discuss the Andean region further on. Before this is done, some further notes on the Egyptian case.

THE EGYPTIAN CASE

The severe aridification that produced the Saharan desert, and also the Negev and Jordan deserts, during the sixth to fourth millennia B.C., strongly affected sedentary life by making it impracticable, except in sites where perennial water sources were present. The Saharan lacustrine basins of the Early Holocene were converted into oases surrounded by deserts, and the groups of fishermen, gatherers, hunters and herders were obliged to migrate to the only permanent source of water; namely the Nile river (Manzanilla 1982, 1985c, 1986b; Butzer 1995). Out of this fortunate confluence of groups of different origins, one of the most outstanding civilizations of ancient times, that of Egypt, emerged about 3000 B.C.

The mixing of groups of different origins gave rise to a heterogenous society in its beginnings, which soon became organized around a mixed economic base, focused on the cultivation of grain and leguminous plants, the breeding of cattle and pigs, the gathering of fruits, river fishing, and hunting of herbivores and aquatic fauna. The Nile was a key factor because it offered a unique system of hydrology, communication and settlement.

In Prehistoric times, elephants, wild cattle, antilopes, zebras, white rhinoceros, oryx, wild ass, ostrich, and giraffes roamed alluvial grazing lands, *wadis*, and desertic plateaus. Analyzing rupestral, low relief, and figurine representations, Butzer showed a first faunal discontinuity around 3500 B.C., with the rarefaction and further disappearance of elephant and giraffe from the Nile Valley around 2700-2500 B.C. (Leclant and Huard 1980:25). Wilson (1964) characterized Egypt as a civilization without cities, due to the fact that population was never congregated into large demographic aggregates, as in the case of Mesopotamia, but was more or less homogeneously distributed along the Nile margins.

Unlike Mesopotamia, Egypt had mineral resources in the Eastern and Western Deserts that directly bordered the Nile Valley. From the earliest periods, Egypt turned inwards, displaying a sense of selfsufficiency and security, as a land of cosmic equilibrium, governed by a god on earth. As lord of Upper and Lower Egypt, the pharaoh was the repository of a dual monarchy, an expression of a peculiar Egyptian manner of understanding the world in dual terms, that is, in terms of a series of pairs of balanced contrasts, in an unchangeable equilibrium: valley-delta, agricultural land-desert, heaven-earth, east bank-west bank of the Nile (Manzanilla 1991b).

While in Mesopotamia the wide open plain resulted in separatist tendencies, in Egypt the unification of the pharaonic state was a relatively easy undertaking due to the monosystemic character of the Nile Valley. While Mesopotamia was an easy prey for invading groups, Egypt had natural desert frontiers that isolated the area.

The lack of true urban centers in Egypt removed the contrast of rural and urban sectors that was so characteristic of Mesopotamia. Information flow along the Nile, between the central government and the provincial administrations, favoured a network of relationships without cities, which were in part unnecessary due to the absence of market exchange.

Centralized storage is also present in the pharaonic state, particularly in the dual storehouses of the central palace: the storehouse of Upper Egypt and that of Lower Egypt. The pharaoh opened these warehouses when calamities came about. Of the very scarce data on Pre- and Protodynastic sites, we may cite the disposition of functional sectors at Ma'adi: the houses are located in the center of the settlement, great storage jars in the north, and semi-subterranean storage areas in the south (Vandier 1952:518). Hoffman (1980:154) considers this site as a manufacturing and mercantile center, and Baumgartel (1955), as a center of diffusion of Palestinian elements and of provision of copper and turquoise from the Sinai.

Bard (1993) proposed that the first state collapse in Egypt, during the late third millennium B.C., was related to climatic change, possibly exacerbated by the socio-political pathologies of the Old Kingdom. "Given a greatly increased population during the Old Kingdom, lower agricultural productivity as a result of disastrously low Nile floods and less floodplain land under cultivation caused widespread famine and anarchy" (Bard 1993). The collapse of centralized control provoked political fragmentation. Butzer (1976, 1984) has also re-examined various texts that refer to catastrophically low Niles between 2200 and 3000 B.C. As Malek (1986:120) has stated, "The worsening climatic conditions, in particular repeated low Niles, would have been a serious blow to Egypt's economy... The area of fields under cultivation diminished, the size of the harvest decreased, and the numbers of livestock were reduced."

Of course this was only one factor within a more complex process of social and political disintegration, that included the collapse of centralized authority and administration, the gradual shift in the ownership of land from the central authority to cult and temple establishments, Egypt's inability to maintain its influence outside its borders (Malek 1986), the social revolution that preluded the First Intermediate Period (Castañeda Reyes 1992), and so forth. As Malek states, "The worsening of climatic conditions, unfortunately, came at a time when Egyptian administration was no longer in a position to react, and so it delivered the decisive blow."

THE ANDEAN REGION

One of the phenomena that has attracted attention with regard to past global changes is the Southern Oscillation of El Niño (ENSO). El Niño events, whose impact affects the Pacific coast, caused severe problems for Peruvian pre-Inca societies; either disasterous droughts or catastrophic rains. Since the Formative Horizon in the Cupisnique Valley of Peru, there is evidence for strong El Niño events, with consequent changes in subsistence and settlement patterns. Domestic middens dated between 1300 and 300 B.C. have been analyzed; tropical molluscs, crustaceans, and fish were associated with warm water incursions. The consequent effects on the biological chains in the Peruvian cold current, and disturbances to the shore fishing technologies (Elera *et al.*, in Orlieb and Macharé 1992) were serious.

Later, the strong rains and floods had considerable effect on the Chimu agricultural system, so that intensive cultivation strategies were adopted, particularly raised-fields (Moore 1991:42). In coastal Peru, El Niño events reduced mollusk populations that constituted the main source of protein for Prehispanic states. Other responses of the Chimu state were the construction of irrigation systems in the Moche Valley and the agricultural expansion into other coastal valleys (Moore 1991). Flood strata are found in some coastal sites of northern Peru, such as Batán Grande, from Chimu times (Moseley 1987:9). Craig and Shimada (1986) correlate a catastrophic El Niño event with these sediments and with ethnohistorical narrations in which the end of the Naymlap dynasty is related to strong rains and catastrophic floods.

Urban phenomena in the Andean Region developed in two regions, the Peruvian valleys and coast, on the one hand, and the Bolivian high plateau, on the other. In the Peruvian valleys, different ecological and altitudinal floors were exploited by the same community due to the autarchic organization of communities. Thus, access to resources from the tropical forest, from the high valleys, and from the coast, was obtained by means of colonies, without the participation of markets. Thus, with some exceptions, there were no real urban centers in these valleys.

The Bolivian high plateau is exceptional for various reasons: Lake Titicaca allowed intensive cultivation in raised fields, a system probably inaugurated by the pre-Inca civilization of Tiwanaku (Kolata 1986) in response to climatic change. There also were copper mines, a fact that favored the emergence of metallurgic centers. Unlike the Peruvian valleys, the Bolivian high plateau is a vast open area that housed the first urban phenomenon, the Tiwanaku civilization, the capital city of which had an area of 400 hectares (Ponce Sanginés 1981). Like the Mesoamerican urban centers, it housed non-farmer specialists.

Our recent research at Tiwanaku has revealed massive human and camelid offerings at Akapana, the site's main pyramid, about A.D. 850/900 (Manzanilla 1992a). We have suggested that this ritual behaviour may have been related to a strong drought that Paulsen (1976:125-127) proposed between A.D. 500 and 1000 for the Andean Region. Recently, Ortloff and

Kolata (1993) have proposed a model to explain the disintegration of the Tiwanaku state, between A.D. 1100-1000. This model takes into consideration radical climate changes, evidence from the Quelccaya ice cap data, and also palynological records of Lake Titicaca. These record drought conditions which would have provoked the deterioration and ultimate abandonment of the Tiwanaku agricultural systems (Ortloff and Kolata 1993:195). On the other hand, Browman (1993) and others have disputed the coincidence between drought conditions and the collapse of civilization.

Thompson *et al.* (1985) presented 1500 years of paleoclimatic information from two ice cores from the summit of the Quelccaya ice cap in southern Peru. Annual variations have been identified by the study of visible dust layers, oxygen isotopes, microparticle concentrations, conductivity, and the identification of historical ash layers (Thompson *et al.* 1986). These cores provide "...information on general environmental conditions including droughts, volcanic activity, moisture sources, temperature, and glacier net balance". The records indicate extended dry periods between A.D. 1200 and 1260, that may have begun between A.D. 520 and 560 (Thompson *et al.* 1985).

In the Andean case, the frequent incidence of climatic disturbances associated with the El Niño phenomenon or with broader climatic changes appear to have provoked changes in settlement patterns, demographic rearrangements, changes in food practices, architectural reconstructions, adoptions of flood control technologies, and agricultural intensification, as well a ideological changes. Lumbreras (1987) proposed that the ritual exchange of the *Spondylus princeps* bivalve (also known as *mullu*, in *quechua*), a mollusk directly related to the warm El Niño currents, served as a climatic indicator to determine rain and drought cycles. The Andean oracle priests used the *mullu* and the observatories as prediction instruments.

John Murra has stated that "when cultivation made its appearance, the calendrical cycle allowed the pooling and redistribution of distinct and geographically sepate resources" (Murra 1987:10). Lumbreras (1987:336-337) has detected from Chavin times onwards (the second half of the second millennium B.C.), new types of public constructions devoted not only to cult purposes, but also to warehouse operations, workshop production, and star observations. Similar complexes are found along the Marañón Andes. Thus, we find here the first hints of archaeological data that supports the existence of an asymmetrical redistributive network, centered in the temple.

In the "vertical archipelago" model, the type of exchange between the highland settlements and its low valley colonies would be reciprocal, and the rights would be claimed through kinship ties, and "periodically reaffirmed ceremonially in the settlements of origin" (Murra 1985b:16).

Ramiro Condarco Morales (in Murra 1985a:6) thought that this type of complementarity generated interrelationships and solidarity that formed the basis of the total unification of the Central Andes by Tiwanaku or the Incas. John Murra (1985b:11) adds that complementarity prevailed in times when there were no marketplaces but many state-operated warehouses and was an excellent means to handle "a multiple environment, vast populations, and hence high productivity"; the key aspect of highland economies being massive storage (Murra 1985:4).

During Inca times, we have archaeological and ethnohistorical evidence with respect to storage facilities. These warehouses are vital when there are continuous frosts or droughts, but also served to maintain state personnel, the army, and state craftsmen (Murra 1975). The deposits were located either inside the settlements or on the mountain slopes (Earle and D'Altroy 1982).

Morris (1978) and Isbell (1978) have detected a difference in the number of warehouses with respect to the site hierarchy and also different products being stored in deposits having either circular or rectangular forms. At Huánuco Pampa—a provincial capital— Morris (1978) detected 497 warehouses constructed and administered by the state, which served to maintain the population of the settlement. He also excavated 40 workshops and 10 related constructions destined to textile production—a key element for reciprocal relations between the Inca (the state) and the people from the communities—and to *chicha* preparation and consumption. In two large plazas located near the public sector of Huánuco Pampa, tons of ceramic vessel fragments were found associated with these activities, and Morris observed that the ceramic production was standardized.

This example is parallel to the Mesopotamian one. Yet, the Andean case differs in the form that redistribution takes place: collective meals versus food rations (Manzanilla 1991a:46). In either process, there is a need for standardized pottery, and thus potters were one of the cathegories of craftsmen that the redistributional circuit sponsored.

When reviewing pre-Inca data on large urban developments, we come necessarily to Tiwanaku, in the Bolivian *altiplano*, where redistribution may have been a key element of the economy.

In recent extensive excavations at the main temple of Tiwanaku (the pyramid of Akapana), we have detected not only cult constructions on its summit, but also multiroom complexes probably devoted to priestly domestic and storage functions (Manzanilla and Woodard 1990; Manzanilla, Barba, and Baudoin 1990; Manzanilla 1992a). Redistributive activities could have been carried out by the priests, involving not only local foodstuff but also goods coming from colonies on the coast and in the tropical sectors to the east of the high plateau (*Chione undatella* clam shells, tropical Sapotaceae or Sapindaceae fruits, etc.).

As in the Mesopotamian examples, this redistributive organization may have also sponsored the maintenance of priests, bureaucrats, and craftsmen, as well as caravan long-distance trade. Further details on this policy will be described in the two last articles of this book.

THE BASIN OF MEXICO

The "economic symbiosis" model could well account for the situation in the Basin of Mexico prior to the emergence of Teotihuacan. From Middle Formative times, we have cases—such as Loma Torremote—where centralized storing activities in the hands of specific households took place (Reyna Robles 1977). In Late Formative times, sites with monumental ceremonial architecture, such as Cuicuilco and Tlapacoya, could have been the distribution centers specified by Sanders' model, and I would add that probably the priests were the group who organized centralized storage.

The priest was certainly a central figure in Teotihuacan society. The frequency of priests' representations, particularly in mural art, is high. René Millon (1967:149-150), for example, states that priests played undoubltedly a very important role and that the integration of the city could have been possible through the pilgrimage-temple-market complex. He also states (Millon 1988:109) that the political realm was sacralized, without a formal differentiation between religious and political spheres. Teotihuacan was a religious center without equal in its time, a sacred city, the center of the cosmos, the place where time began (Millon 1988).

Sanders (1967:134) also argues that perhaps priestly institutions controlled alluvial and piedmont land and that religion was probably one of the most important integrative factors in Teotihuacan. I agree with the idea that the priest was surely the most important figure in the Teotihuacan hierarchy; if there had been secular groups who would have claimed a politically predominant position in society—in a way equivalent to the figure of a king, lord, or ruler—surely there would have been innumerable iconographic representations of them and a cult of the dynastic ruler, as Pasztory (1978:130) has argued for the Maya Lowlands and the Valley of Oaxaca during the Middle Classic period.

I would further propose that the Teotihuacan priesthood centralized the surplus production from communities of the central part of the Basin of Mexico, sponsored full-time craftsmen—probably obsidian workers, some potters who were producing standardized and ritual ceramic types, and sumptuary goods—and also emissaries who established different types of relations with foreign Mesoamerican regions (Manzanilla 1993a). This situation would not be very different from those reviewed formerly, except perhaps by the scale of the phenomenon, which would be closer to that of Tiwanaku that that of the proto-Sumerian centers.

When we review the floral and faunal subsistence data recovered from Teotihuacan excavations, we find that many products could have come from sectors of the Basin of Mexico other that the Teotihuacan Valley. We could cite, for example, lacustrine resources (turtles, fish, and water-fowl)(Starbuck 1987); fresh water snails, and a small rabbit (*Romerolagus diazi*) probably from the Chichinautzin or Nevada Sierras to the south of the Basin of Mexico (Valadez and Manzanilla 1988; Valadez in Manzanilla 1993b). McClung de Tapia (1987:58) shares the same idea with respect to paleobotanical macrofossils, stating that the Teotihuacanos imported basic products from a large sector of the Basin of Mexico.

Much of the subsistence base detected for the urban center of the Classic horizon was already present at Formative villages such as Cuanalan (1985b). I propose, then, that this diversified subsistence base could have been recreated on a larger scale during the Classic horizon, through a regional network of redistributive activities involving groups from different parts of the Basin of Mexico, who were offering their surplus to the Teotihuacan gods (and priests). This type of circulation is not proposed as an exclusive one; direct barter exchange between producers, foreign traders bringing some allochtonous manufactured goods, long-distance elite exchange between temple emissaries, could all have coexisted, involving different goods and social sectors. Yet, in this chapter, I would like to underline that the market would not have been an institution present at Teotihuacan (*contra* Millon 1973), as we shall propose further on.

The Temple of Agriculture's main mural painting at Teotihuacan (Gamio 1922, tomo I, lám. 33) could be one of the particular cases that could reinforce the existence of offering scenes, such as the ones depicted in Uruk period vases from Warka.

The problem of centralized storage of food and raw materials is one that deserves particular attention. In Mesopotamia, the warehouses are integrated architecturally with the sanctuary. In Formative Andean Region and in Mesoamerica, they should be searched for in the immediate vicinity of the ritual structures. I would think that, for example, the low standing row of rooms that closes the southern part of many three-temple complexes at Teotihuacan would be one possible place (Manzanilla 1993b:555-556). Another place would be the "administrative" and/or public constructions along the Street of the Dead.

In the Near East, the appearance of complex administrative activities was a by-product of the temple's redistributional economy. They are represented by seals and their respective clay sealings, tablets, and *bullae*. We do not know what are their counterparts in Central Mexican archaeology.

With respect to storage, one of the particular indicators that has been proposed for Teotihuacan is the concentration of San Martin Orange *amphorae*. Cowgill (1987) states that this type is particularly common in Xolalpan times (A.D. 350-650), specially in the southeastern sector where it is made, in the northwestern sector, where many apartment compounds surrounding three-temple plazas lie (Manzanilla 1993b), and in a band 300 m. to the west of the northern part of the Street of the Dead. For this last sector, I would propose that we could be dealing with centralized storage facilities.

With respect to the redistribution of food, a difference should be made between the regular maintenance of artisans and bureaucrats by the system and the occasional collective ritual meals. For the first case, I would propose that the production of standardized pottery would probably be an indicator. There is, however, little done in this field. If we used the Late Uruk example as suggestive, we should have to study the capacity of bowls in this perspective. Yet, I would also suggest that the handled covers whose distribution is said to be related to high-status architecture, could be another example.

I would invoke here Cowgill's (1967:176-183) original idea that these "covers" served to consume food at a certain distance from where it was prepared, with the possibility that this activity required reheating. If the priests and bureaucrats ate often from these or related vessels, their exceptionally high proportions near the Street of the Dead would be explained.

Yet these covers were not distributed only in high-status residences. They have been found also in clear intermediate-status domestic contexts, at my excavation in Oztoyahualco 15B:N6W3, together with copa vases, censers, Thin Orange pottery, incised ceramics, and other types that have been used as indicators of high status (Manzanilla 1993b).

Ideologically, the redistributional activities in the hands of the priest-administrators devoted to fertility cults would be reinforced by the reception of oblations granted by groups coming from different sectors of the Basin of Mexico and by the offering of communal meals and warehouse openings, such as the ones detected in two large plazas at Huánuco Pampa, Peru (Morris 1978). I would further suggest that the Great Compound at Teotihuacan, more than a market, would be the storage place for the different social sectors and probably also one of the main redistributional *locus* of the city. The regional interests that Sload (1987) invokes for her Great Compound apartment constructions could be precisely the storage of products from specialized sectors—particularly manufactures—and their further pooling into the redistributive network.

It is not by chance that the *Ciudadela* stands just in front of this place, being that ceremonialism is a way of reinforcing ideologically the prodigality of the gods (and their priests). The binome Great Compound and *Ciudadela* would be perhaps a functional one, regarding redistribution of manufactured items and ritual meals, respectively, and the administration of all the network.

Redistribution in the hands of priests could also be reiterated visually through the multiple representations of ritual officials from whose hands come out "falling panels" with *mantenimientos*: seeds, corn cobs, *Cucurbita* fruits and flowers, *tamales, tortillas,* cotton, sea shells, jadeite carvings, and so on (see Manzanilla and Carreón 1991; C. Millon 1973; Miller 1973). Not only in mural paintings, but also in theater censers are there depictions of priests from whose hands food and manufactured items flow.

The redistribution of exotic raw materials would be a restricted circulation circuit that we will mention when speaking of long-distance exchange.

With respect to obsidian workers, obviously not all the workshops depended on the redistributional network. Following Spence's classification (1987), only precinct workshops located near major public structures, and probably regional workshops, were under the priests' control. In the first case, the distribution of precinct workshops would be around the Moon Pyramid, in the Great Compound, and to the northeast of the *Ciudadela* (Spence 1987:434). Regional workshops were also located near major structures or major streets of the city. These would also be sponsored by the priests, to pool their products into the long-distance exchange network that they also controlled, as we will suggest further on.

Thus Spence's (1987:444) impression that the obsidian industry was "administered" and "highly centralized" would be explained by the fact that it was one of the main by-products of the redistributional circuit. And we should add that in his comparison between Classic and Postclassic obsidian industries, the last one is seen as much less centralized and in the hands of part-time specialists (Spence 1987), because it no longer was sponsored by the "temple sphere" and was no longer needed for middle-range exchange.

Certain potters would also be maintained by the system. One of the examples that could be cited is the large workshop of censers' molded parts found just to the north of the Ciudadela (Múnera Bermúdez 1985). Other Matte Ware workshops (for three-prong burners, censers, miniatures, *candeleros*, etc. as well as finely decorated wares) could also belong to this group.

The problem regarding the relationship between Teotihuacan and the rest of Mesoamerica is not a simple one to solve. A recent summary of current data and interpretations has been offered by Millon (1988). I agree with most of them. Yet, I would like to add some considerations on how the flow of exotic goods from regions such as the Maya Lowlands could be seen as a highly controlled movement.

First of all I should say that my model stipulated that there should be no market at Teotihuacan in the way we should expect it at Tlatelolco in Aztec times, nor should there be *pochteca*-like merchants. I am proposing that the high-status raw materials that came from abroad (cacao, shells, feathers, hides, honey, incense, copal, jadeite, serpentine, hematite, cinnabar, malachite, etc.) were all of them products that entered a restricted circulation circuit. Many were used directly in ritual of in conspicuous consumption. So there could have been a direct involvement of the priesthood in their supply.

I am proposing that it was through temple emissaries that the flow was controlled. In particular, four possible colonies could be cited, where Teotihuacan emissaries were perhaps living together with local populations: Matacapan, Kaminaljuyú, Tres Cerritos in Michoacán, and probably a malachite-procurement settlement near Alta Vista, Zacatecas. This type of colony reminds us of the ones established by Tiwanaku in the coastal and lowland valleys in the Central-South Andean Region (Moquegua, in the Peruvian coast, for example).

The tassel headdress that C. Millon (1973) proposes as a symbol of the Teotihuacan polity in foreign regions could be the basic characteristic of these emissaries. This same headdress is portrayed on priests' heads in different mural paintings. We should not be surprised that some of these persons are depicted with weapons in Maya contexts. Traveling so far from the Central Mexican Highlands would not have been an easy endeavor.

Let us speak of obsidian, for example. If Teotihuacan obsidian reached Tikal in such a small quantity (1%) and if it was surely not by marketplace exchange but rather by gift exchange among persons of high status (Sidrys 1977; Spence in Millon 1988:119), then we should think that one of the products that the Teotihuacan emissaries took with themselves was precisely obsidian in the form of prismatic cores and some bifacial products. Fine pottery would be another possibility.

A different circuit would be the one that involved products from the Oaxaca Valley and the Gulf Coast. The Oaxaca and Merchants' *Barrios* at Teotihuacan show goods that are not precisely high-status: pottery and some other manufactured items. Millon (1988:127) has recently asked himself whether these foreigners were really merchants. And even when addressing the subject of Teotihuacan merchants, he recognizes that there is nearly no information.

Barter between producers, foreign people bringing some allochtonous manufactured goods, redistributive networks to assure surplus concentration and craft patronage, long-distance elite exchange between temple emissaries—all are circuits that could have coexisted, involving different goods and social sectors.

Yet, we should not imagine this organization without conflicts. Rural-urban migration towards Teotihuacan was a massive phenomenon, probably exceeding the system's capacity for integrating groups of different origins and interests. There are also hints of conflict probably between groups of priests in what is called the "Mythological Animals' Mural", the change of serpent to jaguar iconography, but also in the dismanteling and covering of the Temple of the Feathered Serpent around A.D. 250.

Some of the causes that Millon (1988:149) evokes for the end of Teotihuacan were the following: a mismanagement of the economy and polity, a rigid inflexibility towards change, an inefficient and incompetent bureaucracy, and the deterioration of exchange networks. Naturally, the complexity of the articulation between all the circuits and social sectors that we have cited, and the enormous scale that the phenomenon adopted, was such that any factor could have broken this fragile equilibrium, where ideology was the main reinforcement agent. We see it also through a moment of great urban vulnerability, when a macroregional drought could have exceeded the system's capacity to manage it (Manzanilla 1992b,1993e, in press).

The changing conditions of the Epiclassic population readjustments, the emergence of palace lordly institutions as economic rivals of the temple sphere, the beginnings of a political realm separated from the religious one—all opened a new perspective in Mesoamerican history: one dominated by the tributary state of the Postclassic period.

The lacustrine basins of the Mexican Neovolcanic Axis are ideal scenarios for paleoclimatic studies and their effects on past human communities, as well as Man-induced environmental changes. Sedimentary series in the Pátzcuaro, Zacapu, Hoya de San Nicolás, Lerma, and Mexico basins have been successfully analyzed by Metcalfe *et al.* (1989, 1991; see also O'Hara 1993) to determine Quaternary climatic variations. Magnetic susceptibility, major cations, total phosphorous, carbon/nitrogen, carbon 13, oxygen 18, diatoms, pollen, and charcoal content have been quantified (Metcalfe *et al.* 1989, Metcalfe *et al.* 1991; Lozano-García 1989). In particular, disturbances have been observed that were due to the adoption of maize cultivation as the main subsistence strategy during the Preclassic Horizon (Metcalfe *et al.*, 1989). In Lake Texcoco of the Basin of Mexico, deforestation due to agricultural field preparation techniques determined the change from pine-oak forest communities to chenopodiaceae-amaranthaceae and grass communities. These were the first Man-induced changes in the peri-lacustrine environment, in Preclassic times.

None of the transformations was so critical as the impact of the urban growth of Teotihuacan. One of the major preindustrial examples of urban phenomena, Teotihuacan was a planned, multi-ethnic city, 20 square kilometers in area, serving as a manufacturing, exchange, and pilgrimage center for all the central highlands. It inaugurated a new era in the settlement history of the Basin of Mexico, with a clear separation between rural and urban sectors. The backcountry was occupied by small farming villages and some secondary centers. To find another urban center, one had to go beyond the ranges ringing the Basin. From this time on, the process of urban growth ultimately culminated with the megalopolis that now covers a vast area of the Basin of Mexico.

Interesting is the fact that the first Teotihuacan urban center was constructed on top of a volcanic flow that covered the northern part of the valley, sparing the alluvial plain to the south for farming. Yet, the urban growth eventually spread onto the alluvial plain, with a loss of economic selfsufficiency. In addition, the buildings of the city were plastered with stucco (a form of calcium carbonate) which implies an immense demand for fuel to burn the requisite lime, so that adjacent pine and oak forest would have suffered severely. Barba's calculations (1995) show enormous volumes of lime plaster used only for domestic purposes (the apartment compounds), and the amount of energy needed for the transformation of limestone into lime was equivalent to 33 days' operation of the nucleoelectric reactor of Laguna Verde. We should add the use of wood for ceramic production, domestic hearths, and roofing of the buildings. Such a scale of destruction of the vegetation cover must have caused soil erosion. Probably at the end of the Teotihuacan era, by A.D. 650, the aridification of the Mezquital Valley in Hidalgo also caused the migration of Otomí hunter-gatherers to the south, contributing to the city's destruction. This epoch is partially coincident to the Mediaeval Warm Period.

On the basis of climatological inferences, García (1974) suggested that, in A.D. 650, an intensive drought in the Basin of Mexico coincided with the worsening of social and political conditions in the Teotihuacan civilization—a situation that can be compared with the Egyptian Old Kingdom and the Andean Tiwanaku collapses. The drought coincided with a moment of great vulnerability of the urban system. Recently, through paleolimnological studies, Metcalfe *et al.* (1989, 1991; see also O'Hara 1993) have detected a drought that affected many of the lacustrine basins of Central Mexico around A.D. 700.

We would like to conclude, thus, saying that the temple organization, centered in an intricate redistributive circuit, could have been the basis for the "urban revolution," and that only in later times, a state centered in the palace as the axis of a tributary circuit and the top of a class society emerges.

REFERENCES

Adams, R. McC., 1960, The Origin of Cities, reprinted from *Scientific American*, September, Reprint 606, W. H. Freeman and Co., San Francisco.
Adams, R. McC., 1966, *The Evolution of Urban Society. Early Mesopotamia and Prehispanic Mexico*, Aldine Publishing Co., Chicago.
Adams, R. McC., 1973, Some Hypotheses on the Development of Early Civilizations, in: *Contemporary Archaeology. A Guide to Theory and Contributions* (M. P. Leone, ed.), Southern Illinois University Press, Carbondale, pp. 359-364.
Adams, R. McC., 1981, *Heartland of Cities*, The University of Chicago Press, Chicago.
Adams, R. McC., and H. J. Nissen, 1972, *The Uruk Countryside. The Natural Settings of Urban Societies*, The University of Chicago Press, Chicago.
Algaze, G., 1993, *The Uruk World System. The Dynamics of Expansion of Early Mesopotamian Civilization*, The Univerisity of Chicago Press, Chicago.
Altschul, J. H., 1981, *Spatial and Statistical Evidence for Social Groupings at Teotihuacan, Mexico*, Ph.D. Dissertation, Brandeis University, University Microfilms, Ann Arbor.
Altschul, J. H., 1987, Social Districts of Teotihuacan, in: *Teotihuacan: Nuevos datos, nuevas síntesis, nuevos problemas* (E. McClung de Tapia and E. C. Rattray, eds.), Serie Antropológica 72, Instituto de Investigaciones Antropológicas, Universidad Nacional Autónoma de México, México, pp. 191-217.
Armillas, P., 1968, Urban Revolution: the Concept of Civilization, reprinted from *The International Encyclopedia of the Social Sciences*, The Macmillan Company and The Free Press:218-221.
Athens, J. S., 1977, 10. Theory Building and the Study of Evolutionary Process in Complex Societies, in: *For Theory Building in Archaeology* (L. R. Binford, ed.), Studies in Archeology, Academic Press, New York, pp. 353.384.
Barba, L., 1995, *Impacto humano en la paleogeografía de Teotihuacan*, Ph.D. Dissertation in Anthropology, Facultad de Filosofía y Letras, Universidad Nacional Autónoma de México, México.
Barba, L., B. Ludlow, L. Manzanilla, and R. Valadez, 1987, La vida doméstica en Teotihuacan. Un estudio interdisciplinario, *Ciencia y desarrollo* año XIII, 77, Consejo Nacional de Ciencia y Tecnología, México:21-32.
Bard, K., 1993, State Collapse in Egypt in the Late Third Millennium B.C., paper presented at the 57th Annual Meeting of the Society of American Archaeology, St. Louis, April 17, 1993.
Baumgartel, E. J., 1955, *The Cultures of Prehistoric Egypt*, London.
Beale, T. W., 1973, Early Trade in Highland Iran: a View from a Source Area, *World Archaeology* 5, 2:133-148.
Beale, T. W., 1978, Bevelled Rim Bowls and their Implications for Change and Economic Organization in the Later Fourth Millennium B. C., *Journal of Near Eastern Studies* 37, 4:289-313.
Blanton, R. E., 1976, Anthropological Studies of Cities, *Annual Review of Anthropology* 5:249-264.
Blanton, R. E., S. A. Kowalewski, G. M. Feinman, and L. M. Finsten, 1993, *Ancient Mesoamerica. A Comparison of Change in Three Regions*, New Studies in Archaeology, Cambridge University Press, Cambridge.
Bradley, R. S. (ed.), 1989, *Global Changes of the Past*, Papers arising from the 1989 OIES Global Change Institute, Boulder, UCAR.

Braidwood, R. J., 1962, *The Near East and the Foundations for Civilization. An Essay in Appraisal of the General Evidence*, Condon Lectures, Oregon State System of Higher Education, Eugene.

Braidwood, R. J., and G. R. Willey, 1962, *Courses toward Urban Life. Archaeological Considerations of Some Cultural Alternates*, Viking Fund Publications in Anthropology 32, Aldine Publishing Co., Chicago.

Braidwood, R. J., and B. Howe, 1972, *Prehistoric Investigations in Iraqi Kurdistan*, Studies in Ancient Oriental Civilization 31, The Oriental Institute of the University of Chicago, Chicago.

Bray, W., 1983, Nine. Landscape with Figures: Settlement Patterns, Locational Models, and Politics in Mesoamerica, in: *Prehistoric Settlement Pattterns. Essays in Honor of Gordon R. Willey* (E. Z. Vogt and R. M. Leventhal, eds.), University of New Mexico Press and Peabody Museum of Archaeology and Ethnology, Cambridge, pp. 167-193.

Broda, J., 1976, Los estamentos en el ceremonial mexica, in: *Estratificación social en la Mesoamérica prehispánica* (P. Carrasco et al., eds.), Secretaría de Educación Pública-Instituto Nacional de Antropología e Historia, México, pp. 37-66.

Browman, D. L., 1993, Climatic Influences in the Titicaca Basin Cultural Sequence, paper presented at the *XIII International Congress of Anthropological and Ethnological Sciences*, Mexico City, August 4, 1993.

Buringh, P., 1957, Living Conditions in the Lower Mesopotamian Plain in Ancient Times, *Sumer* XIII, 1 and 2, Directorate General of Antiquities, Baghdad:30-57.

Butzer, K. W., 1976, *Early Hydraulic Civilization in Egypt. A Study in Cultural Ecology*, The University of Chicago Press, Chicago.

Butzer, K. W., 1980, 11. Pleistocene History of the Nile Valley in Egypt and Lower Nubia, in: *The Sahara and the Nile. Quaternary Environment and Prehistoric Occupation in Northern Africa* (M. A. J. Williams and H. Faure, eds.), G.-P. Maisonneuve et Larose, Paris, pp. 253-280.

Butzer, K. W., 1984, Long-term Nile Flood Variation and Political Discontinuities in Pharaonic Egypt, in: *From Hunters to Farmers* (J. D. Clark and S. A. Brandt, eds.), University of California Press, Berkeley, pp. 102-112.

Butzer, K. W., 1995, Environmental Change in the Near East and the Human Impact on the Land, in: *Civilizations of the Ancient Near East* (J. M. Sasson, ed.), Macmillan, New York, pp. 123-151.

Carneiro, R. L., 1970, A Theory of the Origin of the State, *Science* 169:733-738.

Carrasco, P., 1982, 1. La economía del México prehispánico, in: *Economía política e ideología en el México prehispánico* (P. Carrasco and J. Broda, eds.), Editorial Nueva Imagen, México, pp. 13-17.

Carrasco, P., 1983, IV. Some Theoretical Considerations about the Role of the Market in Ancient Mexico, in: *Economic Anthropology. Topics and Theories* (S. Ortiz, ed.), Society for Economic Anthropology, New York, pp. 67-82.

Castañeda Reyes, J. C., 1992, *Nefer sedem er entet neb. Intento de clarificación del movimiento popular durante el Imperio Nuevo y el Postimperio en el Egypto antiguo*, tesis de Arqueología, Escuela Nacional de Antropología e Historia, México.

Childe, V. G., 1957, Civilizations, Cities, and Towns, *Antiquity* XXXI, 121:36-38.

Childe, V. G., 1964, *Evolución social*, Problemas científicos y filosóficos 29, Universidad Nacional Autónoma de México, México.

Childe, V. G., 1968, *Nacimiento de las civilizaciones orientales*, Historia, Ciencia y Sociedad 31, Ediciones Península, Barcelona.

Childe, V. G., 1971, *Los orígenes de la civilización*, Breviario 92, Fondo de Cultura Económica, México.

Childe, V. G., 1973, The Urban Revolution, in: *Contemporary Archaeology* (M. P. Leone, ed.), Southern Illinois University Press, Carbondale, pp. 43-51.
Claessen, H. J. M., and P. Skalník, 1978, *The Early State*, New Babylon, Studies in the Social Sciences 320, Mouton Publishers, The Hague.
Claessen, H. J. M., 1984, El surgimiento del estado primero (Early State) (La primerísima forma del Estado), *Boletín Mexicano de Derecho Comparado* 50, nueva serie, Año XVII, mayo-agosto, Universidad Nacional Autónoma de México, México:433-479.
Claessen, H. J. M., 1984b, The Internal Dynamics of the Early State, *Current Anthropology* 25, 4:365-379.
Claessen, H. J. M., 1989, Evolutionism in Development. Beyond Growing Complexity and Classification, in: *Kinship, Social Change, and Evolution*. Proceedings of a Symposium held in Honour of Walter Dostal (A. Gingrich, S. Haas, S. Haas, and G. Paleczek, eds.), Wiener Beiträge zur Ethnologie und Anthropologie 5, Verlag Ferdinand Berger & Söhne, Wien, pp. 231-247.
Cohen, M. N., 1975, Archaeological Evidence for Population Pressure in Pre-agricultural Societies, *American Antiquity* 40, 4:471-475.
Cohen, R., and E. R. Service (eds.), 1978, *Originis of the State. The Anthropology of Political Evolution*, Institute for the Study of Human Issues, Philadelphia.
Courty, M.-A., 1993, The Micromorphology of Abrupt Climatic Change, paper presented at the 57th Annual Meeting of the Society of American Archaeology, St. Louis, April 17, 1993.
Cowgill, G. L., 1987, Métodos para el estudio de relaciones espaciales en los datos de la superficie de Teotihuacan, in: *Teotihuacan: Nuevos datos, nuevas síntesis, nuevos problemas* (E. McClung de Tapia and E. C. Rattray, eds.), Serie Antropológica 72, Instituto de Investigaciones Antropológicas, Universidad Nacional Autónoma de México, México, pp. 161-189.
Craig, A. K., and I. Shimada, 1986, El Niño Flood Deposits at Batan Grande, Northern Peru, *Geoarchaeology* 2:29-38.
Dalton, G., 1977, Chapter 11. Aboriginal Economies in Stateless Societies, in: *Exchange Systems in Prehistory* (T. K. Earle and J. E. Ericson, eds.), Studies in Archeology, Academic Press, New York, pp. 191-212.
Doxiadis, C. A., 1968, *Ekistics. An Introduction to the Science of Human Settlements*, Hutchinson and Co., London.
Earle, T. K., 1977, Chapter 12. A Reappraisal of Redistribution: Complex Hawaiian Chiefdoms, in: *Exchange Systems in Prehistory* (T. K. Earle and J. E. Ericson, eds.), Studies in Archeology, Academic Press, New York, pp. 213-229.
Earle, T., 1991, I. The Evolution of Chiefdoms, in: *Chiefdoms: Power, Economy, and Ideology* (T. Earle, ed.), A School of American Research Book, Cambridge University Press, New York, pp. 1-15.
Earle, T. K., and J. E. Ericson, 1977, Chapter 1. Exchange Systems in Archaeological Perspective, in: *Exchange Systems in Prehistory* (T. K. Earle and J. E. Ericson, eds.), Studies in Archeology, Academic Press, New York, pp. 3-12.
Earle, T. K., and T. N. D'Altroy, 1982, Storage Facilities and State Finance in the Upper Mantaro Valley, Peru, in: *Contexts for Prehistoric Exchange* (J. E. Ericson and T. K. Earle, eds.), Academic Press, New York, pp. 265-290.
Espinosa, G., and L. Manzanilla, 1985, Consideraciones en torno a la capacidad de los cuencos troncocónicos de Arslantepé (Malatya), *Quaderni de La Ricerca Scientifica* 112, Scavi e Ricerche Archeologiche degli anni 1976-1979, Consiglio Nazionale delle Ricerche, Roma:139-162.
Flannery, K. V., 1972, The Cultural Evolution of Civilizations, *Annual Review of Ecology and Systematics* 3:399-426.

Flannery, K. V., 1982, Book review: '*In the Land of the Olmec...*' Volumes 1 and 2 by Michael D. Coe and Richard A. Diehl, *American Anthropologist* 84, 2:442-447.
Flannery, K. V., and M. D. Coe, 1972, Social and Economic Systems in Formative Mesoamerica, in: *New Perspectives in Archaeology* (S. R. Binford and L. Binford, eds.), Aldine Publishing Co., Chicago, pp. 267-283.
Frangipane, M., 1990-1991, Spunti per uno studio delle formazioni protostatali: riflessioni con Alba Palmieri, *Origini: Preistoria e Protostoria delle Civiltá Antiche* XV, Bonsignori Editore, Roma:9-21.
Frangipane, M., 1993, Local Components in the Development of Centralized Societies in Syro-Anatolian Regions, in: *Between the Rivers and Over the Mountains. Archaeologica Anatolica et Mesopotamica Alba Palmieri Dedicata* (M. Frangipane, H. Hauptmann, M. Liverani, P. Matthiae, and M. Mellink, eds.), Dipartimento di Scienze Storiche Archeologiche e Antropologiche dell'Antichitá, Universitá di Roma La Sapienza, pp. 133-161.
Frangipane, M., and A. Palmieri, 1987, Urbanisation in Perimesopotamian Areas: The Case of Eastern Anatolia, in: *Studies in the Neolithic and Urban Revolutions: The V. Gordon Childe Colloquium, Mexico 1986* (L. Manzanilla, ed.), BAR International Series 349, British Archaeological Reports, Oxford, pp. 295-318.
Frangipane, M., and A. Palmieri, 1988/89, Aspects of Centralization in the Late Uruk Period in the Mesopotamian Periphery, *Origini* 14, Rome:539-560.
Frankfort, H., 1951a, *The Birth of Civilization in the Near East*, Doubleday and Co., New York.
Frankfort, H., 1951b, The Last Predynastic Period in Babylonia, in: *Cambridge Ancient History* I, 2, Cambridge University Press, Cambridge, pp. 71-92.
Fried, M. H., 1967, *The Evolution of Political Society. An Essay in Political Society*, Studies in Anthropology, Random House, New York.
Fried, M. H., 1974, On the Evolution of Social Stratification and the State, in: *The Rise and Fall of Civilizations. Modern Archaeological Approaches to Ancient Cultures* (C. C. Lamberg-Karlovsky and J. A. Sabloff, eds.), Selected Readings, Cummings Publishing Co., Menlo Park, pp. 26-40.
Friedman, J., 1975, Tribes, States and Transformations, in: *Marxist Analyses and Social Anthropology* (M. Bloch, ed.), ASA Studies 2, Malaby Press, London, pp. 161-202.
Gamio, M., 1922, *La población del Valle de Teotihuacan*, Dirección de Antropología, Secretaría de Agricultura y Fomento, México.
García, E., 1974, Situaciones climáticas durante el auge y la caída de la cultura teotihuacana, *Boletín del Instituto de Geografía* 5, Universidad Nacional Autónoma de México, México:35-69.
Gelb, I. J., 1965, The Ancient Mesopotamian Ration System, *Journal of Near Eastern Studies* 24, 3:231-243.
Gibson, McG., 1973, Population Shift and the Rise of Mesopotamian Civilization, in: *The Explanation of Culture Change. Models in Prehistory* (C. Renfrew, ed.), Duckworth, Gloucester Crescent, pp. 447-463.
Gledhill, J., and M. Larsen, 1982, 13. The Polanyi Paradigm and a Dynamic Analysis of Archaic States, in: *Theory and Explanation in Archaeology* (C. Renfrew, M. J. Rowlands, and B. A. Segraves, eds.), Academic Press, New York, pp. 197-229.
Godelier, M., 1969, *Las Sociedades Primitivas y el Nacimiento de las Sociedades de Clases según Marx y Engels. Un balance crítico*, Editorial La Oveja Negra, Colombia.
Gray, R. F., 1974, Sonjo Lineage Structure and Property, in: *The Family Estate in Africa. Studies in the Role of Property in Family Structure and Lineage Continuity* (R. F. Gray and P. H. Gulliver, eds.), Routledge and Kegan Paul, London, pp. 231-292.
Haas, J., 1982, *The Evolution of the Prehistoric State*, Columbia University Press, New York.

Hardoy, J. E., 1964, *Ciudades precolombinas*, Biblioteca de Planeamiento y Vivienda 7, Ediciones Infinito, Buenos Aires.
Hole, F., 1974, Investigating the Origins of Mesopotamian Civilization, in: *The Rise and Fall of Civilizations. Modern Archaeological Approaches to Ancient Cultures* (C. C. Lamberg-Karlovsky and J. A. Sabloff, eds.), Selected Readings, Cummings Publishing Co., Menlo Park, pp. 269-281.
Hourani, A. H., 1970, Introduction: The Islamic City in the Light of Recent Research, in: *The Islamic City. A Colloquium* (A. H. Hourani and S. M. Stern, eds.), Papers on Islamic History I, Bruno Cassirer, Oxford and the University of Pennsylvania Press, pp. 9-24.
International Geosphere-Biosphere Programme, 1992, *PAGES. Past Global Changes Project:* Proposed Implementation Plans for Research Activities, The International Geosphere-Biosphere Programme, IGBP Global Change, Report 19, Stockholm.
Isbell, W. H., 1978, Environmental Perturbations and the Origins of the Andean State, in: *Social Archeology: Beyond Subsistence and Dating* (C. Redman et al., eds.), Studies in Archeology, Academic Press, New York, pp. 303-313.
Jacobsen, T., 1957, Early Political Development in Mesopotamia, *Zeitschrift für Assyriologie* 52, Leipzig:91-140.
Jacobsen, T., and R. McC. Adams, 1958, Salt and Silt in Ancient Mesopotamian Agriculture, reprinted from *Science* 128, 3334:1251-1258.
Jawad, A. J., 1965, *The Advent of the Era of Townships in Northern Mesopotamia*, E. J. Brill, Leiden.
Jones, G. D., and R. P. Kautz, 1981, *The Transition to Statehood in the New World*, Cambridge University Press, Cambridge.
Kirchhoff, P., 1955, The Principles of Clanship in Human Society, reprinted from *Davidson Journal of Anthropology* I, summer, The Bobbs-Merrill Reprint Series in the Social Sciences A-128), The Davidson Anthropological Society:1-10.
Kirkbride, D., 1975, Umm Dabaghiyah: Fourth Preliminary Report, *Iraq* 37, part 1, London:3-10.
Kolata, A. K., 1986, The Agricultural Foundations of the Tiwanaku State: a View from the Heartland, *American Antiquity* 51, 4:748-762.
Kowalewski, S. A., 1990, The Evolution of Complexity in the Valley of Oaxaca, *Annual Review of Anthropology* 19:39-58.
Krader, L., 1968, *Formation of the State*, Foundation of Modern Anthropology Series, Prentice-Hall, Inc., Englewood Cliffs.
Krader, L., 1975, *The Asiatic Mode of Production*, Van Gorcum, Assem/Amsterdam.
Krader, L., 1979, Etapas de desarrollo del modo de producción asiático, *Antropología y Marxismo* mayo:30-43.
Kraeling, C. H., and R. McC. Adams (eds.), 1960, *City Invincible*. A Symposium on Urbanization and Cultural Development in the Ancient Near East, December 4-7 1958, The University of Chicago Press, Chicago.
Kroeber, A. L., 1953, The Delimitation of Civilizations, *Journal of the History of Ideas* XIV, 2, April, New York:264-275.
Leclant, J., and P. Huard, 1980, *La Culture des Chasseurs du Nil et du Sahara*, Mémoires du Centre de Recherches Anthropologiques, Préhistoriques et Ethnographiques XXIX, C.R.A.P.E., Alger.
Lozano-García, S., 1989, Palinología y paleoambientes pleistocénicos de la Cuenca de México, *Geofísica Internacional* 28-2:335-362.
Lumbreras, L. G., 1987, Childe and the Urban Revolution: The Central Andean Experience, in: *Studies in the Neolithic and Urban Revolutions: The V. Gordon Childe Colloquium, Mexico 1986* (L. Manzanilla, ed.), BAR International Series 349, British Archaeological Reports, Oxford, pp. 327-344.

Maisels, C. K., 1990, *The Emergence of Civilization. From Hunting and Gathering to Agriculture, Cities, and the State in the Near East*, Routledge, London.
Malek, J., 1986, *In the Shadow of the Pyramids. Egypt during the Old Kingdom*, University of Oklahoma Press, Norman.
Manning, S., 1993, End of the Early Bronze Age in the Aegean: Contest, Chronology, Causes, and Effects, Paper presented at the 57th Annual Meeting of the Society of American Archaeology, St. Louis, April 17, 1993.
Manzanilla, L., 1982, *Hypothèses et indices du processus de formation de la civilisation égyptienne (cinquième et quatrième millénaires avant Jésus-Christ)*, PhD Dissertation, Université de Paris IV Sorbonne, Paris.
Manzanilla, L., 1983, La redistribución como proceso de centralización de la producción y circulación de bienes. Análisis de dos casos, *Boletín de Antropología Americana* 7, Instituto Panamericano de Geografía e Historia, México:5-18.
Manzanilla, L., 1985a, Templo y palacio: proposiciones sobre el surgimiento de la sociedad urbana y el Estado, *Anales de Antropología* 22, Instituto de Investigaciones Antropológicas, Universidad Nacional Autónoma de México, México:91-114.
Manzanilla, L., 1985b, El sitio de Cuanalan en el marco de las comunidades pre-urbanas del Valle de Teotihuacan, in: *Mesoamérica y el centro de México. Una antología* (J. Monjarás-Ruiz, R. Brambila, and E. Pérez Rocha, eds.), Colección Biblioteca del Instituto Nacional de Antropología e Historia, México, pp. 133-178.
Manzanilla, L., 1985c, Le développement des sociétés prédynastiques en Egypte: considérations méthodologiques, in: *Studi di Paletnologia in onore di Salvatore M. Puglisi* (M. Liverani, A. Palmieri, and R. Peroni, eds.), Universitá di Roma 'La Sapienza', Roma, pp. 485-494.
Manzanilla, L., 1986a, *La constitución de la sociedad urbana en Mesopotamia: Un proceso en la historia*, Serie Antropológica 80, Instituto de Investigaciones Antropológicas, Universidad Nacional Autónoma de México, México.
Manzanilla, L., 1986b, Cambios en la economía de subsistencia de los grupos prehistóricos del norte de Africa: el Nilo, *Anales de Antropología* XXIII, Universidad Nacional Autónoma de México, México:15-27.
Manzanilla, L., 1987a, The Beginnings of Urban Society and the Formation of the State: Temple and Palace as Basic Indicators, in: *Studies in the Neolithic and Urban Revolutions: The V. Gordon Childe Colloquium, Mexico, 1986* (L. Manzanilla, ed.), BAR International Series 349, Oxford, pp. 271-286.
Manzanilla, L., 1987b, Apuntes para el estudio arqueológico del almacenamiento y el problema de la redistribución, *Cuadernos del Instituto Nacional de Antropología* 12, Buenos Aires:11-24.
Manzanilla, L., 1988-1989, The Study of Room Function in a Residential Compound at Teotihuacan, Mexico, in: *Origini, Giornate di studio in ricordo di Salvatore M. Puglisi: L'interpretazione funzionale dei dati in paletnologia, Preistoria e Protostoria delle Civiltá Antiche* XIV, Universitá degli Studi di Roma 'La Sapienza', Multigrafica Editrice, Roma, pp. 175-186.
Manzanilla, L., 1991a, Redistribución y tributo en el centro de México. Hipótesis y consideraciones generales, *Antropológicas* 6, Instituto de Investigaciones Antropológicas, Universidad Nacional Autónoma de México, México:43-48.
Manzanilla, L., 1991b, Pensamiento político y religión en Egipto y Mesopotamia durante el IV milenio A.C. Dos procesos de formación del Estado, *Anales de Antropología* 28, Instituto de Investigaciones Antropológicas, Universidad Nacional Autónoma de México, México:191-204.

Manzanilla, L., 1992a, *Akapana. Una pirámide en el centro del mundo*, Instituto de Investigaciones Antropológicas, Universidad Nacional Autónoma de México, México.
Manzanilla, L., 1992b, ¿Y si el desastre comenzó en Teotihuacan?, *Antropológicas* 3, julio, nueva época, Universidad Nacional Autónoma de México, México:9-11.
Manzanilla, L., 1993a, The Economic Organization of the Teotihuacan Priesthood: Hypotheses and Considerations, in: *Art, Ideology, and the City of Teotihuacan* (J. C. Berlo, ed.), Dumbarton Oaks Research Library and Collection, Washington D.C., pp. 321-338.
Manzanilla, L., 1993b, *Anatomía de un conjunto residencial teotihuacano en Oztoyahualco*, Instituto de Investigaciones Antropológicas, Universidad Nacional Autónoma de México, México.
Manzanilla, L., 1993c, Daily Life in the Teotihuacan Apartment Compounds, in: *Teotihuacan. Art from the City of the Gods* (K. Berrin and E. Pasztory, eds.), Thames and Hudson, The Fine Arts Museums of San Francisco, San Francisco, pp. 90-99.
Manzanilla, L., 1993d, Surgimiento de los centros urbanos en Mesoamérica, in: *Antropología Breve de México* (L. Arizpe, ed.), Academia de la Investigación Científica, México, pp. 57-82.
Manzanilla, L., 1993e, Cambios climáticos globales del pasado, *Antropológicas* 7, n. e., julio, México, Universidad Nacional Autónoma de México:83-88.
Manzanilla, L., 1995, 24. El Altiplano Central, in: *Historia Antigua de México* (L. Manzanilla and L. López Luján, eds.), Instituto Nacional de Antropología e Historia-Universidad Nacional Autónoma de México-Editorial Miguel Angel Porrúa, México, pp. 139-173.
Manzanilla, L., in press, The Impact of Climatic Change on Past Civilizations. A Revisionist Agenda for Further Investigation, *Quaternary International*.
Manzanilla, L., and E. Woodard, 1990, Restos humanos asociados a la pirámide de Akapana (Tiwanaku, Bolivia), *Latin American Antiquity* 1, 2:133-149.
Manzanilla, L., L. Barba, and M. R. Baudoin, 1990, Investigaciones en la Pirámide de Akapana, Tiwanaku, Bolivia, *Gaceta Arqueológica Andina* V, 20, diciembre, Instituto Andino de Estudios Arqueológicos, Lima:81-107.
Manzanilla, L., and L. Barba, 1990, The Study of Activities in Classic Households: Two Case Studies from Coba and Teotihuacan, *Ancient Mesoamerica* 1, 1, Cambridge University Press:41-49.
Manzanilla, L., and E. Carreón, 1991, A Teotihuacan Censer in a Residential Context. An Interpretation, *Ancient Mesoamerica* 2, 2, Cambridge University Press:299-307.
Marcus, J., 1983, Ten. On the Nature of the Mesoamerican City, in: *Prehistoric Settlement Patterns. Essays in Honor of Gordon R. Willey* (E. Z. Vogt and R. M. Leventhal, eds.), University of New Mexico Press and Peabody Museum of Archaeology and Ethnology, Cambridge, pp. 195-242.
Marcus, J., 1992, Political Fluctuations in Mesoamerica, *National Geographic Research and Exploration* 8, 4:392-411.
McClung de Tapia, E., 1987, Patrones de subsistencia urbana en Teotihuacan, in: *Teotihuacan: Nuevos datos, nuevas síntesis, nuevos problemas* (E. McClung de Tapia and E. C. Rattray, eds.), Serie Antropológica 72, Instituto de Investigaciones Antropológicas, Universidad Nacional Autónoma de México, México, pp. 57-74.
Meillassoux, C., 1974, *Anthropologie Économique des Gouro de Côte d'Ivoire. Del l'économie de subsistance à l'agriculture commerciale*, Le Monde d'Outre Mer, Passé et Présent, Première Série, Études XXVII, Mouton, Paris.
Merpert, N. Y., and R. M. Munchaev, 1969, The Investigation of the Soviet Archaeological Expedition in Iraq in the Spring 1969. Excavations at Yarim Tepe. First Preliminary Report, *Sumer* 25, 1 and 2, Directorate General of Antiquities, Baghdad:125-132.

Metcalfe, S. E., F. A. Street-Perrott, R. B. Brown, P. E. Hales, R. A. Perrot, and F. M. Steininger, 1989, Late Holocene Human Impact on Lake Basins in Central Mexico, *Geoarchaeology* 4, 2, John Wiley and Sons:119-141.

Metcalfe, S. E., F. A. Street-Perrott, R. A. Perrott, and D. D. Harkness, 1991, Palaeolimnology of the Upper Lerma Basin, Central Mexico: a Record of Climatic Change and Anthropogenic Disturbance since 11600 yr BP, *Journal of Paleolimnology* 5, Kluwer Academic Publishers:197-218.

Miller, A. G., 1973, *The Mural Painting of Teotihuacan*, Dumbarton Oaks, Washington D. C.

Millon, C., 1973, Painting, Writing, and Polity in Teotihuacan, *American Antiquity* 38, 3:294-314.

Millon, R., 1967, Teotihuacan, *Scientific American* 216, 6:38-48.

Millon, R., 1988, The Last Years of Teotihuacan Dominance, in: *The Collapse of Ancient States and Civilizations* (N. Yoffee and G. L. Cowgill, ed.), The University of Arizona Press, Tucson, pp. 102-164.

Moore, J. D., 1991, Cultural Responses to Environmental Catastrophes: Post-El Niño Subsistence on the Prehistoric North Coast of Peru, *Latin American Antiquity* 2, 1:27-47.

Morris, C., 1978, The Archaeological Study of Andean Exchange Systems, in: *Social Archeology. Beyond Subsistence and Dating* (C. L. Redman et al., eds.), Studies in Archeology, Academic Press, New York, pp. 315-327.

Moseley, M. E., 1987, The Andes. Punctuated Equilibrium: Searching the Ancient Record for El Niño, *The Quarterly Review of Archaeology*, Fall:7-10.

Moss, R. H., 1992, Research on Global Change and its Human Dimensions, *Global Change Newsletter* 9, March, International Geosphere-Biosphere Programme Secretariat, Sweden:2-5.

Mumford, L., 1970, The natural history of urbanization, in: *Man's Role in Changing the Face of the Earth* I (W. L. Thomas Jr., ed.), The University of Chicago Press, Chicago, pp. 382-398.

Murra, J., 1955, *La organización económica del Estado inca*, Siglo XXI, México.

Murra, J. V., 1975, *Formaciones económicas y políticas del mundo andino*, Instituto de Estudios Peruanos, Lima.

Murra, J. V., 1985a, 'El Archipiélago Vertical' Revisited, in: *Andean Ecology and Civilization: An Interdisciplinary Perspective on Andean Ecological Complementarity* (S. Masuda, I. Shimada, and C. Morris, eds.), University of Tokyo Press, Tokyo, pp. 3-13.

Murra, J. V., 1985b, The Limits and Limitations of the 'Vertical Archipelago' in the Andes, in: *Andean Ecology and Civilization: An Interdisciplinary Perspective on Andean Ecological Complementarity* (S. Masuda, I. Shimada, and C. Morris, eds.), University of Tokyo Press, Tokyo, pp. 15-20.

Neale, W. C., 1957, XI. Reciprocity and Redistribution in the Indian Village: Sequel to Some Notable Discussions, in: *Trade and Market in the Early Empires. Economies in History and Theory* (K. Polanyi, C. M. Arensberg, and H. W. Pearson, eds.), A Gateway Edition, Chicago, pp. 218-236.

Nissen, H. J., 1972, The City Wall of Uruk, in: *Man, Settlement, and Urbanism* (P. J. Ucko, R. Tringham, and G. W. Dimbleby, eds.), Duckworth, Hertfordshire, pp. 793-798.

Nissen, H. J., 1986, *Mesopotamia before 5000 years*, Sussidi Didattici I, Dipartimento di Scienze Storiche, Archeologiche e Antropologiche dell'Antichitá, Universitá degli Studi di Roma 'La Sapienza', Roma.

Oates, J., 1972, Prehistoric Settlement Patterns in Mesopotamia, in: *Man, Settlement, and Urbanism* (P. J. Ucko, R. Tringham, and G. W. Dimbleby, eds.), Gerald Duckworth and Co., Hertfordshire, pp. 299-310.

O'Hara, S. L., F. A. Street-Perrott, and T. P. Burt, 1993, Accelerated Soil Erosion around a Mexican Highland Lake Caused by Prehispanic Agriculture, *Nature* 362, 4 March:48-51.
Ortlieb, L., and J. Macharé, 1992, *Paleo-ENSO Records International Symposium. Extended abstracts*, ORSTOM and Consejo Nacional de Ciencia y Tecnología, Lima.
Ortloff, C. R., and A. L. Kolata, 1993, Climate and Collapse: Agro-Ecological Perspectives on the Decline of the Tiwanaku State, *Journal of Archaeological Sciences* 20, 2:195-221.
Palmieri, A., 1973, Scavi nell'area sud-occidentale di Arslantepe, *Origini* 7, Roma:55-179.
Palmieri, A., 1989, Storage and Distribution at Arslantepe-Malatya in the Late Uruk Period, in: *Anatolia and the Ancient Near East. Studies in Honor of Tahsin Özgüç* (K. Emre *et al.*, eds.), Türk Tarih Kurumu, Ankara, pp. 419-429.
Pasztory, E., 1972, The Gods of Teotihuacan: A Synthetic Approach in Teotihuacan Iconography, *Atti del XL Congresso Internazionale degli Americanisti* I, Rome:147-159.
Pasztory, E., 1978, Artistic Traditions of the Middle Classic Period, in: *Middle Classic Mesoamerica: A.D. 400-700* (E. Pasztory, ed.), Columbia University Press, New York, pp. 108-142.
Paulinyi, Z., 1981, Capitals in Pre-Aztec Central Mexico, *Acta Orientalia Academiae Scientiarum Hungarica* XXXV, 2-3:315-250.
Paulsen, A. C., 1976, Environment and Empire: Climatic Factors in Prehistoric Andean Culture, *World Archaeology* 8, 2:121-132.
Petit-Maire, N., 1991, The Role of Earth Sciences in the Anticipation of Future Climatic Change, *Ciéncia e Cultura* 43, 2, March-April:130-136.
Polanyi, K., 1957, XIII. The Economy as Instituted Process, in: *Trade and Market in the Early Empires. Economies in History and Theory* (K. Polanyi, C. M. Arensberg, and H. W. Pearson, eds.), The Free Press, New York, pp. 243-270.
Ponce Sanginés, C., 1981, *Tiwanaku: Espacio, tiempo y cultura. Ensayo de síntesis arqueológica*, Librería Los Amigos del Libro, La Paz.
Possehl, G., 1993, Climate, Collapse, and Civilization in the Greater Indus Region, Paper presented at the 57th Annual Meeting of the Society of American Archaeology, St. Louis, April 17, 1993.
Price, B. J., 1979, 13. Turning State's Evidence: Problems in the Theory of State Formation, in: *New Directions in Political Economy: An Approach from Anthropology* (M. B. Léons and F. Rothstein, eds.), Greenwich Press, Westport, pp. 269-306.
Raikes, R. L., 1966, The Physical Evidence for Noah's Flood, *Iraq* XXVIII, British School of Archaeology in Iraq, Baghdad:52-63.
Redman, C. L., 1990, *Los orígenes de la civilización. Desde los primeros agricultores hasta la sociedad urbana en el Próximo Oriente*, Editorial Crítica, Barcelona.
Renfrew, C., 1974, Beyond a Subsistence Economy: the Evolution of Social Organisation in Prehistoric Europe, in: *Reconstructing Complex Societies: an Archaeological Colloquium* (C. B. Moore, ed.), Supplement to the Bulletin of the American Schools of Oriental Research 20, Ann Arbor, pp. 69-95.
Renfrew, C., 1975, 1. Trade as Action at a Distance: Questions of Integration and Communication, in: *Ancient Civilization and Trade* (J. A. Sabloff and C. C. Lamberg-Karlovsky, eds.), A School of American Research Book, University of New Mexico Press, Albuquerque, pp. 3-59.
Renfrew, C., 1977, Chapter 4. Alternative Models for Exchange and Spatial Distribution, in: *Exchange Systems in Prehistory* (T. K. Earle and J. E. Ericson, eds.), Studies in Archaeology, Academic Press, New York, pp. 71-90.
Rey, P. P., 1975, The Lineage Mode of Production, *Critique of Anthropology* 3, spring, London:27-79.

Reyna Robles, R. M., 1977, Desarrollo y evolución de la unidad habitacional en una aldea preclásica del Altiplano Central: Loma Torremote como un ejemplo, in: *Los procesos de cambio (en Mesoamérica y áreas circunvecinas)*, I, XV Mesa Redonda, Sociedad Mexicana de Antropología, Guanajuato, pp. 377-383.

Ribeiro, D., 1976, *El proceso civilizatorio (de la revolución agrícola a la termonuclear)*, Editorial Extemporáneos, México.

Rojas, J. L. de, 1987, El control del granero del imperio y la consolidación del estado mexica, in: *Almacenamiento de productos agropecuarios en México* (G. Mummert, ed.), El Colegio de Michoacán, Zamora, pp. 29-38.

Rosen, A. M., 1993, Environmental Stress as a Factor in the Collapse of Early Bronze Age Society in Palestine, Paper presented at the 57th Annual Meeting of the Society of American Archaeology, St. Louis, April 17, 1993.

Rowlands, M., 1987, Chapter 1. Centre and Periphery: a Review of a Concept, in: *Centre and Periphery in the Ancient World* (M. Rowlands, M. Larsen, and K. Kristiansen, eds.), Cambridge University Press, Cambridge, pp. 1-11.

Rowlands, M., 1989, 1. A Question of Complexity, in: *Domination and Resistance* (D. Miller, M. Rowlands, and C. Tilley, eds.), One World Archaeology 3, Unwin Hyman, London, pp. 29-40.

Rowton, M. B., 1973, Urban Autonomy in a Nomadic Environment, *Journal of Near Eastern Studies* 32, 1 and 2:201-215.

Rowton, M. B., 1981, Economic and Political Factors in Ancient Nomadism, in: *Nomads and Sedentary People* (J. Silva Castillo, ed.), El Colegio de México, XXX International Congress of Human Sciences in Asia and North Africa, México, pp. 25-36.

Sanders, W. T., 1967, Life in a Classic Village, in: *Teotihuacan. Onceava Mesa Redonda 1966*, Sociedad Mexicana de Antropología, México, pp. 123-147.

Sanders, W. T., 1968, Hydraulic Agriculture, Economic Symbiosis, and the Evolution of the State in Central Mexico, in: *Anthropological Archeology in the Americas* (B. Meggers, ed.), The Anthropological Society of Washington, Brooklyn, pp. 88-107.

Sanders, W. T., 1971, Cultural Ecology of Nuclear Mesoamerica, in: *Ancient Mesoamerica. Selected Readings* (J. A. Graham, ed.), Peek Publications, Palo Alto, pp. 75-85.

Sanders, W., and B. J. Price, 1968, *Mesoamerica. The Evolution of a Civilization*, Studies in Anthropology AS9, Random House, New York.

Sanders, W. T., and D. Webster, 1978, Chapter 11. Unilinealism, Multilinealism, and the Evolution of Complex Societies, in: *Social Archeology: Beyond Subsistence and Dating* (C. Redman *et al.*, eds.), Studies in Archeology, Academic Press, New York, pp. 249-302.

Sanders, W. T., and D. Webster, 1988, The Mesoamerican Urban Tradition, *American Anthropologist* 90, 3:521-546.

Schädel, R. P., 1968, On the Definitions of Civilization, Urban City and Town in Prehistoric America, *Actas y Memorias del 37º Congreso Internacional de Americanistas* I, Argentina 1966, Departamento de Publicaciones Científicas Argentinas, Buenos Aires, pp. 5-13.

Service, E. R., 1971, *Primitive Social Organization. An Evolutionary Perspective*, Studies in Anthropology, Random House, New York.

Service, E., 1975, *Origins of the State and Civilization. The Process of Cultural Evolution*, W. W. Norton and Co., New York.

Sidrys, R., 1977, Mass-Distance Measures of the Maya Obsidian Trade, in: *Exchange Systems in Prehistory* (T. K. Earle and J. E. Ericson, eds.), Studies in Archeology, Academic Press, New York, pp. 91-107.

Sjoberg, G., 1973, The Origin and Evolution of Cities, in: *Cities, Their Origin, Growth and Human Impact*, Readings from Scientific American, W. H. Freeman and Co., San Francisco, pp. 18-27.
Smith, M. E., 1993, New World Complex Societies: Recent Economic, Social, and Political Studies, *Journal of Archaeological Research* 1, 1:5-41.
Spence, M. W., 1987, The Scale and Structure of Obsidian Production in Teotihuacan, in: *Teotihuacan: Nuevos datos, nuevas síntesis, nuevos problemas* (E. McClung de Tapia and E. C. Rattray, eds.), Serie Antropológica 72, Instituto de Investigaciones Antropológicas, Universidad Nacional Autónoma de México, México, pp. 429-450.
Starbuck, D. R., 1987, Faunal Evidence for the Teotihuacan Subsistence Base, in: *Teotihuacan: Nuevos datos, nuevas síntesis, nuevos problemas* (E. McClung de Tapia and E. C. Rattray, eds.), Serie Antropológica 72, Instituto de Investigaciones Antropológicas, Universidad Nacional Autónoma de México, México, pp. 75-90.
Steward, J. H., 1955, Introducción. El Symposium sobre las Civilizaciones de Regadío, in: *Las Civilizaciones Antiguas del Viejo Mundo y de América*, Estudios Monográficos I, Unión Panamericana, Washington, pp. 1-5.
Steward, J. H., 1972, 11. Development of Complex Societies: Cultural Causality and Law. A Trial Formulation of the Development of Early Civilizations, in: *Theory of Culture Change. The Methodology of Multilinear Evolution*, University of Illinois Press, Urbana, pp. 178-209.
Tainter, J. A., 1990, *The Collapse of Complex Societies*, New Studies in Archaeology, Cambridge University Press, New York.
Terray, E., 1975, Review article: Technology, Tradition and the State, *Critique of Anthropology* 3, spring, London: 80-99.
Thompson, L. G., E. Mosley-Thompson, and B. Morales Arnao, 1984, El Niño-Southern Oscillation Events Recorded in the Stratigraphy of the Tropical Quelccaya Ice Cap, Peru, *Science* 226, 5 October:50-53.
Thompson, L. G., E. Mosley-Thompson, J. F. Bolzan, and B. R. Koci, 1985, A 1500-Record of Tropical Precipitation in Ice Cores from the Quelccaya Ice Cap, Peru, *Science* 229, 6 September:971-973.
Thompson, L. G., E. Mosley-Thompson, W. Dansgaard, and P. M. Grootes, 1986, The Little Ice Age as Recorded in the Stratigraphy of the Tropical Quelccaya Ice Cap, *Science* 234, 17 October:361-364.
Trigger, B. G., 1968, *Beyond History: The Methods of Prehistory*, Studies in Anthropological Method, Holt, Rinehart and Winston, New York.
Trigger, B., 1972, Determinants of Urban Growth in Pre-industrial Societies, in: *Man, Settlement, and Urbanism* (P. J. Ucko, R. Tringham, and G. W. Dimbleby, eds.), Gerald Duckworth and Co., Hertfordshire, pp. 575-598.
Valadez, R., and L. Manzanilla, 1988, Restos faunísticos y áreas de actividad en una unidad habitacional de la antigua ciudad de Teotihuacan, *Revista Mexicana de Estudios Antropológicos* 34, 1, Sociedad Mexicana de Antropología, México:147-168.
Vandier, J., 1952, *Manuel d'Archéologie Egyptienne*, I, Paris.
Webster, D., 1975, Warfare and the Evolution of the State: A Reconsideration, *American Antiquity* 40, 4:464-470.
Webster, D., 1976, On Theocracies, *American Anthropologist* 78, 4:812-828.
Weiss, H., 1993, Abrupt Climatic Change and Mesopotamian Collapse, Paper presented at the 57th Annual Meeting of the Society of American Archaeology, St. Louis, April 17, 1993.
Weiss, H., M.-A. Courty, W. Wetterstrom, F. Guichard, L. Senior, R. Meadow, and A. Curnow, 1993, The Genesis and Collapse of Third Millennium North Mesopotamian Civilization, *Science* 261:995-1088.

Wheatley, P., 1971, *The Pivot of the Four Quarters. A Preliminary Enquiry into the Origins and Character of the Ancient Chinese City*, Aldine Publishing Co., Chicago.
Wheatley, P., 1972, The concept of urbanism, in: *Man, Settlement, and Urbanism* (P. J. Ucko, R. Tringham, and G. W. Dimbleby, eds.), Duckworth, Hertfordshire, pp. 601-637.
Whitehouse, R., 1977, *The First Cities*, Phaidon, Oxford.
Wilson, J., 1964, *La cultura egipcia*, Breviarios 86, Fondo de Cultura Económica, México.
Wittfogel, K. A., 1966, *Despotismo oriental. Estudio Comparativo del Poder Totalitario*, Ediciones Guadarrama, Madrid.
Wittfogel, K., 1967, Review: '*The Evolution of Urban Society: Early Mesopotamia and Prehispanic Mexico*' by Robert McC. Adams, *American Anthropologist* 69, 1:90-92.
Wittfogel, K. A., 1970, The Hydraulic Civilization, in: *Man's Role in Changing the Face of the Earth* I (W. L. Thomas Jr., ed.), The University of Chicago Press, Chicago, pp. 152-164.
Wittfogel, K. A., 1974, Developmental Aspects of Hydraulic Societies, in *The Rise and Fall of Civilizations. Modern Archaeological Approaches to Ancient Cultures* (C. C. Lamberg-Karlovsky and J. A. Sabloff, eds.), Selected Readings, Cummings Publishing Co., Menlo Park, pp. 15-25.
Wolf, E. R., 1990, Distinguished Lecture: Facing Power-Old Insights, New Questions, *American Anthropologist* 92, 3:586-596.
Wright, H. T., 1969, *The Administration of Rural Production in an Early Mesopotamian Town*, Anthropological Papers 38, Museum of Anthropology, University of Michigan, Ann Arbor.
Wright, H. T., and G. A. Johnson, 1975, Population, exchange and early state formation in Southwestern Iran, *American Anthropologist* 77, 2:267-289.
Wright, H. T., 1977a, Recent Research on the Origin of the State, *Annual Review of Anthropology* 6:379-97.
Wright, H. T., 1977b, Toward an Explanation of the Origin of the State, in: *Explanation of Prehistoric Change* (J. N. Hill, ed.), University of New Mexico Press, Albuquerque, pp. 49-67.
Yoffee, N., and G. L. Cowgill (eds.), 1988, *The Collapse of Ancient States and Civilizations*, The University of Arizona Press, Tucson.
Young Jr., T. Cuyler, 1972, Population densities and early Mesopotamian urbanism, in: *Man, Settlement and Urbanism* (P. J. Ucko, G. W. Dimbleby, and R. Tringham, eds.), Gerald Duckworth, Hertfordshire, pp. 827-842.

Part II

Old World

In this part, three articles review some major characteristics of Near Eastern and Asian early urban developments: one centered in redistributional modules and the consequent complex administrative organizations, and the others related to conflictive social environments, and consequent unifications through conquest.

For the first, Mesopotamian examples in the Uruk and Jemdet Nasr periods show the emergence of complex societies through administrative control of temple centralized storage: redistribution of foodstuff and raw materials, massive bowl production in fast-wheels, the emergence of pictographic writing systems as administrative devices, and the auspice of full-time craftsmen.

In Eastern Anatolia, the role played by interregional exchange networks linking the Mesopotamian plains with the Syro-Anatolian regions is emphasized. The emergence of an elite is related with the control of the movement of craft goods and raw materials, more than with the appropriation of subsistence goods.

For the second, Predynastic Egypt unification attempts through conquest show political competition that culminates with the establishment of the pharaonic state, a scenery also present in pre-Shang times in China. The fortified settlement of Wangchenggang, in the central plains of the Yellow River in China, shows the existence of defensive walls and skeletons with physical violence traces; the location of the settlement in elevations and the secular character of the site are mentioned as elements referable to the circumscription model proposed by Carneiro, in which there was an intensification of conflicts provoked by demographic pressures on resources.

Chapter *2*

Arslantepe-Malatya
External Factors and Local Components in the Development of an Early State Society

MARCELLA FRANGIPANE

INTRODUCTION

The mound of Arslantepe, located in the plain of Malatya, Eastern Turkey, not far from the right bank of the Euphrates river, occupied continuously from the Chalcolithic to the Neo-Hittite age, proved to be a key site for the study of both the development of Early State organization in the regions surrounding Mesopotamia, and the formation of complex societies by the widespread interregional relations linking the Mesopotamian plains and the Syro-Anatolian regions in the 4th millennium B.C.

The role of Eastern Anatolia, rich in raw materials, in interregional exchange in the Near East has always been important, and may have determined the structural and organizational characteristics of the first complex societies that occupied these regions. Indeed, in the northern areas the prerogatives of the emerging elite appeared to be linked more to the control of a widespread movement of raw materials and craft products rather than to the actual appropriation of staple goods, unlike what seems

---

MARCELLA FRANGIPANE • Dipartimento di Scienze Storiche, Archeologiche e Antropologiche dell'Antichità, Università di Roma 'La Sapienza', Via Palestro 63, 00185 Roma, Italy.

Emergence and Change in Early Urban Societies, edited by Linda Manzanilla. Plenum Press, New York, 1997.

to have ocurred in the southern Mesopotamian Plain, where the increasing power of dominant social figures appears to be based on the administration of staple products, essentially cereals and livestock products, as far back as the earliest formative phases. This appears to have given rise to a different structure of society, more markedly centralized in the south, and more articulated and less pyramidal in the north. However, these differences, which continued to characterize the two regions over a long period, do not mean that these regions followed completely different trajectories; nor is it possible to imagine, on the contrary, that there was a secondary development in the north based on asymmetrical relationships of interdependency, as hypothesized by some authors (Algaze 1989, 1993).

In the late Chalcolithic period, which precedes the so-called Late Uruk expansion in the north (Figure 1), around the mid-fourth millenium B.C., there was clearly a development of local centers in the Syro-Anatolian regions, which suggests the assertion of groups or institutions with prominent social functions. Sites of this type are present on the Euphrates river, north and south of the Taurus mountains, at Arslantepe and Hacinebi (Frangipane 1993; Stein 1993), on the Balikh river at Hammam et-Turkman (van Loon 1988), on the Khabour at Tell Brak (Oates 1986), and on the Tigris at Tepe Gawra (Tobler 1950).

Although the links with the south indicated by the archaeological material of that period appear to be weaker than in the previous Ubaid period, when a similar type of painted pottery spread from the Persian Gulf to the Upper Euphrates, there are however evident significant parallelisms in the characterization of the little-known southern Early Uruk groups. Suffice it to recall, for instance, the changes in that period—both in the north and in the south—in the organization of pottery manufacture which, with the widespread diffusion of coarse ceramics and mass-production techniques, indicates a parallel change in the socio-economic requirements and therefore a new use for pottery, now predominantely intended as common ware for internal use.

The archaeological evidence therefore suggests that the traditional links between Mesopotamia and the so-called northern peri-Mesopotamian areas, albeit in different ways and with a different intensity, were probably never broken during the course of the fourth millenium, eventhough the two regions had autonomous developments towards "urbanization".

It was maybe precisely the development of complex societies with new organizational capabilities in the Late Chalcolithic which made the further extension of the influence of individual communities possible and consolidate long-distance exchange, and not the other way round. We thus see in the late fourth millenium, in the Late Uruk period, a consistent presence of southern elements in the Syro-Anatolian areas and in Upper Mesopota-

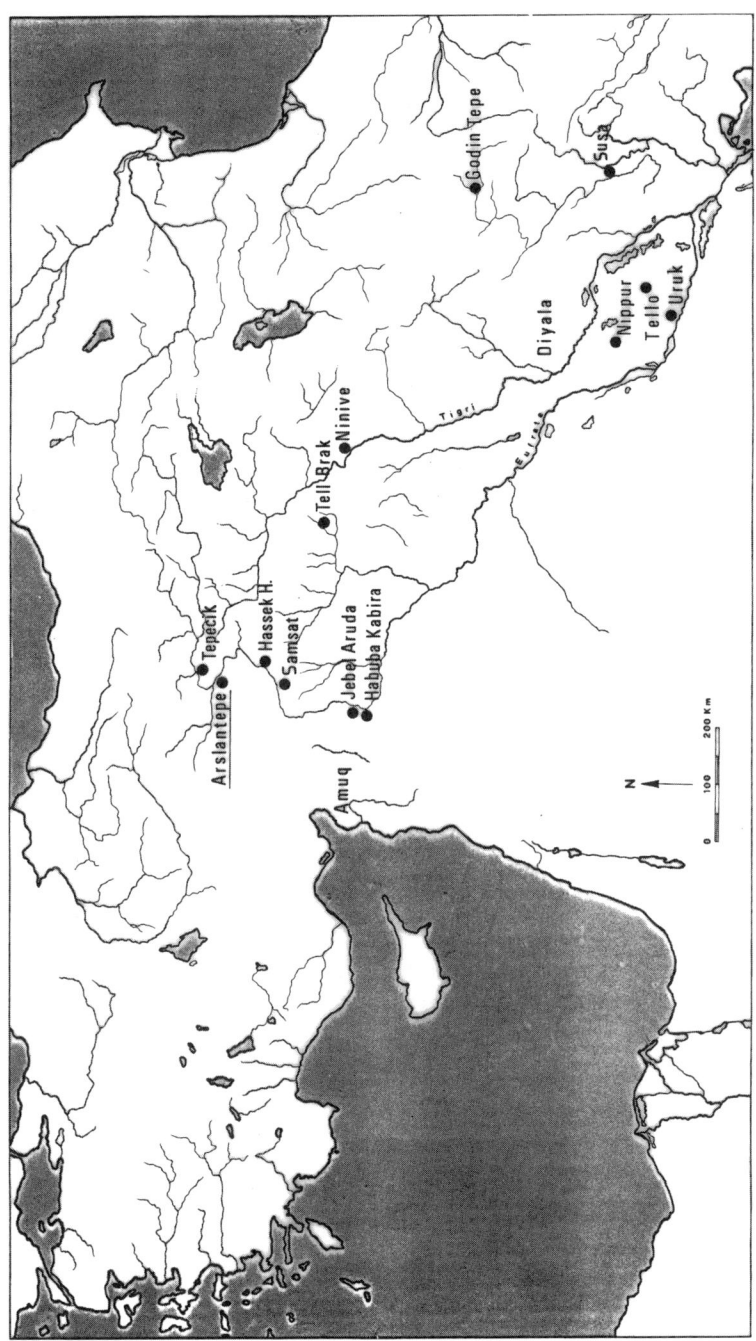

Figure 1. Location of the main Late Uruk sites.

mia which has been interpreted as a true and proper penetration of foreign groups from the south. The settlements along the course of the Tigris and the Euphrates on sites that can be defined as "colonial" due to their characteristics which are very similar to the southern centers, led to the assumption that asymmetrical trade relations existed between north and south, in which it is assumed that the south fixed the rules by obtaining the raw materials it needed from the northern communities in exchange for finished products. These products probably ended up in the hands of the northern elites, thus strengthening their internal power, and at the same time creating increasingly closer links with the stronger communities in the south (Algaze 1993).

This framework may appear simplistic, as the reality is far more complex, with regional differences and a variety of specific situations that differed from site to site, attesting to the complexity of the interactions involved.

ARSLANTEPE IN EASTERN ANATOLIA

The sequence of levels of the fourth and early third millenium at Arslantepe provided important elements in understanding both the level of autonomy reached by the first "urban" development in this area and at the same time the importance of external relations when the urbanization process reached its peak.

The Late Chalcolithic occupation at Arslantepe, characterized by a cultural aspect widespread in the Upper Euphrates and closely correlated with the contemporaneous cultures of the northern Syro-Mesopotamian region, involved the entire areas of the *tell* and showed a different functional characterization of the various sectors of the settlement. Indeed, excavations in the northeasthern area brought to light several levels of small multi-roomed dwelling structures with mud-brick walls (Palmieri 1978). Numerous burials recovered in these levels related to the dwellings contained gifts, mainly consisting of personal ornaments, which, although they differed in several cases by the presence of special objects such as a seal, a silver ring or pottery vessels, provided no obvious proof of any social stratification (Palmieri 1985).

Complex forms of organized labour are suggested, on the contrary, by the presence of mass-produced pottery characterized by fairly hurried manufacture and by the frequent use of potters' marks. The abundance of this production, mainly consisting of coarse bowls varying in size, reflects the rise of new requirements that may be related with the hypothetical development of emergent forms of control over the labour force, with the consequent collective consumption of food beyond the limited family environment.

Craft activities also appear to be fairly developed, as evidenced by the abundant metallurgical material recovered at Arslantepe, including numerous fragments of copper ores and slag that indicate the practice of metallurgical activities in the settlement starting with the initial phases of the metal-making process.

But the most significant indications of a complex organization of society are encountered in the western area of the *tell*, where monumental mud-brick buildings referable to the local Late Chalcolithic are found on what must have been the top of the hill in that period (Frangipane 1993a:136-143). The monumentality and position of these buildings, located directly underneath monumental buildings of the successive period (VI A), suggests the existence, already from the mid-fourth millennium, of a kind of architecturally distiguished, probably public, area, used by the members of the emergent elite. The best preserved building of this period was delimited by mud-brick walls more than one meter thick, coated with white plaster and nearly all decorated with red and black paintings of probably geometric motifs. Along the walls were arranged mud columns covered by a thick layer of clayey plaster, representing an architectural element, in this case presumably a decorative one, new for the period, if we exclude the interesting mention, only of a generic nature for the time being, of the existence of this feature in a building on levels CH 13-14 at Tell Brak, nearly chronologically contemporaneous with that of Arslantepe.

The building was probably modified during the course of time, as we can deduce from the partitions that divided what must have originally have been a large room with columns into four rooms. The largest of these rooms was probably intended for storage, as indicated by the presence of numerous large and middle-sized vessels. No clay-sealings were found, even if a fairly large number of clay lumps, albeit without seal impressions, were found in the adjacent room to the west.

Monumental Architecture

Although the investigations in this part of the Late Chalcolithic settlement have only recently begun, it already appears that around the mid-fourth millennium, Arslantepe showed, through the presence of monumental architecture with special functions, the emergence of an elite that was strong in the region, although maybe not yet capable of centralizing primary resources and means of production.

This developmental process culminates however in the following period (VI A), referable to the late fourth millennium, when Arslantepe appears to be an important administrative center that controls a large part of the economic activities of the region (Frangipane and Palmieri 1983, 1988-89).

In the southwestern area of the mound, excavations have brought to light a series of public monumental buildings in horizontal stratigraphic sequence, occupying an extensive area of the settlement. There is indeed a strong disproportion between the "public" area that appears to be decidedly vast and imposing, and a dwelling area that, although not yet brought to light in the excavation, appears to be fairly small in comparison with the former. This inhabited area does not even reach the northeastern end of the *tell* previously occupied by the Late Chalcolithic settlement. This contrast between a dwelling area that decreases in size with respect to the preceding period and the centralized political, bureaucratic, and economic organization of vast proportions, is a salient feature of the growth of this community. I think, therefore, it would be more correct in this case to refer to the concept of an early state rather than an early urban society.

Although all the public buildings in this period were clearly intended for a number of functions—economic, administrative, and probably political—they have prevailing religious characteristics.

The most recent building is a temple that generically recalls the Mesopotamian typology, also evoked by architectural and decorative features such as niches, a podium-altar, and a plastic wall decoration of concentric ovals obtained by making stamp impressions, which finds parallels in Uruk itself (Sürenhagen 1985). The layout, however, appears to be simplified and rearranged in an original manner, with a large rectangular *cella* and only two smaller rooms on one of the long sides, probably used as storerooms. The smaller room, mainly containing large pots, was probably used as the actual storing place, while the larger one, which contained numerous types of vessels varing in size, including mass-produced wheel-made bowls of the so-called Mesopotamian *flower-pot* type, appears to have been used more for the sorting and movement of goods. A narrow rectangular room opens out into the northeastern corner of the *cella* and, in the final phase of use of the building, had been filled up with rubbish layers containing about a hundred clay sealings bearing the impressions of 25 different seals. This therefore gives us clear indications that a movement of goods (maybe collection and redistribution) under administrative control was taking place in connection with the religious practices.

The temple, constructed on a terrace dug in the southwestern limits of the hill, had cut into part of a previous building (Building III) which was also probably used for religious practices, as indicated by the presence of a kind of quadrangular altar with a hearth in front of it and three small mud basins side by side, close to which were arranged numerous high-stemmed bowls, usually associated with religious activities.

From the adjacent room was recovered an extraordinary assemblage of weapons made of arsenical copper, and consisting of nine swords, some with silver inlay, twelve spearheads and a four-spiral plaque. These outstanding objects, which were probably hanging on the wall, indicate the remarkable role of metals in the reproduction of power. They moreover show the high level of technology reached in metallurgy and, more indirectly, also the importance that Anatolian metal must have had in the fourth millennium interregional exchanges with Mesopotamia.

The oldest of the three public buildings of period VI A (Building IV) appears to be considerable larger than the other two and with a much more articulated layout, characterized by a rectangular monumental gate leading into perpendicular corridors surrounding the building (Figure 2). The first sector closer to the entrance is represented by a complex of adjacent storerooms, each with different functions: the northern room, which is larger and almost exclusively occupied by large containers, appears to have been intended for storage, maybe to supply other rooms; the southern smaller room, which contained, in addition to a few large vessels and some small cooking pots, more than a hundred wheel-made mass-produced bowls and numerous clay-sealings, could have been a kind of store for food to be distributed under administrative control (Frangipane and Palmieri 1988-89; Palmieri 1989). The central room, the only one with access from the corridor, was in fact the entrance to the actual storerooms. Its walls had been painted with figurative motifs represented by the almost obsessive repetition of an anthropomorphic figure with raised up arms, arranged behind a kind of altar and under a richly decorated canopy (Figure 3). The paintings underline the strong ideological, probably religious connotations of the activities connected with centralized storage (Frangipane 1993b).

The ideological/religious basis of the economic centralization in this kind of system is still more clearly evidenced by the identification of the core of the building as a very large temple. The layout of this structure is similar to that of the later temple, but it is more imposing both for its size and the complexity of the building on the whole. The walls along the route leading to the temple—i.e. the northern section of the corridor and the rooms flanking the *cella* on the entrance side—were again decorated with plastic patterns, in this case made of concentric lozenges, and painted motifs.

Administrative System

A concentration of clay-sealings outside the *cella* again stresses the connection of the cult activity with the economic-administrative practices.

Figure 2. Arslantepe-Malatya, Building IV.

Figure 3. Arslantepe. Wall painting in the central room of the store-room complex in Building IV.

The existence of a complex administrative system at Arslantepe is also evidenced by the recovery of thousands of clay-sealings (Figure 4) in a cavity dug out of the western wall of the corridor, opposite the storerooms, where they had been piled in successive rubbish layers as discarded administrative material. The clay sealings, which bore the impression of about 120 different seals and had been affixed on different containers (Figure 5) including storeroom doors, were thrown away according to a precise order which suggested that they had been grouped together before they were discarded (Frangipane and Palmieri 1983:414-444; Ferioli and Fiandra 1983). Such a grouping could have been based on different criteria, for instance the provenance of the sealings from different storeroom sectors or the type of transactions performed; but in any case it reflects a complex recording operation which responds to the need of a sophisticated administrative system.

The complexity of this organization appears to coincide with the size and scale of the economic centralization that must have concerned a large number of activities and above all involved a large number of people, as

Figure 4. Arslantepe. Clay-sealings from the dumping place 206 in Building IV.

indicated by the 157 seals reconstructed from the impressions found in the building. The absolutely predominant use of stamp seals over cylinder seals, the iconography with a clear majority of animal figures, and the styles

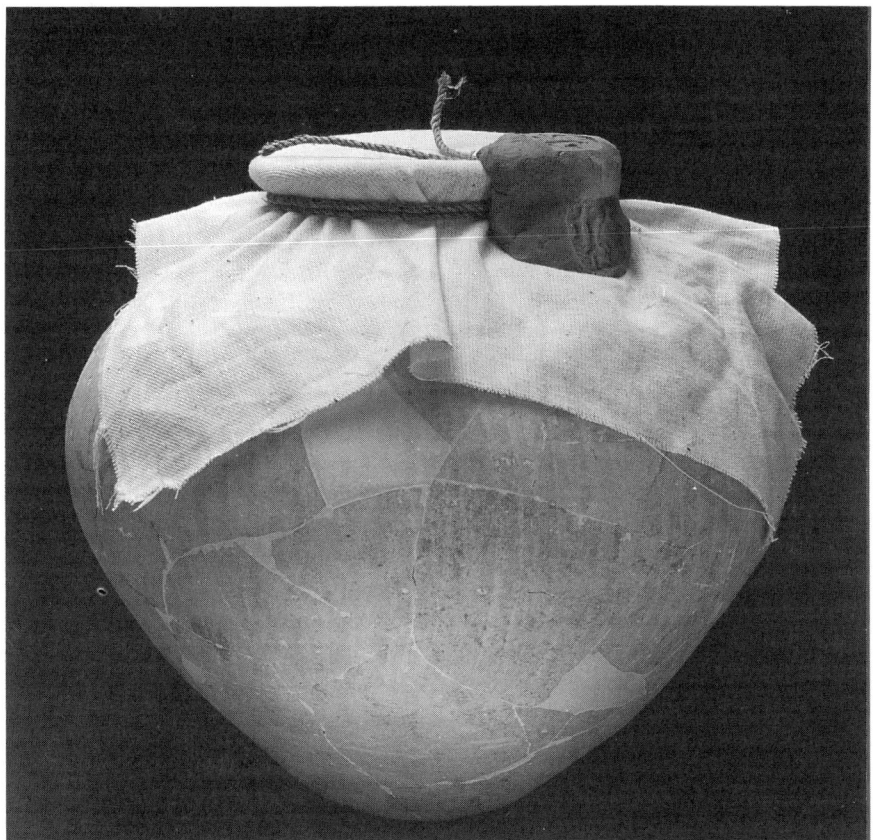

Figure 5. Reconstruction of the clay-sealing affixing system on pots as seen from Arslantepe.

indicate that the glyptics of Arslantepe is fully part of the northern Syro-Mesopotamian tradition, so well represented at Tepe Gawra. However, numerous iconographic and stylistic elements reveal the presence of original characters, suggesting a strong local development of this craft activity. Even where the figures are clearly inspired by the southern Mesopotamian repertoire, such as *tête-bêche* opposite animals or figures of sack and pot bearers, these themes are re-elaborated according to the local taste and repertoire.

In the far less numerous cylinder seals, connections with southern glyptics are more obvious. A particularly striking seal depicts a prominent person being transported on a sledge vehicle with a driver and followed by a procession (Figure 4b). In its iconographic elements, but certainly not in style, the scene recalls similar scenes on seals from Uruk and Susa, indicating significant diffusion among the elites of images intended to symbolize and reinforce their power.

What the exceptional evidence provided by the clay-sealings at Arslantepe does reflect is the presence of an administrative system that is almost identical in its basic structure to the Mesopotamian one, probably even in the details, but at the same time it shows a long tradition of local elaboration, well evidenced in the formal aspects.

Pottery Production

The pottery production is also well in keeping with the increased needs for centrally administered storage, distribution, and religious practices. This is indicated by the more frequent occurrence—with respect to the preceding period—of large necked jars, *pithoi*, and high-stemmed, probably ceremonial, bowls, and by the vast mass production of coarse bowls, now made on the fast wheel and increasingly more standardized, which we hypothetically consider to have been intended for the distribution of food in exchange for work (Frangipane 1989; Espinosa and Manzanilla 1985). The absence of bevelled rim bowls at Arslantepe, but widespread in all Late Uruk contexts, may be due to the existence, in these regions of eastern and southeastern Anatolia, of a long-standing local tradition in the mass production of wheel-made bowls (Figure 6), which is apparently absent in the south before the Late Uruk period. This tradition and the related organization of labour means that Arslantepe directly acquired from the Mesopotamian repertoire the wheel-made flower pot type bowls without having to pass through the technological and organizational step of bevelled rim bowls.

The organization of pottery production also appears to have changed with respect to the Late Chalcolithic period perhaps towards a greater centralization of artisanal activities, which may be indicated by the disappearance of potters' marks. It is the more refined type of southern pottery that is imitated, making a strong selection and simplification in the repertoire by producing mostly necked jars with reserved slip decoration and spouted bottles. On the other hand, coarse ware, both cooking and storage vessels, develops and adapts the local pottery tradition to the new needs. These two types of production are accompanied by black hand-made pottery of clearly central Anatolian inspiration, which underlines the extensive external relations of this community.

Further evidence of centralized control over primary production activities could also be indicated by the great increase in the number of sheep to the detriment of pigs, recovered in the levels of this period, suggesting

Figure 6. Arslantepe. Mass-produced bowls of the local Late Chalcolithic period.

the probably centralized control of herds. This stockraising pattern also occurs in the Late Uruk sites of the south.

CONCLUSIONS

The stratigraphic and architectural continuity observed in the succession of public buildings of the local Late Chalcolithic (period VII) and the subsequent Late Uruk period (period VI A) in the same settlement area, as well as other elements of cultural and organizational continuity, are evidence of the autochthonous roots of the formation of a centralized power both on the site and in the region. However, the nature and the extension of this power appear to be profoundly changed in the society of the Late Uruk period to the extent that it enables us, for the first time, to refer to an early state organization.

It is indeed only in the late fourth millennium that the local elite at Arslantepe takes charge of primary economic activities, the so-called staple finance, through the centralization of resources and labour-force and a complex redistribution system carried out under a sophisticated system of administrative control. Since there is no real urbanization with all the consequences that this concept implies in the general organization of society, the change, in reality, does not appear to involve the basic structure of the community to a notable extent, but rather concerns the capacity of the socially predominant groups to concentrate in their hands economic and perhaps even political power, and to institutionalize their role by intensifying the instruments of ideological pressure.

This change may actually have been stimulated by the new pressure exerted on the northern communities, and particularly on the Anatolian communities, resulting from the demand for raw materials from Mesopotamian centers which, in the second half of the fourth millennium, interact with the northern communities certainly more intensively than before. Even if it is difficult to imagine a model of the type proposed by Algaze, in which the long-distance trade conducted by the southern Late Uruk towns is the principal and almost only reason for the rise of complex societies in the north, it is very likely that trade intensified in this period in relation to the new requirements that emerged not only in the southern societies, but also in northern societies.

Even if the so-called "colonial sites" in the Middle and Upper Euphrates valley (Habuba Kabira, Jebel Aruda, Hassek Höyük) (Strommenger 1980; van Driel 1983; Behm-Blancke 1984), which were characterized by cultural traits identical with those of the Mesopotamian towns, do not give any clear indication they were "trade colonies",[1] at any rate they seem to be the result of the transfer of entire communities or portions of communities to new lands, with which they had traditionally always maintained close relations. Their presence therefore suggests there was an intensification of these relations and a change in the nature thereof. The effects of these new interactions may differ from case to case and from one region to another, according to the level and type of involvement of the individual communities.

At Arslantepe, the participation of the site in the new interregional exchange network, which started in the Late Uruk period, must have had an influence on the direction taken by the early state development of this Anatolian community which, in the late fourth millennium, introduced a clearly Mesopotamian type of economic and administrative system. A

---

[1]On one hand there is no clear evidence of commercial activities in these sites; and on the other, the movement of groups of traders in the historically known cases (see for instance the Assyrian colonies in Cappadocia) does not give rise to the transfer of the entire complex of the original culture to a foreign land.

greater and more regular external demand probably stimulated the development of coordination functions in the central institutions that were forming autonomously, by transforming the external trade of Chalcolithic communities—that was organized on the basis of a limited degree of centralization—into an exchange system under the control of the local centers, and putting the elite in a condition to take over the administration of at least part of the primary economy.

The non-local roots of this substantial change is probably the cause of the crisis that overcame the system after the Late Uruk period, when the centralized organization of Mesopotamian type definitively collapsed, paving the way to the arrival of the East Anatolian/Transcaucasian groups.

Similar situations did not occur in all the northern regions where, according to their own history, certain sites had developments that in no way stopped the early urban and early state phenomena, but were instead the result of their transformation and re-elaboration according to more local patterns.

REFERENCES

Algaze, G., 1989, The Uruk Expansion, *Current Anthropology* 30, 5:571-608.
Algaze, G., 1993, *The Uruk World System*, The University of Chicago Press, Chicago and London.
Behm-Blancke, M. (ed.), 1984, Hassek Höyük, *Istanbuler Mitteilungen* 34:31-111.
Espinosa, G., and L. Manzanilla, 1985, Consideraciones en torno a la capacidad de los cuencos troncocónicos de Arslantepé (Malatya), *Quaderni de La Ricerca Scientifica* 112, Scavi e Ricerche Archeologiche degli anni 1976-1979, I, Roma:139-162.
Ferioli, P., and E. Fiandra, 1983, Clay-sealings from Arslantepe VIA: administration and bureaucracy, in: *Perspectives on Protourbanization in Eastern Anatolia: Arslantepe (Malatya). An Interim Report on 1975-83 Campaings* (M. Frangipane and A. Palmieri, eds.), *Origini* XII, 2, Rome, pp. 455-509.
Frangipane, M., 1989, Produzione di vasellame in serie e distribuzione di razioni alimentari nelle società protourbane del periodo Tardo Uruk-Jemdet Nasr, in: *Il Pane del Re* (R. Dolce and C. Zaccagnini, eds.), Studi di Storia Antica 13, Bologna, pp. 49-63.
Frangipane, M., 1993a, Local components in the development of centralized societies in Syro-Anatolian regions, in: *Between the Rivers and Over the Mountains. Archaeologica Anatolica et Mesopotamica Alba Palmieri Dedicata* (M. Frangipane, H. Hauptmann, M. Liverani, P. Matthiae, and M. Mellink, eds.), Università di Roma 'La Sapienza', Roma, pp. 133-161.
Frangipane, M., 1993b, Dipinti murali in un edificio palaziale di Arslantepe-Malatya: aspetti ideologici nelle prime forme di centralizzazione economica, *Studi Micenei ed Egeo-Anatolici* XXX:143-154.
Frangipane, M., and A. Palmieri, 1983, A protourban centre of the Late Uruk period, in: *Perspectives on Protourbanization in Eastern Anatolia: Arslantepe (Malatya). An Interim Report on 1975-83 Campaings* (M. Frangipane and A. Palmieri, eds.), *Origini* XII, 2, Rome, pp. 287-454.

Frangipane, M., and A. Palmieri, 1988-89, Aspects of centralization in the Late Uruk period in the Mesopotamian periphery, *Origini* XIV, 2:539-560.

Oates, J., 1986, Tell Brak: The Uruk/Early Dynastic sequence, in: *Gamdat Nasr, Period or Regional Style* (U. Finkbeiner and W. Rölling, eds.), Wiesbaden, pp. 245-273.

Palmieri, A., 1978, Scavi ad Arslantepe (Malatya), *Quaderni de 'La Ricerca Scientifica'* 100, Roma:311-373.

Palmieri, A., 1985, Eastern Anatolia and early Mesopotamian urbanization: remarks on changing relations, in: *Studi di Paletnologia in onore di S. M. Puglisi* (M. Liverani, A. Palmieri, and R. Peroni, eds.), Università 'La Sapienza' di Roma, Roma, pp. 191-213.

Palmieri, A., 1989, Storage and distribution at Arslantepe-Malatya in the Late Uruk Period, in: *Anatolia and the Ancient Near East* (K. Emre, B. Hrouda, M. Mellink, and N. Özgüç, eds.), Ankara, pp. 419-430.

Stein, G. J., 1993, Mesopotamian-Anatolian interaction at 4th milennium B.C. Hacinebi, in the Euphrates valley, *Mar Sipri* 6, 1:1, 6-8.

Strommenger, E., 1980, *Habuba Kabira. Eine Stadt vor 5000 Jahren*, Philipp von Zabern, Mainz.

Sürenhagen, D., 1985, Einige Kulturelle Kontakte zwischen Arslantepe VIA und den Frühsumjerisch-hochprotoelamischen Stadtkulturen, in: *Studi di Paletnologia in onore di S. M. Puglisi* (M. Liverani, A. Palmieri, and R. Peroni, eds.), Università 'La Sapienza' di Roma, Roma, pp. 229-236.

Tobler, A. J., 1950, *Excavations at Tepe Gawra*, University of Pennsylvania Press, Philadelphia.

van Driel, G., and C. van Driel Murray, 1983, Jebel Aruda, the 1982 season of excavation, *Akkadica* 33:1-26.

van Loon, M. (ed.), 1988, *Hammam et-Turkman I*, Nederland Historisch-Archeologisch Instituut, Istanbul.

Chapter 3

Urbanism and the Rise of Complex Society and the Early State in Egypt

KATHRYN A. BARD

INTRODUCTION

By *ca.* 3050 B.C. the Early Dynastic state had emerged in Egypt, controlling much of the Nile Valley from the Delta to the First Cataract at Aswan—over 1000 km upriver. This was a centrally controlled polity ruled by a (god-) king from the newly founded capital of Memphis in the north, near Saqqara. Archaeological evidence for state control consists of the names (*serekhs*) of First Dynasty kings on pots, seals, tags (originally attached to containers), and other artifacts found at major Early Dynastic sites in Egypt. Such evidence also suggests a state taxation system in place in the early dynasties, and large quantities of goods and materials marshalled and controlled by the state. The early state in Egypt was highly stratified, with the king at the top of the social pyramid; evidence for such social stratification comes from the highly differentiated burials of this period found throughout Egypt.

The beginning of the First Dynasty was only about 1000 years after the earliest farming villages appeared on the Nile, and the Predynastic period,

---

KATHRYN A. BARD • Department of Archaeology, Boston University, 675 Commonwealth Avenue, Boston, Massachusetts 02215, U.S.A.

Emergence and Change in Early Urban Societies, edited by Linda Manzanilla. Plenum Press, New York, 1997.

during the 4th millennium B.C., was one of fairly rapid social and political evolution. Ancient Egypt is one of the earliest examples of state formation, and Predynastic data should elucidate general processes which may be applicable to other cases of state formation. But we only have a *partial* understanding of the Predynastic, based on different types of data in the north and south. Possibly new and forthcoming evidence from the Delta will provide information on the processes of state formation and unification there, but in the south there is the problem of so many missing settlement data, which are needed in order to make theoretical generalizations.

Unlike much of southern Mesopotamia, which is now sparsely inhabited (Adams and Nissen 1972:1), in part because of soil depletion in earlier periods, the Egyptian Nile Valley is one of the world's most densely populated regions, and has been intensively cultivated for 5000 years. The Nile River has shifted eastward since Predynastic times (Butzer 1976:34-35), with consequences for the preservation of sites on both banks. Modern development and settlements in Egypt have also greatly limited survey and excavation of earlier settlements. There are relatively few data on subsistence for the Predynastic, except from recent fieldwork, and it is unknown when, why, and where agricultural intensification (via irrigation) occurred. Because of alluviation, continuous cultivation, geological conditions, and the modern dense occupation along the river, we may never know much about settlement patterns except from sites preserved above the floodplain. Given that there are so few Predynastic settlement data, causative factors of population increase and population pressure in the rise of the state are highly speculative.

In Upper Egypt there is another reason for the relatively slim evidence for settlements. Located on the low desert, Predynastic cemeteries (with their well preserved burials, some of which contained many grave goods in sometimes exotic materials) were simply of greater interest to earlier excavators than settlements. Early villages and towns have been disturbed by digging for *sebakh* (organic remains used for fertilizing) or destroyed by expanding cultivation on the floodplain. Unless permanent architecture was detected, such as the mudbrick walls excavated by Petrie at Nagada's South Town, more ephemeral Predynastic settlements, which left mainly dense scatters of sherds were interpreted as having been destroyed (see Petrie 1901a:32). In any case, earlier archaeologists working in Egypt did not have the excavation techniques enabling them to understand such sites and their formation processes.

Only more recently has interest in Upper Egypt shifted to the detailed excavation of Predynastic settlements. But such settlements, located on spurs above the floodplain, are deflated, with little or no evidence of permanent architecture. Missing, or perhaps deposited under alluvium, are large (fortified?) sites on higher ground of the floodplain, such as Kemp (1989:33) posits for the late Predynastic. An exception is Nekhen (Hierakonpolis), probably founded on a Nile levee, as shown by coring and sondage in 1984 (Hoffman, Hamroush, and Allen 1986:181).

In northern Egypt, where Predynastic burials of the Maadi culture are relatively unspectacular, with only a few pots, or no burial goods at all, earlier excavations focused equally on settlements. But settlements in the north may also have been better preserved than in the south. Evidence at Maadi of rectangular buildings and subterranean structures suggests good preservation of architecture constructed mainly of wattle and matting (Rizkana and Seeher 1989:75). According to recent excavation reports (Chlodnicki, Fattovich, and Salvatori 1991; Eiwanger 1984, 1988, 1992; van den Brink 1988, 1989, 1992; von der Way 1987, 1988, 1989, 1992), conditions for preservation of stratified remains in the Delta and its margins may be the best in Egypt.

Although there is important evidence from sites such as Hierakonpolis, Predynastic craft production and distribution are mostly known indirectly—from grave goods—as are various technologies (pottery production, metal working, stone carving, and glazing and faience). The rise of political elites can only be suggested from mortuary evidence, and archaeological evidence to demonstrate regional integration and the formation of the earliest state(s) is equivocal. Likewise, the process of unification leading to the Early Dynastic state is uncertain, and the role of warfare in this is only suggested by scenes that appear on late Predynastic palettes. Given that there is so little archaeological evidence for settlements in Predynastic Egypt, the rise of urbanism is also problematic.

URBANISM IN DYNASTIC EGYPT

The majority of people in ancient Egypt were farmers, and the tightly linear geography of the floodplain would have favored more linearly dispersed hamlets of farmers throughout the Valley. Based on population size of Egypt and the number of villages during the medieval Islamic period, Hassan (1993:562) estimates a total rural population of 1,140,000 during the Old Kingdom, with an average village size of 452 persons. It is reasonable to suspect, however, that there were many smaller hamlets of farmers and their families, as there are today in rural areas. Archaeological evidence for such villages is unknown, however, and the remains of towns and cities are scant compared to the evidence from cemeteries and (later) cult centers of Dynastic Egypt.

Although it is no longer believed that early civilization in Egypt was one without cities (see Wilson 1968:34), evidence of Dynastic settlements is missing for the many of the same reasons that it is missing for the Predynastic period. The Dynastic state was certainly organized with a capital, royal residences and estates, nome capitals, and cult centers, and there is textual evidence that all of these existed (see O'Connor 1972, Smith 1972, Wenke 1991:310-315). Terms for settlements were used in Egyptian (*niwt* and *hwt* in the Old Kingdom), but terms differentiating types of settlements did not appear until later, and even then these have problematic meanings (Bietak 1979:99-100; see also Butzer 1976:57-80; Hassan 1993:561).

With the unification of the centralized state (by *ca.* 3050 B.C.), town growth took place in Egypt within the bureaucratic system of the state, through the foundation of temples, royal estates, local redistributive centers, and administrative centers (Kemp 1977:199). During periods of strong centralized control in Egypt (the Old, Middle, and New Kingdoms), the Nile greatly facilitated state control and communication. Given the very arid environment, the population inhabited the floodplain or its margins, and this linear, riverine pattern of occupation facilitated state control of its population through taxation and conscription. During times of collapse of the centralized state (the First, Second, and Third Intermediate Periods), the historical evidence suggests that spatial organization of polities was much more like that of competing city states controlling a much smaller geographic region, as found elsewhere in the ancient Near East. At such times fortified towns with walls are known (O'Connor 1983:248, 1993:579).

Workmen's towns, such as the Middle Kingdom site of el-Lahun and the New Kingdom site of Deir el Medina, are known archaeologically, but the evidence of planned towns for state construction projects is fairly specialized. For security reasons relating to workers who were employed to construct the royal tombs, these workmen's towns were walled, and within these walls there was little room for major changes through time. Also well preserved archaeologically are the Middle Kingdom forts and New Kingdom temple towns that the Egyptians built in Nubia, but again the evidence of such settlements, located outside of Egypt and superimposed on indigenous cultures for the purpose of economic exploitation, is also of a fairly specialized nature.

In addition to planned towns of the state, there were towns with a more 'organic' type of internal development (see Smith 1972:707-709; O'Connor 1993:581). Akhetaten (modern Tell el Amarna), the ephemeral capital in Middle Egypt of the "heretical" pharaoh Akhenaten (*ca.* 1363-1347 B.C.), exhibits planning only in the central quarter ("Central City"), which consists of temples, palace, and government buildings. Most of the population lived in two residential areas to the north and south of the Central City, which, according to Kemp (1989:294), give the overwhelming impression of a "series of joined villages." The city encompassed an area of 16 by 13 km, as delineated by a number of boundary stelae (Kemp 1989:269), but this includes several residential areas and palaces outside the Central City, and a large expanse of low desert which extends to the limestone cliffs on the east, where the Amarna elite built their tombs. Again, the archaeological evidence of Tell el Amarna is fairly specialized, given that its main occupation was very short-lived, and it was deserted by the government after Akhenaten died. However, the lack of centralized planning within a walled settlement, and a more dispersed arrangement of residences (outside the walled compounds of temples or government buildings), as seen at Tell el Amarna, may be more typical of ancient Egyptian cities and towns during periods of strong centralized control. Such an arrangement suggests that the city extended in a dispersed manner from north to south along the floodplain and river, but included a very large area beyond this (east in the case of Akhenaten) in the low desert where the royal and elite tombs were located.

ARCHAEOLOGICAL EVIDENCE OF PREDYNASTIC SETTLEMENTS

Upper Egypt

Dating of the Upper Egyptian (Nagadan) Predynastic has been based on a seriation system devised by Petrie and based on grave goods (1901a:4-12), which he called Sequence Dating (S.D.). Petrie recognized three periods of the Predynastic: Amratian, Gerzean, and Semainean, the last being followed by the First Dynasty (Petrie 1939:9). The Badarian, an earlier phase of the Predynastic, is known from Middle Egypt. More recently, grave goods as well as classes of settlement pottery have been placed in three (slightly different) periods, Nagada I, II, and III, using a modification of Petrie's system devised by Kaiser (1956, 1957; see also Adams 1988). Kings of a unified Egypt immediately preceding the First Dynasty are placed in what is called "Dyn. 0." Since Petrie's initial work, the Predynastic has continued to be mainly defined in periods formed by a seriation of grave goods (see Arkell and Ucko 1965:150-155; Trigger 1968:62-67).

Although many Predynastic sites were excavated long before the advent of radiocarbon dating (Figure 1), some results from recent excavations in the Nagada region are available. Hassan (1984:683) concludes that dates

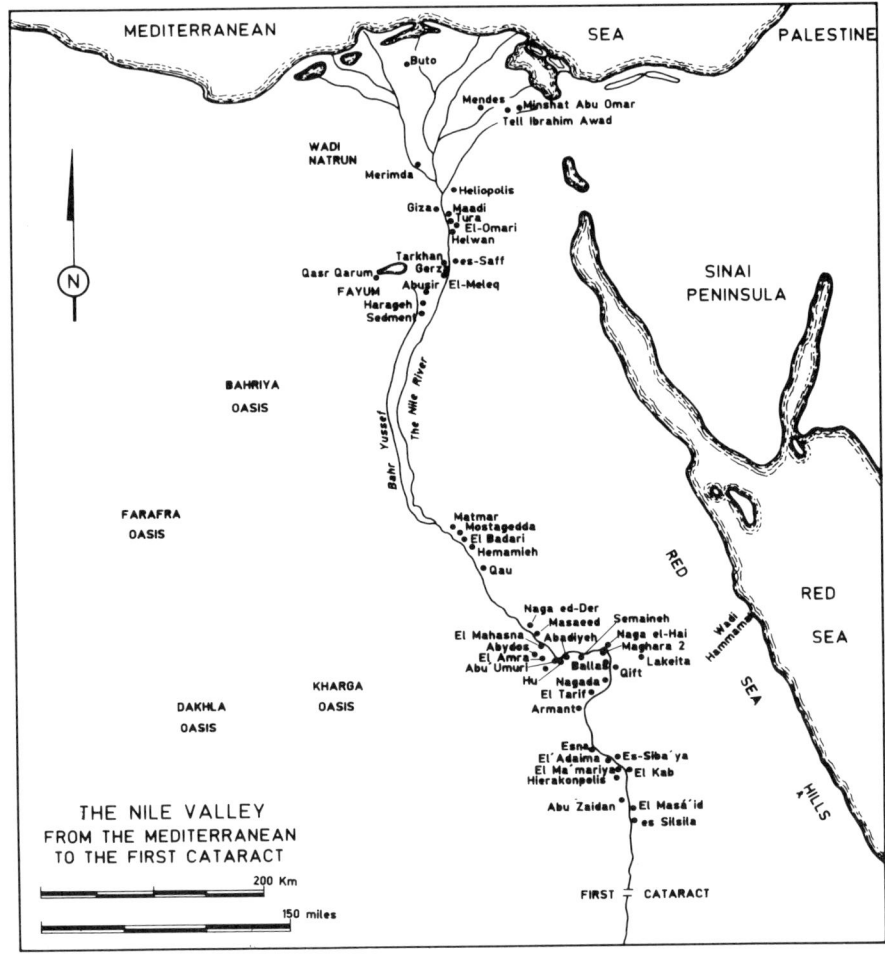

Figure 1. Map of Predynastic sites in the Nile Valley.

from three early Nagada sites provide a midpoint estimate of 3760 ±40 B.C., and dates of the Nagada II zone of South Town provide a range of 3600-3300 B.C. A calibrated radiocarbon date from a Nagada III tomb at Hierakonpolis of 3025 ±80 B.C. (WIS-1180) has been published by Hoffman (1982:42). Chronologies based on king lists place the beginning of the First Dynasty at *ca.* 3050 B.C.[1]

---

[1] A date of 3050 B.C. for the beginning of the First Dynasty is given in an unpublished chronology of the late Klaus Baer's.

In Upper Egypt major towns arose at Hierakonpolis, Nagada, Abydos, and possibly Diospolis Parva (Abadiyeh and Hu). Numerous other Predynastic sites are known in between these as well as farther south to Aswan (see Bard 1994a; Needler 1984:68), but none of these seem to have become large centers.

Hierakonpolis (ancient Nekhen) and its environs, with over 50 Predynastic occupation, industrial, and burial sites (Hoffman 1982:123-127), comprised a major Predynastic center. According to Hoffman's model (Hoffman, Hamroush, and Allen 1986:178-186), Predynastic occupation at Hierakonpolis was early—beginning in the Badarian and Nagada Ia-b periods, *ca*. 4000-3800/3700 B.C., with small scattered farming villages. The Nagada Ic to IIa period (*ca*. 3800/3700-3500/3400 B.C.) was one of regional expansion. Rectangular houses were found in agglomerated settlements, and Hierakonpolis was becoming a center of pottery production. In later Nagada II (b-d) times, *ca*. 3500/3400-3200 B.C., there was a settlement shift from the desert to the edge of areas under cultivation. Basin irrigation may have begun at this time. A large oval courtyard may be the earliest evidence for a Nagada II temple. The Nagada III period, *ca*. 3200-3100 B.C., was a time of political unification, when floods were low and most desert sites were abandoned. The city of Nekhen continued to grow, with "large palace and temple complexes" (Hoffman, Hamroush, and Allen 1986:184).

Well preserved remains of settlements are known from Hierakonpolis—remarkable evidence for Upper Egypt. Both circular and rectangular houses have been excavated by Hoffman; some of these houses had fences and outbuildings (Hoffman 1982:137). A rectangular, semi-subterranean house with postholes representing roof supports was excavated at Locality 29 (Hoffman 1980:130). Elsewhere, beneath the Early Dynastic levels, about 4 m of stratified Predynastic settlement deposits have been found by coring and augering (Hoffman 1989:320). Stratified cultural deposits have also been found via coring under the modern floodplain.

Undoubtedly an Early Dynastic temple also existed at Hierakonpolis. Excavating there in 1897-99, J.E. Quibell and F.W. Green concentrated on the remains of the walled town on the floodplain, with its walled temple precinct of Tuthmose III (New Kingdom) in the southern corner (Quibell and Green 1902:pl. 73). Within the temple area, Quibell found what he termed the "Main Deposit," which included the decorated Maceheads of (king) Scorpion and Narmer, and other artifacts stylistically dating to the late Predynastic/Early Dynastic periods (Quibell and Green 1902:35-44; see also Adams 1974a, 1974b). These artifacts were probably associated with a temple dating to the Early Dynastic period, and were ritually buried when a later temple was built.

Evidence of specialized production, including the production of basalt and diorite vases and microlithic drill bits for bead-making, has also been found at Hierakonpolis (Hoffman 1982:13-14, 130). Pottery kilns have been excavated in the low desert where utilitarian (straw-tempered) wares and Plum Red ware (Black-topped Red class and Polished Red class) were fired (Hoffman, Hamroush, and Allen 1986:183). Vats from two sites at Hierakonpolis suggest the brewing of a wheat-based beer (Geller 1989:52; 1992:21-23).

Mortuary evidence at Hierakonpolis suggests a large center, and Adams and Hoffman (1987:196, 198) estimate there were several thousand Predynastic graves in the region. Southwest of the town site beneath the walls of the "Fort" (a large, elaborately niched, mudbrick structure possibly built in the Second Dynasty), Garstang excavated numerous Predynastic graves (Garstang 1907:136-137) dating mainly to Nagada III, though there were also some Nagada II burials (Kemp 1963:28; see also Adams and Hoffman 1987:180-186). Other Predynastic graves in this cemetery and NE of the Fort had been excavated earlier by de Morgan (Needler 1984:110).

Another Predynastic cemetery area at Hierakonpolis is known in the area of the "Decorated Tomb," south of the Predynastic town (Quibell and Green 1902:20-21). Consisting of a mudbrick-lined pit with painted plaster walls, the tomb dates to the Nagada II period (Case and Payne 1962:10; Payne 1973:31). Green's papers at the University of Cambridge indicate that this was in a small Predynastic cemetery (Adams 1974b:84-111; Payne 1973:31). Sequence dates of pottery from this cemetery are distributed throughout the Nagada II period, and Kaiser (1958:188-192) has suggested that the graves surrounding the Decorated Tomb formed a royal cemetery.

Nine more cemetery areas, dating from Nagada I through Nagada III, have also been located elsewhere in the Hierakonpolis region. One cemetery area (Locality 6), located 2.5 km up the Great Wadi, contained more than 200 Nagada I-II burials, and large Nagada "Protodynastic" (Nagada III/Dyn. 0) tombs, up to 22.75 m^2 in floor area (Adams and Hoffman 1987:196, 202). Burials of elephants, hippopotamuses, crocodiles, baboons, cattle, sheep, goats, and dogs have also been excavated SW of a stone-cut tomb in the western part of this cemetery (Hoffman 1983:50). Evidence of postholes demonstrates that superstructures once covered some of the large tombs in Locality 6, and these tombs were surrounded by fences (Hoffman 1983:49). This may be the earliest association of large elite tombs with a superstructure that symbolized a house/shrine for the deceased. Hoffman (1983:49) states that the Locality 6 tombs belonged to the Protodynastic rulers of Hierakonpolis, and speculates that the largest tomb there was that of (king) Scorpion.

The archaeological evidence at Hierakonpolis, then, suggests the existence of a temple in later Predynastic and Early Dynastic times. Possibly the settlement was becoming agglomerated on the Kom el Ahmar, where the later town is located, but given that much of this early town is buried under the floodplain its size cannot be determined. The late Predynastic and Early Dynastic town may have been little more than a cult center with associated buildings and residences. The existing evidence demonstrates that cemeteries and industrial areas remained dispersed in the Nagada II and III periods. Although desert settlements may have been abandoned in later Predynastic times, settlement may have been more dispersed within and next to the floodplain. Agglomeration (solely) within the town of Nekhen from late Predynastic times and later would have left more evidence of a *tell*, as is found in southern Mesopotamia.

Several Predynastic sites, located 28 km NW of Luxor on the west bank near the modern village of Nagada, were excavated by Petrie in 1894-95. With over 2200 graves, the three Nagada cemeteries ("Great New Race Cemetery," and Cemeteries B and T), along with the estimated 1000 burials excavated by Quibell at Ballas, just north of Nagada, form the largest mortuary area in Predynastic Egypt (Bard 1994b:77).

Two Predynastic settlements, "North Town" and "South Town," were also investigated by Petrie in the Nagada region. Layers of occupation at North Town were very thin, and some flexed burials of children were excavated there (Petrie and Quibell 1896:2). In the northern part of South Town, Petrie found the remains of a thick mudbrick wall, which appeared to be "a fortification with divisions within it" (Petrie and Quibell 1896:54). Test excavations conducted in 1979-1983 at South Town by the Oriental Institute of Naples revealed Predynastic, Early Dynastic, and later Dynastic occupations based on ceramics. Postholes, notches, and grooves cut in the sediment, piles of mudbrick from collapsed walls, and a rounded ditch to the north of the site were identified (Barocas, Fattovich, and Tosi 1989:300-301).

Near the village of el Khattara in the Nagada region, Hassan has located and excavated a number of smaller Predynastic sites. Full excavation reports are forthcoming, but Hays (1976:552) reports previously-unknown Predynastic sites consisting of several mounds of midden deposits. Hassan and Matson's (1989:314) multidimensional scaling of ceramics from Predynastic settlements in the Nagada region indicates an early Nagada group at the el Khattara sites (and a later Nagada II group at South Town and North Town).

The el Khattara sites are located in a linear pattern west of the floodplain. Sites are spaced about 2 km apart (Fekri Hassan, personal communication, 1985). Although there is no evidence of permanent architecture in mudbrick or with stone foundations, domestic features, such as small mud-lined pits, hearths, whole pots, and small wooden posts, have been excavated (Holmes 1989:191).

The Predynastic burials from Nagada, however, are much more spectacular than the poorly preserved remains of settlements. The small Cemetery T that Petrie excavated at Nagada has been considered the burial place of Predynastic chieftains (Case and Payne 1962:15), or kings (Kemp 1973:42). Burials in this cemetery date to Nagada II and III (Davis 1983:21-24; Bard 1994b:81), and include three unusual brick-lined tombs (T15, T23, T29), and a pit with the bones of about 20 dogs (Petrie and Quibell 1896:26). Before Petrie was at Nagada, Jacques de Morgan excavated two "royal" tombs there and a necropolis for "common people" with tombs containing Early Dynastic grave goods (de Morgan 1897:159). This cemetery is located about 6.8 km south of the main Predynastic cemetery (Fekri Hassan, personal communication, 1985). The one well-preserved "royal" tomb, with an elaborately niched mudbrick superstructure, was thought to belong to (king) Aha, dating to the beginning of the First Dynasty (de Morgan 1897:147-202).

About 45 km NW of Nagada, below the Qena bend of the Nile, another major Predynastic center was located at Hu, known as Diospolis Parva in Graeco-Roman times. In 1898-99, Petrie excavated six "prehistoric" cemeteries (U, R, B, C, A, H) in the Hu region, and he noted the remains of prehistoric villages east of the Dynastic cemetery, N, and in the area he called F (Petrie 1901a:31-32). During a reconnaissance survey in 1989, I relocated a Predynastic settlement (HG) near the modern village of Abadiyeh with Predynastic sherds, but no visible architecture, scattered over an area of about 3 ha (Bard 1989:476). I also located another smaller settlement (SH) next to the late Predynastic cemetery at Semaineh, from which the term "Semainean" (Nagada III) was derived. This had thin cultural deposits and no visible architecture except a mudbrick feature, which probably dates to the Old Kingdom.

Site HG was excavated in 1991 (Bard 1992a). Much of this settlement had been disturbed by cultivation in the 1950s and 1960s, and there was no evidence of permanent architecture or even postholes from more perishable architecture. The ceramics date predominantly to Nagada II, and sherds of Predynastic bread molds were also identified (Swain 1992). A lithic workshop was excavated on a small spur to the east of the main village. Artifacts from the workshop included debris from all stages of stone tool manufacture. Finds of a small palette of hard sandstone, and an end fragment of a large, rhomboidal slate palette suggest (small-scale) craft production. Calibrated dates obtained on charcoal from test pits excavated at HG in 1989 place occupation during the Nagada I and II periods: 3700-3370 B.C. (OxA-2183), and 3500-3100 B.C. (OxA-2182) (Bard 1991:130).

A preliminary analysis of the materials found at HG suggests evidence of a widespread exchange network. Beads of agate and carnelian were recovered, as was an unworked piece of green feldspar, also used for bead production in the Predynastic. Agate is found locally in *wadi* deposits, but the green feldspar and carnelian come from the Eastern Desert (Lucas and Harris 1989:387, 391, 394). Two small lumps of copper were recovered, and the nearest copper mines are also in the Eastern Desert (Lucas and Harris 1989:210). A (pierced?) cowrie shell from the Red Sea was also excavated.

Grinding stones collected on the surface of HG consisted of igneous rocks (rhyolite porphyry, basalt, granite) and metamorphic rocks (marble, quartzite) (Mahmoud and Bard 1993:243-244). Marble is found in the Eastern Desert, and the red and grey granites come from Aswan (Lucas and Harris 1989:58, 414). The other igneous and metamorphic rocks are found near Aswan, as well as in the Eastern Desert (Lucas and Harris 1989:61-63, 416).

Complex economic interaction is also suggested by another artifact excavated at HG: a fragment of a mud-sealing. The sealing was created when a mud lump was impressed over three loops of string tied around a jar (or some kind of container). The existence of such a sealing suggests the exchange of valued goods in a regional or long-distance, and not local, exchange network. Such economic evidence from the settlement at HG would also correlate with grave goods excavated by Petrie in sometimes exotic materials, such as lapis lazuli and gold, from the nearby Cemetery B (Petrie 1901a:34).

Downstream from Hu is Abydos, a major center of Predynastic culture in Upper Egypt, and a major cult center in Dynastic times. A study of settlements and cemeteries in the region, dating from the Predynastic through the Old Kingdom, has been conducted by Patch (1984:17), who located seven new Predynastic sites during an archaeological survey in 1982-83. Patch's investigations show a change in settlement patterns through time. In early Nagada times (Nagada Ic and IIa-b) cemeteries of relatively similar size were scattered along the desert edge on both the east and west banks, "implying a similar pattern of settlements" (Patch 1991:306). In later Nagada II times (Nagada IId1-d2) the settlement pattern shows some nucleation, and several cemeteries were no longer in use because of the disappearance of many earlier villages (Patch 1991:307).

Predynastic cemeteries recorded in the Abydos region are in three areas: one near the Osiris temple, the others near the villages of el Mahasna and el Amra (see Ayrton and Loat 1911, Naville 1914, and Randall-MacIver and Mace 1902), from which the term "Amratian" (Nagada I) was derived. In addition to burials, eight Predynastic kilns, which the excavators thought were for parching grain, were excavated in the Cemetery D area of the

Osiris temple (Peet and Loat 1913:1-7). The kilns consisted of two parallel rows of large jars of straw-tempered ware sunk into the ground and containing carbonized organic matter; Geller (1989:47), as noted previously, has evidence from Hierakonpolis that such facilities were for brewing.

The Umm el-Qa'ab at Abydos is where the kings of the First Dynasty built their tombs and "funerary palaces," walled constructions located along the edge of cultivation (O'Connor 1989). Northeast of the identified First Dynasty royal tombs are smaller and less elaborate tombs (B Group) excavated by Petrie (1901b:3-5). Several of these tombs have been identified as belonging to kings immediately preceding, or belonging to the beginning of, the First Dynasty (Iri-Hor, Ka, Narmer, Aha) (Kaiser and Dreyer 1982:241-242). North of the tomb of Aha is another group of tombs (U), one of which (U-j) contained many bone labels with the earliest known hieroglyphs (Dreyer 1992:62-63). The writing on these labels was connected with the delivery of goods (Kaiser 1990:298-299), and probably denotes (royal) estates and administrative districts, with information about the provenience of the vessels to which they were attached and their contents (Dreyer 1992:63, 66).

At Abydos, then, there is evidence of a royal cemetery dating to the end of the Predynastic period (Nagada IIIa-b), possibly of kings whose descendants reigned in the First Dynasty. In the Early Dynastic period there is an enormous increase in the burial population, probably due to an influx of persons belonging to the royal household and associated with the royal burials on the Umm el Qa'ab (Patch 1991:310). The cemetery data, however, suggest that before the Middle Kingdom Abydos was still no larger than a "village" or "small town" (Patch 1991:341), and the main focus of development was mortuary and not urban.

Middle Egypt

In Middle Egypt, Predynastic sites are found in the Badari district, on the east bank of the Nile opposite, and to the south of, Assiut. The earliest class of pottery ("Badarian," a black-topped brown ware with a rippled surface created by pebble burnishing) from prehistoric settlements and cemeteries in this region is thought to be earlier than Petrie's Predynastic classes from Upper Egypt, a chronology demonstrated by Caton Thompson's excavation of the stratified midden at Hemamieh (Brunton and Caton Thompson 1928:73-75).

At El Badari, the remains of Predynastic settlements were located on Spurs 2-12, with cemeteries occurring on Spurs 14-19 (Brunton and Caton Thompson 1928:pl. 2). The small settlement on the north spur at Hemamieh was only 37 × 46 m in area, with some hut (and/or storage) circles, and a midden 2 m deep (Brunton and Caton Thompson 1928:69, 79,

82-88). At Mostagedda, Brunton excavated several small Predynastic villages consisting of hut circles and middens. Cemeteries range in date from Badarian and Predynastic to Dynastic (Brunton 1937:3-4). A recent archaeological survey in the Badari district by Holmes and Friedman has led to the discovery of two Predynastic sites (BD-1 and BD-2), and they noted another at Minshat el Kom el Ahmar (Holmes and Friedman 1989:15). Archaeological evidence in the Badari district is mainly of small settlements, scattered along spurs from Matmar in the north to Qau el Kebir in the south. None of these sites represents Predynastic culture on the scale of that seen at several major sites in Upper Egypt.

North of the Badari district, no Predynastic sites are known south of the Fayum region, over 300 km farther downriver (Middle Egypt is the least surveyed area in the Egyptian Nile Valley, which may in part account for the lack of evidence, but it is also possible that early sites are less well preserved there). Although the major Predynastic sites are found in Upper Egypt, it would be surprising if such settlement suddenly stopped at el Badari. While the Fayum is better known for Neolithic sites on the strandlines representing earlier lake levels, Caton Thompson and Gardner (1934:69-71) excavated a Predynastic site near Qasr Qarun in the SW Fayum. More recently this site was investigated by Wenke, who located two other Predynastic sites to the east. The three sites appear to be "only temporary, seasonally occupied encampments" (Wenke *et al.* 1983:39). Samples of charcoal from hearths obtained in the northern Fayum by the Institute of Archaeology, Jagiellonian University, have yielded (uncalibrated) radiocarbon dates of "the times directly preceding the so-called archaic [Early Dynastic] period" (Dagnon-Ginter *et al.* 1984:65).

The best known Predynastic site in the Fayum region is the cemetery at Gerza, from which the term "Gerzean" (Nagada II) is derived. The site is located on the west bank, about 7 km NE of Meydum. Compared to the major cemeteries in Upper Egypt this was a small cemetery, with only 288 burials, a high percentage of them undisturbed (Petrie, Wainwright, and Mackay 1912:5). No mention is made by Petrie of a Predynastic settlement at Gerza. The Predynastic cemetery at Gerza may represent more permanent occupation than that at the sites located around the shore of the large lake in the Fayum, but it is much smaller than some of the large cemeteries in Upper Egypt, and could not have been associated with anything larger than a (primarily) farming village.

Lower Egypt, Cairo Region

South of Cairo on the east bank, Predynastic evidence of a material culture different from that of Upper Egypt has been found at two major sites, el-Omari and Maadi. On the west of the site of el-Omari (3 km NE of Helwan), which Debono dates from early Nagada I to the beginning of Nagada II, there was a village where the dead were interred in houses. There was a second village with a separate cemetery, where each grave was covered with a mound of stones (Debono 1956:330-331). The western village ("Omari A") extended over a large area and included oval structures of postholes and round, semi-subterranean structures (Debono 1948:562-563). Pottery at el-Omari is unlike that of the Predynastic Nagada culture in the south, but is related to that of Merimde Beni-salâma in the Delta (Debono and Mortensen 1990:39-40). Five calibrated radiocarbon dates on charcoal samples from pits in the "later phases of the settlement" range from 4620 ±220 B.C. to 3540 ±160 B.C. (Mortensen 1992:173).

Maadi, the other major prehistoric site in the Cairo region, is located on a Pleistocene terrace between the mouths of two *wadis* south of modern Cairo. From 1930 to 1953, Cairo University archaeologists excavated four sites: a large settlement (over 40,000 m^2) on the terrace, a cemetery and a settlement at the foot of the terrace, and another Predynastic cemetery 1 km south in the Wadi Digla (Rizkana and Seeher 1984:237; see also Rizkana and Seeher 1989, 1990). More recently, excavations at Maadi have also been conducted in the eastern part of the settlement, which was not excavated earlier (Caneva, Frangipane, and Palmieri 1989:287).

The economy at Maadi was based on farming (emmer wheat and barley) and herding (cattle, sheep, goats, pigs), with considerably less evidence for hunting and fishing. Domesticated dogs and asses were also kept. The presence of many large grinding stones, some weighing more than 50 kg, and hundreds of storage pits and storage jars strongly suggests a permanent settlement subsisting mainly by farming (Rizkana and Seeher 1989:75-76).

Settlement debris at Maadi was found in an area 1300 m long and 100-130 m wide. Evidence from the recent Maadi excavations suggests shifting occupation within the settlement (Caneva, Frangipane, and Palmieri 1989:287), with earlier occupation in the eastern part and later occupation to the west (Caneva, Frangipane, and Palmieri 1987:113). There is no evidence of a planned settlement, and houses consisted mainly of wattle and matting, sometimes covered with mud. Some rectangular buildings were noted, and four subterranean structures were found in the NW part of the site. Interpretations of the excavated settlement data are hampered by earlier digging for *sebakh*, and by problems with understanding the earlier excavations (Rizkana and Seeher 1989:74).

Over 80% of the pottery excavated at Maadi is of a local ware not found in Upper Egypt, which "clearly underlines the difference between Lower and Upper Egypt in Predynastic times" (Rizkana and Seeher 1987:78). This pottery has datable parallels in Upper Egypt from the Nagada I and II periods, and Rizkana and Seeher (1987:78) propose an end to occupation at Maadi by late Nagada II times (the end of Nagada IIc). Four radiocarbon dates from the recent excavations at Maadi are "grouped around 3650 B.C. (MASCA calibrated)" (Caneva, Frangipane, and Palmieri 1987:106).

Among the artifacts from Maadi are a few goods that most likely were imports from Upper Egypt, where they are much more numerous: rhomboid slate palettes, and maceheads and wide-brimmed jars of diorite (Rizkana and Seeher 1989:77). Much more frequent, however, are palettes of limestone in different sizes and shapes, probably made locally (Rizkana and Seeher 1984:244). The numerous black basalt vases at Maadi in shapes similar to locally produced pottery suggest a Lower Egyptian source (Rizkana and Seeher 1989:77). Maadi has also been regarded as a center of copper production, as Hayes (1965:128) suggests. Rizkana and Seeher (1984:238-239), however, think that this is an exaggerated view, given the actual finds: two copper axes, and small objects (pins, chisels, wires, and fish-hooks). Three large pieces of copper, which may have been ingots, were also found at Maadi, and a site of copper smelting has only been tentatively identified (Rizkana and Seeher 1984:239). The copper ore found in all areas and layers at Maadi was probably not for smelting, but it was most likely used for its "colouring properties" (Rizkana and Seeher 1989:13, 18).

There were few grave goods in the 76 graves in the cemetery next to the Maadi settlement: 27 pots, some potsherds, a flint flake, and 2 aspatharia shells (Rizkana and Seeher 1990:26). In the cemetery at the mouth of the Wadi Digla ("Maadi South") 468 human burials and 14 animal burials were excavated (Rizkana and Seeher 1987:19). These graves were simple oval pits, with either a few pots or entirely without grave goods (Rizkana and Seeher 1989:74).

Although archaeological evidence at Maadi and Maadi-related sites is mainly from settlements, unlike most of the surviving evidence for the Nagada culture in Upper Egypt, what is known about Maadi suggests a material culture very different from that in the south. The cemetery at Maadi, with its very simple human burials, is also very different from Predynastic cemeteries in Upper Egypt. Some contact with southwest Asia is demonstrated by the imported coarse-tempered ware at Maadi, which may have been a northern Egyptian center for trade with Palestine (see Seeher 1990:153-154), but this did not require the development of a large urban center.

Both Maadi and el-Omari were farming villages, and although Maadi is a much larger site than el-Omari, the archaeological evidence there does not suggest much socioeconomic complexity. The settlement at Maadi was primarily a farming village that shifted horizontally through time, but it seems difficult now to determine the extent of occupation at Maadi in any one period. The architectural remains are only of small domestic structures, and there is no evidence of a cult center or major economic institutions controlling craft production or large-scale trade with Upper Egypt or southwest Asia.

Lower Egypt, the Delta

On the western fringe of the Delta, about 60 km NW of Cairo, is the large prehistoric site of Merimde Beni-salâma (Junker 1928, 1929, 1930, 1932, 1933, 1934, 1940). Junker dug here from 1928 to 1939, but most of the excavation notes were lost during World War II (Baumgartel 1965:503). Junker thought that the *ca.* 160,000 m^2 of living debris was occupied continuously, but Kemp (1968:27) states that, given the almost complete absence of anything suggesting communal organization, there probably was horizontal displacement of the settlement through time. Average age estimates of radiocarbon dates for Merimde are *ca.* 4800 B.C. (early Neolithic), and 4400 B.C. (late Neolithic) (Hassan 1985:95). These dates are considerably earlier than the recent radiocarbon dates reported for Maadi. Given horizontal displacement of the Merimde settlement through time, Kemp (1968:26) thinks it questionable as to what extent the intra-settlement burials and houses were contemporary. Unlike Predynastic burials, the Merimde ones were without grave goods, and many were of children (Kemp 1968:23, 26).

More recent excavations have been conducted by Eiwanger at Merimde, between and to the north of the eastern and western areas excavated by Junker (Eiwanger 1984, 1988, 1992). Although Junker identified three phases of occupation at Merimde, Eiwanger has identified five, with a discernible change in the lithics and ceramics between the first and subsequent phases (Eiwanger 1988:51-54). Postholes of small oval houses were found in all five phases (Eiwanger 1982:68). Fish bones along with numerous artifacts used in fishing, such as net weights, harpoons, and fish hooks, suggest one important subsistence activity (Eiwanger 1982:80). Storage pits are known from Phases II-V, and emmer wheat and barley were the most abundant plant remains (Wetterstrom 1993:213). Although the archaeological evidence at Merimde certainly represents long-term occupation, it in no way suggests anything more than a farming and fishing village.

Judging by reports of recent excavations in the Delta and its margins, conditions for preservation of stratified remains may be the best in Egypt (Chlodnicki, Fattovich, Salvatori 1991; Eiwanger 1984, 1988, 1992; van den Brink 1988, 1989, 1992; von der Way 1987, 1988, 1989, 1992). Surveys conducted in the Sharqiya province of the NE Delta since 1984 by van den Brink have yielded evidence of sites of the Old Kingdom and earlier (van den Brink 1987:17). Italian archaeologists who conducted a survey in this region in 1987 recorded more than 30 sites, dating in the 4th and 3rd millennia B.C. and late Roman times (Chlodnicki, Fattovich, and Salvatori 1991:6). Excavations at Tell el-Farkha have demonstrated a clear break between the Predynastic and Protodynastic (Nagada III/Dynasty 0-1) phases, with a change in pottery fabrics, and a stratigraphic marker composed of an aeolian bed representing settlement abandonment between the Predynastic and Protodynastic occupations (Chlodnicki, Fattovich, and Salvatori 1991:23).

At Tell Ibrahim Awad the stratigraphy shows an uninterrupted sequence from the late Predynastic, with no mudbrick architecture, to the Early Dynastic, with substantial mudbrick architecture (van den Brink 1988:76-77; 1989:59-64; 1992:50-54). Initial excavations reveal the "occurrence of certain ceramics clearly differing from contemporary sites in the Nile Valley, and therefore possibly reflecting an original Delta culture" (van den Brink 1988:77). Phase A pottery at Tell Ibrahim Awad is comparable to the straw-tempered ware from Tell el Fara'in/Buto, farther west in the Delta, but the former disappears and is replaced by "different ware groups" known from Nagada III and Early Dynastic sites in the Delta and the Nile valley (van den Brink 1989:70-71). Grave goods in several burials can be dated to the early First Dynasty, and a number of copper artifacts in one burial suggests intensive contact with Early Bronze Age II copper-mining settlements in the Sinai (van den Brink 1988:78).

At Minshat Abu Omar, *ca.* 150 km NE of Cairo, a cemetery with Predynastic/Early Dynastic graves has been excavated by Wildung, Kroeper, and Krzyzaniak, and archaeological evidence for these periods can be attested at other sites in the NE Delta (Kroeper and Wildung 1985:97; Krzyzaniak 1989). Aside from the 370 early burials at Minshat Abu Omar, no other graves are found at this cemetery until the Graeco-Roman period (Kroeper 1988:11). With the exception of classes of pottery dating to the early (Nagada I) Predynastic of Upper Egypt, all other southern Predynastic classes of pottery are present in these burials. These classes of pottery span the Nagada II and III periods, continuing into the First Dynasty (Wildung 1984:267). The latest graves, which date to the early First Dynasty, have many more carved stone vessels than the earlier ones, and two of these graves were roofed and built of mudbricks, which partitioned 2-3 rooms (Kroeper 1988:16-17). Some 400-700 m from the cemetery at Minshat Abu Omar, remains of a settlement of late Predynastic/Early Dynastic date were located by systematic auguring (Krzyzaniak 1992:151-152). Future excavations are planned for this settlement, and should help to explain the presence in the NE Delta of graves and burial goods typical of the late Predynastic of Upper Egypt (Nagada II-III).

Finally in the northern Delta, archaeological evidence has recently been excavated below the water table at Tell el-Fara'in/Buto by von der Way. Below levels dating to the 3rd millennium B.C. was a settlement of "Lower Egyptian culture" of the second half of the 4th millennium B.C. (von der Way 1988:247). Most of the wares at Tell el Fara'in were also found at Maadi, and the same type of black basalt jars were found at both sites. At two sites about 3 km SW of Tell el-Fara'in, Ezbet el-Qerdahi East and West, more ceramics of the same wares as found at Maadi and Tell el-Fara'in have also been excavated (Wunderlich, von der Way, and Schmidt 1989:313-316).

Pottery of Upper Egyptian classes was only found in "one small place" at Tell el-Fara'in, which von der Way (1988:248) thinks may be a kind of trade depot. Pottery of the 'Amuq F period from northern Syria was also imported to the site. Above the two layers at Buto with ceramics of Lower Egyptian tradition is a transitional layer with decreasing amounts of these ceramics and, for the first time, Upper Egyptian (Nagada IId) style pottery (von der Way 1991:420-423, 1992:3). In this transitional layer (IIIa) forms "suddenly occur" which are typical of the Lower Egyptian tradition but are manufactured in the "Nagada manner" (Kohler 1992b:17-18). Von der Way (1992:4) interprets this as evidence of "cultural superposition by assimilation," which was followed in the Nagada IIIa period by "the final struggle" for political unification. Kohler (1992a:5), however, suggests that there were not two different cultures in Upper and Lower Egypt during the Nagada II period, but that "style" separated these two regions, and by late Nagada II times both regions had nearly the same utilitarian pottery and lithics. Not enough of the site of Buto has yet been excavated to determine the extent of the settlement and its development through time, however. Other recently excavated sites in the Delta of Predynastic date likewise need more study to determine the nature of socioeconomic development, the chronology and extent of the Delta/Maadi culture, and the crucial period of transition to a material culture of Upper Egyptian origin.

DISCUSSION

Despite the problem of limited settlement data in Upper Egypt, the emerging picture of Egypt in the 4th millennium B.C. is of two different material cultures with different belief systems: the Predynastic Nagada culture of Upper Egypt and the Maadi culture of Lower Egypt (see Bard 1992b). Archaeological evidence in Lower Egypt consists mainly of village settlements, with very simple burials in cemeteries, and suggests no great socioeconomic complexity. This is in contrast to the evidence from Upper Egypt, where large cemeteries with elaborate burials are found.

Archaeological evidence also points to the origins of the state which emerged by the First Dynasty in the Nagada culture of Upper Egypt, where grave types, pottery, and artifacts demonstrate an evolution of form from the Predynastic to the First Dynasty. This cannot be demonstrated for the material culture of Lower Egypt, which was eventually displaced by that originating in Upper Egypt. Hierarchical society with much social and economic differentiation, as symbolized in the Nagada II cemeteries of Upper Egypt, does not seem to have been present in Lower Egypt, a fact which also supports an Upper Egyptian origin for the unified state.

With the rise of the Nagada culture in Upper Egypt in the early 4th millennium B.C., simple farming communities evolved into more complex societies. Archaeological evidence, mainly from cemeteries, suggests a core area of the Nagada culture that extended from Abydos in the north to Hierakonpolis in the south. Major centers developed at Abydos, Nagada, Hierakonpolis (Nekhen), and possibly at Hu (Diospolis Parva), but only toward the end of the Predynastic period were some of these centers becoming (walled) settlements which might be called cities.

In Lower Nubia there are numerous burials of the A-Group culture which contain many Nagadan craft goods, but these were probably obtained through trade (see Nordstrom 1972:25; Smith 1991:108; Trigger 1976:38-39). Luxury raw materials, such as ivory, ebony, incense, and exotic animal skins, all greatly desired in Dynastic times as well, came from farther south and passed through Nubia. A-Group chieftains may have benefitted economically from the trade in such raw materials, but sociopolitical complexity as was occurring in Upper Egypt is unlikely (contra Williams 1986:177).

Differentiation in the Predynastic cemeteries of Upper Egypt (but not Lower Egypt) is symbolic of status display and status rivalry (Trigger 1987:60), which probably represent the earliest processes of competition and the aggrandizement of local polities in Egypt as economic interaction occurred regionally. The importation of exotic materials for craft goods found in burials may have become a political strategy, and the control of prestige goods would have reinforced the position of a chief among his supporters (Kirch 1990:282). Craft specialization was thus partly related to the production of ritual paraphernalia [for burials], and the conversion of exotic raw materials into craft goods which expressed status (Marcus 1989:191).

While the rich grave goods in the major cemeteries in Upper Egypt represent the acquired wealth of higher social strata, the economic sources of this wealth cannot be satisfactorily determined because there are so few settlement data, though the larger cemeteries were probably associated with centers of craft production (for which there is some evidence at Hierakonpolis). Trade and exchange of finished goods and luxury materials from the Eastern and Western Deserts and Nubia would also have taken place in such centers. Elites must have assumed greater control of the economy along with the establishment of control mechanisms for procurement, manufacturing/processing, and distribution of goods and materials exchanged in regional and long-distance trade networks.

A motivating factor for Nagada culture expansion into northern Egypt would have been to directly control the lucrative trade with other regions in the eastern Mediterranean (Trigger 1983:49). But more importantly, large boats were the key to control and communication on the Nile and large-scale economic exchange, and timber for the construction of such boats (cedars) did not grow in Egypt, but came from the Levant. Gold was an *Upper* Egyptian resource (Trigger 1983:39), along with various kinds of stone used for carved vessels and beads—highly desired goods and materials in long-distance exchange. Villages in Lower Egypt did not have such resources, and in a configuration of trading partners in the eastern Mediterranean, would only have been (expendable) middlemen. Possibly there was first a more or less peaceful(?) movement or migration(s) of Nagada culture peoples from south to north. Trigger (1987:61) proposes that this expansion was the result of refugees emigrating from the developing states in the south, or the presence of Nagada traders involved in the commerce with southwest Asia.

The (final) unification may have been achieved through a military conquest in the north (see Hassan 1988:172-173). Archaeological evidence, however, suggests a system much too complex for the southern expansion to be explained by military conquest alone, and an earlier unification of southern polities may represent a series of alliances (Trigger 1987:61). According to Kaiser (1964, 1985, 1990; contra Trigger 1987:61), the unification took place much earlier than the period immediately preceding the beginning of the First Dynasty, and the northern culture may have made important contributions to the unified polity which emerged (Seeher 1991:318). One result of this expansion of Nagada culture throughout northern Egypt would have been a greatly elaborated (state) administration, and by the beginning of the First Dynasty this was managed in part by the invention of writing, used on seals and tags affixed to state goods (see Dreyer 1992). Concomitant with the emergence of the newly unified state was also a shift in settlement patterns, and by the First Dynasty the north was much more densely inhabited than the south (Mortensen 1991:24).

What is truly unique about the early state in Egypt is the integration of rule over an extensive geographic region, in contrast to contemporaneous polities in Nubia, Mesopotamia, Palestine, and the Levant. There was undoubtedly heightened commercial contact with southwest Asia in the late 4th millennium B.C., but the Early Dynastic state which emerged in Egypt was unique and indigenous in character. The focus of development shifted from south to north (Wenke 1989:142), and Memphis, the main administrative seat of the government, was founded. Tombs of high officials are found in nearby North Saqqara (Emery 1949, 1954, 1958), and officials of all levels were buried at other sites in the Memphis region. Memphis undoubtedly became a large town or city, but the remains of its earliest occupation which have not been quarried away are well beneath the water table (see Kemp 1977:192-196), and therefore very difficult to excavate. In the south, Abydos remained the most important cult center, and the kings of the First Dynasty were buried there (Dreyer 1992; Petrie 1900, 1901b), another indication of the Upper Egyptian origins of this state. According to Kemp (1977:189), the scattered Predynastic villages in the Abydos region were replaced by a single town (see also Patch 1991:306-310), and this process is also thought to have occurred at Hierakonpolis (Hoffman, Hamroush, and Allen 1986:184).

Urbanization was unquestionably a part of the process of state formation and unification in Egypt as the bureaucracy and mechanisms of state control were being established. But the majority of the population must have continued to live in small farming villages in or on the edge of the Nile Valley, for which there is very little archaeological evidence. The capital and state administrative (nome) centers were certainly urban communities, but they were probably less agglomerated in plan than the contemporaneous city states in southern Mesopotamia. In Egypt there is simply much less archaeological evidence of urban settlements than there is for these centers' cemeteries and cults, which were mainly mortuary, and the nature of early urbanism continues to be poorly known.

ACKNOWLEDGMENTS

I would like to thank Rodolfo Fattovich and Joyce Marcus, who read and commented on earlier versions of this article.

REFERENCES

Adams, B., 1974a, *Ancient Hierakonpolis*, Aris & Phillips, Warminster.
Adams, B., 1974b, *Ancient Hierakonpolis*. Supplement, Aris & Phillips, Warminster.
Adams, B., 1988, *Predynastic Egypt*, Shire Publications, Aylesbury.

Adams, B., and M. A. Hoffman, 1987, Analysis and Regional Perspective, in: *The Fort Cemetery at Hierakonpolis* (B. Adams, ed.), KPI, London, pp. 176-202.

Adams, R. McC., and H. Nissen, 1972, *The Uruk Countryside*, University of Chicago Press, Chicago.

Arkell, A. J., and P. J. Ucko, 1965, Review of Predynastic Development in the Nile Valley, *Current Anthropology* 6:145-166.

Ayrton, E. R., and W. L. S. Loat, 1911, *The Predynastic Cemetery at El Mahasna*, Egypt Exploration Fund, London.

Bard, K. A., 1989, Predynastic Settlement Patterns in the Hu-Semaineh Region, Egypt, *Journal of Field Archaeology* 16:475-478.

Bard, K. A., 1991, Egypt. Halfiah Gibli and Semaineh H, Hiw, *Archaeometry* 33:129-130.

Bard, K. A., 1992a, Preliminary Report:The 1991 Boston University Excavations at Halfiah Gibli and Semaineh, Upper Egypt, *Newsletter of the American Research Center in Egypt* 158/159:11-15.

Bard, K. A., 1992b, Toward an Interpretation of the Role of Ideology in the Evolution of Complex Society in Egypt, *Journal of Anthropological Archaeology* 11:1-24.

Bard, K. A., 1994a, The Egyptian Predynastic: A Review of the Evidence, *Journal of Field Archaeology* 21, 3:265-288.

Bard, K. A., 1994b, *From Farmers to Pharaohs. Mortuary Evidence for the Rise of Complex Society in Egypt*, Sheffield Academic Press, Sheffield.

Barocas, C., R. Fattovich, and M. Tosi, 1989, The Oriental Institute of Naples' Expedition to Petrie's South Town (Upper Egypt), 1977-1983: An Interim Report, in: *Late Prehistory of the Nile Basin and the Sahara* (L. Krzyzaniak and M. Kobusiewicz, eds.), Muzeum Archeologiczne W. Poznaniu, Poznan, pp. 295-301.

Baumgartel, E. J., 1965, What Do We Know About the Excavation at Merimde?, *Journal of the American Oriental Society* 85:501-511.

Bietak, M., 1979, Urban Archaeology and the 'Town Problem' in Ancient Egypt, in: *Egyptology and the Social Sciences* (K. Weeks, ed.), American University in Cairo Press, Cairo, pp. 97-144.

Brunton, G., 1937, *Mostagedda and the Tasian Culture*, British Museum Expedition to the Middle East, London.

Brunton, G., and G. Caton Thompson, 1928, *The Badarian Civilization*, British School of Archaeology in Egypt, London.

Butzer, K. W., 1976, *Early Hydraulic Civilization in Egypt*, University of Chicago Press, Chicago.

Caneva, I., M. Frangipane, and A. Palmieri, 1987, Predynastic Egypt:New Data from Maadi, *African Archaeological Review* 5:105-114.

Caneva, I., M. Frangipane, and A. Palmieri, 1989, Recent Excavations at Maadi, in: *Late Prehistory of the Nile Basin and the Sahara* (L. Krzyzaniak and M. Kobusiewicz, eds.), Muzeum Archeologiczne W. Poznaniu, Poznan, pp. 287-293.

Case, H., and J. C. Payne, 1962, Tomb 100:The Decorated Tomb at Hierakonpolis, *Journal of Egyptian Archaeology* 48:5-18.

Caton Thompson, G., and E. W. Gardner, 1934, *The Desert Fayum*, The Royal Anthropological Institute of Great Britain and Ireland, London.

Chlodnicki, M., R. Fattovich, and S. Salvatori, 1991, Italian Excavations in the Nile Delta: Fresh Data and New Hypotheses on the 4th Millennium Cultural Development of Egyptian Prehistory, *Rivista di Archeologia* 15:5-33.

Dagnon-Ginter, A., B. Ginter, J. K. Kozlowski, M. Pawlikowski, and J. Sliwa, 1984, Excavations in the Region of Qasr el-Sagha, 1981. Contribution to the Neolithic Period, Middle

Kingdom Settlement and Chronological Sequences in the Northern Fayum Desert, *Mitteilungen des Deutschen Archaeologischen Instituts Abteilung Kairo* 40:33-102.

Davis, W., 1983, Cemetery T at Nagada, *Mitteilungen des Deutschen Archaeologischen Instituts Abteilung Kairo* 39:17-28.

Debono, F., 1948, El-Omari (près d'Hélouan). Exposé Sommaire, *Annales du Service des Antiquités de l'Egypte* 48:561-583.

Debono, F., 1956, La Civilization Prédynastique d'el Omari (Nord d'Hélouan). Nouvelles Données, *Bulletin de l'Institut d'Egypte* 37:329-339.

Debono, F., and B. Mortensen, 1990, *El Omari. A Neolithic Settlement and Other Sites in the Vicinity of Wadi Hof, Helwan,* Philipp von Zabern, Mainz.

Dreyer, G., 1992, The Royal Tombs of Abydos, in: *The Near East in Antiquity III* (S. Kerner, ed.), Goethe-Institut, Amman, pp. 55-67.

Eiwanger, J., 1982, Die neolithische Siedlung von Merimde-Benisalame: vierter Bericht, *Mitteilungen des Deutschen Archaeologischen Instituts Abteilung Kairo* 38:67-82.

Eiwanger, J., 1984, *Merimde-Benisalame I. Die Funde der Urschicht,* Philipp von Zabern, Mainz.

Eiwanger, J., 1988, *Merimde-Benisalame II. Die Funde der Mittleren Merimdekultur,* Philipp von Zabern, Mainz.

Eiwanger, J., 1992, *Merimde-Benisalame III. Die Funde der jungeren Merimde-kultur,* Philipp von Zabern, Mainz.

Emery, W. B., 1949, *Great Tombs of the First Dynasty I,* Government Press, Cairo.

Emery, W. B., 1954, *Great Tombs of the First Dynasty II,* Egypt Exploration Society, London.

Emery, W. B., 1958, *Great Tombs of the First Dynasty III,* Egypt Exploration Society, London.

Garstang, J., 1907, Excavation at Hierakonpolis, at Esna, and Nubia, *Annales du Service des Antiquités de l'Egypte* 8:132-148.

Geller, J. R., 1989, Recent Excavations at Hierakonpolis and Their Relevance to Predynastic Production and Settlement, in: *Sociétés Urbaines en Egypte et au Soudan,* Cahiers de Recherches de l'Institut de Papyrologie et d'Egyptologie de Lille 11, Lille, pp. 41-52.

Geller, J. R., 1992, From Prehistory to History: Beer in Egypt, in: *The Followers of Horus. Studies Dedicated to Michael Allen Hoffman* (R. Friedman and B. Adams, eds.), Oxbow Monograph 20, Oxford, pp. 19-26.

Hassan, F. A., 1984, Radiocarbon Chronology of Predynastic Settlements, Upper Egypt, *Current Anthropology* 25:681-683.

Hassan, F. A., 1985, Radiocarbon Chronology of Neolithic and Predynastic Sites in Upper Egypt and the Delta, *African Archaeological Review* 3:95-116.

Hassan, F. A., 1988, The Predynastic of Egypt, *Journal of World Prehistory* 2:135-185.

Hassan, F. A., 1993, Town and Village in Ancient Egypt: Ecology, Society and Urbanization, in: *The Archaeology of Africa. Food, Metals and Towns* (T. Shaw et al., eds.), Routledge, London, pp. 551-569.

Hassan, F. A., and R. G. Matson, 1989, Seriation of Predynastic Potsherds from the Nagada Region, in: *Late Prehistory of the Nile Basin and the Sahara* (L. Krzyzaniak and M. Kobusiewicz, eds.), Muzeum Archeologiczne W Poznaniu, Poznan, pp. 303-315.

Hayes, W. C., 1965, *Most Ancient Egypt,* University of Chicago Press, Chicago.

Hays, T. R., 1976, Predynastic Egypt: Recent Field Research, *Current Anthropology* 17:552-554.

Hoffman, M. A., 1980, A Rectangular Amratian House from Hierakonpolis and its Significance for Predynastic Research, *Journal of Near Eastern Studies* 39:119-137.

Hoffman, M. A., 1982, *The Predynastic of Hierakonpolis. An Interim Report,* Egyptian Studies Association Publication 1. Cairo.

Hoffman, M. A., 1983, Where Nations Began, *Science* 83, 4, 8:42-51.

Hoffman, M. A., 1989, A Stratified Predynastic Sequence from Hierakonpolis (Upper Egypt), in: *Late Prehistory of the Nile Basin and the Sahara* (L. Krzyzaniak and M. Kobusiewicz, eds.), Muzeum Archeologiczne W. Poznaniu, Poznan, pp. 317-323.

Hoffman, M. A., H. A. Hamroush, and R. O. Allen, 1986, A Model of Urban Development for the Hierakonpolis Region from Predynastic through Old Kingdom Times, *Journal of the American Research Center in Egypt* 23:175-187.

Holmes, D. L., 1989, *The Predynastic Lithic Industries of Upper Egypt. A Comparative Study of the Lithic Traditions of Badari, Nagada and Hierakonpolis*, BAR International Series 469 (i, ii), British Archaeological Reports, Oxford.

Holmes, D. L., and R. F. Friedman, 1989, The Badari Region Revisited, *Nyame Akuma* 31:15-19.

Junker, H., 1928, Bericht über die von der Akademie der Wissenschaften in Wien nach dem Westdelta entsendete Expedition (20. Dezember 1927 bis 25. Februar 1928), *Anzeiger der Akademie der Wissenschaften in Wien*, philosophisch-Historische Klasse 65, Wien.

Junker, H., 1929, Vorlaufiger Bericht über die Grabung der Akademie der Wissenschaften in Wien auf der neolithischen Siedlung von Merimde-Benisalame (Westdelta) vom 1. bis 30 Marz 1929, *Anzeiger der Akademie der Wissenschaften in Wien*, philosophisch-historische Klasse 66, Wien:156-248.

Junker, H., 1930, Vorlaufiger Bericht über die zweite Grabung der Akademie der Wissenschaften in Wien auf der vorgeschichtlichen Siedlung Merimde-Benisalame vom 7. Februar bis 8. April 1930, *Anzeiger der Akademie der Wissenschaften in Wien*, philosophisch-historische Klasse 67, Wien:21-82.

Junker, H., 1932, Vorbericht über die von der Akademie der Wissenschaften in Wien in Verbindung mit dem Egyptiska Museet in Stockholm unternommenen Grabungen auf der neolithischen Siedlung von Merimde-Benisalame vom 6. November 1931 bis 20. Januar 1932, *Anzeiger der Akademie der Wissenschaften in Wien*, philosophisch-historische Klasse 69, Wien:36-82.

Junker, H., 1933, Vorlaufiger Bericht über die von der Akademie der Wissenschaften in Wien in Verbindung mit dem Egyptiska Museet in Stockholm unternommenen Grabungen auf der neolithischen Siedlung von Merimde-Benisalame vom 2. Januar bis 20. Februar 1933, *Anzeiger der Akademie der Wissenschaften in Wien*, philosophisch-historische Klasse 70, Wien:54-82.

Junker, H., 1934, Vorbericht über die fünfte Grabungen von der Akademie der Wissenschaften in Wien und dem Egyptiska Museet in Stockholm unternommene Grabung auf der neolithischen Siedlung Merimde-Benisalame vom 13. Februar bis 26. Marz 1934, *Anzeiger der Akademie der Wissenschaften in Wien*, philosophisch-historische Klasse 71, Wien:118-132.

Junker, H., 1940, Vorbericht über die siebente Grabung der Akademie der Wissenschaften in Wien auf der vorgeschichtlichen Siedlung Merimde-Benisalame vom 25. Januar bis 4. April 1939, *Anzeiger der Akademie der Wissenschaften in Wien*, philosophisch-historische Klasse 77, Wien:3-17.

Kaiser, W., 1956, Stand und Probleme der ägyptischen Vorgeschichtsforschung, *Zeitschrift für ägyptische Sprache und Altertumskunde* 81:87-109.

Kaiser, W., 1957, Zur inneren Chronologie der Naqadakultur, *Archaeologia Geographica* 6:69-77.

Kaiser, W., 1958, Zur vorgeschichtlichen Bedeutung von Hierakonpolis, *Mitteilungen des Deutschen Archaeologischen Instituts Abteilung Kairo* 16:183-192.

Kaiser, W., 1964, Eine Bermerkungen zur ägyptischen Frühzeit, *Zeitschrift für ägyptische Sprache und Altertumskunde* 91:86-125.

Kaiser, W., 1985, Zur Südausdehnung der vorgeschichtlichen Deltakulturen und zur frühen Entwicklung Oberägyptens, *Mitteilungen des Deutschen Archaeologischen Instituts Abteilung Kairo* 41:61-87.

Kaiser, W., 1990, Zur Entstehung des gesamtägyptischen Staates, *Mitteilungen des Deutschen Archaeologischen Instituts Abteilung Kairo* 46:287-299.

Kaiser, W., and G. Dreyer, 1982, Umm el-Qaab. Nachuntersuchungen im frühzeitlichen Königsfriedhof. Vorbericht, *Mitteilungen des Deutschen Archaeologischen Instituts Abteilung Kairo* 38:211-269.

Kemp, B. J., 1963, Excavations at Hierakonpolis Fort, 1905: A Preliminary Note, *Journal of Egyptian Archaeology* 49:24-28.

Kemp, B. J., 1968, Merimde and the Theory of House Burial in Prehistoric Egypt, *Chronique d'Egypte* 43, 85:22-33.

Kemp, B. J., 1973, Photographs of the Decorated Tomb at Hierakonpolis, *Journal of Egyptian Archaeology* 59:36-43.

Kemp, B. J., 1977, The Early Development of Towns in Egypt, *Antiquity* 51:185-200.

Kemp, B. J., 1989, *Ancient Egypt. Anatomy of a Civilization.* Routledge, London.

Kirch, P. V., 1990, *The Evolution of the Polynesian Chiefdoms*, Cambridge University Press, Cambridge.

Kohler, C., 1992a, Evidence for Interregional Contacts between Late Prehistoric Lower and Upper Egypt—a View from Buto, paper presented at the International Symposium, Interregional Contacts in the Later Prehistory of Northeastern Africa, Poznan, Poland, 8-12 September, 1992.

Kohler, C., 1992b, The Pre- and Early Dynastic Pottery of Tell el-Fara'in (Buto), in: *The Nile Delta in Transition: 4th.-3rd. Millennium B. C.* (E. C. M. van den Brink, ed.), The Israel Exploration Society, Jerusalem, pp. 11-22.

Kroeper, K., 1988, The Excavations of the Munich East-Delta Expedition in Minshat Abu Omar, in: *The Archaeology of the Nile Delta. Problems and Priorities* (E. C. M. van den Brink, ed.), Netherlands Foundation for Archaeological Research in Egypt, Amsterdam, pp. 11-19.

Kroeper, K., and D. Wildung, 1985, *Minshat Abu Omar. Münchner Ostdelta-Expedition Vorbericht 1978-1984*, Karl M. Lipp, München.

Krzyzaniak, L., 1989, Recent Archaeological Evidence on the Earliest Settlement in the Eastern Nile Delta, in: *Late Prehistory of the Nile Basin and the Sahara* (L. Krzyzaniak and M. Kobusiewicz, eds.), Muzeum Archeologiczne W. Poznaniu, Poznan, pp. 267-285.

Krzyzaniak, L., 1992, Again on the Earliest Settlement at Minshat Abu Omar, in: *The Nile Delta in Transition: 4th.-3rd. Millennium B. C.* (E. C. M. van den Brink, ed.), The Israel Exploration Society, Jerusalem, pp. 151-155.

Lucas, A., revised by J. R. Harris, 1989, *Ancient Egyptian Materials and Industries*, Histories and Mysteries of Man, London.

Mahmoud, A. M. A., and K. A. Bard, 1993, Sources of the Predynastic Grinding Stones in the Hu-Semaineh Region, Upper Egypt, and Their Cultural Context, *Geoarchaeology* 8:241-245.

Marcus, J., 1989, Zapotec Chiefdoms and the Nature of Formative Religions, in: *Regional Perspectives on the Olmec* (R. J. Sharer and D. C. Grove, eds.), Cambridge University Press, Cambridge, pp. 148-197.

de Morgan, J., 1897, *Recherches sur les Origines de l'Egypte. Ethnographie Préhistorique et Tombeau Royal de Negadah*, Ernest Leroux, Paris.

Mortensen, B., 1991, Change in the Settlement Pattern and Population in the Beginning of the Historical Period, in: *Ägypten und Levante II* (M. Bietak, ed.), Osterreichishchen Akademie der Wissenschaften, Wien, pp. 11-37.

Mortensen, B. 1992, Carbon-14 Dates from El Omari, in: *The Followers of Horus. Studies Dedicated to Michael Allen Hoffman* (R. Friedman and B. Adams, eds.), Oxbow Monograph 20, Oxford, pp. 173-174.

Naville, E., 1914, *The Cemeteries of Abydos*. Part I. 1909-1910, Egypt Exploration Fund, London.

Needler, W., 1984, *Predynastic and Archaic Egypt in the Brooklyn Museum*, The Brooklyn Museum, Brooklyn.

Nordstrom, H.-A., 1972, *Neolithic and A-Group Sites*, Scandinavian University Books, Stockholm.

O'Connor, D., 1972, The Geography of Settlement in Ancient Egypt, in: *Man, Settlement, and Urbanism* (P. J. Ucko, R. Tringham, and G. W. Dimbleby, eds.), Gerald Duckworth, London, pp. 681-698.

O'Connor, D., 1983, New Kingdom and Third Intermediate Period, 1552-664 B. C., in: *Ancient Egypt. A Social History* (B. G. Trigger, B. J. Kemp, D. O'Connor, and A. B. Lloyd), Cambridge University Press, Cambridge, pp. 183-278.

O'Connor, D., 1989, New Funerary Enclosures (Talbezirke) of the Early Dynastic Period, *Journal of the American Research Center in Egypt* 26:51-86.

O'Connor, D., 1993, Urbanism in Bronze Age Egypt and Northeast Africa, in: *The Archaeology of Africa. Food, Metals and Towns* (T. Shaw et al., eds.), Routledge, London, pp. 570-586.

Patch, D. C., 1984, Preliminary Report on the 1983 Field Season of the Pennsylvania-Yale Expedition to Abydos, *American Research Center in Egypt Newsletter* 126:14-20.

Patch, D. C., 1991, *The Origin and Early Development of Urbanism in Ancient Egypt. A Regional Study*, Ph.D. Dissertation, University of Pennsylvania, University Microfilms International, Ann Arbor.

Payne, J. C., 1973, Tomb 100: The Decorated Tomb at Hierakonpolis Confirmed, *Journal of Egyptian Archaeology* 59:31-35.

Peet, T. E., and W. L. S. Loat, 1913, *The Cemeteries of Abydos. Part III*. 1912-1913, Egypt Exploration Fund, London.

Petrie, W. M. F., 1900, *The Royal Tombs of the First Dynasty. 1900*. Part I, Egypt Exploration Fund, London.

Petrie, W. M. F., 1901a, *Diospolis Parva. The Cemeteries of Abadiyeh and Hu*, Egypt Exploration Fund, London.

Petrie, W. M. F., 1901b, *The Royal Tombs of the Earliest Dynasties. 1901*. Part II, Egypt Exploration Fund, London.

Petrie, W. M. F., 1939, *The Making of Egypt*, Sheldon Press, London.

Petrie, W. M. F., and J. E. Quibell, 1896, *Naqada and Ballas*, British School of Archaeology in Egypt, London.

Petrie, W. M. F., G. A. Wainwright, and E. Mackay, 1912, *The Labyrinth, Gerzeh and Mazguneh*, British School of Archaeology in Egypt, London.

Quibell, J. E., and F. W. Green, 1902, *Hierakonpolis II*, Egypt Research Account, London.

Randall-MacIver, D., and A. C. Mace, 1902, *El Amrah and Abydos*, Egypt Exploration Fund, London.

Rizkana, I., and J. Seeher, 1984, New Light on the Relation of Maadi to the Upper Egyptian Cultural Sequence, *Mitteilungen des Deutschen Archaeologischen Instituts Abteilung Kairo* 40:237-252.

Rizkana, I., and J. Seeher, 1987, *Maadi I. The Pottery of the Predynastic Settlement*, Philipp von Zabern, Mainz.

Rizkana, I., and J. Seeher, 1989, *Maadi III. The Non-lithic Small Finds and the Structural Remains of the Predynastic Settlement*, Philipp von Zabern, Mainz.

Rizkana, I., and J. Seeher, 1990, *Maadi IV. The Cemeteries of Maadi and Wadi Digla*, Philipp von Zabern, Mainz.
Seeher, J., 1990, Maadi—eine prädynastische Kulturgruppe zwischen Oberägypten und Palästina, *Prähistorische Zeitschrift* 65:123-156.
Seeher, J., 1991, Gedanken zur Rolle Unterägyptens bei der Herausbildung des Pharaonenreiches, *Mitteilungen des Deutschen Archaeologischen Instituts Abteilung Kairo* 47:313-318.
Smith, H. S., 1972, Society and Settlement in Ancient Egypt, in: *Man, Settlement, and Urbanism* (P. J. Ucko, R. Tringham, and G. W. Dimbleby, eds.), Gerald Duckworth, pp. 705-719.
Smith, H. S., 1991, The Development of the A-Group Culture in Northern Lower Nubia, in: *Nubia from Prehistory to Islam* (W. V. Davies, ed.), British Museum Press, London, pp. 92-111.
Swain, S., 1992, Hu, *Bulletin de Liaison du Groupe International d'Etude de la Céramique Egyptienne* 16:23-24.
Trigger, B. G., 1968, *Beyond History: The Methods of Prehistory*, Holt, Rinehart, and Winston, New York.
Trigger, B. G., 1976, *Nubia under the Pharaohs*, Thames & Hudson, London.
Trigger, B. G., 1983, The Rise of Egyptian Civilization, in: *Ancient Egypt. A Social History* (B. G. Trigger, B. J. Kemp, D. O'Connor, and A. B. Lloyd), Cambridge University Press, Cambridge, pp. 1-70.
Trigger, B. G., 1987, Egypt: A Fledgling Nation, *Journal of the Society for the Study of Egyptian Antiquities* 17:58-66.
van den Brink, E. C. M., 1987, A Geo-Archaeological Survey in the North-Eastern Nile Delta, Egypt; the First Two Seasons, a Preliminary Report, *Mitteilungen des Deutschen Archaeologischen Instituts Abteilung Kairo* 43:7-31.
van den Brink, E. C. M., 1988, The Amsterdam University Survey Expedition to the Northeastern Nile Delta (1984-1986), in: *The Archaeology of the Nile Delta, Egypt: Problems and Priorities* (E. C.M. van den Brink, ed.), Netherlands Foundation for Archaeological Research in Egypt, Amsterdam, pp. 65-114.
van den Brink, E. C. M., 1989, A Transitional Late Predynastic-Early Dynastic Settlement Site in the Northeast Nile Delta, *Mitteilungen des Deutschen Archaeologischen Instituts Abteilung Kairo* 45:55-108.
van den Brink, E. C. M., 1992, Preliminary Report on the Excavations at Tell Ibrahim Awad, Seasons 1988-1990, in: *The Nile Delta in Transition: 4th.-3rd. Millennium B. C.* (E. C. M. van den Brink, ed.), The Israel Exploration Society, Jerusalem, pp. 43-68.
von der Way, T., 1987, Tell el-Fara'in-Buto. 2. Bericht, *Mitteilungen des Deutschen Archaeologischen Instituts Abteilung Kairo* 43:241-257.
von der Way, T., 1988, Investigations Concerning the Early Periods in the Northern Delta of Egypt, in: *The Archaeology of the Nile Delta. Problems and Priorities* (E. C. M. van den Brink, ed.), Netherlands Foundation for Archaeological Research in Egypt, Amsterdam, pp. 245-249.
von der Way, T., 1989, Tell el-Fara'in-Buto. 4. Bericht, *Mitteilungen des Deutschen Archaeologischen Instituts Abteilung Kairo* 45:275-308.
von der Way, T., 1991, Die Grabungen in Buto und die Reichseinigung, *Mitteilungen des Deutschen Archaeologischen Instituts Abteilung Kairo* 47:420-424.
von der Way, T., 1992, Excavations at Tell el-Fara'in/Buto, in: *The Delta in Transition: 4th.-3rd. Millennium B. C.* (E. C. M. van den Brink, ed.), The Israel Exploration Society, Jerusalem, pp. 1-10.
Wenke, R. J., 1989, Egypt: Origins of Complex Societies, *Annual Review of Anthropology* 18:129-155.

Wenke, R. J., 1991, The Evolution of Early Egyptian Civilization: Issues and Evidence, *Journal of World Prehistory* 5:279-329.

Wenke, R. J., P. Buck, J. R. Hanley, M. E. Lane, J. Long, and R. Redding, 1983, The Fayyum Archaeological Project: Preliminary Report of the 1981 Season, *American Research Center in Egypt Newsletter* 122:25-40.

Wetterstrom, W., 1993, Foraging and Farming in Egypt: The Transition from Hunting and Gathering to Horticulture in the Egyptian Nile Valley, in: *The Archaeology of Africa. Food, Metals and Towns* (T. Shaw et al., eds.), Routledge, London, pp. 165-226.

Wildung, D, 1984, Terminal Prehistory of the Nile Delta: Theses, in: *Origin and Early Development of Food-producing Cultures in North-eastern Africa* (L. Krzyzaniak and M. Kobusiewicz, eds.), Polska Akademia Nauk-Oddzial W. Poznaniu, Poznan, pp. 265-269.

Williams, B., 1986, *Excavations between Abu Simbel and the Sudan Frontier. The A-Group Royal Cemetery at Qustal: Cemetery L*, The Oriental Institute of the University of Chicago, Chicago.

Wilson, J. A., 1968, *The Culture of Ancient Egypt*, University of Chicago Press, Chicago.

Wunderlich, J., T. von der Way, and K. Schmidt, 1989, Neue Fundstellen der Buto-Maadi Kultur bei Ezbet el-Qerdahi, *Mitteilungen des Deutschen Archaeologischen Instituts Abteilung Kairo* 45:309-318.

Chapter **4**

China's First Cities
The Walled Site of Wangchenggang in the Central Plain Region of North China

WALBURGA WIESHEU

INTRODUCTION

It was in the Yellow River Valley that the Chinese civilization came into being. Here, especially in the *Zhongyuan* or Central Plain region—that is the area around the middle course of the Yellow River (Figure 1)—the first dynasties mentioned in early historical sources had their area of geographical distribution. Recent archaeological studies carried out in this region were able to identify a local sequence evolving directly from the Henan Longshan Culture (2600-2000 B.C.), into the Erlitou Culture, the latter being supposed to include the remains of the semi-legendary Xia (approximately 21st to 17th centuries B.C.), China's first recorded dynasty and perhaps also its earliest state formation.

In the same Central Plain region, the earliest rammed-earth (*hangtu*) walled sites were found (Figures 2 and 3), dating back to more than 4000 years ago.[1] In addition to the site of Hougang, unearthed as early as 1931, from 1976 onward a whole new series of such walled sites have been

---

[1]Walled sites have also been found in the lower course of the Yellow River, pertaining to the Shandong Longshan Classical Culture; but these seem to be later than the fortified centers of the Central Plain region. On the other hand, the earliest walled sites have been discovered in the Inner Mongolian region; these even seem to date back to 3000 B.C., but are built of stone, not of rammed earth.

WALBURGA WIESHEU • Escuela Nacional de Antropología e Historia, Periférico y Zapote s/n, Delegación Tlalpan, México D.F. 14030

Emergence and Change in Early Urban Societies, edited by Linda Manzanilla. Plenum Press, New York, 1997.

87

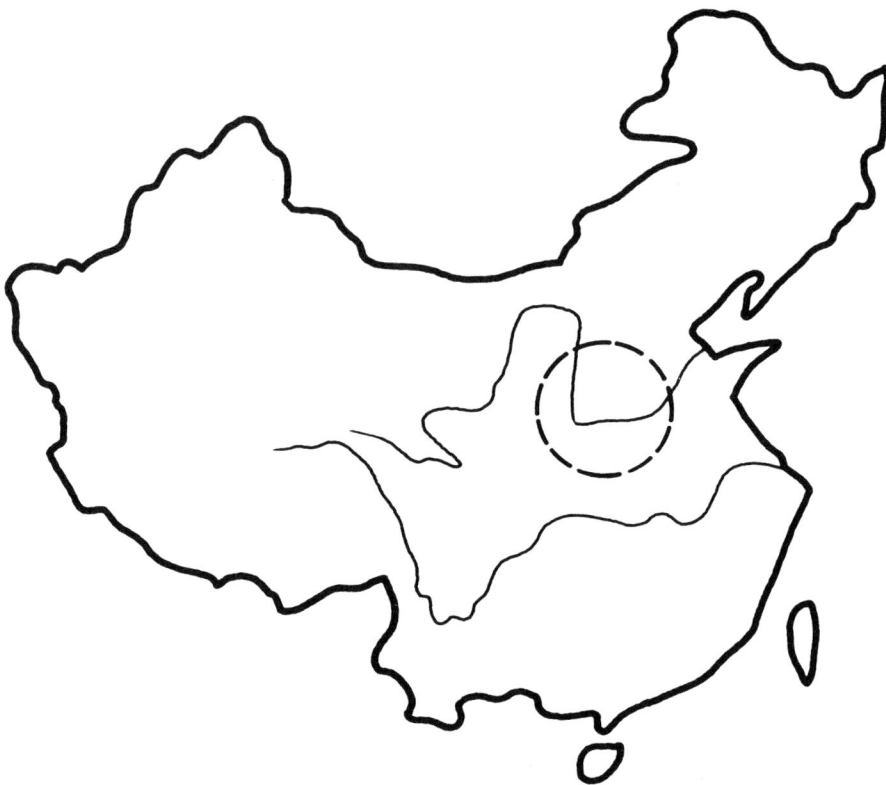

Figure 1. Location of the Central Plain (*Zhongyuan*) Cultural Region around the middle reaches of the Yellow River.

discovered and partially excavated. The results of these investigations are considered as highly relevant to the study of the origin and development of the city in ancient China, where the term city (*cheng*) generally referred to a dwelling site enclosed by walls.[2]

As a matter of fact, in recent years the topic of the origins of the city has become an important new research issue in Chinese archaeology.

Perhaps the earliest of such rammed-earth walled settlements in the Central Plain region is the site of Wangchenggang, located at the Dengfeng

---

[2] As a definition taken generally from China's earliest dictionary, the Shuowen Jie Zi, compiled during the Han dynasty.

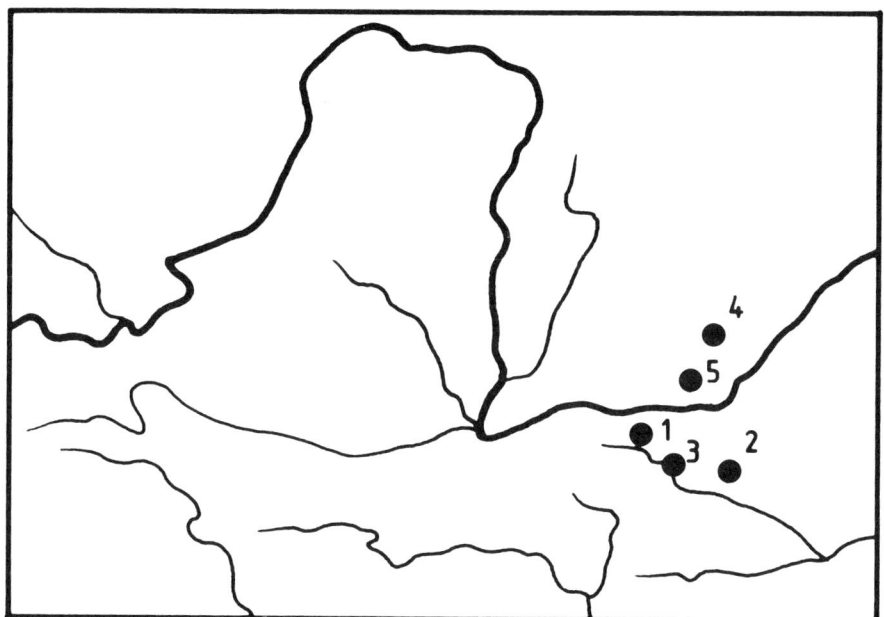

Figure 2. Distribution of Henan Longshan Culture walled settlements. 1. Wangchenggang; 2. Pingliangtai; 3. Haojiatai; 4. Hongang; 5. Mengzhuang.

County in the western part of Henan province. Its archaeological exploration since 1977 is considered as one of the most important activities and results of Chinese archaeology in the last decade, in particular as the excavators of the site have suggested that Wangchenggang was possibly the first capital site of Yu, the founder of the Xia dynasty (Henan Archaeological Research Institute and The Archaeology Department of the Museum of Chinese History, 1992).

According to historical sources such as the Bamboo Annals or The Roots of the Generations, Yu lived at a place named Yangcheng. Besides, in early textual references and geographical studies, this place is said to have been located around the Songshan mountains and the rivers of Wudu and Ying, near the present day town of Gaocheng in Dengfeng County. As in recent years, through archaeological survey and excavation in the surroundings of Gaocheng, the Yangcheng sites of the Zhou and Han periods have been found, it is for the Chinese archaeologists no accident that just to the west of the latter and separated only by the Wudu River, a walled settlement dating back at least to the late phase of the

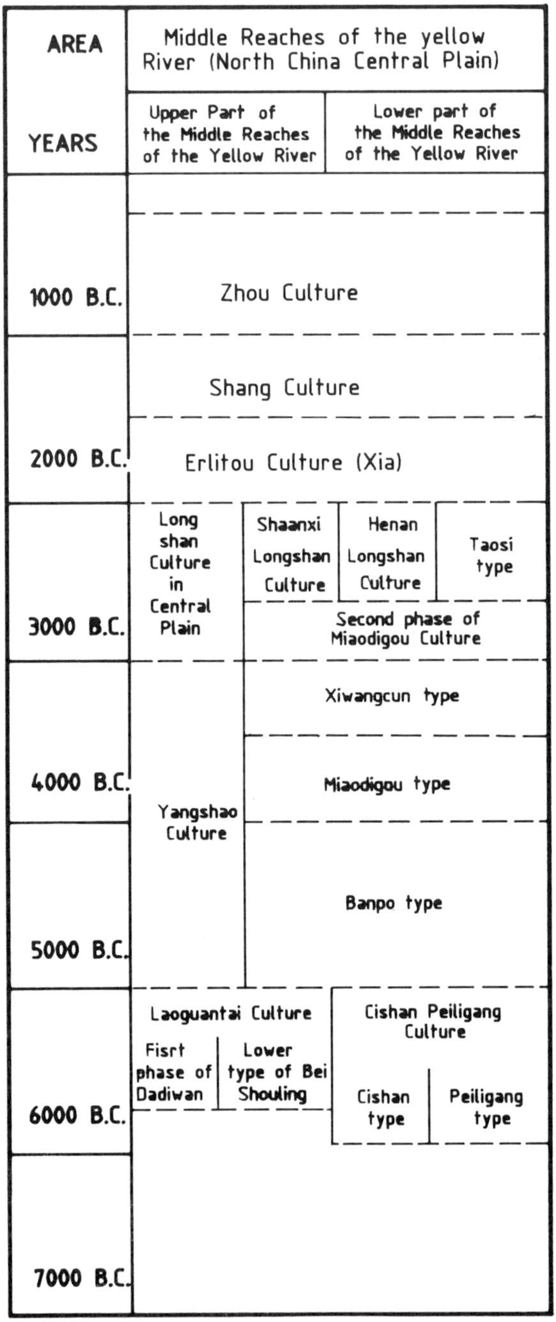

AREA	Middle Reaches of the yellow River (North China Central Plain)	
YEARS	Upper Part of the Middle Reaches of the Yellow River	Lower part of the Middle Reaches of the Yellow River
1000 B.C.	Zhou Culture	
	Shang Culture	
2000 B.C.	Erlitou Culture (Xia)	
3000 B.C.	Long shan Culture in Central Plain	Shaanxi Longshan Culture / Henan Longshan Culture / Taosi type — Second phase of Miaodigou Culture
4000 B.C.	Yangshao Culture	Xiwangcun type
		Miaodigou type
5000 B.C.		Banpo type
6000 B.C.	Laoguantai Culture — First phase of Dadiwan / Lower type of Bei Shouling	Cishan Peiligang Culture — Cishan type / Peiligang type
7000 B.C.		

Figure 3. Chronological Sequence in the *Zhongyuan* Region.

Longshan period, was found: the same phase, as more recently some archaeologists have proposed, might have already formed part of the initial Xia period.³

But whereas for the Yangcheng site of Zhou times there is reliable confirming evidence, in the form of more than thirty pottery fragments into which inscriptions like "Yangcheng" or "Inventory of the Yangcheng Storehouse" had been incised, Wangchenggang's identification as the first residence or capital site of the Xia dynasty is still difficult to attest at this moment. In this context, authors like An Jinhuai (1982) think that since the local name of Wangchenggang actually means "Royal City Mound", and was transmitted as such from generation after generation, this site could have indeed functioned as a royal seat. Thus, Wangchenggang in fact could have been the locality of Yangcheng of Yu.

THE SITE OF WANGCHENGGANG

Located in an area of fertile land and abundant water resources, the site of Wangchenggang is only half a kilometer northwest of the modern town of Gaocheng (see Figure 4). There it lies in an elevated area above the confluence of the Ying and the Wudu Rivers. The Ying River flows approximately 400 m to the south of the site, while the Wudu River is right to its east side. The Jishan and Songshan mountains are to the south and north, respectively. Unfortunately, the site has suffered serious destruction by the westward shift of the course of the Wudu River and the mountain torrents rushing down from the mountains in the north and northeast.

This site with remains of Peiligang, Yangshao and the Wangwan subtype of the Henan Longshan periods, is divided into five phases, with Phase II including the remains of the rammed-earth walls. Actually, the site of Wangchenggang consists of two adjoining walled enclosures, called by the excavators Western City and Eastern City, respectively (see Figure 5).

Most of the remains of the Eastern City have been washed away by the Wudu River. There the original surface wall bodies do not exist any longer; only the rammed earth in the foundation ditches of the southwestern corner, the western section of the southern wall and the southern section of the western wall are partly left. The remaining western section is 30 m long,

---

³There is a strong debate as to which particular archaeological culture could be considered as the remains of the Xia dynasty. Whereas some scholars think that the whole sequence of Erlitou coincides with Xia, others attribute different phases of it to the Xia or the Early Shang, respectively. And recently there is a trend to push the beginnings of the Xia back to the late Longshan period. For these different views, see for example An Jinhuai 1989b.

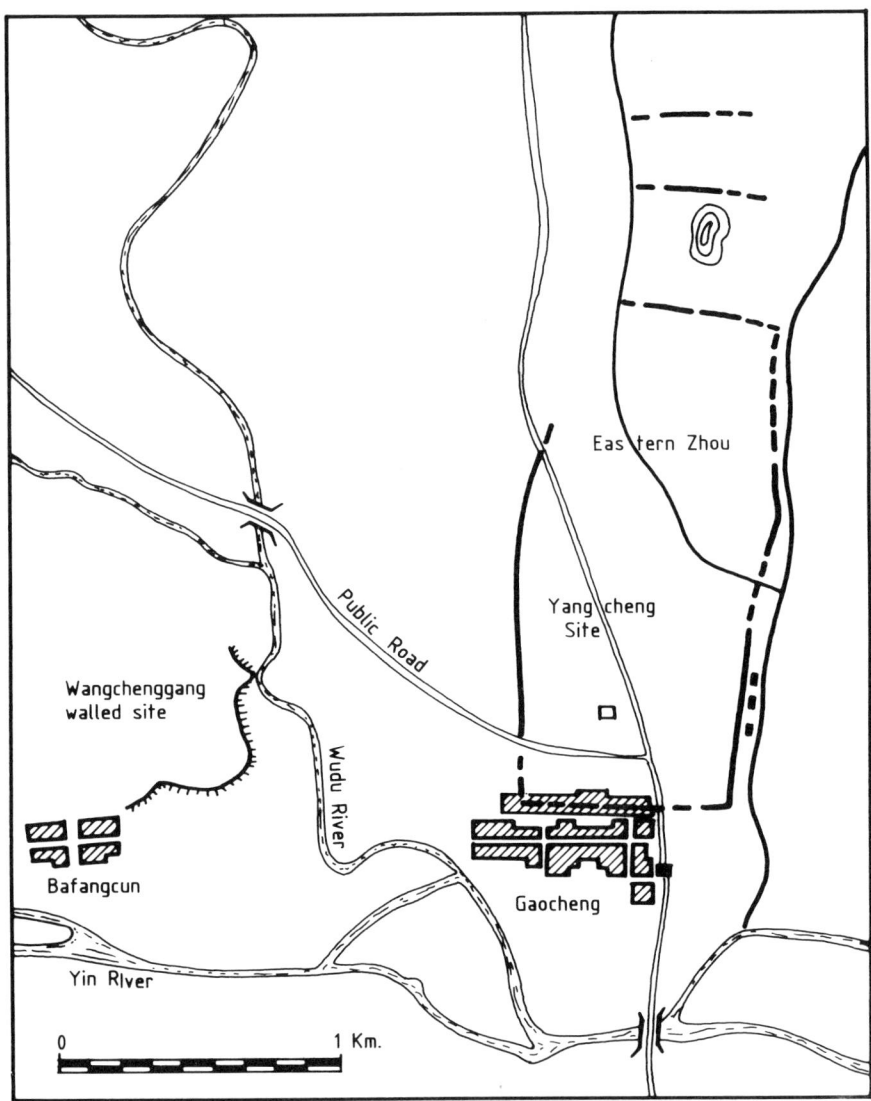

Figure 4. Location of the Longshan Period Wangchenggang and Eastern Zhou Yangcheng sites (according to 1992's excavation report).

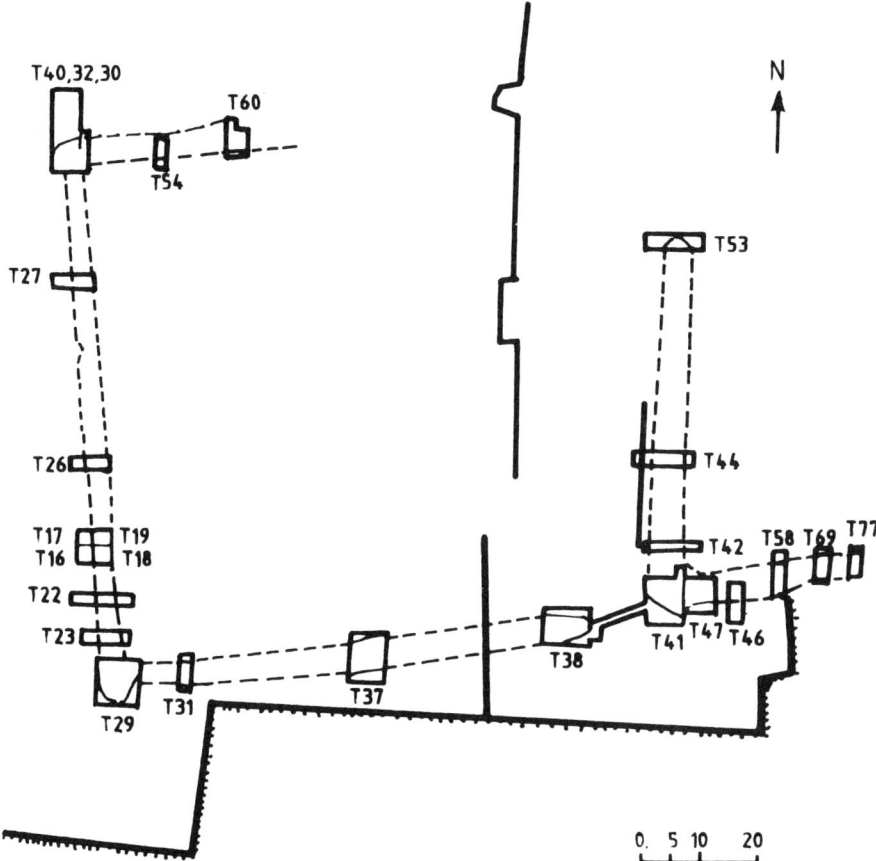

Figure 5. Wangchenggang's western and eastern walled encloures (*Wenwu* 3, 1983:14).

whereas the southern section of the western wall is preserved to a length of 65 m According to the excavation report from 1992 (*op. cit.*), these two walls cross at an angle of 88 degrees, with the corner rounded inside and extending about two meters outward, which seems to suggest to the excavators of the site the existence of some kind of defensive projections of the city walls. Originally, the walls of the Eastern City probably formed a square.

Perhaps it was due to the destruction of the eastern enclosure by floods that the Western City was built. In its construction the latter incorporated the western wall of the former as its eastern wall. To the extent the *hangtu*-layers are preserved, its southern and western walls were 82.4 and 92 m long, respectively. The northern section has been destroyed by the mountain torrents coming from the northwest and only a foundation ditch with rammed earth is left at a length of 29 m, also rounded inside and projecting two meters outwards. According to the excavation report (*Ibid.*), the four walls of the Western City also formed an approximate square, with the sides measuring about 90 m each and enclosing an area of circa 10,000 m^2.

Between the eastern end of the southern wall of the Western City and the southwestern corner of the Eastern City, the excavators detected a gap of 9.5 m in length, which in their view may have been the remains of the southern gate of the western enclosure.

As was revealed by test excavations into the walls of the Western City, the method of construction of the enclosure consisted in digging a trapezoidal foundation trough with sloping walls wider at the top than at the bottom.[4] In these troughs, earth was laid and stamped solid layer after layer; the thickness of the layers was not uniform, measuring an average of from 10 to 20 cm. Between each of the stamped layers, a layer of fine sand about one centimeter thick was laid. On top of these sand layers, traces of the pounding pestles were preserved. An (l982) implies the use of a still quite rudimentary earth-pounding method, which was to undergo continuous improvement and further development in the Erlitou palace-constructions and the building of Shang cities at Yanshi and Zhengzhou.

According to a carbon sample collected from a refuse pit inside the western enclosure and contemporary with the city walls, a radiocarbon date of 4010 ±85 B.P. was obtained, which is corrected to 4415 ±140 after the application of tree-ring calibration.

The excavations within the walled area yielded house foundations, ash pits and many objects of stone, ceramics, bone and shell. Contemporary with the phase of construction and use of the *hangtu*-walls, 11 plots of rammed earth were identified, as well as 13 rammed-earth pits and 13 rammed-earth foundation pits. But due to the fact that above all the house remains had suffered serious damage by succeeding levels of occupation, it is difficult to draw any conclusions concerning their original layout. Nevertheless, as there is a dense distribution of *hangtu*-platform remains especially in parts inside the enclosure in its central western portion and on a somewhat elevated area, according to the form of the *hangtu*-pits under these constructions—some of which even were found to be connected—it is possible to infer that these were the remains of important buildings. Some of these buildings apparently were of quite a large size; the

---

[4]For example in Test Pit WT22, dug into the western wall, the foundation trough was 3.4 m wide at the top and 2.9 m wide at the bottom, and up to 2.4 m deep.

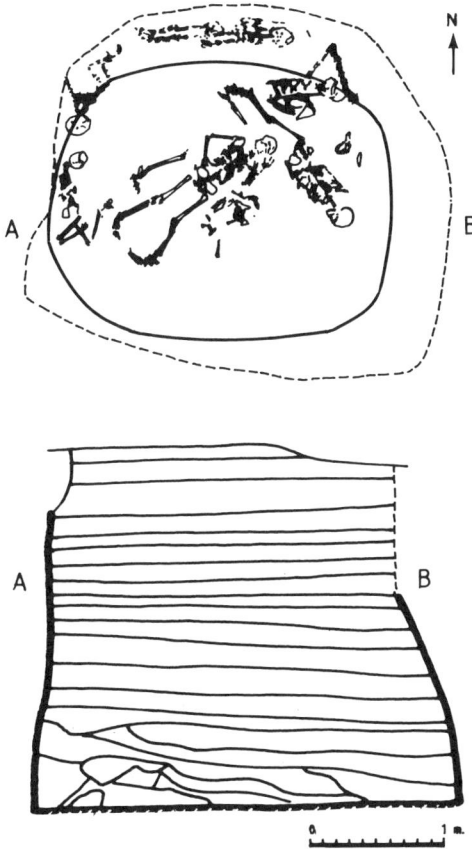

Figure 6. Foundation Pit n. 1 at Wangchenggang's western city (*Wenwu* 3, 1983:15).

excavation report from 1992 mentions that one of these constructions has possibly an area of 70 m², while a second one had up to 150 m².

What mostly survived from Phase II, were the rammed-earth foundation pits under the *hangtu*-platforms of such buildings. In the foundation pits, skeletons of human beings have been found buried between layers of stamped earth. In one of them, seven skeletons of male and female adults as well as children have been identified (Figure 6). The whole site of Wangchenggang revealed more than 20 such skeletons, some of which showed signs of physical violence, with the skull or the limbs separated from the body. The excavators of the site deduce that these were victims of foundation-laying ceremonies of the constructions inside the walled enclosures. Due to the partial excavation of this kind of remains, we have only a very fragmentary picture of the overall situation to be found in such foundation pits.[5]

With respect to the remains of refuse pits, these had different forms and contained ceramics, as well as stone, bone and shell artifacts. Ornaments of turquoise have also been recovered from such pits, which as a whole could have been simple houses or storage pits. Most were re-used in Phase II, a phase of general decline and partial abandonment of the fortified setlement. In one of the refuse pits, an object of metal, probably a fragment of a tripod vessel, was found. This is taken by some archaeologists as a proof for the conclusion that the walled site of Wangchenggang had already entered the Bronze Age, but in fact this find has nothing to do with the period of the construction and use of the city walls, as the metal fragment is from Phase IV. As we have stated earlier, the *hangtu*-walls of Wangchenggang were erected in Phase II of the site, which dates back more or less to the middle of late phase of the Henan Longshan Culture.

OTHER HENAN LONGSHAN SITES

Approximately at the same time as the Wangchenggang "twin city" was built, but belonging to different local cultural subtypes of the same Henan Longshan Culture, other walled centers appeared in the Central Plain region, both to the north and south of the Yellow River. Thus, besides Wangchenggang, walled Henan Longshan settlements up to now include the sites of Pingliangtai in eastern Henan, and of Hougang and Haojiatai in northern Henan; moreover, in this latter portion of the same province, only very recently a new site of this type, called Mengzhuang, was discovered.[6]

Unfortunately, due to the recent nature of the discovery of most of these sites, and above all the limited amount of excavation carried out in them, the archaeological information available at this moment is still very scarce or not yet published at all, so that all conclusions about the general nature of the site must have necessarily a tentative character. Nevertheless, although it is difficult at this moment to assess and deduce details about the overall layout and internal organization of these early walled centers,

---

[5]In order to preserve the data of the *hangtu*-wall level, the digging work generally stopped when reaching such a level. As for refuse pits and foundation-laying pits, when uncovering skeletons or bones, only 1/3 or 1/4 of them were excavated. For this reason, and taking into account the big destruction the site has suffered, the general picture of the city and the evidence related to the area inside the walls remains quite incomplete.

[6]This information appeared in a short article in China's Cultural Relics Newspaper *Zhongguo Wenwu Bao*, December 6th, l992:1.

we believe that it is already possible to discern some of the features shared by them.

To begin with, all of these Henan Longshan walled settlements were preferably located on an elevated terrain above the fertile alluvial plain of tributaries of the Yellow River. According to An (1982) such a topographic choice of the location of ancient Chinese cities and in particular of the sites of capitals, responded to the fact that these not only had to be close to a river in a location not endangered by inundations, but also that high elevations were easily defended against attacks from the outside. Thus, in addition to a pattern of favourable ecological conditions, we observe a preference for strategic locations, mostly above the confluence of two rivers and in a position high enough to protect against floods as well as against enemies.

The total area covered by these walled enclosures was rather small, with an average of perhaps 30,000 m^2 and with the site of Wangchenggang being the smallest of all of them. The overall plan in all these cases seems to respond to an approximate square or a rectangular shape, as well as a general orientation along the four cardinal directions. The entrance to the city seems to have been located to the south, or both to the north and south, so that a north-south axis perhaps already existed. This is quite obvious in the case of the walled site of Pingliangtai in eastern Henan province, which had a gate both to the north and to the south side (see Figure 7); moreover, here the southern gate not only had guardhouses on both sides of the entrance to the city, but also showed remains of an underground drainage system that consisted of pottery pipes covered with small rocks and earth, and paved over by a road surface.[7]

The fragmentary nature of the archaeological information available makes it difficult to estimate the population that lived inside the Longshan walled enclosures. Although the size of these compounds was rather small, authors like Qu Yingjie (1989) believe that they already contained a dense and compact population and that the socio-economic composition of its inhabitants was rather complex. From the remains of 39 houses unearthed in an area of 600 m^2 within the walled enclosure of Hougang, of which ten houses belonged to the middle and late phase of the Henan Longshan Culture, this archaeologist infers the existence of a population of up to 3000 persons. To him this seems comparable to population densities equivalent to those calculated for the early urban centers of Mesopotamia and the Indus Valley. Of course, such an estimate seems far too exaggerated and in this respect for example Sui Yuren

---

[7] For more details concerning the site of Pingliangtai, we refer in particular to the preliminary report of the trial excavations published in *Wenwu* 1983:321-36.

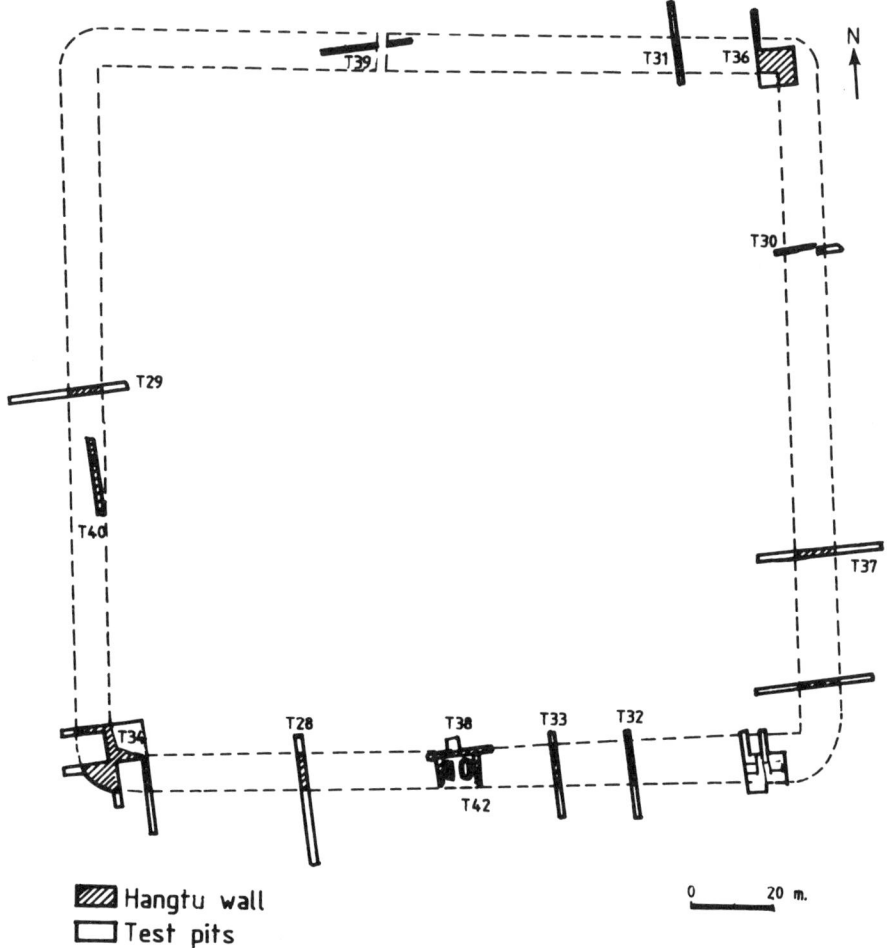

Figure 7. City wall at the site of Pingliangtai (*Wenwu* 3, 1983:27).

(1988) thinks that small walled enclosures such as Wangchenggang contained even less than one hundred persons.

On the other hand, Qu (1989) deduces from the types of objects found inside the enclosures that a high degree of differentiation between distinct kinds of professions already existed and that the bulk of the population within the walled areas were craftsmen. At the site of Pingliangtai, three pottery kilns were found inside the walled area, while some of these early walled settlements also revealed metal fragments as well as slag left from the smelting of metal. Based on this evidence of metal remains, Chinese archaeologists tend to jump to the conclusion that China had already entered the Bronze Age at this early stage. But, as already mentioned, the metal fragment recovered at Wangchenggang stemmed from a relatively late phase of occupation while the discoveries of metal remains at other sites are still too sporadic. This is why, among other, Yan Wenming (1987) recently has reclassified the Longshan cultural horizon as belonging rather to a Chalcolithic stage of development. While we agree on the fact that the finds of metal objects at the period in question are still too sporadic to speak of a Bronze Age or even of the existence of a sector of the population specialized in the manufacture of bronze objects, we should also take into account K. C. Chang's observation in relation to the fact that the location of sites like Wangchenggang and, in general, the early capitals of China's first dynasties coincided with the distribution of mineral resources needed for the smelting of metal (Chang 1985).

Unfortunately, questions concerning the distribution of resources in relation to the location of sites have recieved little attention in Chinese archaeology and it seems particularly difficult to reconstruct patterns of economic organization during the Longshan period.

From the discovery of turquoise objects at Wangchenggang and of jade and shell artifacts at this and other Longshan sites, some authors (for example, Qu 1989) conclude that some kind of exchange activities must have existed. Qu even allows the possibility of the existence of a market in Longshan times,[8] but there is—as of now—no archaeological proof for the existence of such an institution at such an early time. So far no archaeological field work has emphasized the discerning of patterns of production and circulation in a prehistoric context. With regard to the Central Plain area, most resources were probably locally available, so that mechanisms of exchange and redistribution might have played a minor role in the rise of China's early urban centers.

The information regarding patterns of social stratification in these early urban centers is also very limited. The evidence based on burials is not at all clear, mostly because the partial excavations have yielded only few burials inside the walled compounds.[9] Nevertheless, from the discovery of sacrificial victims in house foundation pits and of skeletons abandoned in refuse pits, Chinese archaeologists conclude that in middle and late Longshan times we observe the transition to class society and the emergence of

---

[8]Scholars relying on historical sources see some confirming evidence for the early existence of markets in textual references according to which the legendary hero Shennong established markets. See, e.g. Qu 1989.
[9]The cemeteries were probably located outside the walled areas.

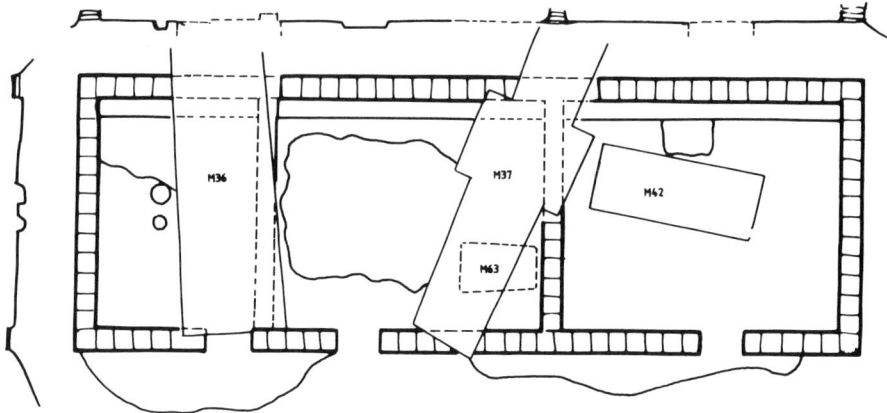

Figure 8. Adobe brick multi-room building above a platform, at the walled site of Pingliangtai (*Wenwu* 3, 1983:30).

the first slave-holder state of the Xia (An 1989a). In this context, it is generally affirmed that the mutilated skeletons found in Wangchenggang could have been those of slaves.[10]

The archaeological data in relation to house remains are also still very fragmentary, although we think that the presence in particular of *hangtu*-platforms like those unearthed at Wangchenggang and Pingliangtai (Figure 8), as well as the use of qualitatively distinct building materials, such as sun-dried clay bricks for the construction of house walls or the plastered lime floors detected in some remains at several Longshan sites, may indicate the existence of an already quite complex social stratification. Those qualitatively distinct house remains were perhaps those of important public buildings or even of a type of elite residences where the members of a socially privileged sector lived.[11] In our view, if the *hangtu*-platforms sup-

---

[10] There are different attempts to classify the period of the rise of these walled centers according to the stage of social evolution. Whereas some authors hold the opinion that these formed part of a late phase of primitive community, especially of a phase of a so-called military democracy—where the cultural heroes of Yao, Shun and Yu lived—see, e.g. Cao Guiling 1985; Sui Yuren 1988, authors like An Jinhuai speak of a phase of dissolution of the primitive community and the emergence of a class society in a slave-state.

[11] As we have already mentioned, the house remains at Wangchenggang are difficult to reconstruct; but at Pingliangtai at least one house was a multi-room building of adobe bricks above a platform, while another one—built also with adobe bricks and standing on a platform 72 cm high—had even a surface area of almost 90 m^2 (see Figure 8).

ported public buildings of the palace-type, the rise of a state society in China could be pushed back to the Longshan period.[12]

On the other hand, apart from foundation-laying ceremonies, up to now the Henan Longshan walled centers provide little evidence of religious activities; on the contrary, these early urban centers must have had a predominantly secular character. As is stated by Qu Yingjie (1989) there is no indication of altars or temple constructions, although he thinks that these kind of structures must have existed. Also, in this early phase of urban formation, such features as an orientation according to the four cardinal directions with an emphasis on a north-south axis seem to have had no major cosmological significance. In North China, such features may have simply responded to geographical considerations of protection against the wind coming from the north and of facing the main side of the buildings towards the sun.

Thus, the hypothesis of a religious origin of Chinese urban centers as proposed by Paul Wheatley (1971), finds little support in the archaeological data coming from the Central Plain region. At the same time, here, at the birthplace of the Chinese civilization no major importance of a shamanistic cosmological system based chiefly on animals as ritual items, or of the use of divination practices by way of scapulimancy, as emphasized by K. C. Chang (l986), can be attested;[13] for us, these seem to be rather elements coming from diverse Neolithic cultures situated on the periphery and incorporated later into the cultural system of the core area of Chinese civilization.[14]

CONCLUSIONS

In this context, most Chinese authors would affirm that the appearance of walled settlements like that of Wangchenggang was closely linked to the germination and development of class society. Walls are seen as the product of an irresolvable conflict between two opposing classes. As is

---

[12]We conceive palace buildings as one of the most important archaeological indicators for the emergence of a state society; see Wiesheu, l990 and in press. Up to now, the earliest identified palace buildings found in China are those of Palace n. 1 and n. 2 at the Erlitou site. Moreover, just recently, a new one was discovered at the same site, dating probably to the early phase of the Erlitou Culture (*Zhongguo Wenwu Bao*, February 28th, 1993).

[13]Chang (1986) thinks that the rise of the Chinese civilization was associated to a differentiated access to the means of communication, based on the control of such ritual elements.

[14]In Chinese archaeological literature it is often stated that in the Henan Longshan Culture the use of oracle bones for divination was already a common practice. But, as a matter of fact, I found that from the first walled sites, so far only one fragment—coming from the Hougang site—is reported.

argued for example by An Jinhuai (1982), the technology of building *hangtu*-precincts and walls became an instrument at the service of the ruling class who tried to protect its wealth accumulated inside the walls and ward off attacks from the outside. As such, the walls basically had a defensive function, whose origin can be even traced back to the moats that encircled Yangshao sites. Thus, according to most Chinese archaeologists, as wealth increased, the emerging ruling class of Longshan society took refuge in such rammed-earth walled settlements. But some other scholars doubt that such sites, more specifically called in the Chinese literature "fortification sites" (*chengbao*), could be considered true cities, in particular as these are of a very small size. A real city (*chengshi*), with large dimensions and the establishment of a market system, developed only in Zhou times. In this sense, the "*chengbao*"-earthen fortifications of the Longshan period are seen as merely embryonic types of cities, that originally had only defensive functions, but which in the course of a gradual and long-term development adopted additional economic, political and religious functions (for this view, see for examplem Du Yu 1983 and He Zhengfeng 1989). And only from Han times onward did the urban plan and layout reflect the imperial ideology of the "four quarters" cosmology!

However, the question as to whether or not the Longshan walled sites were real cities is difficult to answer at the present stage of research. We think it is quite possible that such walled enclosures were only a kind of inner or "palace-city" (*gongcheng*), which at later stages of Chinese urban development were clearly differentiated from an outer encirclement (*guocheng*). As such, the Longshan walled compounds contained perhaps only the most important public buildings as well as the elite residential precincts. This is even suggested by our site of Wangchenggang, where in a zone extending from the western enclosure to the Ying River, there is still an unexcavated site of 12,000 to 20,000 m^2 also dating back to the Longshan period (Jia E. 1984).

Thus in general—and on this we agree mostly with the Chinese scholars—the emergence of urban centers in China was associated chiefly with elements of a secular kind. However, our point of view differs from theirs in considering processes like the accumulation of wealth and the formation of a class society as a consequence of the constitution of such urban centers. Why, then, did the necessity for building walled centers like Wangchenggang arise?

In its beginnings, the erection of moats and walls appears to have been aimed, at least in part, at protecting the settlement against the danger of floods caused by the frequent shifts in river courses.[15] In the case of Wang-

---

[15] In Ancient China, the protection from water was presumably more important than the control of this factor for its use in irrigating agricultural fields (see Wiesheu 1991).

chenggang, this factor was certainly also important, though there is rather a more definitive proof about floods causing the decline and partial abandonment of this site in Phase IV when it was reconverted to a modest village site.[16] While the choice of the city site in a location not endangered by inundations played certainly an important role in Chinese urban development—and floods presumably were mostly responsible for the frequent move of ancient Chinese capitals[17]—we however assume that considerations related to military protection provided by the erection of walled centers in a strategic location were predominant.

Thus, conceived originally as an idea when digging canals and embankments around Yangshao sites, the building of walled enclosures and the adoption of the *hangtu*-technology in its construction during the middle or late Longshan period, could be viewed as a result of the need for establishing defensive installations in a period of increasing internal or external conflict.

If, in addition, we take into account the favourable environmental conditions of the fertile alluvial plain and the great variety of resources locally available, the Central Plain region could be considered as another instance of environmental circumscription, as stated in Carneiro's theory of the origin of state (1970 and 1987). Together with the intensification of conflict in Longshan times, as evidenced in particular in the defensive projections of the walls around strategic sites and the indications of violence in skeletons, and as a process triggered off by population stress, these factors led eventually to the formation of China's earliest societies. Although the existence of a demographic stress is difficult to discern at this moment from the archaeological record, there should be indications of a considerable population growth in absolute terms. In addition to more compact sites in Longshan times, there is a definite dense distribution of sites contemporary with Wangchenggang in this core area of Chinese civilization.[18]

---

[16]In this respect, Dong Qi (1986) argues that not only a great part of the eastern enclosure was washed away by floods, but that also within the northern and southwestern portion of the western enclosure, there was a considerable amount of silts deposited as a consequence of inundations.

[17]For a different view, see K. C. Chang, who feels that the shifts of capital sites in ancient China was due to the frequent exhaustion of copper and tin mines (Chang 1985 and 1986).

[18]Especially in the surroundings of the Songshan mountains where Wangchenggang is located, many other contemporary sites have been discovered; these include Cuoli, Meishan, Xinchai, Baiyuan, Wadian, Chengya, Erqilu, etc. Unfortunately, no studies of regional settlement patterns have been undertaken. Besides a more detailed investigation of the overall community pattern with digging work also carried out in the area outside the city walls, it would be interesting to have data about the hierarchy of sites as derived from a regional type of analysis.

Like in most other centers of pristine civilizations, in China, too, the necessity of mediating military conflict appears to have been a major factor for the institutionalization of kingship and the emergence of urban societies associated with state formation. As we had already tentatively concluded in an earlier paper (Wiesheu 1991), the Xia state was perhaps not the earliest and not the only one among several local political entities of this type. In this context, the citadel-like center of Wangchenggang might have functioned as a political and military seat of a very early embryonic state formation that even predated the Xia by a few centuries.

Instead of being the Yangcheng site of the semi-legendary flood-controller and first sovereign of the Xia, was Wangchenggang then the site of a capital established by Yu's father Gun, or even that of the prestigious "cultural hero" Huangdi? One of the alleged achievements of these two legendary figures consisted precisely in having built Ancient China's first cities.

REFERENCES

An, J., 1982, The Shang-City at Cheng-chou and Related Problems, in: *Studies of Shang Archaeology. Selected Papers from The International Conference on Shang Civilization* (K. C. Chang, ed.), Yale University Press, New York and London, pp. 15-48.
An, J., 1983, Jin nian lai Henan Xia-Shang wenhua kaogu de xin shouhuo, *Wenwu* 3:1-7.
An, J., 1989a, Shilun Henan diqu Longshan wenhua de shehui xingzhi, *Zhongyuan Wenwu* 1:20-24.
An, J., 1989b, Shi nian lai Henan Xia-Shang kaogu de faxian yu yanjiu, *Huaxia Kaogu* 3:11-16.
Cao, G., 1985, Lun Longshan wenhua gu cheng de shehui xingzhi, in: *Zhongguo kaoguxue hui, di wu ci nian lunwenji*, Wenwu Press, Beijing, pp. 1-7.
Cao, G., 1990, Huaiyang Pingliangtai yizhi shehui xingzhi tanxi, *Zhongyuan Wenwu* 2:89-92.
Carneiro, R. L., 1970, A Theory of the Origin of State, *Science* 169:733-738.
Carneiro, R. L., 1987, Further Reflections on Resource Concentration and its Role in the Rise of the State, in: *Studies in the Neolithic and Urban Revolutions. The V. Gordon Childe Colloquium, Mexico 1986* (L. Manzanilla, ed.), BAR International Series, BAR, Oxford, pp. 245-260.
Chang, K. C., 1985, Guanyu Zhongguo chuqi chengshi zhe ge gainian, *Wenwu* 2:61-67.
Chang, K. C., 1986, *The Archaeology of Ancient China*, Fourth Edition, revised and enlarged, Yale University Press, New Haven and London.
Dong, Q., 1986, Wangchenggang chengbao yinyin chutan, *Kaogu yu Wenwu* 1:32-35.
Dong, Q., 1988, Shi wo guo shiqian shiqi de chengbao, *Beifang Wenwu* 4:17-21.
Dong, Q., 1989, Wangchenggang chengbao zhuqiang jishu yuanliu, *Jianghan Kaogu* 1:48-53.
Du, Y., 1983, Zhongguo gudai chengshi de qiyuan yu fazhan, *Zhongguo Shiqian Yanjiu* 1:149-157.
He, Z., 1989, You guan wo guo zaoqi chengshi tansuo zhong de ji ge wenti, *Kaogu yu Wenwu* 4:91-96.
Henan Archaeological Research Institute and The Archaeology Department of The Museum of Chinese History, 1983, Dengfeng Wangchenggang yizhi de fajue, *Wenwu* 3:8-20.
Henan Archaeological Research Institute and The Archaeology Department of The Museum of Chinese History, 1992, *Dengfeng Wangchenggang yu Yangcheng*, Wenwu Press, Beijing.

Henan Archaeological Research Institute and Yancheng County Memorial Hall of Xu Shen, 1992, Yancheng Haojiatai yizhi de fajue, *Huaxia Kaogu* 3:62-91.
Henan Archaeological Research Institute and The Relics Section of the Bureau of Culture at Zhoukou Prefecture, 1983, Henan Huaiyang Pingliangtai Longshan wenhua chengzhi shifa jianbao, *Wenwu* 3:21-36.
Jia, E., 1984, Guanyu Dengfeng Wangchenggang yizhi ji ge wenti de tantao, *Wenwu* 1:63-68.
Ma, S., 1988, Shilun cheng de chuxian ji qi fangyu zhineng, *Zhongyuan Wenwu* 1:66-71.
Ma, S., 1992, Zhong-wai wenming qiyuan wenti duibi yanjiu, *Zhongyuan Wenwu* 3:58-66.
n.a., 1992, Huixian Mengzhuang faxian Longshan wenhua chengzhi, *Zhongguo Wenwu Bao* December 6:1.
n.a., 1993, Erlitou zaoqi daxing jianzhu jizhi de faxian ji qi yiyi, *Zhongguo Wenwu Bao* February 28:3.
Qu, Y., 1989, Lun Longshan wenhua shiqi gu chengzhi, in: *Zhongguo yuanshi wenhua lunji* (T. Changwu and S. Xingbang, eds.), Wenwu Press, Beijing, pp. 267-289.
Shi, J., 1986, Jianlun Zhongguo gudai chengshi buju guihua de xingcheng, *Zhongyuan Wenwu* 2:91-99.
Sui, Y., 1988, Huanghe zhong-xia you Longshan wenhua chengbao chuta, *Zhongyuan Wenwu* 4:46-52.
Wheatley, P., 1971, *The Pivot of the Four Quarters*, Aldine, Chicago.
Wiesheu, W., 1990, El problema del origen del Estado en China, *Estudios de Asia y Africa* 81, 1, El Colegio de México:105-115.
Wiesheu, W., 1991, *El origen del Estado y de la civilización en China: El caso de la dinastia Xia*, Master's Degree Thesis, Center of African and Asian Studies, El Colegio de México, México.
Wiesheu, W., in press, *Cacicazgo y Estado arcaico: Evolución y distinción antropológica de organizaciones sociopolíticas complejas*, Instituto Nacional de Antropología e Historia, México.
Yan, W., 1987, Zhongguo shiqian wenhua de tongyixing yu duoyangxing, *Wenwu* 3:38-50.
Yang, Z., 1989, Jin shi nian Henan yuanshi shehui kaogu de zhongyao faxian yu yanjiu', *Huaxia Kaogu* 3:1-10.

Part **III**

New World

For Mesoamerica, three articles show a variety of early urban developments, all centered around control through the ideological use of monumental space. Teotihuacan, a huge capital, was a strategic site controlling obsidian mines and fresh-water springs, a locus of specialized crafts, a vast planified settlement, a redistributional center, but also a model of the Mesoamerican cosmos which render it as the main pilgrimage site in Central Mexico.

The Oaxaca example also states ideology, power, and inequality but in an actor-based approach. It emphasizes the role played by the changing behavior of elites, particularly the role of ideology as prime mover in the origin and development of urban society. Ideology made people move to unstable ecological zones, pushed the nobles to establish contact with distant elites to obtain exotic materials, was used to extract resources, and finally provoked collapse.

Oxkintok was also a model of Maya cosmos, related to the Sun God dynastic iconography. In a monumental setting, the disposition of architectural groups bears resemblance to the symbolic representation of the cosmos; power systems, relations, capacity, and exercise are materialized in architectural symbols. The author proposes that the Maya constructed their cities as images of ideological models to evidence divine sanctions to the social organization.

For the Andean area, two contemporaneous major urban developments are discussed: Huari and Tiwanaku. The first stresses the transformation of a religious into a military settlement; the process that originated Huari began in the concentration of hamlets and villages, transformed when ceremonial complexes emerge. Theocratic leadership created an ideological and spatial unification. The emergence of orthogonal patterns imposed on the landscape is viewed as imposed by military lords who were transformed into architects and administrators.

For Tiwanaku, two aspects are mentioned: one is related to the provincial linkages of the Tiwanaku policy; the areas under Tiwanaku influence show different types of relationships with the core: exchange, economic interdependence, the establishment of provinces, monoethnic colonies, multiethnic colonies, and military conquest. The other discusses three models related to the establishment of complex society: the vertical archipelago, the *Altiplano* mode of production, and the agricultural production model. Thus, the expansion of Tiwanaku is seen not as the result of complementing limited altiplano resources with goods from other ecological zones, but as the procurement of basic foodstuff due to pressures on the existent productive system.

Chapter 5

Teotihuacan
Urban Archetype, Cosmic Model

LINDA MANZANILLA

INTRODUCTION

Life in urban centers and cities was a characteristic of civilized life in Mesoamerica and Mesopotamia. In spite of differences in form and function (Marcus 1983), the majority of the Mesoamerican cities included a civic, administrative, and ceremonial core; they were also demographic concentrations that offered goods and services to the productive surrounding territories.

Yet there was a difference between urban centers in the Central Mexican Highlands and those of the Mayan Area, which lay in the importance assigned to craft production and specialization within the core itself, in the demographic density, and in the articulation of foreign groups to urban life.

According to Freidel (1981), in cities of the Basin of Mexico, such as Teotihuacan, the main goal of large-scale nucleation was to control people, whereas the main goal of residential dispersion in the Mayan Area was the control of the distribution of goods and services.

The cities of Central Mexico were multiethnic centers that took advantage of the occupation qualities of foreign groups, which shared residence and occupation with local inhabitants, but maintained distinctive traits particularly evident in funerary practices and ritual behavior.

LINDA MANZANILLA • Instituto de Investigaciones Antropológicas, UNAM, Ciudad Universitaria, 04510 México D.F.

Emergence and Change in Early Urban Societies, edited by Linda Manzanilla. Plenum Press, New York, 1997.

Central Mexican main settlements were planified perhaps incorporating astronomical standards or ritual axes (Tichy 1983). Adding to their symbolic preëminence and their concentration of power, they may have represented cosmic models which had a terrestrial sacred space, a synthesis of the four courses of the cosmos represented by the four divisions of the city; a celestial sphere depicted by the summits of the temples and the sky itself; and an underworld represented by a system of tunnels or caves under the settlement.

The Prehispanic megacenters of the Basin of Mexico—Teotihuacan and Tenochtitlan—were the capitals of large states, which nevertheless differed in organization, administration, coercive power, and settlement hierarchy. They inaugurated a process of geopolitical importance of the region as the core of the macroarea which lasts until the XXth century. They both belong to Marcus' (1983) sectorial model, in which the wedges represent sectors with social and economic differences. They are also main exchange locuses.

TEOTIHUACAN

This city (Figure 1) was one of the hugest and most important urban developments of preindustrial times. It was the main pilgrimage and manufacturing center of the Classic horizon. Its main features will be discussed briefly.

Strategic Site

The location of Teotihuacan was chosen due to its nearness to the Otumba and Pachuca obsidian deposits, to the fresh-water spring concentration of Puxtla at San Juan, to the Texcoco Lake, and to its priviledged position in the easiest access route from the Gulf Coast to the Basin of Mexico. Nevertheless the location of the first urban center in the northwestern part of the valley surprises because the sector is deprived of running water, unless the disponibility of building material was the cause.

A Great Demographic Concentration

As a result of the eruption of the Xitle volcano in the southwestern portion of the Basin of Mexico, Cuicuilco—one of the largest Formative centers—was deserted. The Popocatepetl volcano was also erupting in the last centuries B.C., and covering large Formative sites (Uruñuela y Ladrón de Guevara and Plunket Nagoda 1995). The consequent demographic re-

Figure 1. View of the Street of the Dead and the Pyramid of the Sun from the Moon Plaza.

arrangements provoqued massive migrations to the northern part of the basin. Yet, one of the possible phenomena associated with the early history of Teotihuacan was the reallocation of population and its channeling to huge constructive enterprises, such as the Pyramids of the Sun and the Moon.

From then on, the main settlement of Central Mexico was Teotihuacan, with the consequent ruralization of the rest of the region. It concentrated around half of the population of the Basin of Mexico, which was devoted mainly to craft production. One may think that the valleys of Toluca, Tlaxcala, and eastern Morelos were dependent from Teotihuacan, and were probably sending cotton, avocado, Thin Orange wares, as well as other products to the city.

Monumentality

As we already mentioned, the first urban center of the Teotihuacan Valley was located in the northwestern sector. It was characterized by a dispersed distribution of three-temple plazas surrounded by the dwellings of the inhabitants. After some time, came the construction of the Pyramids of the Sun (Figure 2) and the Moon. And soon after, during the first centuries AD, the Street of the Dead is planned, and so is the orthogonal grid of the city. The population formerly living in the northwestern sector

Figure 2. Pyramid of the Sun.

moves to fringe the main avenue. The city then grows steadily until it reached 20 km².

The monumentality of its constructions was a main investment in the ideological importance of the settlement. It was the creation of sacred space, and maybe also the symbolic instauration of sacred time—the ritual calendar—as represented in the building of the Temple of the Feathered Serpent (Figure 3) (López Austin, López Luján, and Sugiyama 1991).

Millon (1993:25) states that the constructions of the Pyramids of the Sun and Moon, the Ciudadela, as well as the "Street of the Dead" are "...dramatic demonstrations, dramatic realizations of the exercise of power during a time of strong rulers...". Eventhough we yet do not have concrete data that supports the hypothesis of strong individual rulers, we yet know that the two main pyramids were built not with volcanic scoria, as the rest of the city was, but with tons of organic earth, as if all the northern half of the city's subsoil was scraped, leaving the volcanic tuff (*tepetate*) as the floor from which the foundations of all the constructions were placed (Manzanilla 1994). This huge enterprise, probably related to the construction of "mountains of sustenance" copying the neighboring mountain profiles, soon after the volcanic events of the beginnings of the Era, can also

Figure 3. Temple of the Feathered Serpent.

be seen as a major investment in the symbolic power of the city, as well as a means of preventing collapse during earthquakes.

Urban Planning

For the Tlamimilolpa phase, but not before, elements of urban planning at the site were clearly defined, as well as domestic life in apartment compounds (Millon 1973). These elements include:

1. The existence of streets and axes, as part of an orthogonal grid oriented to 15 degrees east of north (see Figure 1). This was perhaps traced by the use of circular markers in the nearby hills and in the city itself (Aveni, Hartung, and Buckingham 1978). Millon proposes the existence of two axes: the Street of the Dead and the East-West Avenue that divide the city in four quadrants. Tichy (1983) adds that this orientation is related to the beginnings of the rainy season in May, creating thus a radial system of visual lines relative to the sun's position in the horizon. The center of the system was the Pyramid of the Sun.
2. The presence of a water supply and drainage system.

3. Administrative and public constructions placed along the Street of the Dead. The rest of the city was built around three-temple plazas, that could have been wards' centers.
4. The existence of craftsmen and foreign *barrios*. Around the main core, there were a number of multifamily apartment compounds that consisted of several rooms at slightly different levels, disposed around open spaces (courtyards, backyards, and light wells); these last were places for ritual, pluvial water collection, partial refuse disposal, and light provision (Figure 4). The compounds consisted of different apartments joined by passages for circulation; they have domestic sanctuaries, and the entire structure is enclosed within an exterior wall.

It is believed that these compounds could have been occupied by corporate groups sharing kinship, residence, and occupation, for it has been archaeologically observed that craftsmen dedicated to the manufacture of different products lived in separate compounds (Spence 1966; Millon 1968). Yet, scarce evidence has been published until now in this respect.

Because life in multifamily apartment compounds was a highligh of urban Teotihuacan, we will devote some pages to its analysis.

The compounds vary considerably in surface area. Apartments within the compound could be isolated either taking into consideration the circulation alleys or access points, or by mapping the different food consumption *loci* for each particular household. In adition, each household seems to have had its own storage, refuse, sleeping, and cult areas. There are other spaces where the entire family group gathered to participate in common activities, particularly related to family group ritual.

Some of the apartment compounds in the central area of the city have been excavated—among them: Tlamimilolpa, Xolalpan, Atetelco, Tepantitla, La Ventilla, Tetitla (see Figure 4), Zacuala, Bidasoa, San Antonio Las Palmas, El Cuartel, and structure 15B:N6W3 at Oztoyahualco. We also have information from Tlajinga 33 (Storey and Widmer 1989, Storey 1992) and Maquixco on the outskirts of the city (Sanders 1994, 1995).

Domestic life in large urban centers has been a major interest in our projects. From 1985 to 1988 we carefully dissected an apartment compound at Oztoyahualco (Figure 5)—the northwestern boundary of the city—in Millon's N6W3 square (Barba *et al.* 1987; Manzanilla 1988-89; Manzanilla and Barba 1990; Manzanilla 1993; Manzanilla, in press a). We planned a strategy that took into consideration chemical traces of activities on the plastered floors, as well as microscopic and macroscopic evidence related to specific activities.

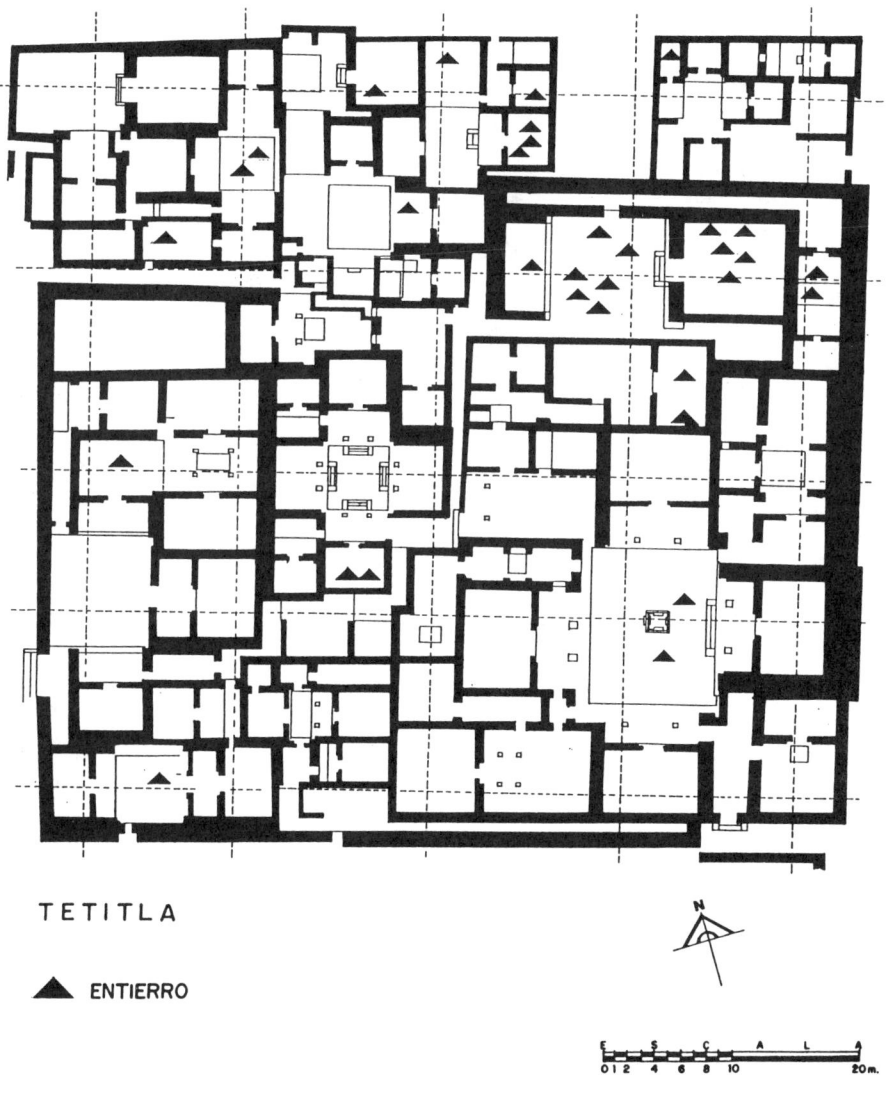

Figure 4. Map of Tetitla, an elite apartment compound (redrawn from Séjourné 1966).

Each apartment within the compound included a zone for food preparation and consumption, sleeping quarters, storage areas, sectors for refuse, patios for cult activities, and funerary areas. Additionally, there were

Figure 5. Aerial view of Oztoyahualco 15B:N6W3 (photograph by Linda Manzanilla).

zones in which the entire family group gathered to share activities, particularly those related to ritual and perhaps to the raising of domestic animals.

We suspect that members of different families participated in specialized activities with respect to the rest of the city. In the compound that we studied, the family group probably specialized in the stucco finishing of neighboring three-temple plazas, as well as other constructions at Oztoyahualco. Other family groups were devoted to ceramic, textile, obsidian working or painting activities.

With respect to diet, the Mesoamerican plant complex was present in our as well as in the other apartment compounds [maize, amaranth, beans, squash, hot peppers, *Chenopodium*, *Portulaca*, *Physalis*, cactus, Mexican hawthorn, and Mexican cherries (McClung 1979, 1980:162-163; Manzanilla 1985; Manzanilla 1993; Manzanilla, in press a; Storey 1992:64)]. Some cases of medicinal plants could be cited, particularly related to white sapodilla, wild potatoes, and probably some Compositae (Manzanilla 1988-89).

The presence of *Nicotiana* at San Antonio Las Palmas (Monzón 1989), avocado at Teopancazco (McClung 1979), cotton at Tlamimilolpa (Linné 1942) and Teopancazco (McClung 1979), and related Malvaceae at Tetitla (McClung 1979) and Tlajinga 33 (Storey and Widmer 1989) probably suggest differential access to certain botanical resources, associated with manufactures and ritual consumption.

Faunal subsistence depended on rabbits and hares, deer, dogs, and turkey, supplemented by duck and fish (Starbuck 1975; Valadez and Manzanilla 1988). At Oztoyahualco 15B:N6W3, we had a wide variety of rabbit and hare species. We even detected young individuals, so we have proposed a breeding locus for rabbits in Room 10. We also had four young dogs, particularly present in child burials (Valadez and Manzanilla 1988; Valadez, in Manzanilla 1993, v. II), so we have also proposed dog raising. The high amount of rabbits and hares in subsistence also had an ideological counterpart in a small rabbit sculpture that stood on a temple model in one of the ritual courtyards, probably as a patron deity (Manzanilla 1988-1989; Manzanilla and Ortiz 1991; Manzanilla 1993; Manzanilla, in press a).

Yet, one difference between domestic units that should be pointed out is the presence of different hunting techniques represented in the technological repertoire, particularly in the percentages of projectile points of various sizes to cope with small, medium, and large animals with respect to blow-gun projectiles.

In Xolalpan times, there could probably have been shortages in meat distribution in response to population pressure. Maybe one of the relevant responses is the breeding of rabbits together with turkeys and dogs at Oztoyahualco 15B:N6W3. Another could have been the consumption of freshwater fish at Tlajinga 33.

Plant species were generally gathered for food, medicinal purposes, fuel, and construction. Varieties included hawthorn, purslane, wild potatoes, wild reeds, umbelliferous plants, white sapodilla, pine, oak, juniper, ditch reeds, and bulrushes.

Each nuclear family had a specific area for cooking that was recognized in the archaeological record by dark, circular spots on the stucco floor, where the wood-fueled, portable stove was placed, and where its pH was changed due to the nearness of fire. Concentrations of phosphates may be seen around these stains that mark the area of food consumption. Grinding stones and other implements, as well as carbonized seeds and animal bones, related to food preparation were found around the consumption areas.

Distinct storage sectors were located, in the neighborhood of the food consumption areas, where San Martin storage amphorae were present, together with several plant macrofossils. There are also evidences of differential use of pottery wares and other activities by each household, within the Oztoyahualco compound we excavated.

There are also occupational differences between domestic units, including: lapidary work (Widmer 1991), ceramic manufacture (Krotser and Rattray 1980), obsidian biface production and prismatic blade extraction,

Figure 6. Burial 8 at Oztoyahualco 15B:N6W3 (Manzanilla 1993).

figurine production, textile manufacture, probably basket making, hide and fiber-work, mural painting, stucco polishing, etcetera.

There are some hints of a differential usage of wares with respect to each nuclear family unit. This could probably reflect differential access to pottery production in the urban setting for each nuclear family (Manzanilla [ed.] 1993). There are also differences in: the realm of family group or nuclear family activities, suggesting group and family specializations; the number of high-status products, particularly the decorated ceramic tripods or the mural paintings; the quality of the construction itself. Nevertheless, without approaching the problem of the different circulation spheres properly, the differential access issue will remain unconcluded.

Burials are rich in domestic contexts. However, with the exception of Tlajinga 33 and probably La Ventilla, the number of adults interred in each one of the compounds is too low, relative to the area of the compound, to account for most of its inhabitants. For example, seven burials are recorded for Xolalpan, thirteen for Tlamimilolpa, and eighteen for our compound at Oztoyahualco. Perhaps other adults, particularly women, were buried in other places.

Certain burials in each compound had very rich offerings. At Oztoyahualco, Burial 8 (Figure 6) was exceptional for it contained a male adult, twenty-two years of age, with an intentionally deformed skull, in association with an impressive theater-type incense burner (Manzanilla and Carreón 1991). In what seems to represent a funerary ritual, the incense burner appliqués were removed from the lid, and all were placed around the deceased. The chimney was deposited toward the west, and the lid and the figure to the east of the skull; representations of plants and sustenance (ears of corn, squash, squash flowers, cotton, *tamales*, corn bread, and perhaps amaranth bread) to the south; the four-petaled flowers, roundels representing feathers, and mica disks to the east and west.

Although Oztoyahualco had only 18 burials, and not as much information as that provided by Tlajinga 33 (Storey 1992) or by La Ventilla "B" (Serrano and Lagunas 1974), there are important conclusions regarding this type of data. We observed an over-representation of burials belonging to particular apartments of the compounds, a phenomenon also noted for Xolalpan, where nearly all the burials are concentrated in the southwestern section; at Tlamimilolpa, nearly all are grouped in the central-southern section; at Tetitla, they are concentrated in the northeastern section. It seems that there is one family that is well represented with respect to funerary practices, and all the rest seem to be under-represented.

One should also mention the presence of foreign raw materials such as mica, slate, and marine shells in burials at Xolalpan, Tlamimilolpa, and Oztoyahualco 15B:N6W3. The difference lies in their quantity, and in the proportion of Pacific versus Atlantic shell species.

I have a remark on domestic cult. It has been proposed that a superposition of deities on two levels occurred for the first time at Teotihuacan. Lineage gods were patrons of lines of descent, and above them was the deity Tlaloc as god of place, protector of the territory, and patron of the city and the "caves" (López Austin 1989). This opinion contrasts with another which places the Great Goddess at the summit of the sacred hierarchy (Pasztory 1976, 1992).

Among the deities present at Teotihuacan, the Fire God (Huehuetéotl), who was known from the Formative Horizon, always appears associated with the eastern portions of apartment compounds. Another deity present in domestic contexts is the Fat God, generally represented in figurines or appliquéd on tripod vessels. The Butterfly God is presented on incense burners and is probably linked to death and fertility (Manzanilla and Carreón 1991; Paulinyi 1995).

The state god Tlaloc was represented on a domestic level in figurines with goggles and elaborate headdresses. However, at Oztoyahualco 15B:N6W3, we also had evidence of patron gods related to particular families. A stucco rabbit sculpture was found on a basalt, Teotihuacan miniature temple-shaped shrine in one of the ritual patios of the compound.

Around the domestic ritual courtyards of the compound—one for each household—some activity areas related to ritual preparation have been detected. There were also numerous funerary and offering pits.

Religion should be seen as a sphere of sociopolitical integration organized into a hierarchy in which the patron gods of family groups, *barrio* and occupational deities, the gods of specific priestly groups, and finally, state deities such as Tlaloc are superposed.

The Teotihuacan society was integrated mainly through religion. The conception of the four courses of sacred space permeated also the domestic domain of Teotihuacan (Manzanilla 1993; Manzanilla, in press a). Spatial patterning seems to have been established for the disposition of functional sectors, which extended beyond the framework of individual households. We wish to emphasize that the affinity for order so patently manifest in the grid system of the city finds its correspondence on the domestic level.

The three-temple complexes that we find throughout the city may have been the centers of *barrio*-groups, where the cult and exchange activities would have taken place for a number of specialized corporate groups living in apartment compounds around them.

Manufacturing Center

Teotihuacan manufactures had prestige all over Mesoamerica during the Classic Horizon. Particularly green obsidian prismatic blades and high-quality pottery were distributed among elites. Other products, such as those derived from cactus and *Agave*, as well as ritual paraphernalia, could have been exchanged with foreign groups (Millon 1993:28). In the city, distinct manufacturing wards have been individuated, specifically those regarding blade production around the Pyramid of the Moon, or ceramic manufacturing sectors in the southeastern part of the city. Obsidian production was specialized to the level of the type of artifact produced. There were also censers' plaque workshops around the Ciudadela, probably items of conspicuous consumption.

Lapidary, shell, textile, and feather-working workshops have been individuated. Paulinyi (1981) suggests the existence of districtal groups which may have had a part in co-rulership: one located to the west of the Great Compound; the second, in the northwestern part of the valley; the third to the east of the Street of the Dead; the fourth, in the eastern fringe of the city; the fifth, to the south of the San Lorenzo river.

The Merchants' and the Oaxaca *Barrios* were two foreign wards, but maybe not the only ones. Recently, West Mexican pottery and figurines have been located in the western part of the city (Rubén Cabrera, personal communication, 1992). The Merchants' *Barrio* was probably inhabited by merchants from the Gulf Coast that lived in round houses, and brought in Maya pottery and Gulf Coast products. The Oaxaca *Barrio* may have been involved in the distribution of shell ornaments (Rattray 1987, 1988, 1993).

Redistributive Center

In our reconstruction of the economic organization of the Teotihuacan priesthood (Manzanilla 1992), we have proposed that the collective entity that administered Teotihuacan created different redistributive circuits to assure the maintenance of the bureaucracy as well as the full-time State craftsmen. These redistributive networks maybe ran parallel to other types of exchange systems: barter between producers, long-distance elite exchange, direct provisioning of sumptuary goods in enclaves, foreign merchants using the city's distributive system, etcetera.

Teotihuacan was also the central place for a wide distribution of goods, following definite routes. One of them, maybe the best defined, has been located in the Puebla-Tlaxcala Region, where 80 Teotihuacan settlements are arranged in a corridor relating Teotihuacan to Cholula, and then to the Oriental Basin and the Gulf Coast (García Cook 1981).

Sumptuary goods included feathers, jadeite and other greenstone minerals, cacao beans, incense (*copal*), rubber (Millon 1993), Atlantic and Pacific shells, avocado, cotton, perhaps also honey, animals from the tropical forest, *Amate* paper, and other products.

Political Capital

Nobody can contest that Teotihuacan was the capital of an incomparable State that established enclaves in remote provinces of Mesoamerica. Yet, there are discrepancies with respect to its type of government. There are some that believe that Teotihuacan was headed by a single lord or maybe two (*i.e.* Cabrera, Cowgill, and Sugiyama 1990). There are others that propose a priestly collective government (Manzanilla 1992; Pasztory 1992).

Paulinyi (1981) mentions the idea that Teotihuacan and Tula inaugurated a type of government characterized by the co-regency of three to seven lords. López Austin (1989) proposes that Teotihuacan was the first place were the transformation from lineage to State took place, a process in which the old lineage heads detached themselves from common people to form an autonomous group of bureaucrats, redistributers, and nobles. The birth of the State would be derived from the presence of groups of diverse origin and from the use of power over a territory.

With respect to coercion mechanisms, these seem to be evident until the last phases of Teotihuacan history. Yet, around the third century AD, there seem to be vast sacrificial consacration acts, such as the one evident in the foundation of the Temple of the Feathered Serpent (Cabrera, Cowgill, and Sugiyama 1990; López Austin, López Luján, and Sugiyama 1991). There were also power struggles between the heads of the government; these are evident in the dismantlement and covering of the Temple of the Feathered Serpent, the iconographical change from serpents to jaguars in the Street of the Dead Compound (Morelos García 1993:104), and also in the Mythological Animals Mural (Miller 1973:71-72; Cabrera Castro 1987). Millon (1993:31) adds that there is evidence of two military wards at Teotihuacan: one centered in Atetelco, in the southwestern part of the city, and the other—Techinantitla—in the northeastern section.

Nevertheless, recently there is an excesive statement of war and sacrifice for Teotihuacan (Carlson 1991), evidencing a lack of diachronic analysis as well as concrete archaeological contextual data to support these ideas.

Sacred Capital

Teotihuacan was planned to be harmonious with the natural scenery. The main pyramids echo the profiles of the main mountains to the north, south and west. The procession avenue redimensions the importance of the Moon Pyramid with respect to Cerro Gordo, probably a sacred mountain.

The four sectors of the city in the horizontal dimension, the presence of an underworld particularly related to Tlaloc, a terrestrial and a celestial domains in the vertical one, as well as the astronomical orientation following the heliacan setting of the Pleyades in the summer solstice, suggest that Teotihuacan was planned as a reproduction of the cosmos (Manzanilla 1994).

Since the discovery of the tunnel of the Pyramid of the Sun, the importance of caves and tunnels has been considered, particularly relating underground spaces with the world of the dead, the Tlalocan, and the womb of the earth (Heyden 1981; Manzanilla *et al.* 1989; Manzanilla 1994, 1994b)(Figures 7, 8, and 9).

In recent *nahuat* myths registered by Knab (1991) in the Northern Sierra of Puebla, the geography of the underworld or *Talokan* is described. It is interesting to observe that the four entrances to the underworld have names related to toponyms in the Teotihuacan Valley and surroundings (Manzanilla *et al.* 1989):

–In the myth, the southern entrance is called *Atotonican* and is a place of warmth; it is a hot spring that produces vapor and clouds, in the back of

Figure 7. *Varillas* tunnel, behind the Pyramid of the Sun (Manzanilla 1994).

a cave. In the Teotihuacan Valley, it is well known that a vast area of springs is situated to the southwest.

–The eastern access of the mythic underworld is called *Apan*, a large lake in the underworld that joins the sea. And actually the lacustrine basin of Apan is located to the east of the Teotihuacan Valley.

–The mythic western entrance is located at a place called *Tonalan*, a mountain where the sun stops on its voyage. The western entrance to the underworld is on top of the mountain that captures the sun, only allowing it to pass after midnight. We have visited Mount Tonalan in the northwestern boundary of the Teotihuacan Valley; it is a small mountain located between Cerro Gordo and Cerro Malinalco.

–The northern entrance to the underworld, *Mictalli* or *Miquitalan*, is represented by a "cave of the winds" and the access to the world of the dead. Tobriner (1972) refered to a gorge on the northeastern slope of Cerro Gordo with a cave that emitted a sound of water. A map dating to 1580 represents this gorge on the southeastern portion of the hill. Tobriner also suggested that the Street of the Dead in Teotihuacan was built pointing towards Cerro Gordo because of the association of this mountain with the God of Water. It should be noted that the geographic distribution of these four elements in Teotihuacan follow the pattern northeast, northwest,

Figure 8. Child burials in the *Pirul* tunnel, behind the Pyramid of the Sun (Manzanilla 1994; Manzanilla, López, and Freter, in press).

southwest and east, possibly aligned with the Teotihuacan axis of 15.5° azimuth.

It is probable that the myth of the *Nahuat*-speakers in the Sierra de Puebla is derived from a version based on the sacred geography of the Teotihuacan Valley, but it is equally probable that both have their source in an archetypical Mesoamerican conception of the underworld. Our recent research in the tunnels behind the Pyramid of the Sun supports the existence of a *Tlalocan*—perhaps the first in Prehispanic history—in Teotihuacan (Manzanilla 1994; Manzanilla, López, and Freter, in press).

Teotihuacan could have also been the place where sacred time—the ritual calendar—was created, as was recently proposed for the Temple of the Feathered Serpent (López Austin, López Luján, and Sugiyama 1991). Millon (1993:23) also suggests that the tunnel under the Pyramid of the Sun "...came to be seen as the focus of a creation myth in which it was portrayed as the place where the present era began, where humankind came into being, and where the present cycle of time was born".

Teotihuacan society was integrated mainly through religion. The conception of the four courses of sacred space permeated also the domestic domain of Teotihuacan (Manzanilla 1993; Manzanilla, in press a). Religion was represented in three levels: state cult, district or barrio gods, and lineage deities.

Figure 9. Dog skeletons buried near the child burials in Figure 8, as guides of the dead in the underworld (Manzanilla 1994).

Teotihuacan was thus the archetype of the Mesoamerican civilized city, the most sacred realm, and probably the mythic *Tollan* where crafts flourished. It inaugurated a new era in the settlement pattern of the region, an era that has not ended.

A DIACHRONIC VIEW

We consider that in Teotihuacan history there were two epochs. The first belongs to the Patlachique-Tzacualli phases, with sparse settlement in the so-called 'Old City', the northwestern sector of the valley. This sector is characterized by a vast tongue of pyroclastic materials where different tunnels were excavated by the Teotihuacanos to extract the porous volcanic materials for their constructions (Manzanilla 1994).

Three-temple plazas were the main architectural groups of this first settlement and may be also the congregational centers of ward groups. The Pyramids of the Sun and the Moon also belong to three-temple plazas. These groups could be related to the system of tunnels that may have crossed the northern part of the city (Manzanilla 1994; Manzanilla *et al.* 1989; Manzanilla, López, and Freter, in press).

The settlement density of this epoch was light, and not continuous. The San Juan alluvial plain was devoted to cultivation, and all the constructions were placed in the northern half of the valley.

Millon (1993:25) believes that this first epoch was an era of strong rulers that demonstrated their power by building huge constructions such as the main pyramids, the Ciudadela, and the "Street of the Dead". As Millon (1993:24) states, "ideology would have played a critical integrative role, supporting the state in maintaining order in a city now swollen with thousands of ethnically diverse newcomers...".

The Moon Pyramid, probably dedicated to a Great Goddess—perhaps related to flowing water and springs—would have been the culmination of the Street of the Dead, and would have been framed by the sacred mountain, the Cerro Gordo (Millon 1993:24). The Pyramid of the Sun, according to Millon, would have been devoted to the Great Goddess and to the Storm God. Nevertheless, for us the Pyramid of the Sun would have been dedicated to Tonacatecuhtli, an advocation of Tlaloc, as god of sustenance and fertility (Manzanilla 1994).

The construction of the Temple of the Feathered Serpent would have been, in Millon's view (1993:25), an enterprise related to "an ambitious new ruler with a passion for immortality...", and would have been related to the planet Venus and a cult of sacred war and sacrifice, that has been called the "star war". This view—recently a mode common between art historians—lacks concrete archaeological contextual evidence.

In our view, during the second epoch, beginning in 250 AD, the city acquires an orthogonal configuration. From the Tlamimilolpa phase onwards, elements of urban planning are clear in the new city. The multifamily apartment compounds represent the new domestic architectural unit.

Millon (1993:26-27) has proposed that there was a period of reaction and political reform, which transformed rulership into collective leadership, and intensified religiosity. Expansion continued to other parts of Mesoamerica.

The city grows and invades the alluvial plain. Excesive rural-urban migration, deforestation of nearby mountains to obtain wood for construction and fuel for domestic use and lime burning, soil erosion, over-exploitation of acquifers, problems with food poduction, a deficiency of the system to harmonize ethnic and social groups of so diverse interests, etc. could have been present at the end of this second epoch.

The core of the city is burned and looted. Incursions of nomadic groups, agricultural collapse, powerful marginal groups, and the blocking of supply routes have all been cited as factors involved in the city's collapse.

Millon (1988) also mentiones that the causes of Teotihuacan's end were bad administration, inflexibility with respect to change, the existence of an inefficient bureaucracy, and the deterioration of exchange routes.

If a long drought was present during the sixth or seventh centuries AD (García 1974), it struck when urban vulnerability was at its height (Manzanilla, in press b).

ACKNOWLEDGMENTS

I thank the following people for their participation in particular studies in the domestic archaeology project: Luis Barba and Agustín Ortiz for the geophysical and geochemical prospection, as well as for the chemical studies; Raúl Valadez for the paleofaunal analysis; Neusa Hidalgo, Javier González, and Emily McClung for the paleobotanical data; Beatriz Ludlow and Emilio Ibarra for the pollen information; Judith Zurita for the phytolith analysis; Magalí Civera and Mario Millones for the osteological analyses; Cynthia Hernández for the lithic analyses; Miguel Angel Jiménez for the ceramic distributional maps; Edith Ortiz for the domestic ideology research, and the Graphic Department of the Institute of Anthropological Research of the National Autonomous University of Mexico for their invaluable help. This interdisciplinary research was funded by the Institute of Anthropological Research of the National Autonomous University of Mexico (UNAM).

I would also like to thank doctors Zoltán de Cserna and Gerardo Sánchez Rubio of the Institute of Geology; José Lugo Hubp of the Institute of Geography; Jaime Urrutia and Dante Morán of the Institute of Geophysics, National Autonomous University of Mexico, for their advice and suggestions at different stages of research on tunnels and caves at Teotihuacan. We also thank the students of the Engineering Faculty of the University and the ones of the National School of Anthropology and History for their participation. The text was translated to English by Dr. Emily McClung de Tapia. This research was funded by the Institute of Anthropological Research and by Grant DGAPA-UNAM IN214694 of the National Autonomous University of Mexico (UNAM); by Grants n. P218CC00892832, H9106-0060, and 400358-5-5412-S of the National Council of Science and Technology of Mexico (CONACYT), and by Grant FAMSI n. 95007 of the Foundation for the Advancement of Mesoamerican Studies, Inc., and it was undertaken with permission of the Archaeological Council of the National Institute of Anthropology and History (INAH). The geophysical work was also partially supported by an internal grant IGF-02-9102.

REFERENCES

Arzate, J. A., L. Flores, R. E. Chávez, L. Barba, and L. Manzanilla, 1990, Magnetic Prospecting for Tunnels and Caves in Teotihuacan, México, in: *Geotechnical and Environmental Geophysics, Volume III: Geotechnical* (S. H. Ward, ed.), Investigations in Geophysics 5, Society for Exploration Geophysicists, pp. 155-162.

Aveni, A. F., H. Hartung, and B. Buckingham, 1978, The Pecked Cross Symbol in Ancient Mesoamerica, *Science* 202, 4365:267-279.

Barba, L., B. Ludlow, L. Manzanilla, and R. Valadez, 1987, La vida doméstica en Teotihuacan. Un estudio interdisciplinario, *Ciencia y desarrollo* 77, año XIII, noviembre-diciembre:21-23.

Barba, L. A., L. Manzanilla, R. Chávez, L. Flores, and A. J. Arzate, 1990, Chapter 24. Caves and Tunnels at Teotihuacan, México; A Geological Phenomenon of Archaeological Interest, in: *Centennial Special, 4, Archaeological Geology of North America* (N. P. Lasca and J. Donahue, eds.), Geological Society of America, Boulder, pp. 431-438.

Cabrera, R., 1987, La secuencia arquitectónica del Edificio de los Animales Mitológicos en Teotihuacan, in: *Homenaje a Román Piña Chan* (B. Dahlgren, C. Navarrete, L. Ochoa, M. C. Serra, and Y. Sugiura, eds.), Universidad Nacional Autónoma de México, México, pp. 349-371.

Cabrera, R., G. L. Cowgill, and S. Sugiyama, 1990, El Proyecto Templo de Quetzalcóatl y la práctica a gran escala del sacrificio humano, in: *La Epoca Clásica: Nuevos Hallazgos, Nuevas Ideas* (A. Cardós de Méndez, coord.), Instituto Nacional de Antropología e Historia, México, pp. 123-146.

Freidel, D. A., 1981, 15. The Political Economics of Residential Dispertion among the Lowland Maya, in: *Lowland Maya Settlement Patterns* (W. Ashmore, ed.), School of American Research Advanced Seminar Series, University of New Mexico Press, Albuquerque, pp. 371-382.

García Cook, A., 1981, 8. The Historical Importance of Tlaxcala in the Cultural Development of the Central Highlands, in: *Supplement to the Handbook of Middle American Indians, Archaeology* I (J. A. Sabloff, ed.), University of Texas Press, Austin, pp. 244-276.

García, E., 1974, Situaciones climáticas durante el auge y la caída de la cultura teotihuacana, *Boletín del Instituto de Geografía* 5, Universidad Nacional Autónoma de México:35-69.

Heyden, D., 1975, An Interpretation of the Cave Underneath the Pyramid of the Sun in Teotihuacan, Mexico, *American Antiquity* 40, 2:131-147.

Heyden, D., 1981, Caves, Gods, and Myths: World Views and Planning in Teotihuacan, in: *Mesoamerican Sites and World Views* (E. P. Benson, ed.), Dumbarton Oaks Research Library and Collection, Washington, pp. 1-39.

Kirchhoff, P., 1985, El imperio tolteca y su caída, *Mesoamérica y el centro de México* (J. Monjarás-Ruiz, R. Brambila, and E. Pérez Rocha, eds.), Colección Biblioteca del INAH, Serie Antropología, Instituto Nacional de Antropología e Historia, México, pp. 249-272.

Knab, T. J., 1991, Geografía del inframundo, *Estudios de Cultura Náhuatl* 21:31-57.

Krotser, P., and E. Rattray, 1980, Manufactura y distribución de tres grupos cerámicos de Teotihuacan, *Anales de Antropología* 17, Universidad Nacional Autónoma de México:91-104.

Linné, S., 1934, *Archaeological Researches at Teotihuacan, Mexico*, Ethnographical Museum of Sweden, Stockholm.

Linné, S., 1942, *Mexican Highland Cultures. Archaeological Researches at Teotihuacan, Calpulalpan and Chalchicomula in 1934-35*, New Series, Publication 7, The Ethnographical Museum of Sweden, Stockholm.

López Austin, A., 1989, 1. La historia de Teotihuacan, in: *Teotihuacan*, El Equilibrista, Citicorp/Citibank, México, pp. 13-35.
López Austin, A., L. López Luján, and S. Sugiyama, 1991, The Temple of Quetzalcoatl at Teotihuacan. Its Possible Ideological Significance, *Ancient Mesoamerica* 2, 1:93-105.
Manzanilla, L., 1985, El sitio de Cuanalan en el marco de las comunidades pre-urbanas del Valle de Teotihuacan, in: *Mesoamérica y el Centro de México* (J. Monjarás-Ruiz, E. Pérez Rocha, and R. Brambila, eds.), Colección Biblioteca del INAH, Instituto Nacional de Antropología e Historia, México, pp. 133-178.
Manzanilla, L., 1988-89, The Study of Room Function in a Residential Compound at Teotihuacan, Mexico, *Origini* XIV, *Giornate in onore di Salvatore Maria Puglisi*, Roma:175-186.
Manzanilla, L., 1992, The Economic Organization of the Teotihuacan Priesthood, in: *Art, Ideology, and the City of Teotihuacan* (J. C. Berlo, ed.), Dumbarton Oaks Research Library and Collection, Washington, pp. 321-338.
Manzanilla, L. (ed.), 1993, *Anatomía de un conjunto residencial teotihuacano en Oztoyahualco*, Instituto de Investigaciones Antropológicas, Universidad Nacional Autónoma de México, México, 2 v.
Manzanilla, L., 1994, Geografía sagrada e inframundo en Teotihuacan, *Antropológicas* 11, julio, Universidad Nacional Autónoma de México:53-65.
Manzanilla, L., 1994b, Las cuevas en el mundo mesoamericano, *Ciencias* 36, octubre-diciembre, Universidad Nacional Autónoma de México:59-66.
Manzanilla, L., in press a, Corporate Groups and Domestic Activities at Teotihuacan, *Latin American Antiquity* September, 1996.
Manzanilla, L., in press b, The Impact of Climatic Change on Past Civilizations. A Revisionist Agenda for Further Investigation, *Quaternary International*.
Manzanilla, L., and L. López Luján (eds.), 1989, *Atlas histórico de Mesoamérica*, Serie Referencias, Ediciones Larousse, México.
Manzanilla, L., L. Barba, R. Chávez, J. Arzate, and L. Flores, 1989, El inframundo de Teotihuacan. Geofísica y Arqueología, *Ciencia y desarrollo* XV, 85, CONACYT, México:21-35.
Manzanilla, L., and L. Barba, 1990, The Study of Activities in Classic Households. Two Case Studies from Coba and Teotihuacan, *Ancient Mesoamerica* 1, 1:41-49.
Manzanilla, L., and A. Ortiz, 1991, Los altares domésticos en Teotihuacán. Hallazgo de dos fragmentos de maqueta, *Cuadernos de Arquitectura Mesoamericana* 13, octubre, Universidad Nacional Autónoma de México:11-13.
Manzanilla, L., and E. Carreón, 1991, A Teotihuacan Censer in a Residential Context. An Interpretation, *Ancient Mesoamerica* 2, 2:299-307.
Manzanilla, L., and L. López Luján (eds.), 1994, *Historia antigua de México*, INAH-UNAM-Miguel Angel Porrúa Editor, México, 3 v.
Manzanilla, L., L. Barba, R. Chávez, A. Tejero, G. Cifuentes, and N. Peralta, 1994, Caves and Geophysics: an Approximation to the Underworld of Teotihuacan, Mexico, *Archaeometry* 36, 1, Oxford University Press:141-157.
Manzanilla, L., C. López, and A. Freter, Dating Results from Excavations in Quarry Tunnels behind the Pyramid of the Sun at Teotihuacan, *Ancient Mesoamerica*, Cambridge University Press, Fall, 1996.
Marcus, J., 1983, Ten. On the Nature of the Mesoamerican City, in: *Prehistoric Settlement Patterns. Essays in Honor of Gordon R. Willey* (E. Z. Vogt and R. M. Leventhal, eds.), University of New Mexico Press and Peabody Museum of Archaeology and Ethnology, Cambridge, pp. 195-242.
Marcus, J., 1992, Political Fluctuations in Mesoamerica, *National Geographic Research and Exploration* 8, 4:392-411.

McClung de Tapia, E., 1979, *Plants and Subsistence in the Teotihuacan Valley A.D. 100-750*, PhD Dissertation, University Microfilms, Ann Arbor.

McClung de Tapia, E., 1980, Interpretación de restos botánicos procedentes de sitios arqueológicos, *Anales de Antropología* XVII, Universidad Nacional Autónoma de México:149-165.

Miller, A. G., 1973, *The Mural Painting of Teotihuacan*, Dumbarton Oaks, Washington, D. C.

Millon, R., 1968, Urbanization at Teotihuacan: The Teotihuacan Mapping Project, in: *Actas y Memorias del XXXVII Congreso Internacional de Americanistas* 1, Departamento de Publicaciones Científicas, Buenos Aires, pp. 105-120.

Millon, R., 1973, *Urbanization at Teotihuacan. The Teotihuacan Map*. Part One: Text, The Dan Danciger Publication Series, University of Texas Press, Austin.

Millon, R., 1988, V. The Last Years of Teotihuacan Dominance, in: *The Collapse of Ancient States and Civilizations* (N. Yoffee and G. L. Cowgill, eds.), The University of Arizona Press, Tucson, pp. 102-164.

Millon, R., 1993, The Place Where Time Began. An Archaeologist's Interpretation of What Happened in Teotihuacan History, in: *Teotihuacan. Art from the City of the Gods* (K. Berrin and E. Pasztory, eds.), Thames and Hudson, The Fine Arts Museums of San Francisco, San Francisco, pp. 16-43.

Monzón, M., 1989, *Casas prehispánicas en Teotihuacan*, Instituto Mexiquense de Cultura, Toluca, México.

Morelos García N., 1993, *Proceso de producción de espacios y estructuras en Teotihuacán*, Colección Científica 274, Instituto Nacional de Antropología e Historia, México.

Múnera, C., 1985, *Un taller de cerámica ritual en la Ciudadela*, tesis de licenciatura en Arqueología, Escuela Nacional de Antropología e Historia, México.

Pasztory, E., 1976, *The Murals of Tepantitla*, A Garland Series: Outstanding Dissertations in the Fine Arts, Garland Publishing Inc., New York.

Pasztory, E., 1992, Abstraction and the Rise of a Utopian State at Teotihuacan, in: *Art, Ideology, and the City of Teotihuacan* (J. C. Berlo, ed.), Dumbarton Oaks Research Library and Collection, Washington D.C., pp. 281-320.

Paulinyi, Z., 1981, Capitals in Pre-Aztec Central Mexico, *Acta Orientalia Academiae Scientiarum Hung*. XXXV, 2-3:315-350.

Paulinyi, Z., 1995, El pájaro del Dios Mariposa de Teotihuacan: análisis iconográfico a partir de una vasija de Tiquisate, Guatemala, *Boletín del Museo Chileno de Arte Precolombino* 6:71-110.

Rattray, E. C., 1987, Los barrios foráneos de Teotihuacan, in: *Teotihuacan. Nuevos datos, nuevas síntesis y nuevos problemas* (E. McClung de Tapia and E. Childs Rattray, eds.), Universidad Nacional Autónoma de México, México, pp. 243-273.

Rattray, E. C., 1988, Nuevas interpretaciones en torno al Barrio de los Comerciantes, *Anales de Antropología* 25:165-182.

Rattray, E. C., 1993, *The Oaxaca Barrio at Teotihuacan*, Monografías Mesoamericanas 1, Instituto de Estudios Avanzados, Universidad de las Américas-Puebla, Cholula.

Sánchez Alaniz, J. I., 1989, *Las unidades habitacionales en Teotihuacan: el caso de Bidasoa*, Tesis de licenciatura en Arqueología, Escuela Nacional de Antropología e Historia, México.

Sanders, W. T., 1966, Life in a Classic Village, in: *Teotihuacan, Onceava Mesa Redonda*, Sociedad Mexicana de Antropología, México, pp. 123-147.

Sanders, W. T. (ed.), 1994, *The Teotihuacan Valley Project. Final Report: Volume 3, The Teotihuacan Occupation of the Valley. Part 1. The Excavations*, Occasional Papers in Anthropology 19, Matson Museum of Anthropology, The Pennsylvania State University, University Park.

Sanders, W. T. (ed.), 1995, *The Teotihuacan Valley Project. Final Report: Volume 3, The Teotihuacan Occupation of the Valley. Part 2. Artifact Analyses*, Occasional Papers in Anthropology 20, Matson Museum of Anthropology, The Pennsylvania State University, University Park.

Sanders, W. T., J. R. Parsons, and R. S. Santley, 1979, *The Basin of Mexico. Ecological Processes in the Evolution of a Civilization*, Academic Press, New York.

Séjourné, L., 1966, *Arquitectura y pintura en Teotihuacán*, Siglo XXI, México.

Serrano, C., and Z. Lagunas, 1974, Sistema de enterramiento y notas sobre el material osteológico de La Ventilla, Teotihuacan, México, *Anales del Instituto Nacional de Antropología e Historia* 7a, Instituto Nacional de Antropología e Historia: 105-144.

Spence, M., 1966, Los talleres de obsidiana de Teotihuacan, in: *XI Mesa Redonda: El Valle de Teotihuacan y su entorno*, Sociedad Mexicana de Antropología, México, pp. 213-218.

Spence, M., 1987, The Scale and Structure of Obsidian Production in Teotihuacan, in: *Teotihuacan. Nuevos datos, nuevas síntesis, nuevos problemas* (E. McClung de Tapia and E. Childs Rattray, eds.), Universidad Nacional Autónoma de México, México, pp. 429-450.

Starbuck, D., 1975, *Man-Animal Relationships in Pre-Columbian Central Mexico*, PhD Dissertation, Department of Anthropology, Yale University.

Storey, R., 1992, *Life and Death in the Ancient City of Teotihuacan. A Modern Paleodemographic Synthesis*, The University of Alabama Press, Tuscaloosa.

Storey, R., and R. J. Widmer, 1989, Household and Community Structure of a Teotihuacan Apartment Compound: S3W1:33 of the Tlajinga Barrio, in: *Households and Communities* (S. MacEachern, D. J. W. Archer, and R. D. Garvin, eds.), Chacmool, The Archaeological Association of the University of Calgary, Calgary, pp. 407-415.

Tichy, F., 1983, El patrón de asentamiento con sistema radial en la meseta central de México: ¿'sistemas ceque' en Mesoamérica?, *Jahrbuch für Geschichte von Staat, Wirtschaft und Gesellschaft Lateinamerikas* 20., Böhlau Verlag, Köln Wien:61-84.

Tobriner, S., 1972, The Fertile Mountain: an Investigation of Cerro Gordo's Importance to the Town Plan and Iconography of Teotihuacan, in: *Teotihuacan. XI Mesa Redonda*, Sociedad Mexicana de Antropología, México, pp. 103-115.

Uruñuela y Ladrón de Guevara, G., and P. Plunket Nagoda, 1995, Proyecto Tetimpa. Informe técnico al Consejo de Arqueología. Primera temporada (noviembre 1993-julio 1994), Archivo Técnico del Instituto Nacional de Antropología e Historia, Universidad de las Américas-Puebla, México.

Valadez, R., and L. Manzanilla, 1988, Restos faunísticos y áreas de actividad en una unidad habitacional de la antigua ciudad de Teotihuacan, *Revista Mexicana de Estudios Antropológicos* XXXIV, 1:147-168.

Widmer, R. J., 1991, Lapidary Craft Specialization at Teotihuacan: Implications for Community Structure at 33:S3W1 and Economic Organization in the City, *Ancient Mesoamerica* 2, 1:131-147.

Chapter 6

Ideology, Power, and State Formation in the Valley of Oaxaca

ARTHUR A. JOYCE

INTRODUCTION

Archaeological research in the Valley of Oaxaca has shown that the Late/Terminal Formative period (500 B.C.-A.D. 200) was a time of dramatic social change, perhaps culminating in the formation of the first state polity in the Americas (Blanton 1978; Blanton et al. 1982; Flannery and Marcus 1983a; Kowalewski et al. 1989; Winter 1989). This period began about 500 B.C. with the founding of the political center of Monte Albán located on a previously unoccupied ridgetop, 300-400 m above the valley floor where the three arms of the Valley of Oaxaca intersect (Figure 1). The size, architectural complexity, and political importance of the site increased rapidly through the Late/Terminal Formative (Acosta 1965:814-824; Blanton 1978:33-56; Flannery 1983a). While there has been debate on the precise timing of the emergence of a state polity at Monte Albán (e.g., Flannery and Marcus 1983a; Sanders and Nichols 1988), there can be no doubt that the Late/Terminal Formative was a tumultuous period marked by the emergence of many of the features that have traditionally been used to define the

---

ARTHUR A. JOYCE • Department of Anthropology, Vanderbilt University, Box 6050-Station B, Nashville, Tennessee, 37235 U.S.A.

Emergence and Change in Early Urban Societies, edited by Linda Manzanilla. Plenum Press, New York, 1997.

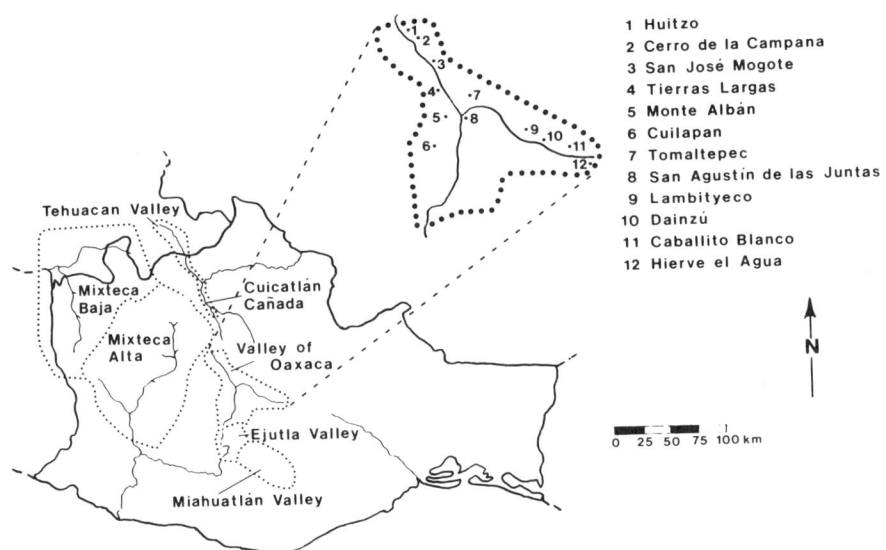

Figure 1. Oaxaca state showing regions and sites mentioned in the text.

state (Blanton 1978:33-56; Blanton et al. 1982:37-84; Flannery and Marcus 1983a; Kowalewski et al. 1989:85-200; Spencer 1982:12-31).

While there have been some disagreements concerning the social developments of the Late/Terminal Formative in the Valley of Oaxaca, the most heated debate has centered on theoretical explanations for these events (Blanton 1980, 1990; Sanders and Nichols 1988; Santley 1980). Explanations for the social developments of this period, including the formation of the state, have been advanced by researchers using both cultural ecology (Sanders and Nichols 1988) and ecological systems theory (Spencer 1982; Wright 1977). As useful as cultural ecology and systems theory have been for modeling social evolution, they have been criticized on a variety of theoretical and empirical grounds by biologists, ecologists, and anthropologists (Athens 1977; Brumfiel 1992; Colinvaux 1973; Slobodkin 1972; Vayda and McCay 1975; Williams 1966). In this article, Late/Terminal Formative period social change in the Valley of Oaxaca is addressed using an actor-based theoretical perspective that avoids many of the problems inherent in systems theory and cultural ecology. This actor-based approach views people as dynamic actors in social process rather than components in a system or passive responders to the environment. Social developments during the Late/Terminal Formative are considered from this perspective and an explanatory model for these developments is presented.

THEORETICAL BACKGROUND

Explanations for the origins and development of the Monte Albán polity have been derived primarily from cultural ecology (Sanders and Nichols 1988) and ecological systems theory (Spencer 1982; Wright 1977). Despite theoretical differences between these two schools (e.g., Sanders and Nichols 1988), both approaches share a materialist perspective which assumes that human social groups (variously modeled as societies, cultures, or populations) are the units that drive social developments such as urbanization and state formation (Dunnell 1980; Orlove 1980). Cultural ecology and ecological systems theory differ in the degree to which they stress environmental versus social and ideological factors as determinants of sociocultural change (Orlove 1980), and this has been the source of much of the debate amongst proponents of these two approaches (Sanders and Nichols 1988). Both approaches, however, make an "organismic analogy" where the society, culture, or ecological community is likened to a functioning organism. Social evolution occurs when the response of the cultural or ecological system to socio-environmental stress reaches a threshold and the system shifts to a new organizational level characterized by a greater regulatory capacity. The different organizational levels are often equated with traditional neoevolutionist categories of political organization such as bands, tribes, chiefdoms, and states.

The most damaging critiques of cultural ecology and systems theory involve their teleological and systems-stability assumptions. The assumption that systems exist at the level of populations, cultures, or ecosystems requires both a demonstration that the boundaries of the system actually exist, and a theory to account for the creation of teleological processes at that level. However, critics have shown that regulatory functions and systemic goals are assumed rather than demonstrated and boundaries of systems are usually drawn arbitrarily rather than empirically (McCay 1978; Orlove 1980; Peoples 1982; Richerson 1977; Vayda 1986; Vayda and McCay 1975). The position that a population, culture, or ecosystem acts as a functioning unit also requires a theory of group selection to account for its evolution (Richerson 1977:3). Evolutionary biologists, however, have rejected theories of group selection on both theoretical and empirical grounds (Alexander and Borgia 1978; Grafen 1984; Lack 1966; Lewontin 1970; Williams 1966). In addition, a focus on population-level systems ignores the goal-driven behavior of social-actors as well as intrasocietal (gender, class, ethnic, racial) conflict among those actors (Brumfiel 1992; Friedman and Rowlands 1978; Mithen 1989; Orlove 1980; Vayda and McCay 1975).

In ecological anthropology, critiques of cultural ecology and systems theory have led to a series of new approaches that focus on individual actions and decision making (e.g., Orlove 1980; Vayda 1986; Winterhalder and Smith 1981). These processual actor-based approaches include applications of economics of flexibility (McCay 1978, 1981), economic decision making (Laughlin 1974, Rutz 1977), and optimal foraging theory (Keegan 1986; McCay 1981; Winterhalder and Smith 1981). Intrasocietal conflicts of interest, especially involving class distinctions, are also gaining attention (Bloch 1975; Brumfiel 1983; Conrad and Demarest 1984; Friedman and Rowlands 1978; Godelier 1978; Kolata 1992; Patterson and Gailey 1987). Archaeologists have participated in the critique of systems theory (Brumfiel 1992; Dunnell 1980; Joyce 1991:598-603; Mithen 1989; Rindos 1984; Wenke 1981) and are beginning to consider actor-based approaches (Brumfiel 1992; Jochim 1976; Joyce 1994a; Joyce and Winter 1993; Keene 1981; Schortman 1989; Schortman and Urban 1987).

An Actor-Based Approach to Social Change

This section outlines an actor-based approach to social change that can be applied to the archaeological record. This approach argues that individuals rather than social or ecological systems are the agents that cause changes in the properties of social groups. I follow other actor-based approaches in anthropology by examining individual-level behavioral strategies in the context of opportunities and constraints posed by the biophysical and sociocultural environment (see McCay 1978, 1981; Orlove 1980; Vayda 1986; Winterhalder and Smith 1981). It is assumed that people pursue particular behavioral strategies to acquire and utilize resources, including information, for themselves and their close kin in competition with other people (Joyce 1991:603-616, 1994a; Joyce and Winter 1993). I stress, however, that behavioral strategies are defined culturally and that the actors should not be modeled as optimally adapted. Instead, it is crucial to gain an understanding of the cultural environment and how it may have defined goals differently from those of the economic optimum. Population-level phenomena such as social organization and subsistence patterns are, therefore, viewed as the outcome of the behavioral stategies of individuals developed in the context of their biophysical and sociocultural environments. By tracking changes in behavioral strategies through time, hypotheses can be evaluated concerning the environmental conditions that fostered these changes. As people adopt novel behavioral strategies, these strategies, as well as their material and ideological correlates, in turn become part of the sociocultural environment.

Adaptive strategies and their relative success in terms of controlling, acquiring, storing, and using resources are operationalized here using the concept of social identity (Joyce 1991, 1994a; Joyce and Winter 1993; cf. McGuire 1983; Schortman 1989). Social identities consist of two types of parameters: social roles which describe individual-level strategies and social statuses that describe the relative success of those strategies (Joyce 1991:269-281, 602-707; cf. Blau 1977; McGuire 1983; Rapoport 1976:19; Schortman 1989:54). Social roles specify behavioral strategies used by people to control, acquire, store, and utilize both material resources and information. Social roles include behaviors defined by factors such as gender, occupation, kinship, ethnicity, community affiliation, and religion. Social status is a measure of an individual's ability to control material resources and information relative to other members of society. Social roles and statuses can covary, as when an occupation or lineage defines status, or they can be independent of one another (McGuire 1983).

Social status reflects two usually related factors: power and wealth. Power is the ability to control resources, including other people and information, and is often a means to obtain wealth. Wealth is a measure of the amount of resources that a person has accumulated relative to other individuals. Differences in wealth and power exist in all types of societies ranging from small-scale kinship-based ones to large nation-states. Status differences may be continuous within a society or there can be distinct breaks in status creating clearly defined social classes. While power and wealth usually covary, they can also be decoupled as when religious practitioners are restricted from using their power for the accumulation of personal wealth. For the purposes of this article, however, power and wealth are assumed to covary with status.

Social identities can be reconstructed because their effects are archaeologically visible, especially the effects of identities adopted by many people (e.g., low-status farmers) or those used by a few people who had a great impact on society (e.g., rulers). While archaeological data do not allow the delineation of all social identities of the past, they do permit access to the more visible, institutionalized, and widely shared ones such as occupations, ethnic affiliations, and status (Schortman 1989).

Variation in social identities also provides a means for defining social complexity through estimates of heterogeneity and inequality (Blau 1977; McGuire 1983). Societies become more complex with increases in heterogeneity and inequality, which measure variability in the social identities of group members. Heterogeneity is a measure of the frequency of distinct social roles and status levels in a society. Generally, heterogeneity increases with the number and degree of independence of social roles and statuses. The development of craft and other types of economic specializations as well as the differentiation of administrative roles among political elites are examples of increases in heterogeneity. Inequality is a measure of status differentiation within society.

Heterogeneity and inequality also provide a means to define the state. Using essentially the same criteria as Spencer (1982:2; 1990) and Wright (1977:385), the state is defined as a polity with variation in the administrative roles of political elites (i.e., specialized decision-making or government) as well as great inequalities in statuses implying social stratification and political centralization. In addition, as discussed by Flannery (1972:404), the power of political elites is usually manifest in their ability to draft soldiers, levy taxes, and exact tribute. Taxes and tribute are used in part to construct and/or maintain public buildings, works, and services, including the institutions and personnel of a state religion. The next section examines the power relations that support status inequalities in complex societies since, as will be argued later in the article, the consolidation of power by elites was a key factor in the social developments of the Late/Terminal Formative.

Ideology, Power, and Inequality

The unequal social relations that largely define complex societies such as states must be understood in terms of the flow of resources among individuals channelled by power differentials. In non-industrial societies such as those of prehispanic Mesoamerica, wealth accumulation above a relatively low level must be the result of the labor of other people. Inequalities in these societies largely involve the ability to create, legitimate, and institutionalize a positive net flow of resources from other people. Relationships of power within societies are created, legitimated, and institutionalized by the material benefits they provide to the less powerful and/or by ideologies that make the relationships seem beneficial and unalterable. Power is generally derived through three overlapping types of social interactions: reciprocity, coercion, and ideology.

Power through reciprocity occurs when lower-status individuals (non-elites) provide material resources to high-status individuals (elites) in return for benefits in the form of information. This information often involves some type of administrative input that allow individuals to more efficiently coordinate their actions and/or more accurately predict future environmental contingencies (e.g., scientific knowledge). In a reciprocal relationship, the information input provided by elites results in real material benefits for non-elites. Elites gain disproportionately in material resources due to the extra share they take in return for their administrative efforts. However, non-elites also gain relative to their likely condition in the absence of elite administration. Conditions that encourage power through reciprocity include: (1) economic and political specializations that promote centralized management; (2) high risk from natural hazards promoting centralized storage as insurance; (3) risk from human hazards (e.g., military threats, crime) promoting the centralized coordination of force; and (4) technologies that require heavy investments of capital and/or labor thereby promoting centralized pooling of these resources (e.g., large-scale irrigation facilities).

Coercive power involves the use of threats to compel people to cooperate and provide resources. The threat can include potential physical harm as in a police state or it can involve the withholding of critical resources. Physical threats require some type of legitimate coercive apparatus such as a police or military force under elite control.

Ideological power depends on the concealment of elite interests through ideology. Ideology is defined here in its more restricted sense (Giddens 1979:165-197; Larrain 1983), as ideas that represent and mask the interests of factions within society. Ideology conceals interests by representing those interests as universal, by denying intrasocietal conflicts of interest, and by naturalizing the present to preserve the dominant position of the elite (Giddens 1979:193-197). Elements of ideology that legitimate inequality can include religious (Conrad and Demarest 1984; Demarest 1989; Spores 1983a), political (Cohen 1981; Johnson 1986, 1987), and economic ideas (Weber 1986), although these categories usually overlap. It is difficult to separate a dominant ideology that masks inequality from an overall ethos that explains many elements of existence for people at all status levels (Giddens 1979:184-196). Ideology is not only a means to legitimate relationships of power, but is also a dynamic factor in creating and maintaining those relationships. This process often involves the cooptation and transformation of pre-existing ideas and symbols. Ideologies often promote abstract symbols of authority such as deities, flags, and patriotism that cloud the relationship between elite interests and decision making (Cohen 1981; Edelman 1964; Mack 1983). The psychology of dominance/deference relations may also help to reinforce ideological power since humans seem to be prone to relinquishing power and autonomy to authority figures, especially during times of crisis (Becker 1973; Freud 1922; Milgram 1974; Volkan 1985). However, to the extent that people are able to penetrate a dominant ideology, elite power will fail unless supported by coercive or reciprocal forms of power.

In practice, the generation and maintenance of power may simultaneously involve aspects of coercion, reciprocity, and ideology. In addition, risk, uncertainty, and the unintended consequences of human actions often result in unforeseen outcomes (Cancian 1980; Hewitt 1983; Ortiz

1980; Vayda 1986). However, reciprocal, coercive, and ideological relationships of power should be measurable archaeologically to the degree that they become incorporated in aspects of social identities that are expressed materially and preserved in the archaeological record.

The following section examines social developments in the Valley of Oaxaca during the Late/Terminal Formative in terms of changes in social roles and statuses. This discussion provides a background for examining changes in power relations within the Valley of Oaxaca during this period.

LATE/TERMINAL FORMATIVE PERIOD SOCIAL CHANGE IN THE VALLEY OF OAXACA

While researchers have debated the precise time when a state polity arose in the Valley of Oaxaca (e.g., Blanton et al. 1982:69-71; Sanders and Nichols 1988; Spencer 1982), it is clear that social complexity increased significantly during the Late/Terminal Formative. Survey data suggest that shortly after its founding Monte Albán was the largest community in the Valley of Oaxaca (Blanton 1978; Blanton et al. 1982; Kowalewski et al. 1989). Monte Albán's political importance was reflected in its size, monumental architecture, high-status burials, and numerous carved stone monuments, including some of the earliest examples of hieroglyphic writing known for Mesoamerica (Marcus 1976, 1983a, 1992). Evidence for increasing interpolity conflict and indications that some regions were conquered by the Valley of Oaxaca, have led several researchers to argue that Monte Albán may have been the capital of a conquest empire (Marcus 1983a; Flannery 1983b; Redmond 1983; Spencer 1982).

This section examines the evidence for changes in social complexity in the Valley of Oaxaca during the initial development of the Monte Albán polity through the examination of inequality and heterogeneity. The period of interest includes Periods Ia (500-300 B.C.), Ic (300-100 B.C.), and II (100 B.C.-A.D. 200) in the Valley of Oaxaca ceramic chronology (Caso et al. 1967; Kowalewski et al. 1978).

Inequality

Archaeological data suggest that status inequalities during Periods I and II were considerably greater than previously and seem to have increased through this period (Joyce 1991:644-648; Joyce and Winter 1993). Wealth differences can be inferred from mortuary data through the analysis of variation in the quantity and quality of burial offerings, as well as the amount of energy expended in the preparation of the grave (Autry 1973;

Chapman et al. 1981; Peebles and Kus 1977; Rathje 1970). Variation in the spatial distribution of high-status markers such as prestige goods (e.g., imported ceramics, greenstone), high-status burials, caches, and expensive ceramics as well as elaborate residences and other architectural features also suggest wealth differences. Inequalities in power are inferred primarily from evidence suggesting that certain individuals exerted control over the resources and labor of others.

Mortuary data from the Valley of Oaxaca suggest significant differences in status by Periods I and II (Autry 1973; Drennan 1976a: Appendix XIV; Whalen 1981:102-103, 1988:300-302; Winter 1989:40). The majority of burials at this time were interred in simple graves that occasionally lacked offerings, but which usually included from one to three ceramic vessels and at times other items such as ground stone tools, obsidian blades, and shell artifacts. A smaller number of burials, which were the interments of high-status individuals, were usually in formal tombs with abundant offerings of items such as ceramic vessels, jade, shell, and obsidian. The ceramic vessels interred with high-status individuals were also usually more elaborate than those in lower-status burials.

Disparities between elite and non-elite burials in the Valley of Oaxaca were increasingly marked from Period I to II (Acosta 1965; Autry 1973; Caso et al. 1967; Kuttruff and Autry 1978; O'Brien et al. 1982; Winter 1974). Period II tombs were usually better made than those of Period I; the latter were often made of adobe rather than stone. There also appears to have been a general increase in the wealth of offerings in elite burials during the Late/Terminal Formative, while those in low-status interments did not change significantly. Presumably, the increasing inequality in the wealth of burial offerings is a reflection of status differences during people's lives.

The distribution of probable high-status markers also suggests rising wealth differences during the Late/Terminal Formative. Elaborate ceramics were increasingly restricted to elites as demonstrated by stronger correlations between the amount of such pottery and monumental architecture at sites from Period I to II (Feinman 1980:172, 1986:368-369; Kowalewski et al. 1989:181, 195). Kowalewski and his colleagues (1989:149) argue that the high proportion of "artifact poor" sites in piedmont and rural areas, especially during Period Ic, suggest material poverty in these regions. The subsequent abandonment of piedmont settlements during Period II, due at least in part to erosion and soil depletion (Joyce and Mueller 1992; Mueller and Joyce 1993), was undoubtedly a further hardship to these communities.

While data on the size and complexity of Period I and II residences in the Valley of Oaxaca are not abundant, the available evidence also suggests status differences (Whalen 1981; Winter 1972, 1974, 1986). Late/Terminal

Formative houses excavated at the sites of Monte Albán, Tomaltepec, and Tierras Largas usually consisted of small rectangular stone foundations not exceeding 7.5 m x 4.0 m with earthen floors. The size and complexity of these non-elite households as well as the composition of associated artifacts and features were similar to patterns noted during the Middle Formative and appear to have remained relatively constant during Periods I and II. In contrast, elite residences including *Plataforma* 1 and *Plataforma* E at Huitzo, Household unit 1c-1 at Tomaltepec, and a house excavated at San Agustín de las Juntas were built on low platforms and had foundation walls that measured approximately 20 m on a side with plaster floors. By Period II, the first true "palace" in the Valley of Oaxaca may be represented by Structure 17 on Mound 8 at San José Mogote with dimensions exceeding 30 m on a side, a façade made of limestone blocks each weighing approximately one ton, plaster floors, and at least one sunken patio (Flannery and Marcus 1983b:113). In addition, during the Late/Terminal Formative high-status residences were increasingly set-off with public buildings in elite-administrative precincts. By Period Ic, elite-administrative precincts with monumental architecture occur even at lower-order sites such as Tomaltepec (Whalen 1981, 1988; Winter 1984:194). The monumentality of public buildings also rose dramatically during this period (Acosta 1965:814-824; Flannery 1983a; Flannery and Marcus 1976a:213-221, 1983c; Winter and Joyce 1994).

A more crucial indication of rising status inequalitites in the Valley of Oaxaca involves evidence for differences in power. The rising wealth of the elite during the Late/Terminal Formative demonstrate that they had the power to mobilize greater quantities of material resources such as pottery and obsidian. However, a more crucial resource that elites increasingly gained control over was human labor provided by commoners to support elites and their institutions.

The increasing power of elites to control labor in the Valley of Oaxaca must be understood in the context of demographic changes accompanying the early development of Monte Albán. By the end of Period Ia, Monte Albán was the largest site in the valley with an estimated one-third of the region's population (Kowalewski et al. 1989:107). The ability of the founders of Monte Albán to attract large numbers of followers to the previously unoccupied ridgetop demonstrates that elites already had considerable power. However, the location of Monte Albán on a barren ridgetop also suggests that elites had sufficient power to mobilize labor in surrounding areas to provision the occupants of the urban center (Feinman and Nicholas 1990:102-104). The thin soils and rocky slopes of Monte Albán would not have produced sufficient food to support the resident population (Nicholas 1989). People living at Monte Albán could have traveled down the hillside and farmed several productive areas on the valley floor beneath the site. However, living at Monte Albán and farming the surrounding land would have been energetically more costly than remaining on the valley floor, and probably would not have solved the provisioning problem (Nicholas 1989). If the people living at Monte Albán were unable to produce sufficient food to support themselves, then they would have had to be provisioned through tribute provided by other settlements in the Valley of Oaxaca.

The problem worsened during Period Ic as estimates suggest a tripling in population in the valley, with 75% of the increase occurring in a core area within 20 km of Monte Albán (Kowalewski et al. 1989:123-126). Much of the increase in population in the core region can be attributed to expansion into the piedmont, rather than onto the valley floor. Several lines of evidence have led Blanton and his colleagues (Blanton et al. 1982:69-70; Feinman et al. 1985:345-349; Kowalewski et al. 1989:123-126) to argue that Monte Albán was provisioned by settlements in the core, especially the new piedmont sites. The evidence for the provisioning of Monte Albán through this "piedmont strategy" includes: (1) a large population living on the infertile slopes of Monte Albán (estimated at 10,200 to 20,400 for Period Ic; Blanton 1978:44); (2) settlement over much of the agricultural land surrounding the site that limited the land that could have been farmed by people from Monte Albán; (3) a large amount of monumental architecture requiring considerable non-farming labor input at the site; and (4) the development of small-scale irrigation facilities in the piedmont, thereby increasing agricultural production. The provisioning of Monte Albán and the population expansion into the piedmont may have required a shift from mono-cropping to double-cropping (Blanton et al. 1981:71; Feinman et al. 1984:173).

Agricultural expansion into the piedmont during Period Ic would have been a high-risk strategy, given both large yearly fluctuations in productivity and the greater susceptibility of the topsoil to erosion (Feinman et al. 1985:346; Kirkby 1973; Kowalewski et al. 1989). By Period II, settlement pattern data suggest that the piedmont strategy had collapsed, probably as a result of erosion and soil depletion (Joyce and Mueller 1992; Mueller and Joyce 1993; Kowalewski et al. 1989). The core area, especially the piedmont sites surrounding Monte Albán, experienced a marked drop in population, while site locations shifted away from Monte Albán and into the three arms of the valley (Blanton et al. 1982; Kowalewski et al. 1989).

In summary, the demographic data from Monte Albán suggest that the urban center was provisioned by agricultural intensification requiring greater expenditures of labor by non-elites. Monte Albán was probably provisioned primarily by people in the core region during Period I. How-

Figure 2. The Main Plaza at Monte Albán looking north from the South Platform.

ever, with the collapse of the unstable piedmont strategy during Period II, Monte Albán must have been supplied by communities elsewhere in the valley. These data suggest that by Period II the rulers of Monte Albán had established connections with elites elsewhere in the valley that allowed for the provisioning of the site. The linkage of elites is further suggested by the similarity in the form of public buildings (Flannery and Marcus 1976a; Spencer 1982:24-28) and ritual paraphernalia (e.g., urns) in the valley during Period II.

In addition to the increased agricultural output of non-elites, the massive amount of monumental architecture built at Monte Albán and smaller centers would have required large amounts of corvée labor (Acosta 1965:814-824; Blanton 1978; Flannery 1983a; Flannery and Marcus 1976a, 1983c; Kowalewski et al. 1989; Winter 1989). The North Platform area went through a major period of construction during Periods I and II (Blanton 1978:46; Caso et al. 1967:90-106; Winter and Joyce 1994). The Main Plaza at Monte Albán (Figure 2) was laid out and plastered during Period II, and would have required a tremendous labor expenditure involving both the levelling of rock outcrops and the filling of deep depressions (Acosta 1965:818). Early versions of many of the structures on the Main Plaza were begun during Period II, including Buildings G, H, I, J, and the ballcourt as well as continuing construction activities at Buildings K and M. The adoratory east of Building H and the tunnel running east from Building I were apparently built at this time. Other sites with evidence for the construction of multiple monumental structures during Period II include San José Mogote (Flannery and Marcus 1983b), Dainzú (Bernal and Oliveros 1988), Cerro de la Campana (Kowalewski et al. 1989:182-198), and Cuilapan (Flannery and Marcus 1983d; Kowalewski et al. 1989:182-198).

In addition to their increasing inputs of tribute and labor to the elite, most non-elites also appear to have experienced a loss of economic, religious, and political autonomy. Some types of craft production were removed from local control during the Late/Terminal Formative as certain communities began to specialize in the production of pottery, chipped stone tools, salt, and lime (Feinman 1986; Feinman et al. 1984; Hewitt et al. 1987; Kowalewski et al. 1989; Parry 1987; Whalen 1988:301-304). Access to public buildings and ritual paraphernalia was also increasingly restricted to the elite (Flannery and Marcus 1976b, 1983a:82). By the end of Period II, non-elites in most settlements in the Valley of Oaxaca would have been dependent on specialists for the production of certain ceramic and lithic artifacts as well as the performance of important public rituals. The loss of autonomy by non-elites was in part related to a rising heterogeneity of social roles which included the emergence of both craft and religious specialists.

Heterogeneity

In addition to increasing inequality, rising social complexity in the Valley of Oaxaca during the Late/Terminal Formative is indicated by evidence for greater heterogeneity. This section examines the evidence for changes in heterogeneity during the Late/Terminal Formative.

The heterogeneity of non-elite social roles rose during Periods I and II in the Valley of Oaxaca with the first appearance of craft and possibly military specialists. The earliest evidence for community specialization in ceramic production dates to Period Ia (Feinman 1980, 1986; Feinman et al. 1984; Whalen 1988:301-304; Winter 1984). Ceramic production at these sites was large-scale and may reflect full-time craft specialization by at least some members of the community. Evidence of large-scale salt production has been found at the sites of Lambityeco, 30 kilometers east of Monte Albán, and Hierve el Agua, 60 kilometers east of Monte Albán (Hewitt et al. 1987; Parry 1987; Winter 1984:199; however see Neely et al. 1990). Specialized quarrying and production of worked chert and onyx, lime, and certain foods may also have occurred during the Late/Terminal Formative in the Valley of Oaxaca (Winter 1984:198-200). The evidence for widespread conflict, including the possible conquest of the Cuicatlán Cañada region, suggests that there may also have been military specialist roles among non-elites (Spencer 1982:243-246).

While Periods I and II were marked by the development of craft and possibly military specialists, the social roles of most people in the Valley of Oaxaca would have continued to be focused on agricultural production. The social changes of the Late/Terminal Formative, however, would have affected economic strategies within households. As discussed above, non-elite social roles, especially in the core region, would have involved an increased input of labor for agricultural production (double-cropping and small-scale irrigation) as well as corvée labor for the construction of monumental structures at Monte Albán. One response to these changes in social roles may have been the development of the *tortilla* as suggested by the first appearance of *comales* (ceramic griddles). *Tortillas* provided an easily transportable and durable food source suggesting a significant change in the economics of non-elite households (Blanton et al. 1981:71-72; Kowalewski et al. 1989:108; Winter 1984:213). *Tortillas* could have been transported to Monte Albán as tribute and laborers would have been able to bring their own food when working at the capital.

Craft specialization, and perhaps the development of markets, may have resulted from the increased labor demands on non-elites. Some individuals or communities may have begun to specialize in certain crafts, such as ceramics and stone tools, taking advantage of the fact that most people would have had less time to carry out the full array of productive tasks that they had previously undertaken (Feinman 1986; Feinman et al. 1984; Kowalewski et al. 1989:149-151). People would have developed markets to provide a central location to obtain products manufactured by specialists. Increased labor demands may also explain the rapid growth in population during Period I, especially in the core region. Thus, population growth may have been a result of the changes in social relations during Period I, rather than a cause of those changes as argued by cultural ecologists (Sanders and Nichols 1988:51).

Elite social roles also appear to have changed during the Late/Terminal Formative with elites increasingly monopolizing the role of religious specialists for their subjects. Data from Periods I and II suggest a significant change in access to public buildings and ritual paraphernalia. During the Early and Middle Formative public buildings were generally integrated into the community and ritual paraphernalia was distributed throughout all levels of the status hierarchy (Drennan 1983a; Flannery 1976; Flannery and Marcus 1976a). By the Late/Terminal Formative, however, there is evidence for a stronger association of elite residences and public buildings in elite-administrative precincts separated from non-elite residential areas (Flannery and Marcus 1983c; Whalen 1981:104, 1988; Winter 1974).

Ethnohistoric data indicate that the public buildings in elite-administrative precincts (e.g., two-room temples and ballcourts) had religious functions (Flannery 1983c:132). Symbols and artifacts used in ritual contexts, including hieroglyphic writing, calendrics, urns, and incense burners, are found almost exclusively in elite-administrative precincts of the largest sites in the valley (Feinman 1986:365; Marcus 1976; Winter 1989:48-61). Elites or craftspeople attached to elite households also probably specialized in the construction of monumental architecture and carved stones as well as certain prestige items like ceramic urns.

Ethnohistoric data indicate that prestige goods sought by elites played important roles in religious practices (King 1988; Marcus 1983b; Monaghan 1994; Nicholson 1971; Schele and Miller 1986; Spores 1984; Whitecotton 1977). For example, obsidian blades were closely associated with prehispanic ritual bloodletting. Shell and greenstone ornaments and exotic foods were also involved with ritual practices.

Architectural evidence suggests that politico-religious roles may have varied among elites. By the Terminal Formative, public buildings in the Valley of Oaxaca exhibited considerable formal and, presumably, functional differentiation (Flannery and Marcus 1976a; Spencer 1982:24-28). Three distinct types of public buildings have been recognized for Period II in the Valley of Oaxaca (Flannery and Marcus 1976a:217-219): (1) rectangular two-room temples such as at Mound X at Monte Albán and Building 13 at San José Mogote; (2) arrowhead-shaped buildings including Building J at Monte Albán and Mound O at Caballito Blanco; (3) ballcourts such as in the Main Plaza at Monte Albán and in Mound 7 at San José Mogote. This architectural variation in public buildings may reflect differences in the politico-religious decision-making roles of elites which would be consistent with the emergence of a state polity in the Valley of Oaxaca during Period II (Spencer 1982:24-28).

Overall, the data from Periods I and II suggest a significant increase in social complexity as measured by heterogeneity and inequality. Craft, religious, and possibly military specialization as well as a powerful and wealthy elite class were created and institutionalized in Valley of Oaxaca society during this period. Politico-religious authority appears to have been increasingly vested in a small number of elites. The most powerful of these elites undoubtedly resided at Monte Albán where they exercised political authority over the core region and beyond. While it may not be possible to demonstrate heterogeneity in the roles of political decision-makers and thereby determine precisely the time of state emergence, the data indicate that the *process* of state formation was well on its way during this period. In the next section, this process is examined in more detail and an explanatory model for Late/Terminal Formative period social development is offered based on the actor-based theoretical perspective outlined above.

THE CONSOLIDATION OF POWER AT MONTE ALBÁN

The data from the Valley of Oaxaca suggest that the bahavioral strategies of elites during the Late/Terminal Formative generated increasing wealth and power. The outcome of elite strategies is consistent with the assumption that people compete to acquire resources. It is not obvious, however, why so many non-elites would have moved their homes to ecologically risky areas in and around Monte Albán and provided food and labor to the elite. I argue that a key theoretical problem raised by the early development of Monte Albán is to explain this trend in behavioral strategies of non-elites towards living in denser communities and supporting an emerging elite class, both of which were often detrimental to the former. Non-elites must have been compelled to support the social changes of the Late/Terminal Formative through reciprocity, coercion, and/or ideology. In this section, each of these factors will be assessed as a potential cause of the rising differentials in wealth and power in the Valley of Oaxaca.

Reciprocal Power

Ecological systems theory and cultural ecology often argue that elites consolidate power through the reciprocal benefits they provide by coordinating economic, military, and political matters, especially under conditions of stress (Flannery 1972; Johnson and Earle 1987; Peebles and Kus 1977:426-427; Sanders and Nichols 1988; Wright 1977). For example, when stress occurs due to factors such as population-resource imbalances and economic uncertainty, elites can act to pool and redistribute resources or redirect and intensify agricultural production. There is no evidence, however, for conditions of economic stress during the Middle Formative Rosario phase that might have provided an opportunity for the elite to manage agricultural production, storage, or distribution. Archaeologists generally agree that population in the Valley of Oaxaca was well below carrying capacity during the Rosario phase and Period Ia, and many areas of productive land remained only sparsely settled (Blanton et al. 1982:70; Feinman et al. 1985:340-348; Kowalewski 1980; Nicholas 1989:491-494; Nicholas et al. 1986:151-154; Sanders and Nichols 1988). Rather than ameliorating economic risk, the founding of Monte Albán seems to have caused increasing economic uncertainty and possibly localized population-resource imbalances due to the piedmont strategy and the need to provision the hilltop center.

The management of both irrigation and market systems has also been proposed as a source of reciprocal power for elites (Sanders 1968; Sanders and Nichols 1988; Steward 1955; Wittfogel 1957). Irrigation in the Valley of Oaxaca, however, was never more than small-scale and there is no evidence that the management of irrigation systems by elites had a significant unifying effect (O'Brien et al. 1982; Flannery 1983d). Craft specialization and markets did not cause, but rather appear to have resulted from Late/Terminal Formative social change. Craft specialization and markets probably resulted from increasing demands on rural producers during Period I (Feinman et al. 1984; Kowalewski et al. 1989), rather than the direct promotion of these new economic relationships by the elite. While lower-level elites may have influenced local production and market relations, Kowalewski and his colleagues (1983, 1989:199) conclude that the most powerful elites at Monte Albán apparently had little direct control over these matters.

Once Monte Albán was established, the most likely economic problem requiring administrative input would have been the provisioning of the site's occupants (Blanton et al. 1982; Feinman et al. 1985; Kowalewski 1980; Nicholas 1989; Nicholas et al. 1986). The dense settlement in the core region during Period Ic would have further limited the land available to farmers living at Monte Albán. Population expansion and agricultural intensification in the piedmont would have increased the economic interdependence of these communities because of the year-to-year uncertainty of piedmont farming (Nicholas 1989). The elite at Monte Albán could have served a reciprocal role by administering the provisioning of the hilltop center as well as managing risk and social conflict in the piedmont communities. This hypothesis is supported by a distributional analysis of elite/administrative centers that suggests Monte Albán elites directly administered most of the core region during Period Ic (Kowalewski et al. 1989:138). The promotion of economic interdependence by the elite would have been a logical strategy in the consolidation of power in the Valley of Oaxaca, but it does not explain why non-elites would have acquiesced to these materially unfavorable economic relationships.

Coercive Power

Coercion seems to be unlikely as the primary source of elite power during the Late/Terminal Formative. Several researchers have argued that the rulers of Monte Albán initiated a series of extraregional conquests in order to provision themselves and their subjects through tribute extraction following the collapse of the piedmont strategy (Kowalewski et al. 1989:198-200; Spencer 1982:210-211). The cost of conquering and administering hinterland regions, however, coupled with the inefficiency of interregional transport of subsistence goods (Drennan 1984), would have made the provisioning of Monte Albán through interregional conquest highly risky, if not impossible (Feinman and Nicholas 1990:232; Joyce 1991:590-592). If the elite of Monte Albán had the political authority to raise an imperial army to subjugate hinterland regions, it seems more likely that they could have coerced people within the valley to provide tribute (Sanders and Nichols 1988:73).

It appears that Monte Albán must have been provisioned primarily through tribute payments from people within the valley. It is unlikely, however, that coercion through military force could have been the primary means through which people were initially compelled to migrate to Monte Albán, or the core region, and pay tribute in the form of crops and labor. This would have required a large, well-organized military force which probably would have been beyond the capacity of Rosario phase or Period Ia polities in the Valley of Oaxaca. In addition, there is no evidence for a forced resettlement of people or for widespread conflict before the formation of Monte Albán. Coercion through military force, however, may have been an instrument for neutralizing competing elites within the valley.

Ritual and Ideological Power

Instead of reciprocal or coercive power, I argue that elite power during the Late/Terminal Formative resulted from ideological changes, probably initiated by elites, that resulted in their emerging role as ritual specialists. The ritual role of elites gave them a greater ability to influence the workings of the natural and supernatural world and to intercede on the behalf of non-elites (Conrad and Demarest 1984; Demarest 1992; Freidel and Schele 1988; Grove and Gillespie 1992a; King 1988; Masson et al. 1992; Monaghan 1990, 1994; Orr 1993; Schele and Freidel 1990; Spores 1983a). Elites served as mediators with the forces that controlled the cosmos, acting on behalf of their followers through the practice of certain rituals such as bloodletting, human sacrifice, divination, and shamanistic transformation. Political power and wealth resulted from religious practices, since non-elites provided productive resources, such as foodstuffs and labor, to the elite often in ritualized contexts which supported the elite and their special abilities to affect the cosmos. Since these affairs were tied intimately to production, health, and well-being, the intervention of elites counterbalanced the loss of resources by non-elites. This created a situation of material obligation and deference on the part of non-elites towards elites.

Power through religious ideology has deep roots in Mesoamerican culture and predates the founding of Monte Albán (Drennan 1976b; 1983a; Flannery and Marcus 1983e:64; Grove and Gillespie 1992a, 1992b). Grove and Gillespie (1992a) argue that high-status was legitimated by the ritual role of elites as far back as the Early Formative (1500-800 B.C.), especially in the Gulf coast lowlands. Religious ritual may be fundamental to power relations in chiefdoms since elite power appears to be dependent on public demonstrations of sanctity and sacred knowledge, especially the ritual redistribution of prestige goods (Earle 1991; Feinman 1991; Helms 1979, 1988; Steponaitis 1991; Sahlins 1958; Service 1975:291-296). Prestige goods signify sanctity and status, and often are seen as containing an "inherent" sacred value (Helms 1979). Chiefs obtain prestige goods through the efforts of a retinue of craft specialists and/or obtain them by long distance exchange with other elites. In part, the ritual power of non-local prestige goods is often seen as the result of their having originated from a distant sacred place (Helms 1987). If chiefs are unable to provide sufficient quantities of prestige goods, then their sanctity is suspect and their deceptive power is compromised, making them vulnerable to uprisings by lower-status chiefs (see Earle 1978:171-184; Goldman 1970; Helms 1979:24-37). In this sense, prestige goods can be considered the currency of power in chiefly societies.

Archaeolgocial and ethnohistorical data from Oaxaca are consistent with the existence of religious ideologies similar to that discussed above for chiefdoms. Intersite and intrasite comparisons of the distribution of exotics for the Middle/Late Formative in the Valley of Oaxaca (Blanton et al. 1982:57; Drennan 1976a:133; Pires-Ferreira 1975:35; Winter 1984:201; Whalen 1981:74, 85-87) and in other nearby regions (Feinman and Nicholas 1993; Joyce 1991:272-281; Redmond 1983:73-81; Spencer 1982:167-174; Spores 1974; Winter 1984:206-207; Zeitlin 1993) are consistent with the mutual exchange and preferential control of prestige goods by elites. An ideology involving the ritualistic control of nature is suggested in ethnohistoric data from Oaxaca (Marcus 1983b; Monaghan 1994; Paso y Troncoso 1982:217-218; Spores 1983a, 1983b, 1984) as well as other regions of Mesoamerica (Durán 1964:112; Conrad and Demarest 1984). Elites extracted tribute from commoners at least in part to sponsor religious ceremonies and support practitioners (Monaghan 1994; Spores 1984:74-75). Using ethnohistorical data, Monaghan (1994) has shown in detail how prehispanic Mixtec elites used religion and especially ritual sacrifice to extract resources from the citizenry in exchange for insuring the fertility of the natural world.

The existence of an ideology involving redistribution of prestige goods as well as the ritualistic control of natural and supernatural forces would explain the actions of non-elites in the Valley of Oaxaca at the beginning of Period I. The establishment of a politico-religious center at Monte Albán would have drawn followers interested in maintaining good relations with natural and supernatural powers through their participation in the ritually important network of redistribution (see Helms 1979; Millon 1974; Sanders and Webster 1988). Since the elite controlled the acquisition of prestige goods and represented the apex of the redistributive/ritual network, their movement to Monte Albán would have provided a strong inducement for non-elites to relocate.

The early years of Monte Albán, however, involved more than simply the migration of elites and their followers. The increasingly restricted association of ritual paraphernalia with indications of high-status during Periods I and II suggests that the elite manipulated the pre-existing ideology so that primarily only they administered religious affairs (see Flannery and Marcus 1976b:383). Elites acted as ritual specialists, and would have directed the most important public ceremonies, although non-elites continued to perform private, household rituals much as they do today throughout Mesoamerica. It appears that rather than participating, albeit as inferiors, in a ritual redistributive network, by Period II the role of non-elites in public ceremonies was primarily to provide tribute to the elite to assure that natural and supernatural forces were appeased. Prestige goods like greenstone artifacts, obsidian eccentrics, urns, and elaborate shell ornaments continued to be exchanged in ritualized contexts among the elite. Yet as symbols of the separateness of royalty, exotics may have been less available to commoners than previously. The increasing control of ritual knowledge and authority by the elite would have given them greater power to convince people to relocate and provide tribute in the form of agricultural surpluses and corvée labor.

The ideological transformation of the Late/Terminal Formative almost certainly involved the sanctification of elite social roles and/or the religious institutions that they controlled (see Drennan 1976b:348). Elites consolidated power by making their role as ritual specialists part of the sacred, unquestionable assumptions of the Zapotec ethos. The most sacred of institutions may have been the Monte Albán hilltop itself, which visually and perhaps symbolically dominated the valley. Throughout Mesoamerica hilltops were often seen as sacred places and several scholars have argued that prehispanic pyramids were representations of sacred hills (Schele and Freidel 1990). The Zapotec place glyph, seen earliest in the Period II "conquest-slabs" from Building J, is in the form of a hill. The founding of Monte Albán was probably a key event in the ideological transformations at the end of the Formative.

The sanctity of the elite was expressed by the development of highly standardized and elaborate forms of symbolic expression that represented a growing body of esoteric knowledge accessible only to the elite, thereby restricting non-elite ritual participation. The most elaborate symbolic expressions involved hieroglyphic and calendric inscriptions as well as an interest in marking astronomical phenomena. Late/Terminal Formative hieroglyphic inscriptions relating to the 365-day solar calendar occurred at Monte Albán and may have been linked to the pre-existing 260-day ritual calendar, producing the first example of the 52-year calendar round (Marcus 1976). The Late/Terminal Formative also marks the earliest appearance of pottery vessels with representations of Cocijo, the Zapotec god of lightning. Representations of Cocijo occur only on elaborate vessels, including urns, usually recovered from high-status burials, public buildings, or elite residences (Caso and Bernal 1952; Caso et al. 1967). Ethnohistoric sources show that Cocijo was perhaps the most powerful Zapotec supernatural, with control over natural forces such as clouds, wind, and rain (Marcus 1983b). Cocijo also figured prominently in the Zapotec calendar. Many lords took Cocijo as part of their name, and royalty, especially royal ancestors, were seen as having special relationships with this deity. Therefore, literacy, calendric and astronomical knowledge, as well as associations with Cocijo were symbols of an emerging elite identity separate from that of commoners. In addition, there were almost certainly elements of dress and speech that visibly set Zapotec elites apart from commoners.

Militarism and Ideological Power

In addition to the ritual responsibilities of elites, the coordination of defensive measures may have served as a source of power and an inducement for people to surrender autonomy and tribute. In the Valley of Oaxaca, evidence for militaristic and defensive considerations occur at Monte Albán beginning with the earliest phase of occupation (Joyce 1994b; Joyce and Winter 1993). The central position of Monte Albán within the valley and its elevation above the valley floor made it an excellent location for both political control and defense (Figure 3). Militaristic themes are depicted in carved stones from the Main Plaza at Monte Albán (Figure 4). During Period I more than 310 carved stones were erected in the Main Plaza that seem to represent themes of conflict (Scott 1978). These carved stones, known as the "danzantes," were arranged as an outside gallery set into Building L, a monumental public structure. The danzantes depict male figures in various contorted positions and often include brief hieroglyphic inscriptions. Considering general iconographic conventions in prehispanic

Figure 3. View of the Valley of Oaxaca looking north from Monte Albán's Main Plaza. The hills in the foreground are part of Monte Albán.

Mesoamerica, the most reasonable interpretations of the danzantes are that they depict slain or sacrificed individuals (Coe 1962; Marcus 1976, 1983a).

Evidence for militaristic concerns at Monte Albán continues, and perhaps intensifies, during the Terminal Formative. At the end of Period Ic or during Period II defensive considerations are attested by the construction of a wall around the north, northwest, and part of the western sides of Monte Albán proper (Blanton 1978:52-54). Construction of the Period II ballcourt in the Main Plaza at Monte Albán might also reflect military activities since the prehispanic ballgame seems to have acted as a boundary mechanism symbolically expressing and resolving both inter- and intrasocietal conflict (Gillespie 1991; Schele and Miller 1986). During Period II another set of over 50 carved stones depicting militaristic themes was erected in the Main Plaza. These carved stones, known as "conquest slabs," were inset in Building J on the Main Plaza and have been interpreted as depictions of places conquered by and/or paying tribute to Monte Albán (Caso 1947; Marcus 1976, 1983a; 1992:394-400).

The creation of over 360 carved stones depicting themes of conflict during the Late/Terminal Formative at Monte Albán is consistent with elites promoting the perception of external threats. The carved stones from the main plaza at Monte Albán represent the largest single corpus of carved stone monuments for Formative Mesoamerica and constitute approxi-

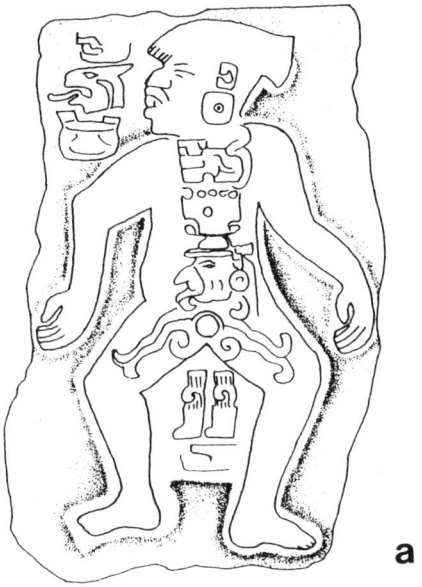

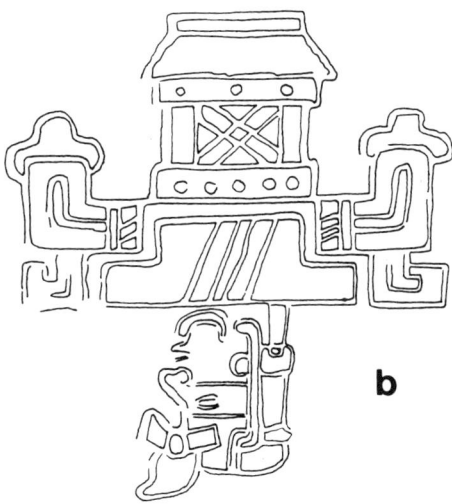

Figure 4. Late/Terminal Formative carved stones from the Main Plaza at Monte Albán: a = danzante D55 (redrawn from Scott 1978); b = glyph from the Building J conquest slab (Lápida 4; redrawn from Caso 1947).

mately 90% of the total monument record from Monte Albán (see Marcus 1974). Marcus states:

> This early effort probably coincides with the time when the rulers of Monte Albán would have felt the greatest need to legitimize their power and sanctify their position. Perhaps by creating a large gallery of prisoners, they were able to convince both their enemies and their own population of their power, although it was not yet institutionalized or completely effective (1974:90).

Thus, the danzantes and the conquest slabs would have carried with them a forceful message of the consequences of opposing the elite, either from within or without. The construction of defensive walls around Monte Albán would have gone beyond their most obvious utility (i.e., to keep enemies out), serving also as a form of propaganda promoting the external threat and enhancing messages of control and exclusivity of the precinct.

Conflict with polities outside the Valley of Oaxaca is supported by evidence for the conquest of the Cuicatlán Cañada region by Monte Albán (Redmond 1983; Spencer 1982). Other regions such as the Ejutla and Miahuatlán Valleys and mountainous areas near the Oaxaca Valley may have been integrated into the Monte Albán polity (Drennan 1983b; Feinman and Nicholas 1990:230-234; Winter 1989:63). In the Mixteca Alta and Baja regions as well as in the Tehuacán Valley there is evidence for an increase in interpolity conflict, although the identity of the combatants has not been determined (Joyce 1991:563-567, 593-594).

The promotion of external threats may have provided the rulers of Monte Albán with another source of ideological power. The presence of an external threat provides elites with power through the organization of military measures including the formation of an army and the construction of defensive works. External threats also tend to unify the populace and unite them around their rulers. To the degree that the threats are real and unprovoked the elite are acting in a reciprocal fashion with non-elites for collective defense. However, these conditions also make it advantageous for the elite to promote the perception of external threats through propaganda in order to extract resources from commoners. While the promotion of the threat often leads to actual conflict, the nature of elite power under these circumstances is ideological and potentially coercive. Several studies on state formation in Western Europe have focused on the promotion of perceived external threats as a means to power (Bean 1973; Lane 1966; Tilly 1975, 1985). Tilly states:

> To the extent that the threats against which a given government protects its citizens are imaginary or are consequences of its own activities, the government has organized a protection racket. Since governments themselves commonly simulate, stimulate, or even fabricate threats of external war and since the repressive and extractive activities of governments often

constitute the largest current threats to the livelihoods of their own citizens, many governments operate in essentially the same way as racketeers (1985:171).

Viewed in this way, the promotion of interpolity conflict in the Valley of Oaxaca would have been beneficial to the elite, regardless of the quantity of resources obtained from conquered or intimidated regions.

Ideology and Power at Monte Albán

The two main sources of elite power, religion and warfare, were part of a complex ideology. Archaeological and ethnohistoric data demonstrate that religion and warfare were interconnected throughout prehispanic Mesoamerica (Conrad and Demarest 1984; Freidel 1986; Schele 1984; Schele and Miller 1986; Sugiyama 1993). In Tilly's terminology, the linkage of militarism with religion provides the elite with two types of protection rackets. The promotion of interpolity conflict allowed elites to provide protection from external human threats. The control of ritual knowledge and authority allowed the elite to provide protection from natural and supernatural threats. A major link between religion and warfare with deep roots in prehispanic Mesoamerica was the ritual sacrifice of war captives (Boone 1984; Freidel 1986).

There is some evidence to suggest that religion and warfare might have been linked in a similar fashion during the Late/Terminal Formative in Oaxaca. If the danzantes represent sacrificed war captives then the sacrifices may have taken place among the monumental public buildings of the main plaza in ritual contexts (Marcus 1992:394; Masson et al. 1992). The danzantes also included some of the earliest hieroglyphic texts and calendric dates known for Mesoamerica, further suggesting considerable ritual significance (Flannery and Marcus 1983c; Marcus 1992). The appearance of ballcourts during Period II may also reflect the linkage between religion and warfare (Orr 1993). Ballcourts seem to have been involved in boundary maintenance with other competing polities and between elite and non-elite segments of society (Gillespie 1991; Kowalewski et al. 1991; Trinkaus 1987).

In summary, many of the social changes of the Late/Terminal Formative in the Valley of Oaxaca were the result of an elite strategy to consolidate power that was facilitated by ideological change (Joyce 1991; Joyce and Winter 1993). This ideological transformation involved the promotion of interpolity conflict and the increasing control of ritual knowledge and authority by the elite. Both of these factors could have convinced non-elites to provide greater amounts of resources in return for the apparent protective services of the elite. The promotion of external threats would have allowed elites to extract resources for the organization of military measures, including formation of an army and construction of defensive works. The control of ritual knowledge and authority would have allowed the elite to provide protection from perceived natural and supernatural threats. This ideology created and legitimated the power of the elite to exploit resources more successfully from non-elites, leading directly to rising status inequalities and, indirectly, to increasing heterogeneity, population growth, and interpolity conflict.

CONCLUSIONS

The changes in sociopolitical organization, religion, and warfare of the Late/Terminal Formative represent the beginnings of a pattern that reached its apogee with the Classic Period state in the Valley of Oaxaca (Flannery and Marcus 1983f; Joyce and Winter 1993; Kowalewski et al. 1989; Winter 1974, 1989). Evidence for many of the features that have been used to define the state first occur in the Valley of Oaxaca by Period II (see Flannery and Marcus 1983a; Redmond 1983; Spencer 1982). These features include: emergence of distinct social strata, political centralization, elite control of a centralized religion, elite control of production in the form of tribute extraction, elite sponsored warfare, and a four-tiered administrative hierarchy. It seems clear from discussions in the preceding pages that the Valley of Oaxaca was well on its way to state formation during this period.

This article views the emergence of an urban, state society in the Valley of Oaxaca as resulting from changes in behavioral strategies of social actors as well as the cultural and ecological conditions that affected them. While I have focused on the role of ideology in state formation, it does not mean that I see ecological and economic factors as unimportant. Obviously, large populations with complex social organization arose in regions like the Valley of Oaxaca because of productive ecological conditions. Economic factors like craft specialization, exchange, markets, and tribute extraction were also clearly crucial in state formation and development.

I argue, however, that the manipulation of ideology was a driving force behind the origins of the state because it created and legitimated unequal social and economic relations. The ideological changes of the Late/Terminal Formative allowed elites to extract resources, leading to rising inequalities, a key element in state formation. Elite strategies involved the manipulation of ideology so that they increasingly took on the role of ritual specialist, acting as mediators between commoners and the devine forces that were believed to control the cosmos. The special ritual role of the elite created and legitimated their political power and convinced commoners to provide materials and labor as tribute. Ideology compelled people to move to urban centers and into ecologically unstable piedmont areas, both of which had economic and ecological consequences. Elites also appear to have promoted conflict as a means of unifying people and extracting resources for military measures.

While elite strategies were successful in mobilizing resources, non-elites pursued their own strategies. Archaeologically visible changes in social roles of most non-elites involved practicing more intensive forms of agriculture and providing corvée labor to the elite. The benefit in terms of resource acquisition that the change in non-elite social roles ostensibly accomplished was to assure the "protective" services of their rulers. In the cultural milieu in which they were operating, non-elites were gaining both the ritual services of the elites as well as protection from human enemies. Of course, non-elites probably got few material resources in return for their investment since the elite had little empirical control over natural forces and may have been exaggerating the threat of interpolity conflict for their own ends. With many non-elites increasingly focused on intensive agriculture and corvée labor, an opportunity arose for some people to specialize in the production of certain craft goods. Specialization may also have allowed some commoners to avoid paying other kinds of tribute to nobles such as corvée labor. The emergence of these economic specialists increased the heterogeneity of non-elite social roles.

The ideological transformation of the Late/Terminal Formative was part of a changing world view into which commoners and elites alike were enculturated. These ideological changes grew out of an ethos with deep roots in prehispanic Mesoamerica. Evidence from the Early and Middle Formative suggest that elites were viewed as having had special ritual abilities (Grove and Gillespie 1992a), although they did not monopolize ritual authority to the extent that they would during later periods. From an archaeological perspective it is difficult to assess the degree to which the changing ideologies of the Late/Terminal Formative were radical breaks with the past for the actual actors. There is evidence for continuity in ideological themes such as sacrifice and the sacred value of exotic goods. Nevertheless, ideological change during the Late/Terminal Formative was a key factor in the rise of the Monte Albán state which would continue to flourish and develop until the end of the Classic period.

ACKNOWLEDGMENTS

I would like to thank Wendy Ashmore, Henri J. M. Claessen, Arthur Demarest, Annabeth Headrick, John Monaghan, Heather Orr, Damon

Peeler, and Marcus Winter for discussions concerning the ideas contained in this chapter. I also want to thank Linda Manzanilla for inviting me to participate in this volume. The article was written while the author was a Kalbfleisch Research Fellow at the American Museum of Natural History. An earlier version of the paper was presented at the 59th Annual Meeting of the Society for American Archaeology, Anaheim, California.

REFERENCES

Acosta, J. G., 1965, Preclassic and Classic architecture of Oaxaca, in: *Handbook of Middle American Indians, vol. 3: Archaeology of Southern Mesoamerica, part 2* (R. Wauchope and G. R. Willey, eds.), University of Texas Press, Austin, pp. 814-836.

Alexander, R. D. and G. Borgia, 1978, Group selection, altruism, and the levels of organization of life, *Annual Review of Ecology and Systematics* 9:449-474.

Athens, J. S., 1977, Theory building and the study of evolutionary process in complex society, in: *For Theory Building in Archaeology* (L. R. Binford, ed.), Academic Press, New York, pp. 353-384.

Autry, W. O., Jr., 1973, *Post Formative Burial Practices: Valley of Oaxaca, Mexico*. Unpublished honors thesis; University of North Carolina, Chapel Hill.

Bean, R., 1973, War and the birth of the nation state. *Journal of Economic History* 33:203-221.

Becker, E., 1973, *The Denial of Death*, The Free Press, New York.

Bernal, I. and A. Oliveros, 1988, *Exploraciones arqueológicas en Dainzú, Oaxaca*. Colección Científica 167 Instituto Nacional de Antropología e Historia, Mexico.

Blanton, R. E., 1978, *Monte Albán: Settlement Patterns at the Ancient Zapotec Capital*, Academic Press, New York.

Blanton, R. E., 1980, Cultural ecology reconsidered. *American Antiquity* 45,1:145-151.

Blanton, R. E., 1990, Theory and practice in Mesoamerican archaeology: A comparison of two modes of scientific inquiry, in: *Debating Oaxaca Archaeology* (J. Marcus, ed.), Museum of Anthropology, University of Michigan Anthropological Papers 84, Ann Arbor, pp. 1-16.

Blanton, R. E., S. A. Kowalewski, G. Feinman, and J. Appel, 1981, *Ancient Mesoamerica: A Comparison of Change in Three Regions*. Cambridge University Press, Cambridge.

Blanton, R. E., S. A. Kowalewski, G. Feinman, and J. Appel, 1982, *Monte Albán's Hinterland, part I: Prehispanic Settlement Patterns of the Central and Southern Parts of the Valley of Oaxaca, Mexico*. Prehistory and Human Ecology of the Valley of Oaxaca, vol. 7, Memoirs of the University of Michigan Museum of Anthropology 15, Ann Arbor.

Blau, P. M., 1977, *Inequality and Heterogeneity: A Primitive Theory of Social Structure*. The Free Press, New York.

Bloch, M. (editor), 1975, *Marxist Analysis and Social Anthropology*. Malaby Press, London.

Boone, E. (editor), 1984, *Ritual Human Sacrifice in Mesoamerica*. Dumbarton Oaks, Washington, D.C.

Brumfiel, E. M., 1983, Aztec state making: Ecology, structure, and the origin of the state. *American Anthtopologist* 85,2:261-284.

Brumfiel, E. M., 1992, Distinguished lecture in archaeology: Breaking and entering the ecosystem-gender, class, and faction steal the show. *American Anthropologist* 94,3:551-567.

Cancian, F., 1980, Risk and uncertainty in agricultural decision-making. In *Agricultural Decision Making* (P. F. Bartlett, ed.), Academic Press, New York, pp. 161-176.

Caso, A., 1947, Calendario y escritura de las antiguas culturas de Monte Albán. *Obras completas de Miguel Othón de Mendizábal*, 1,116-143, Mexico.
Caso, A. and I. Bernal, 1952, *Urnas de Oaxaca*. Memorias del Instituto Nacional de Antropología e Historia 2, Mexico.
Caso, A., I. Bernal, and J. R. Acosta, 1967, *La cerámica de Monte Albán*. Memorias del Instituto Nacional de Antropología e Historia 13, Mexico.
Chapman, R., I. Kinnes, and K. Randsborg, 1981, *The Archaeology of Death*. Cambridge University Press, Cambridge.
Coe, M. D., 1962, *Mexico*. Praeger, New York.
Cohen, A., 1981, *The Politics of Elite Culture*. University of California Press, Berkeley.
Colinvaux, P. A., 1973, *Introduction to Ecology*. Wiley, New York.
Conrad, G. W. and A. A. Demarest. 1984. *Religion and Empire: The Dynamics of Aztec and Inca Expansionism*. Cambridge University Press, Cambridge.
Demarest, A. A., 1989, Ideology and evolutionism in American Archaeology: Looking beyond the economic base, in: *Archaeological Thought in America* (C. C. Lamberg-Karlovsky, ed.), Cambridge University Press, New York, pp. 89-102.
Demarest, A. A., 1992, Ideology in ancient Maya cultural evolution: The dynamics of Galactic Polities, in: *Ideology and Pre-Columbian Civilizations* (A. A. Demarest and G. W. Conrad, eds.), Sante Fe, NM, pp. 135-158.
Drennan, R. D., 1976a, *Fábrica San José and Middle Formative Society in the Valley of Oaxaca*. Prehistory and Human Ecology of the Valley of Oaxaca, vol. 4, Memoirs of the University of Michigan Museum of Anthropology 8, Ann Arbor.
Drennan, R. D., 1976b, Religion and social evolution in Formative Mesoamerica, in: *The Early Mesoamerican Village* (K. V. Flannery, ed.), Academic Press, New York, pp.345-368.
Drennan, R. D., 1983a, Ritual and ceremonial development at the early village level, in: *The Cloud People: Divergent Evolution of the Zapotec and Mixtec Civilizations* (K. V. Flannery and J. Marcus, eds.), Academic Press, New York, pp. 46-50.
Drennan, R. D., 1983b, Monte Albán I and II settlement in the mountain survey zone between the valleys of Oaxaca and Nochitlán. In *The Cloud People: Divergent Evolution of the Zapotec and Mixtec Civilizations* (K. V. Flannery and J. Marcus, eds.), Academic Press, New York, pp. 110-111.
Drennan, R. D., 1984, Long-Distance movement of goods in the Mesoamerican Formative and Classic. *American Antiquity* 49,1:27-43.
Dunnell, R. C., 1980, Evolutionary theory and archaeology, in: *Advances in Archaeological Method and Theory* (Vol. III) (M. B. Schiffer, ed.), Academic Press, New York, pp. 35-99.
Durán, D., 1964, *The Aztecs: The History of the Indies of New Spain*. Translated by D. Heyden and F. Horcasitas. Orion Press, New York.
Earle, T., 1978, *Economic and Social Organization of a Complex Chiefdom: The Halelea District, Kaua'i Hawaii*. Museum of Anthropology, University of Michigan Anthropological Papers 64, Ann Arbor.
Earle, T., 1991, The evolution of chiefdoms, in: *Chiefdoms: Power, Economy, and Ideology* (T. Earle, ed.), Cambridge University Press, Cambridge.
Edelman, M., 1964, *The Symbolic Uses of Politics*. University of Illinois Press, Urbana.
Feinman, G. M., 1980, *The Relationship between Administrative Organizations and Ceramic Production in the Valley of Oaxaca, Mexico*. Ph.D. dissertation, Department of Anthropology, City University of New York, New York.
Feinman, G. M., 1986, The emergence of specialized ceramic production in Formative Oaxaca, in: *Economic Aspects of Prehispanic Highland Mexico* (B. Isaac, ed.), JAI Press, Greenwich, pp. 347-373.

Feinman, G., 1991, Demography, surplus, and inequality: Early political formations in highland Mesoamerica, in: *Chiefdoms: Power, Economy, and Ideology* (T. Earle, ed.), Cambridge University Press, Cambridge, pp. 229-262.

Feinman, G. M., R. E. Blanton, and S. A. Kowalewski, 1984, Market system development in the prehispanic Valley of Oaxaca, Mexico, in: *Trade and Exchange in Early Mesoamerica* (K. G. Hirth, ed.), University of New Mexico Press, Albuquerque:, pp. 157-178.

Feinman, G. M., S. A. Kowalewski, L. Finsten, R. E Blanton, and L. Nicholas, 1985, Long-term demographic change: A perspective from the Valley of Oaxaca. *Journal of Field Archaeology* 12:333-362.

Feinman, G. M. and L. M. Nicholas, 1990, At the margins of the Monte Albán state: Settlement patterns in the Ejutla Valley, Oaxaca, Mexico. *Latin American Antiquity* 1,3:216-246.

Feinman, G. M. and L. M. Nicholas, 1993, Shell-ornament production in Ejutla: Implications for highland-coastal interaction in Ancient Oaxaca. *Ancient Mesoamerica* 4:103-119.

Flannery. K. V., 1972, The cultural evolution of civilizations. *Annual Review of Ecology and Systematics* 3:399-426.

Flannery, K. V., 1976, Contextual analysis of ritual paraphernalia from Formative Oaxaca, in: *The Early Mesoamerican Village* (K. V. Flannery, ed.), Academic Press, New York, pp. 333-345.

Flannery, K. V., 1983a, The development of Monte Albán's Main Plaza in Period II, in: *The Cloud People: Divergent Evolution of the Zapotec and Mixtec Civilizations*. (K. V. Flannery and J. Marcus, eds.), Academic Press, New York, pp.102-104.

Flannery, K. V., 1983b, Monte Negro: A reinterpretation, in: *The Cloud People: Divergent Evolution of the Zapotec and Mixtec Civilizations* (K. V. Flannery and J. Marcus, eds.), Academic Press, New York, pp.99-102.

Flannery, K. V., 1983c, The legacy of the Early Urban period: An ethnohistoric approach to Monte Albán's temples, residences, and royal tombs, in: *The Cloud People: Divergent Evolution of the Zapotec and Mixtec Civilizations*. (K. V. Flannery and J. Marcus, eds.), Academic Press, New York, pp.99-102.

Flannery, K. V., 1983d, Precolumbian farming in the Valleys of Oaxaca, Nochixtlan, Tehuacan, and Cuicatlán: A Comparative Study, in: *The Cloud People: Divergent Evolution of the Zapotec and Mixtec Civilizations* (K. V. Flannery and J. Marcus, eds.), Academic Press, New York, pp.323-338.

Flannery, K. V. and J. Marcus, 1976a, Evolution of the public building in Formative Oaxaca, in: *Cultural Change and Continuity: Essays in Honor of James Bennett Griffin* (C. E. Cleland, ed.), Academic Press, New York, pp. 205-221.

Flannery, K. V. and J. Marcus, 1976b, Formative Oaxaca and the Zapotec cosmos. *American Scientist* 64:374-383.

Flannery, K. V., and J. Marcus, 1983a, Editors' introduction: The origins of the state in Oaxaca, in: *The Cloud People: Divergent Evolution of the Zapotec and Mixtec Civilizations* (K. V. Flannery and J. Marcus, eds.), Academic Press, New York, pp.79-83.

Flannery, K. V. and J. Marcus, 1983b, San José Mogote in Monte Albán II: A secondary administrative center, in: *The Cloud People: Divergent Evolution of the Zapotec and Mixtec Civilizations* (K. V. Flannery and J. Marcus, eds.), Academic Press, New York, pp. 111-113.

Flannery, K. V. and J. Marcus, 1983c, The earliest public buildings, tombs, and monuments of Monte Albán with notes on the internal chronology of Period I, in: *The Cloud People: Divergent Evolution of the Zapotec and Mixtec Civilizations* (K. V. Flannery and J. Marcus, eds.), Academic Press, New York, pp. 91-96.

Flannery, K. V. and J. Marcus, 1983d, Cuilapan, in: *The Cloud People: Divergent Evolution of the Zapotec and Mixtec Civilizations* (K. V. Flannery and J. Marcus, eds.), Academic Press, New York, pp. 204-206.

Flannery, K. V. and J. Marcus, 1983e, The growth of site hierarchies in the Valley of Oaxaca: Part I, in: *The Cloud People: Divergent Evolution of the Zapotec and Mixtec Civilizations* (K. V. Flannery and J. Marcus, eds.), Academic Press, New York, pp. 53-64.

Flannery, K. V. and J. Marcus (editors), 1983f, *The Cloud People: Divergent Evolution of the Zapotec and Mixtec Civilizations*. New York: Academic Press.

Freidel, D. A., 1986, Maya warfare: An example of peer-polity interaction, in: *Peer Polity Interaction and Socio-Political Change* (C. Renfrew and J. F. Cherry, eds.), Cambridge University Press, Cambridge, pp. 93-108.

Freidel, D. A. and L. Schele, 1988, Kingship in the Late Preclassic Maya Lowlands. *American Anthropologist* 90,3:547-567.

Freud, S. 1922. *Group Psychology and the Analysis of the Ego*. Norton, New York.

Friedman, J. and M. Rowlands, 1978, Notes towards an epigenetic model of the evolution of civilization, in: *The Evolution of Social Systems* (J. Friedman and M. Rowlands, eds.), University of Pittsburgh Press, Pittsburgh, pp. 201-278.

Giddens, A., 1979, *Central Problems in Social Theory*. University of California Press, Berkeley.

Gillespie, S. D., 1991, Ballgames and boundaries, in: *The Mesoamerican Ballgame* (V. L. Scarborough and D. R. Wilcox, eds.), The University of Arizona Press, Tucson, pp. 317-346.

Godelier, M., 1978, Infrastructures, societies, and history. *Current Anthropology* 19:763-771.

Goldman, I., 1970, *Ancient Polynesian Society*. University of Chicago Press, Chicago.

Grafen, A., 1984, Natural Selection, Kin Selection and Group Selection, in: *Behavioral Ecology: An Evolutionary Approach* (J. R. Krebs and N. B. Davies, eds.), Sinauer, Sunderland, pp. 62-84.

Grove, D. C. and S. D. Gillespie, 1992a, Ideology and evolution at the pre-state level: Formative Period Mesoamerica, in: *Ideology and precolumbian civilizations* (A. A. Demarest and G. W. Conrad, eds.), School of American Research Press, Sante Fe, NM, pp. 15-36.

Grove, D. C. and S. D. Gillespie, 1992b, Archaeological indicators of formative period elites: A perspective from central Mexico, in: *Mesoamerican Elites: An Archaeological Assessment* (D. Z. Chase and A. F. Chase, eds.), University of Oklahoma Press, Norman and London, pp. 191-205.

Helms, M. W., 1979, *Ancient Panama: Chiefs in Search of Power*. University of Texas Press, Austin.

Helms, M. W., 1987, Thoughts on public symbols and distant domains relevant to the chiefdoms of lower Central America. Paper presented at the Conference on Wealth and Hierarchy in the Intermediate Area, Dumbarton Oaks, Washington, D.C.

Helms, M. W., 1988, *Ulysses' Sail*. Princeton University Press, Princeton, NJ.

Hewitt, K., 1983, *Interpretations of Calamity*. Allen & Unwin Inc., Boston.

Hewitt, W. P., M. C. Winter, and D. A. Peterson, 1987, Salt production at Hierve el Agua, Oaxaca. *American Antiquity* 52,4:799-815.

Jochim, M. A., 1976, *Hunter-Gatherer Subsistence and Settlement: A Predictive Model*. Academic Press, New York.

Johnson, A. W. and T. Earle, 1987, *The Evolution of Human Societies: From Foraging Group to Agrarian State*. Stanford University Press, Stanford, CA.

Johnson, G. R., 1986, Kin selection, socialization, and patriotism: An integrating theory. *Politics and the Life Sciences* 4,2:127-154.

Johnson, G. R., 1987, In the name of the Fatherland: An analysis of kin term usage in patriotic speech and literature. *International Political Science Review* 8,2:165-174.

Joyce, A. A., 1991, *Formative Period Occupation in the Lower Río Verde Valley, Oaxaca, México: Interregional Interaction and Social Change*. Ph.D. dissertation, Department of Anthropology, Rutgers University, New Brunswick, NJ.

Joyce, A. A., 1994a, Late Formative community organization and social complexity on the Oaxaca coast. *Journal of Field Archaeology* 21,2:147-168.

Joyce, A. A., 1994b, Ideology, power, and state formation at Monte Albán. Paper presented at the 59th Annual Meeting of the Society for American Archaeology, Anaheim, CA.

Joyce, A. A. and R. G. Mueller, 1992, The social impact of anthropogenic landscape modification in the Río Verde drainage basin, Oaxaca, Mexico. *Geoarchaeology* 7,6:503-526.

Joyce, A. A. and M. C. Winter, 1993, Ideology, power, and urban society in Prehispanic Oaxaca. Paper presented at the 13th International Congress of Anthropological and Ethnological Sciences, Mexico City, Mexico.

Keegan, W. F., 1986, The optimal foraging analysis of horticultural production. *American Anthropologist* 88,1:92-107.

Keene, A. S., 1981, *Prehistoric Foraging in a Temperate Forest: A Linear Programing Model*. Academic Press, New York.

King, M. B., 1988, *Mixtec Political Ideology: Historical Metaphors and the Poetics of Political Symbolism*. Ph.D. dissertation, Department of Anthropology, University of Michigan, Ann Arbor.

Kirkby, A. V. T., 1973, *The Use of Land and Water Resources in the Past and Present Valley of Oaxaca, Mexico*. Prehistory and Human Ecology of the Valley of Oaxaca, vol. 1, Memoirs of the University of Michigan Museum of Anthropology 5, Ann Arbor.

Kolata, A. L., 1992, Economy, ideology, and imperialism in the South-Central Andes, in: *Ideology and Pre-Columbian Civilizations* (A. A. Demarest and G. W. Conrad, eds.), School of American Research, Sante Fe, NM, pp. 65-86.

Kowalewski, S. A., 1980, Population-resource balances in Period I of Oaxaca, Mexico. *American Antiquity* 45,1:151-165.

Kowalewski, S., C. Spencer, and E. Redmond, 1978, Appendix II. Description of ceramic categories, in: *Monte Albán: Settlement Patterns at the Ancient Zapotec Capital* (R. E. Blanton, ed.), Academic Press, New York, pp. 167-193.

Kowalewski, S. A., R. E. Blanton, G. Feinman, and L. Finsten, 1983, Boundaries, scale, and internal organization. *Journal of Anthropological Archaeology*, 2:32-56.

Kowalewski, S. A., G. Feinman, L. Finsten, and R. E. Blanton, 1991, Pre-Hispanic ballcourts from the Valley of Oaxaca, Mexico, in: *The Mesoamerican Ballgame* (V. L. Scarborough and D. R. Wilcox, eds.), University of Arizona Press, Tucson, pp. 25-44.

Kowalewski, S. A., G. Feinman, L. Finsten, R. E. Blanton, and L. M. Nicholas. 1989. *Monte Albán's Hinterland, part II: Prehispanic Settlement Patterns in Tlacolula, Etla, and Ocotlán, the Valley of Oaxaca, Mexico*. Memoirs of the University of Michigan Museum of Anthropology 23, Ann Arbor.

Kuttruf, C. and W. O. Autry, Jr., 1978, Test excavations at Terrace 1227, in: *Monte Albán: Settlement Patterns at the Ancient Zapotec Capital* R. E. Blanton, ed.), Academic Press, New York, pp. 167-193.

Lack, D. 1966. *Population Studies of Birds*. Clarendon Press, Oxford.

Lane, F. C., 1966, The economic meaning of war and protection, in: *Venice and History: The Collected Papers of Frederic C. Lane* (F. C. Lane, ed.), Johns Hopkins University Press, Baltimore.

Larrain, J., 1983, *Marxism and Ideology*. Macmillan, London.

Laughlin, C. D., 1974, Maximization, marriage and residence among the So. *American Ethnologist* 1:129-141.

Lewontin, R. C., 1970, The Units of Selection. *Annual Review of Ecology and Systematics* 1:1-18.
Mack, J. E., 1983, Nationalism and the self. *Psychohistory Review* 11,2-3:47-69.
Marcus, J., 1974, The iconography of power among the Classic Maya. *World Archaeology* 6,1:83-94.
Marcus, J., 1976, The iconography of militarism at Monte Alban and neighboring sites in the Valley of Oaxaca, in: *The Origins of Religious Art and Iconography in Preclassic Mesoamerica* (y H. B. Nicholson, ed.), UCLA, Latin American Center, Los Angeles, pp. 123-139.
Marcus, J., 1983a, The conquest slabs of Building J, Monte Alban, in: *The Cloud People: Divergent Evolution of the Zapotec and Mixtec Civilizations* (K. V. Flannery and J. Marcus, eds.), Academic Press, New York, pp.106-108.
Marcus, J., 1983b, Zapotec religion, in: *The Cloud People: Divergent Evolution of the Zapotec and Mixtec Civilizations* (K. V. Flannery and J. Marcus, eds.), Academic Press, New York, pp. 345-351.
Marcus, J., 1992, *Mesoamerican Writing Systems: Propaganda, Myth, and History in Four Ancient Civilizations*. Princeton University Press, Princeton.
Masson, M. A., H. Orr, and J. Urcid, 1992, Building dedication, nagual transformation, and captive sacrifice at Monte Albán: Programs of sacred geography. Paper presented at the 57th Annual Meeting of the Society for American Archaeology, Pittsburgh, PA.
McCay, B. J., 1978, Systems ecology, people ecology, and the anthropology of fishing communities. *Human Ecology* 6,4:397-422.
McCay, B. J., 1981, Optimal foragers or political actors? Ecological analysis of a New Jersey fishery. *American Ethnologist* 8,2:356-382.
McGuire, R. H., 1983, Breaking down cultural complexity: Inequality and heterogeneity. In *Advances in Archaeological Method and Theory* (Vol. VI) (M. B. Schiffer, ed.), Academic Press, New York, pp. 91-142.
Milgram, S., 1974, *Obidience to Authority*. Harper & Row, New York.
Millon, R., 1974, The study of urbanism at Teotihuacan, Mexico, in: *Mesoamerican Archaeology: New Approaches* (N. Hammond, ed.), University of Texas Press, Austin, pp. 335-362.
Mithen, S., 1989, Evolutionary theory and post-processual archaeology. *Antiquity* 63:483-494.
Monaghan, J., 1990, Sacrifice, death, and the origins of agriculture in the *Codex Vienna*. *American Antiquity* 55,3:559-569.
Monaghan, J., 1994, Sacrifice and power in Mixtec kingdsoms. Paper presented at the 59th Annual Meeting of the Society for American Archaeology, Anaheim, CA.
Mueller, R. A. and A. A. Joyce, 1993, The effects of human landscape degradation in highland Oaxaca. Paper presented at the 92nd meeting of the American Anthropological Association, Washington, D.C.
Neely, J. A., S. C. Caran, and B. M. Winsborough, 1990, Irrigated agriculture at Hierve el Agua, Oaxaca, Mexico, in: *Debating Oaxaca Archaeology* (J. Marcus, ed.), pp. 115-190. Museum of Anthropology, University of Michigan Anthropological Papers 84, Ann Arbor.
Nicholas, L., 1989, Land use in prehispanic Oaxaca, in: *Monte Albán's Hinterland, Part II: Prehispanic Settlement Patterns in Tlacolula, Etla, and Ocotlán, the Valley of Oaxaca, Mexico* (S. A. Kowalewski, G. Feinman, L. Finsten, R. E. Blanton, and L. M. Nicholas, eds.), pp. 449-506. Memoirs of the University of Michigan Museum of Anthropology 23, Ann Arbor.
Nicholas, L., G. Feinman, S. A. Kowalewski, R. E. Blanton, and L. Finsten, 1986, Prehispanic colonization of the Valley of Oaxaca, Mexico. Human Ecology 14,2:131-162.
Nicholson, H. B., 1971, Religion in pre-Hispanic central Mexico, in: *Handbook of Middle American Indians, Vol. 10: Archaeology of Northern Mesoamerica, Part 1* (R.

Wauchope, G. F. Ekholm, and I. Bernal, eds.), University of Texas Press, Austin, pp. 395-446.
O'Brien, M. J., R. D. Mason, D. E. Lewarch, and J. A. Neely, 1982, *A Late Formative Irrigation Settlement below Monte Albán*. Austin: Institute of Latin American Studies, University of Texas.
Orlove, B. S., 1980, Ecological anthropology. *Annual Review of Anthropology* 9:235-273.
Orr, H. S., 1993, The ballplayers of Dainzú: Evidence for inter-site elite competition in the Late Formative Valley of Oaxaca. Paper presented at the 58th meeting of the Society for American Archaeology, St. Louis, MO.
Ortiz, S., 1980, Forecasts, decisions, and the farmer's response to uncertain environments, in: *Agricultural Decision Making* (P. F. Bartlett, ed.), Academic Press, New York, pp. 177-202.
Parry, W. J., 1987, *Chipped Stone Tools in Formative Oaxaca, Mexico: Their Procurement, Production and Use*. Museum of Anthropology, University of Michigan, Memoirs 20, Ann Arbor.
Paso y Troncoso, F. (editor), 1982. *Papeles de Nueva España, tomo IV*. Facsimile of 1905 edition. Mexico: Banca Comfía.
Patterson, T. C. and C. W. Gailey. (editors), 1987, *Power Relations and State Formation*. Archaeology Section/American Anthropological Association, Washington.
Peebles, C. S. and S. M. Kus, 1977, Some archaeological correlates of ranked societies. *American Antiquity* 42,3:421-446.
Peoples, J. G., 1982, Individual or group advantage? A reinterpretation of the Maring ritual cycle. *Current Anthropology* 23,3:291-310.
Pires-Ferreira, J. W., 1975, *Formative Mesoamerican Exchange Networks with Special Reference to the Valley of Oaxaca*. Prehistory and Human Ecology of the Valley of Oaxaca, vol. 3, Memoirs of the University of Michigan Museum of Anthropology 7, Ann Arbor.
Rathje, W. L., 1970, Socio-political implications of lowland Maya burials: Methodology and tentative hypotheses. *World Archaeology* 1,3:359-375.
Rapoport, A., 1976, Sociocultural aspects of man-environment studies, in: *The Mutual Interaction of People and their Built Environment: A Cross-Cultural Perspective* (A. Rapoport, ed.), Mouton, The Hague, pp. 7-35.
Redmond, E. M., 1983, *A fuego y sangre: Early Zapotec Imperialism in the Cuicatlán Cañada, Oaxaca*. Museum of Anthropology, University of Michigan, Memoir 16, Ann Arbor.
Richerson, P. J., 1977, Ecology and human ecology: A comparison of theories in the biological and social sciences. *American Ethnologist* 4:1-26.
Rindos, D., 1984, *The Origins of Agriculture: An Evolutionary Perspective*. Academic Press, New York.
Rutz, H. J., 1977, Individual decisions and functional systems: Economic rationality and environmental adaptation. *American Ethnologist* 4:156-74.
Sahlins, M., 1958, *Social Stratification in Polynesia*. University of Washington Press, Seattle .
Sanders, W. T., 1968, Hydraulic agriculture, economic symbiosis and the evolution of states in central Mexico, in: *Anthropological Archaeology in the Americas* (B. J. Meggars, ed.), Anthropological Society of Washington, Washington, D.C., pp. 88-107.
Sanders, W. T. and D. L. Nichols, 1988, Ecological theory and cultural evolution in the Valley of Oaxaca. *Current Anthropology* 29,1:33-80.
Sanders, W. T. and D. Webster, 1988, The Mesoamerican urban tradition. *American Anthropologist* 90:521-546.
Santley, R. S., 1980, Disembedded capitals reconsidered. *American Antiquity* 45:132-145.
Schele, L., 1984, Human sacrifice among the Classic Maya, in: *Ritual Human Sacrifice in Mesoamerica* (E. Boone, ed.), Dumbarton Oaks, Washington, D.C., pp. 6-48.

Schele, L. and D. A. Freidel, 1990, *A Forest of Kings: The Untold Story of the Ancient Maya*. William Morrow, New York.
Schele, L. and M. E. Miller, 1986, *The Blood of Kings, Dynasty and Ritual in Maya Art*. Kimbell Art Museum, Fort Worth, TX.
Schortman, E. M., 1989, Interregional interaction in prehistory: The need for a new perspective. *American Antiquity* 54,1:52-65.
Schortman, E. M. and P. Urban, 1987, Modeling interregional interaction in prehistory, in: *Advances in Archaeological Method and Theory* (Vol. XI) (M. B. Schiffer, ed.), Academic Press, San Diego, pp. 37-95.
Scott, J. F., 1978, *The Danzantes of Monte Albán. Part II: Catalogue*. Dumbarton Oaks, Studies in Pre-Columbian Art & Archaeology No. 19, Washington, D.C.
Service, E. R., 1975, *Origins of the State and Civilization: The Process of Cultural Evolution*. Norton, New York.
Slobodkin, L. B., 1972, On the inconstancy of ecological efficiency and the form of ecological theories. *Transactions of the Connecticut Academy of Sciences* 44:293-305.
Spencer, C. S., 1982, *The Cuicatlán Cañada and Monte Albán*. Academic Press, New York.
Spencer, C. S., 1990, On the tempo and mode of state formation: Neoevolutionnism reconsidered. *Journal of Anthropological Archaeology* 9:1-30.
Spores, R., 1974, *Stratigraphic Excavations in the Nochixtlán Valley, Oaxaca*. Vanderbilt University Publications in Anthropology 11, Nashville.
Spores, R., 1983a, The origin and evolution of the Mixtec system of social stratification, in: *The Cloud People: Divergent Evolution of the Zapotec and Mixtec Civilizations* (K. V. Flannery and J. Marcus, eds.), Academic Press, New York, pp. 227-238.
Spores, R., 1983b, Mixtec religion, in: *The Cloud People: Divergent Evolution of the Zapotec and Mixtec Civilizations* (K. V. Flannery and J. Marcus, eds.), Academic Press, New York, pp. 342-345.
Spores, R., 1984, *The Mixtecs in Ancient and Colonial Times*. University of Oklahoma Press, Norman.
Steponaitis, V., 1991, Contrasting patterns of Mississippian development, in: *Chiefdoms: Power, Economy, and Ideology* (T. Earle, ed.), Cambridge University Press, Cambridge, pp. 193-228.
Steward, J. H., 1955, *The Theory of Culture Change*. University of Illinois Press, Urbana.
Sugiyama, S., 1993, Worldview materialized in Teotihuacán, Mexico. *Latin American Antiquity* 4(2):103-129.
Tilly, C., 1975, *The Formation of Nation States in Western Europe*. Princeton University Press, Princeton.
Tilly, C., 1985, War making and state making as organized crime, in: *Bringing the State Back In* (P. B. Evans, D. Rueschemeyer, and T. Skocpol, eds.), Cambridge University Press, Cambridge, pp. 169-191.
Trinkaus, K. M. (editor), 1987, *Politics and Partitions: Human Boundaries and the Growth of Complex Societies*. Arizona State University Anthropological Research Papers, No. 37, Tucson.
Vayda, A. P., 1986, Holism and individualism in ecological anthropology. *Reviews in Anthropology* 13:295-313.
Vayda, A. P. and B. J. McCay, 1975, New directions in ecology and ecological anthropology. *Annual Review of Anthropology* 4:293-306.
Volkan, V. D., 1985, The need to have enemies and allies: A developmental approach. *Political Psychology* 6,2:219-247.
Weber, M., 1986, Domination by economic power and by authority, in: *Power* (S. Lukes, ed.), New York Univerisity Press, New York, pp. 28-36.

Wenke, R. J., 1981, Explaining the evolution of cultural complexity: A review, in: *Advances in Archaeological Method and Theory* (Vol. IV) (M. B. Schiffer, ed.), Academic Press, New York, pp. 79-127.

Whalen, M. E., 1981, *Excavations at Santo Domingo Tomaltepec: Evolution of a Formative Community in the Valley of Oaxaca, Mexico*. Prehistory and Human Ecology of the Valley of Oaxaca, vol. 6, Memoirs of the University of Michigan Museum of Anthropology 12, Ann Arbor.

Whalen, M. E., 1988, Small community organization during the Late Formative Period in Oaxaca, Mexico. *Journal of Field Archaeology* 15:291-306.

Whitecotton, J. W., 1977, *The Zapotecs: Princes, Priests, and Peasants*. University of Oklahoma Press, New York and London.

Williams, G. C., 1966, *Adaptation and Natural Selection*. Princeton: Princeton University Press, Princeton, NJ.

Winter, M. C., 1972, *Tierras Largas: A Formative Community in the Valley of Oaxaca, Mexico*. Unpublished Ph.D. dissertation, Department of Anthropology, University of Arizona, Tucson.

Winter, M., 1974, Residential patterns at Monte Albán, Oaxaca, Mexico. *Science* 186,4168:981-987.

Winter, M., 1984, Exchange in Formative highland Oaxaca, in: *Trade and Exchange in Early Mesoamerica* (K. G. Hirth, ed.), University of New Mexico Press, Albuquerque, pp. 179-214.

Winter, M., 1986, Unidades habitaciones prehispánicas de Oaxaca, in: *Unidades habitacionales mesoamericana y sus áreas de actividad* (L. Manzanilla, ed.), pp. 325-374. Instituto de Investigaciones Antropológicas, Serie Antropológica:76. Mexico: Universidad Nacional Autónoma de México.

Winter, M., 1989, *Oaxaca: The Archaeological Record*. Mexico: Minutiae Mexicana.

Winter, M. C. and A. A. Joyce, 1994, Early political development at Monte Albán: Evidence from recent excavations. Paper presented at the 93nd meeting of the American Anthropological Association, Atlanta, GA.

Winterhalder, B. and E. A. Smith (editors), 1981, *Hunter-Gatherer Foraging Strategies*. Chicago: The University of Chicago Press.

Wittfogel, K., 1957, *Oriental Despotism*. Yale University Press, New Haven.

Wright, H., 1977, Recent research on the origin of the state. *Annual Review of Anthropology* 6:379-397.

Zeitlin, R. N., 1993, Pacific coastal Laguna Zope: A regional center in Terminal Formative Oaxaca prehistory. *Ancient Mesoamerica* 4,1:85-102.

Chapter 7

Clues to the System of Power in the City of Oxkintok*

MIGUEL RIVERA DORADO

INTRODUCTION

Power, systems of power, and the capacity and practices of power have, through the course of history, left their symbolic imprints to posterity in a number of ways: in language and the written text, in dress and food habits, in the conventions of protocol, and in the extravagances of the elite. On this occasion, our objective is to show the importance of architectural symbols in the investigation of power relations; that is, of the relative positions of rank and dominance, and their ideological justifications. The place chosen for these speculations is the pre-Hispanic city of Oxkintok, in the north of the Yucatan peninsula. In this ensemble of ruins (Figure 1), which is at a distance of around 50 kilometers from Mérida, the present-day capital of Yucatan, and at some 30 kilometers from the well-known city of

---

*Translated from Spanish by Niall Binns.

MIGUEL RIVERA DORADO • Departamento de Antropología y Etnología de América, Facultad de Geografía e Historia, Universidad Complutense, Ciudad Universitaria, Madrid 28040, España

Emergence and Change in Early Urban Societies, edited by Linda Manzanilla, Plenum Press, New York, 1997.

Figure 1. The Satunsat of Oxkintok.

Uxmal—a model of settlements in the mountainous region (the Puuc) during the Terminal Classic Period (*ca*. 850-1000 AD)—excavations have been carried out in recent years, unearthing new information which I shall use in this chapter (and part of which has already been published by the Spanish Ministry of Culture, in a series called OXKINTOK).

The drawing up of a new map of the site (Figure 2), and the cleaning and restoration of more than twenty architectural structures, has not led to an automatic understanding of the buildings, nor to any explanation of the urban layout or the processes of growth and reform in the constructed spaces. The accumulation of supposed data in the so-called archaeological record would have extended still further the inventory of monuments and objects of the ancient Mayan civilization had it not been restricted and channelled by prior consideration of problems and theoretical guidelines, which led to the adoption of specifically selected strategies of investigation, and consequently of excavation and analysis. This means that the decision to investigate certain sectors, the area of excavation, and the number of buildings to be explored in specific locations was taken on the basis of the particular objectives we were pursuing, which were largely concerned with urban design and development in antiquity. Our aim was to find out if there existed a type of planning dependent on the governing minority's desire

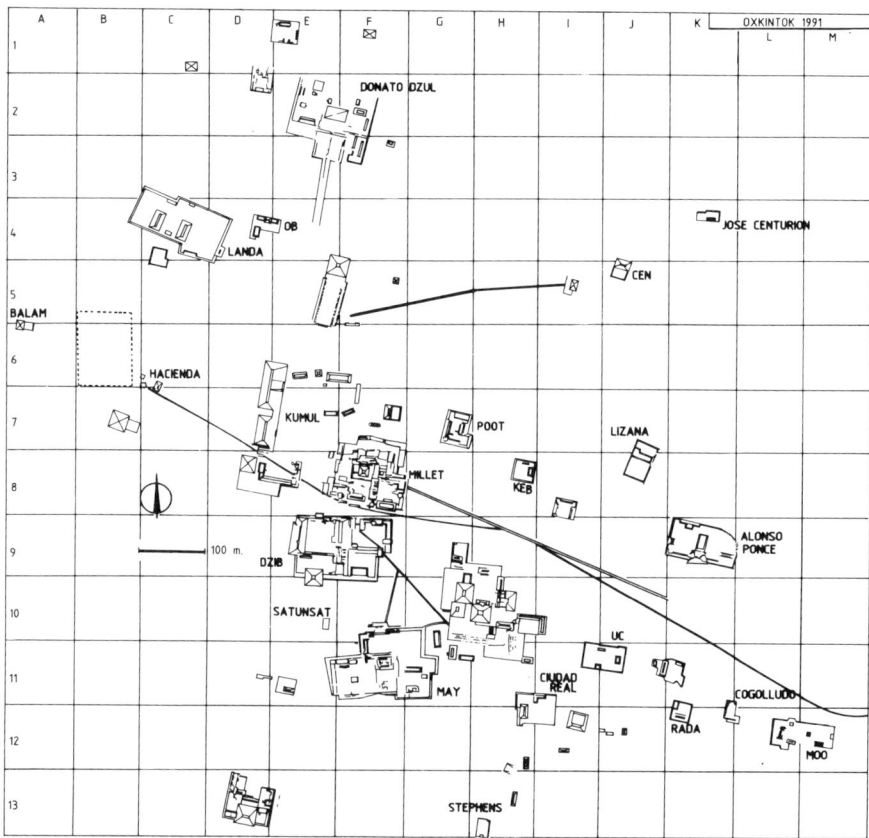

Figure 2. Map of Oxkintok.

for political expression—taking it for granted that such an expression was to be revealed in the form of special constructions. This idea is not new in other parts of the ancient world, even in Mesoamerica, as is clearly documented by European chroniclers of the 16th century, in their descriptions of cities such as Tenochtitlan or, in the Mayan region, Tayasal, which stress that specific buildings were assigned to institutions of political and religious power. However, this is by no means evident in the urban development in the lowlands of Guatemala and Yucatan during the Classic Period, when Mayan archaeological culture, in its most typical form, was at its prime. Moreover, although it can be argued that all monumental stone constructions were related to the ruling minorities, no one has been able to form any characterization of the system of government, of the practices of the authority and its legitimation, from the meticulously detailed descriptions of those buildings, which have filled, and which continue to fill, hundreds of pages of printed reports. Now, however, beyond the platitude that monumental architecture is a typical feature of stratified societies, and that its existence and use is related to the elites of those societies, the time has come to consider it an essential source of information on political typologies and on models of power.

Let us briefly consider a prior factor which is vital to our analysis: in a universe containing dozens of settlements of very diverse class and condition, as is the case in the tropical lowlands of Southeastern Mesoamerica, the first task will be to discover the general rules of grouping, integration, and relative hierarchy which exist among these settlements, and to define the model by which different levels of local and regional power are manifested. It is clear that the presumed existence of a "radial" or "pyramidal" system of government over a continuous territory in the pre-Hispanic Mayan area is due both to the ethnocentric prejudice which comes from experience of the modern state, and also to historical observation of the distribution of authority in the world, in regions—great or small—where there have been administrations of an "imperial" character. After more than a century of investigations and debates, there is still no agreement among Mayanists on this matter, nor are there any propositions which are more than hypothetical and, naturally, questionable.

Demarest (1984) suggests that the political and territorial organization of the Mayas since the Late Pre-Classic Period corresponds to the Southeast Asian model of "pulsating galactic polities," whose distinctive characteristic is the manner in which subordinate centers expand and contract, thus modifying the overall territory, but without challenging the continued control of a principal site. This model is apparently based on the configuration of the "mandala" in Oriental cosmology. The degree of the state's centralization, the leaders' power, and the whole network of political loyalties are upheld by personal and family relations of influence and control, which radiate from the administrative center to subordinate centers, arranged around it in the form of a constellation. This same system is duplicated and repeated, on a smaller scale, around the lesser sites. The basic feature of this model is that subordinate centers can move easily inside or outside the orbit of the principal site, changing their alliances and loyalties. Such a model may well account—more convincingly than a linear one—for the parallel rise and fall of different settlements throughout the Mayan lowlands, and can explain, for example, why El Mirador declines in the Early Classic whereas Tikal grows during the same period.

The difficulty of widespread territorial control in the tropical rain forests of Central America, added to the strength of traditions of organization based on kinship ties—which had sufficiently displayed their ability to adapt since Formative times—explains the lack of imperialistic political and territorial tendencies among the Mayan monarchies of the Classic Period. The integration needed to produce economic benefits (joint exploitation of the floodlands (*bajos*), cooperation in public works, greater ease in commercial trade, etc.) and social benefits (reduction in conflicts, greater spacial movement, identification and solidarity with large groups to increase security, etc.) could be achieved perfectly by mechanisms for exchanging people and merchandise, and by a loose system of political loyalties based on relative prestige, on status within a kinship unit, and on the objective resources of power (greater wealth, larger population, greater strength in arms, better ideological justifications). As a result, the argument that political relations between different sites must have been conditioned by the distance between them (Houston 1987) is particularly useful. The tabbing of different types of relationship between sites (e.g., relations of explicit subordination, hostility, or marriage) reveals that war and marriage occur between sites at an average distance of 38.62 and 38.83 kilometers, respectively. Sites of a subordinate political class are at an average distance of 11.36 kilometers from the dominant site. The average distance between autonomous centers is of 40 kilometers in 8.18.0.0.0, 62.5 kilometers in 9.3.0.0.0, 58.33 kilometers in 9.8.0.0.0, 59.54 kilometers in 9.13.0.0.0, and 52.18 kilometers in 9.18.0.0.0; in other words, between approximately 396 and 790 A.D., throughout the Classic Period, the real power of a governor extended little more than 50 kilometers from the capital in which he was based (cf. Mathews 1979).

It was particularly difficult for the Mayan kings to stop their delegates and lieutenants in smaller and dependent centers from splitting away from the kingdom, and seizing absolute power in the territory under their control; this process must have been the cause of numerous wars, but the most efficient way of conserving power over subordinate sites, from which the capital expected tribute and loyal cooperation, was precisely by slackening the ties of dependence and allowing them all the paraphernalia of dynastic rites, which included the vindication of the authority of their ancestry, and the religious and iconographic exaltation of their governer. The temptation of seeking independence could be restricted by bonds of family and marriage, by economic alliances, and by joint participation in specific rituals which reaffirmed socially shared myths. The preservation of political and territorial unity was at stake in this subtle game of give and take, this "dyanamic equilibrium," and great effort and teaching was dedicated to it, as can be seen clearly from art and epigraphy of the epoch. The sequences of sculpted monuments and of dates from the Initial Series, the raising of stelae, and the remodelling of architectural structures show, in their continuity or discontinuity, in their duration and vicissitudes, those moments of equilibrium and instability which each center underwent in its particular situation within a greater unit or constellation, or kingdom, as we have called it. All of this must necessarily be symbolized in the design of the forms and volumes of the city, just as it is in "ornamental" manifestations, in graphic expression, and in the selection and location of sculptural and pictorial realistic images. The "grammar" of the elements in the urban space is that of the power relations transmuted into cosmological symbols, with the sun-king as the polarizing element and the Upper Sky and the Lower Sky as sacred keys to the hierarchical structure, whose origin stems from the nature of the world, from the primeval order ordained by the gods.

In the Old World tradition, the house of god is the image of the house of man: the god enters society by occupying his place in the hierarchical order, the largest, most luxurious, and most central house, as corresponds to his importance. In the Mayan area, gods and human beings are related, and although there existed a strictly hierarchical organization, the house of god is above all the house of the father of men and, as the founder and ancestral forefather, his figure is inseparably united to the social structure. This is why the buildings which we call temples seem to have been dedicated solely to the cult of kings or noble families; in reality they were at the same time, and perhaps most importantly, temples to the gods, and therefore also to their descendants, among whom were the kings and dignitaries. These were the *present-day* representatives of the gods, and for that reason their images outnumber those of their divine forefathers in the temples. A perfect example is that of the temples of Palenque, but something similar occurs in Tikal and elsewhere. Moreover, since popular worship was performed in the open air, the "temple," insofar as it is the house of the god, a sacred space, refers to the whole group of buildings, and perhaps to the entire city. But in Oxkintok, the principal groups of buildings, often raised on basal platforms, tend to have one or more of these pyramids, which are generally thought to be temples; likewise there are obvious associations between these groups of buildings and the stelae, whose sculptures appear to refer to events and people linked to the specific groups. In my opinion, the capital city of the ancient Mayans of Yucatan is a symbolic cosmos which represents all the social units involved in the government of the kingdom, both in the main and in the secondary centers. In the same way, each lesser city had to reproduce this scheme, but in relation to the third class centers which in turn depended on them, and so on successively. Thus, the key to the real power of each family or corporate social unit can be found in the relative importance of their group of buildings in the capital city, in their temple, which is the same as to say their god and their lineage. Dimensions, number of buildings, orientation, proximity or distance from the group of buildings belonging to the king's family, quantity and variety of sculptures and hieroglyphic inscriptions, size and quality of the templar pyramid: these are the signs which indicate that relative importance, the level of each of the units within the hierarchy, and hence the magnitude and the category of the city in their power within the radius of 50 kilometers mentioned above.

THE SITE OF OXKINTOK

In Oxkintok there are five architectural groups with important pyramids. Others do exist, but they are small, too far from the center or of a very late date. The Classic groups (approximately A.D. 350-750) which contain pyramids are called Donato Dzul, Dzib, May, Xanpol, and Ah Canul (see Rivera *et al*. 1991). Recent excavations included three of these groups, and with the other two we can conjecture without excessive risk. In all of them, the pyramid occupies a preeminent and focal postion, although rarely exceeding twenty meters in height (this includes their platforms); in three of them, the pyramid faces the north, and in one the south. The Ah Canul group is special because it has at least three pyramids, which are positioned almost at the edge of the rest of the buildings, as though they were an annex, and which face north, east, and west. It can be supposed that the disproportion—in three groups the pyramid faces north, whereas in only one it faces south—is significant, and this is confirmed by the fact that the Xanpol, May, and Dzip groups are all located in the southern half of the city, whereas the Donato Dzul group, the only of the big groups whose temple faces the south, is located in the north of the city. If we accept the idea that the groups represent social units (see also Kurjack and Garza 1981), it seems clear that these are organized in two parts, two halves, and that the southern half is larger and more powerful than the northern. This hypothesis is further strengthened by the fact that the Ah Canul group is also in the southern half, and there is little doubt that this is the group of greatest symbolic importance in the whole city. Besides, the ball game is located in what is approximately the center of the city, in the middle of the north-south axis around which the distribution of the buildings is arranged; because of this, I am inclined to believe that here the game is an expression and regulating mechanism of the basic social interactions of a dualist collectivity organized in moieties. Since a symbology of the game has been proposed which relates it to Venus, it is feasible to suggest that the respective appearances of the planet, as the star of the morning and of the evening, represent the two halves of the community; of course, the dual Venus may likewise be the sun and the moon, as can be seen from a literal reading of Popol Vuh, but to my mind there is a general assimilation of these symbols, so that the two Venuses and the sun and the moon are interchangeable—which puts an end to the confusion originating from the identification of the divine twins of the Quiché book.

In short, the southern half of the city of Oxkintok is, according to the analysis of its buildings and the symbolic value which we attribute to them, more important than the northern half. The Ah Canul group contains, in addition to the three pyramids, the largest palace of the site, which is also full of splendid lintels sculpted with fine dynastic iconography and hieroglyphics. Furthermore, in the southern half is the Satunsat (see Figure 1), a building of a labyrinthine plan, whose religious and political significance is enormous (Rivera 1989). In the Ah Canul group, paving was found with the painted mat-design, which was a symbol of royalty among the Mayas. In the May group there was a glyph on a wall of royal character, which reads *ahau*, indicating the importance of the building. In the Dzib group can be found the ball-game, and also two flights of stairs with hieroglyphic signs. The only governor of the city who is known at present, and whom we call Walas, is mentioned in the inscriptions of the Ah Canul and Dzib groups. The majority of the city's best stelae, and those which provide the best information, were in their day located in the southern half of the site, in the Ah Canul, May, and Dzib groups. As a result, and despite the fact that the northern Donato Dzul group is yet to be excavated, it seems clear that the southern half is the more important.

Of the three groups investigated in the south, one of them is undoubtedly the most important: Ah Canul. I believe that this was the seat of maximum power during the Classic Period, and therefore the seat of the power which governed the entire kingdom of Oxkintok—Walas would be an example of such a governor. The other two groups are obviously specialized: one possesses the ball-game, which makes it extremely important in the expression of social order, of power relations, and of the legitimation of the monarchy. At the end of the Classic Period, various causeways were built in the city: one of them joined the Dzib group directly to Ah Canul, and that relation is also vital in classifying the architectural group, and its occupants, in second place in the hierarchy. The May group provided very few hieroglyphic inscriptions, and its most representative building, the MA-1sub structure, belongs to the Early Classic Period, and was later hidden by the templar pyramid that was raised above it. MA-1sub was a strange palace, just as labyrinthine as the Satunsat, but was destroyed by the later, standard temple, as though an effort had been made to transfer to another group, presumably Ah Canul, the predominance held by May before the sixth century—that is perhaps why four fifth-century lintels, carved with hieroglyphics and dates from the Initial Series, were taken to Ah Canul. This probably meant that the May group and its occupants came to fill the third place in the hierarchy. At present, it would be almost impossible to apply this preliminary classification of the users of the architectural groups to the territory of the kingdom of Oxkintok; the region is almost unexplored, and we know very little of the archaeology of important centers at a distance of 20 or 30 kilometers. Certainly, we can be sure that Uxmal, a city at some 30 kilometers from Oxkintok, was not part of this kingdom; on the other hand, it is quite possible that Chunchucmil was. A worthwhile investigation could be made of the connections between the lesser sites around Oxkintok and the groups mentioned in the capital itself; if such relations could be corroborated by a detailed analysis of the symbols which identify the respective social unit in both the sites and the groups, a giant step forward would be made, I believe, in our knowledge of the political system of the Mayas and of the methods of territorial government.

Moving on to another subject, there can be no doubt that the relation between the divine Mayan monarchy and the sun-god is more complex than a simple assimilation of the king with the powerful star, thus investing his activity with life-giving, fertile, or luminous qualities. The appearance of the sun as founder of time and space is also of transcendental importance in studying the attributes of earthly power, of he who governed the world and of the destiny of time—that very time which inexorably brushes away all the components of perceptible reality. The king, like the sun, is above that destiny which makes all that has been created perishable: his existence continues after his death, and in his apotheosis he accompanies the gods in their starry travels, like the Egyptian pharaoh. Therefore, in the symbolism of the royal city, of the kingdom's capital, the finest solar dedications, the most outstanding material ornaments, and the most elevated and striking expressiveness must be found, since, as I have said, the urban space is probably the faithful reflection of the heavens and the cosmos. The first sign is that of the orientation of representative buildings, such as, in Oxkintok, the Satunsat, with its façades to the East and the West, the latter specially prepared for observing and measuring the equinox, and for trapping solar light in the interior of the labyrinth; also there are the causeways which go in the directions north-south and east-west, like solar paths among the constellations of architectural structures; and the ball-game, with its court facing north-south, so that the ball imitates the annual itinerary of the sun in its comings and goings. It is worth pointing out that the urban spaces which can be linked to the apparent movements of the sun or which are connected to its symbology, are those which best display the monumental appearance of political power. Wherever the sun is, the king is also. Sadly, however, all too often we are still unable to discern the symbols, or we lack sufficiently complete or precise maps of numerous cities, or the looting and the elements have wiped out the clearest remains. My opinion is that the Maya city, at least in certain regions and in specific periods, was a representation of the heavens—day and night, assuredly, corresponding to upper and lower spaces—and that within it, like in the immense expanse of stars which the earth-dweller beholds, the sun plays a primordial role. The king who in reliefs holds up the ceremonial bar, emblem of the sky, is the sun which shows itself in the celestial city through his works. Directions, axes, and gaps in the architecture related to the king, are all planned around the model of the sun's behavior. In Oxkintok, the architectural group in which many of the possibilities of solar projection can be proved is Ah Canul; there indeed the sculpted effigies of the sun and the moon—which is the sun of the night—appeared, Kinich Ahau and Ix Chel in the late terminology, and there are temples which face the rising and the setting sun, the same as the gates of the grand palace—of over 30 meters in length—which contains the images of the governing family.

CONCLUSIONS

The Mayan city, and specifically Oxkintok, lived in a state of constant remodelling. The Mayas were not only excellent builders; moreover, they never stopped building. As well as new constructions, they worked permanently at amplifying, reforming, and demolishing. What could be the cause of this constant, and at times seemingly compulsive, unrest in the building of their cities? We know of the obligation of certain rulers in the Altiplano to re-pave, re-plaster and re-adorn. In the lowlands, I believe that the unceasing construction is related to the symbolization of kinship ties and the cult of the ancestors. The ancestors placed the first stones, and each successive ruler established with other stones his links with the founding fathers. Thus, the architectural history of a site, or of a group, is evidence of this ideology. The value of sequential works was that they offered a way of making history in pre-Hispanic times, of adding a new thread to the social loom, of legitimizing the place and the role of each member in the order of the collectivity. The chain of construction was the chain of the generations. For us, the links in the chain constitute the explicit reasoning of the Mayans in questions of rank and hierarchy. Constructing is the expression of kinship ties and of the laws of stratification, and each building is the reaffirmation of some lineage, the memory of its existence and the justification of its power.

REFERENCES

Demarest, A., 1984, Conclusiones y especulaciones, in: The Harvard El Mirador Project, 1982-1983, *Mesoamérica* 7:136-160.

Houston, S. D., 1987, Notes on Caracol Epigraphy and its Significance, in: *Investigations at the Classic Maya City of Caracol, Belize: 1985-1987* (A. F. Chase and D. Z. Chase, eds.), Monograph 3, Pre-Columbian Art Research Institute, San Francisco, pp. 85-100.

Kurjack, E., and S. Garza, 1981, Pre-Columbian Community Form and Distribution in the Northern Maya Area, in: *Lowland Maya Settlement Patterns* (W. Ashmore, ed.), University of New Mexico Press, Albuquerque, pp. 287-309.

Mathews, P., 1979, On the glyphs "West" and "Mah K'ina", *Maya Glyph Notes* 6.

Rivera, M., 1989, El laberinto maya, Paper presented at the First International Congress of Mayanists, San Cristóbal de las Casas.

Rivera, M., *et al.*, 1991, *Oxkintok, una ciudad maya de Yucatán*, Sociedad Estatal Quinto Centenario y Misión Arqueológica de España en México, Madrid.

Chapter 8

Reconstructing Huari
A Cultural Chronology for the Capital City

WILLIAM H. ISBELL

INTRODUCTION

During the sixth through ninth centuries, a distinctive ceramic style and iconography were spread through much of Peru. Archaeological research clearly shows the center of dispersal to have been the site of Huari (Menzel 1964, 1968, 1977; Knobloch 1991). During these same centuries it is also clear that Huari became one of the largest cities of the precolumbian Andes (Isbell 1978, 1983, 1984, 1985, 1986; Isbell, Brewster-Wray and Spickard 1991; Rowe 1963). Furthermore, centers with Huari style architecture appeared intrusively in distant parts of the Peruvian highlands—probably the first prehistoric Andean evidence for provincial administrative centers (Isbell 1977, 1989, 1991a, 1991b; Isbell and Schreiber 1978; Lumbreras 1974; McEwan 1984, 1991; Rowe 1956, 1963; Schreiber 1978, 1987a, 1987b, 1991, 1992; J. Topic 1991; Topic and Topic 1985a). Finally, at least one Huari fortress has been identified, ensconced deep inside Tiahuanaco territory (Watanabe 1984; Moseley, Feldman, Goldstein, and Watanabe 1991). I know of no comparable evidence for military conquest and occupation of enemy land at an earlier date in the Andes.

While the archaeological record would seem to leave little doubt about the evolutionary and political importance of Huari for Andean culture,

---

WILLIAM H. ISBELL • Department of Anthropology, State University of New York at Binghamton, Binghamton, New York 13902-6000, U.S.A.
Emergence and Change in Early Urban Societies, edited by Linda Manzanilla. Plenum Press, New York, 1997.

some Andean prehistorians still ignore Huari, treat it as no more than many other regional capitals of the time, or subjugate it to another center, *altiplano* Tiwanaku or coastal Pachacamac, for example (Bawden and Conrad 1982; Bueno 1982; Kolata 1983; Shady 1982, 1988, 1989, Shady and Ruiz 1979). While Michael Moseley (1992) has abandoned an interpretation implying that Tiwanaku somehow controlled Huari (Moseley (1978, 1983) he still wants to separate Huari from the evolutionary trajectory that led to coastal Andean states such as Moche by creating two tracks, one to "intensive" states (Moche) and the other to "extensive" states (Huari).

I believe that such minimization of Huari cannot be understood in terms of a positivist approach to the past, that assumes a real past about which archaeologists learn through objective collection and evaluation of data. Too many data have been dismissed, ignored or manipulated for the process to be considered objective. Rather, I find the rejection of Huari's importance to relate to political, economic and social contexts, and to the histories and financing of archaeological research within these contexts. Prehistoric pasts are not discovered through objective scientific investigation, but constructed by contemporary people—scientists, nationalists, international capitalists, etc.— for real purposes, and certainly in some modicum of conformity with information revealed by archaeological investigation.

Let me consider briefly an example. The Spanish colonial government was interested in the Incas primarily to discount their political legitimacy. In subsequent republican Peru, Inca integration became a basis for a new nationalist identity. In the early 20th century, multinational academics whose interests were contrary to the promotion of nationalistic identities began championing a science of diffusionism, constructing a single origin for agriculture and civilization in the entire New World. In this way scholars like Max Uhle and Herbert Spinden (Spinden 1928; Uhle 1922) severed the Peru's precolumbian roots for nationalism by unifying Andean/Peruvian culture with Mesoamerica. Peruvian scholar Julio C. Tello (1942, 1943) confronted the multinationals by constructing "Chavín" as an early autochthonous cultural tradition, a great art style, and a time period, named for a Peruvian site that was believed to be the tradition's "origin center." The Chavín construction provided national roots for Peruvian identity, while the Inca construct promoted national unity.

"Tiwanaku" is another politically, economically and socially powerful construct that resembles Chavín and Inca rolled together. It includes an "origin center" city, an iconographic horizon, a cultural tradition divided into phases, a series of ceramic styles, an ancient state and imperial government, a collection of architectural forms and technologies, and more recently a mode of production based on hierarchically administered ridged fields as well as a regional settlement system (Kolata 1985, 1986, 1987, 1993; Ponce 1969, 1976, 1980). Since its promotion in the 1950's as part of a political party's ideology, Tiwanaku has been constructed as a symbol of Bolivian national identity and autochthonous origins. The priority, power and prestige of the Tiwanaku "origin center" within a south Andean sphere are not research questions for investigation, but assumptions built into the Tiwanaku construct. Consequently, only certain kinds of pasts can be constructed for Tiwanaku. And these pasts progressively reinforce the "origin center" construct.

Huari has not participated in pasts constructed by any politically, economically or socially powerful interests. In fact, the most popular construction of Huari has been in the interest of counter-cultural, counter-nationalist, and even counter-internationalist goals. Initially Huari was the subject of multinational academics (Bennett 1953; Rowe, Collier and Willey 1950; Schaedel 1948), but it subsequently passed into the hands of Peruvian Luis G. Lumbreras (1959, 1960, 1969. 1974), and his Ayacucho colleagues (Benavides 1984; González 1982). Their Huari construct was not in promotion of nationalism but in protest against state and class organization, as well as against Peru's participation in world capitalism and the consequent oppression of Andean peoples. It was not in promotion of big, technocratic, governments that direct vast development schemes, but in support of small-scale production units that employ intimate knowledge and careful conservation. It also attributed great worth to highland Indians and their culture. Led by Lumbreras and a core of Marxist Ayacucho scholars, Huari was conceptualized as a militaristic empire of highland origin based on the forceful appropriation of surplus from efficient small producers by an oppressive and dominant elite. These small farmers became soldiers for the state, and Huari rapidly conquered and systematically reorganized and exploited almost all the regional cultures of Peru. In this construction, the type site capital was built quickly at the expense of the subjugated. But it endured only briefly for its internal contradictions soon brought about its downfall.

This is the threatening "Huari" past eagerly rejected or ignored by nationalist and multinational scholars alike. For the nationalist it attacks technocratic rule and challenges the conviction that big government promotes big development and big production. It challenges multinational/North American evolution and process archaeology by refusing to attribute the success of Huari to superior adaptations to the natural environment. To the contrary, Huari was oppressive and exploitive. Second, the military and administrative take-over of technocratic bureaucracies of coastal states by rustic highlanders is offensive and counter-intuitive to scholars whose construction of the Andean past assumes that the rich, irrigated coast (the Europeanized, developed region of today) has always been the only progressive and civilized area, and has always clashed with the less productive and backward highlands (today, the stronghold of indigenous culture). Anti-Indian racism supports these feeling. Third, and closely related is a sense that seems to underlie some scholars' reactions to the Marxist construction of Huari—that it promotes the Maoist Shining Path guerrillas, also of Ayacucho origin. Thinking apparently runs as follows: attributing prehistoric military prowess to Ayacucho peasant soldiers, and ascribing to them the ability to conquer and control virtually all of Peru is a statement about Peru today. It must be predicting that Ayacucho peasant guerrillas of the Shining Path will destroy the modern government and rule in its place. Consequently, the possibility of Huari victories must be denied, even if the events being constructed occurred more than a millennium before the Shining Path, or its ideology, existed. Finally, and equally unattractive to oligarchic interests is the Ayacucho Marxist construction of "Huari" as an episode of violent, repressive government that spawned an opulent urban elite unable to reproduce itself, and destined to collapse in favor of classless, egalitarian organization.

Clearly, accounts of the past are not unbiased, scientific descriptions. They go beyond the data, that consist of counts and measurements of artifacts. They construct "meanings" that express values and goals conditioned by social, economic and political contexts. Pasts are constructed for reasons. Sometimes the reasons are very clear, like national identity, but sometimes the reasons are more opaque, like the value placed on technocratic government and its efficient administration of big, successful development programs. Only when we realize that much funding of archaeological research is in the hands of technocratic government agencies—and as in the case of recent investigations of Tiwanaku, development oriented agencies— do the political motives become apparent.

Because different pasts are constructed for different reasons, they are rarely comparable with one another. Tiwanaku is a concept constructed to promote nationalist origins and political unity. More recently it has become involved in the promotion of technocratic administration and high cost/big credit development programs. As such it emphasizes a privileged origin center responsible for cultural tradition, political integration, and the development and management of production. Huari is a concept constructed in critique of nationalism and political hierarchy, in favor of a class of oppressed highland Indians. It emphasizes revolt, the violence and oppression of hierarchical administration, and the inefficiency of big development schemes in favor of small producers. Finally it emphasizes the failure inherent in elite centers and state domination.

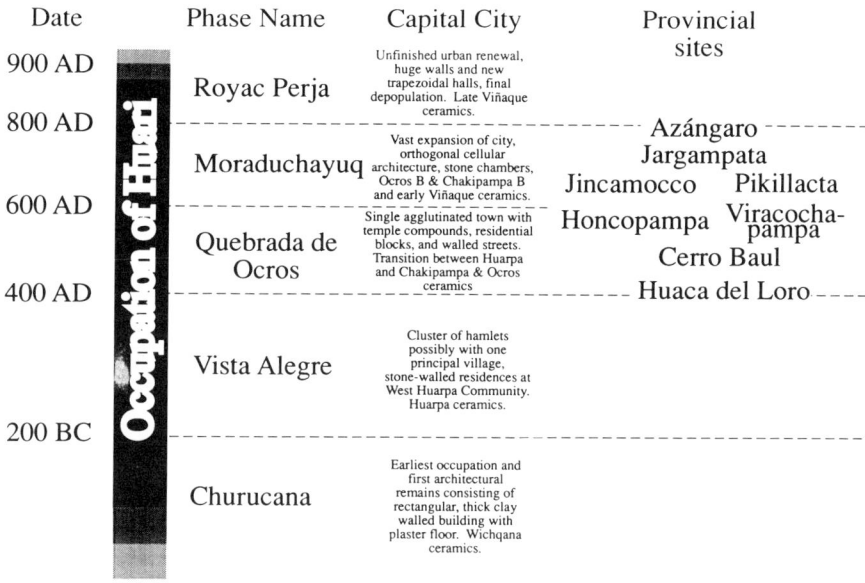

Figure 1. Huari chronological sequence.

In order to undertake meaningful comparison of different archaeological pasts we must throw off politicized images and reconstruct depoliticized pasts explicitly for the purpose of comparison. Richard Burger (1992) has had considerable success in his program to reinvestigate and effectively, to "reconstruct" Chavín. His initial effort to depoliticize this highly charged image centered on the creation of a relatively neutral chronology of absolute time, ceramic styles, and cultural conditions at Chavín de Huántar. He deliberately sought to eliminate nationalist meanings previously ascribed to Chavín. Something similar is needed for Huari, for Tiwanaku, and for other politically loaded pasts.

I will begin the task of creating a less politicized Huari past, and one that can more meaningfully be compared with depoliticized pasts of other cities, by seeking to construct a chronology of absolute time, ceramic styles, and cultural conditions for the type site. In contrast to the politicized past constructed for Huari—that views the site as constructed quickly by oppressed workers-Huari has a long, *in situ* history spanning more than 1500 years. I divide this into 5 phases (Figure 1). For each phase I construct a characterization of the city based on my evaluation of the archaeological findings of the Huari Urban Prehistory Project. I also try to consider some of the changes that probably took place during each phase. It is important to point out that the chronology I am presenting is for the Huari city. It was developed around architectural forms and superimpositions found at the site. I have sought to synchronize this essentially architectural sequence with the existing sequence of ceramic styles, focusing on the late Early Intermediate Period and Middle Horizon Epochs 1 and 2, that were developed primarily from the study of coastal Huari materials (Menzel 1964, 1966, 1977). My effort to test and refine Menzel's coast-based sequence at Huari itself went far (Brewster-Wray 1983, 1990; Cook 1983, 1987; Isbell 1977; Knobloch 1976, 1981, 1991; Wagner 1981), but unfortunately, this ceramic analysis is complex and guerrilla conflict in Ayacucho made it impossible to continue long enough to reach the level of understanding that I desire. Finally, I try to synchronize the Huari architectural and ceramic phases with (uncorrected) radiocarbon dates from Huari as well as other sites with related architecture and ceramics. This makes it necessary to briefly review information about the sites that have been considered Huari provincial administrative centers.

THE HUARI SITE

The ruins of Huari are located in Peru's central highlands (Figure 2), constructed on a ridge projecting from the east flank of the Huamanga Basin of the Ayacucho Valley Figure 3). An inventory of the standing walls and a survey of pottery sherds and other prehistoric trash littering the ground show that it may be the biggest archaeological zone in South America (see Figures 8 and 9 for the location and extent of the site). The remains of buildings cover some two and a half square kilometers, constituting what I call the "architectural core" (Figure 4) and lesser traces of masonry as well as pottery fragments spread over that much area again. Across much of another 10 km^2, ceramic sherds and other broken items discarded by prehistoric residents can be found where erosion has not reduced the surface to bedrock. Of course, Huari's 15 km^2 archaeological zone represents more than 1500 years of occupation, and at no time was all of it occupied simultaneously. Conservative techniques for estimating prehistoric population suggest 10,000 to 20,000 people in the city at its peak, and more liberal assumptions imply as many as 35,000 to 70,000 inhabitants (Isbell 1984, 1985, 1991b).

Division of Huari's 1500 years of occupation into phases can employ any number of criteria, but I have chosen to define the phases in terms of architectural changes documented in our limited archaeological record,

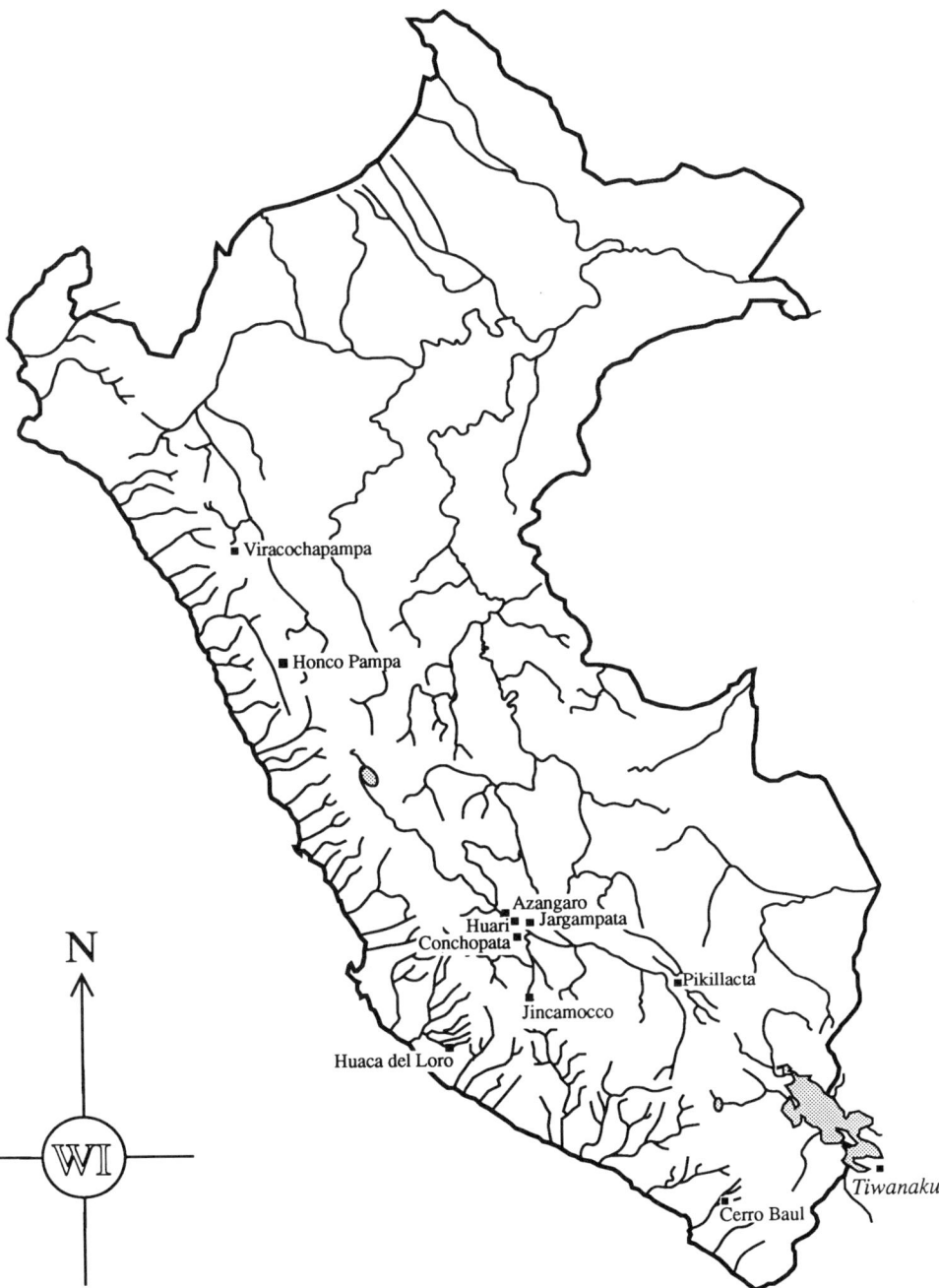

Figure 2. Huari and Huari sites.

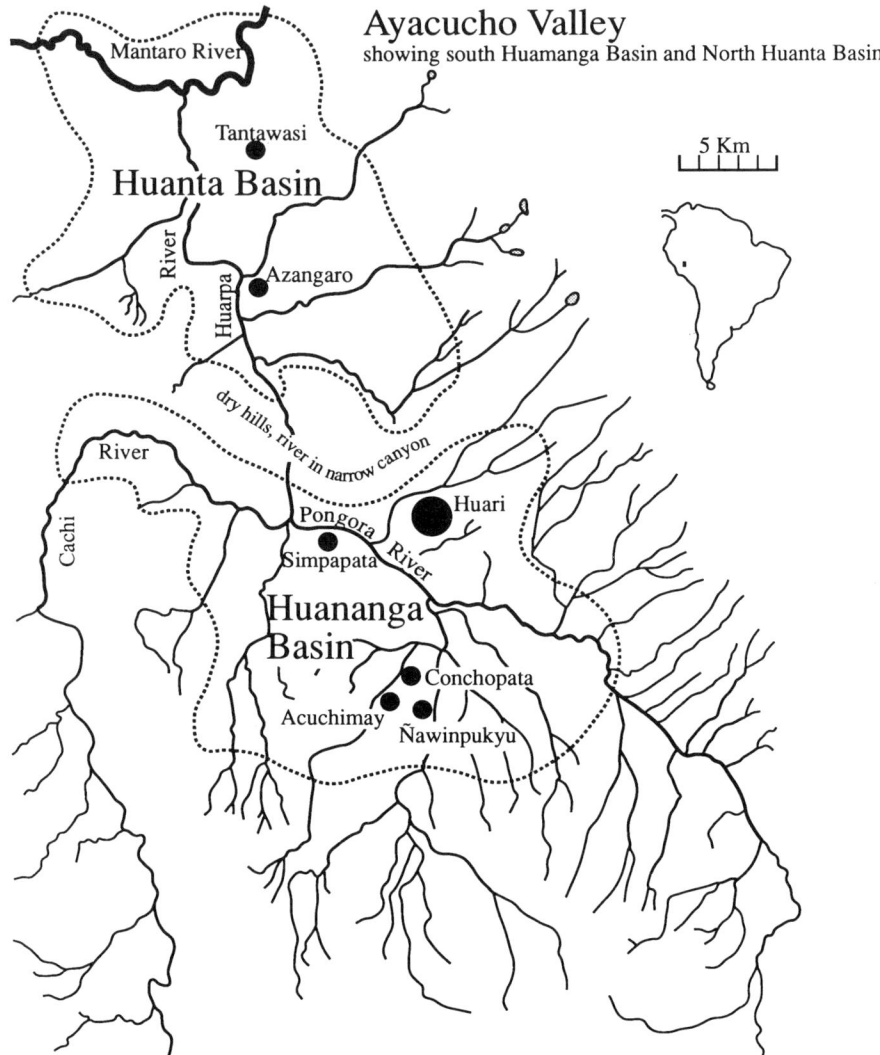

Figure 3. Ayacucho Valley showing south Huamanga Basin and north Huanta Basin.

and implied by formal variation recorded while mapping surface remains. I could name the phases Huari I, Huari II, Huari III, Huari IV, and Huari V to construct a past that promotes Huari as a long and independent tradition rather than the brief florescence followed by downfall emphasized by the Marxist scholars. This would also make Huari seem more comparable

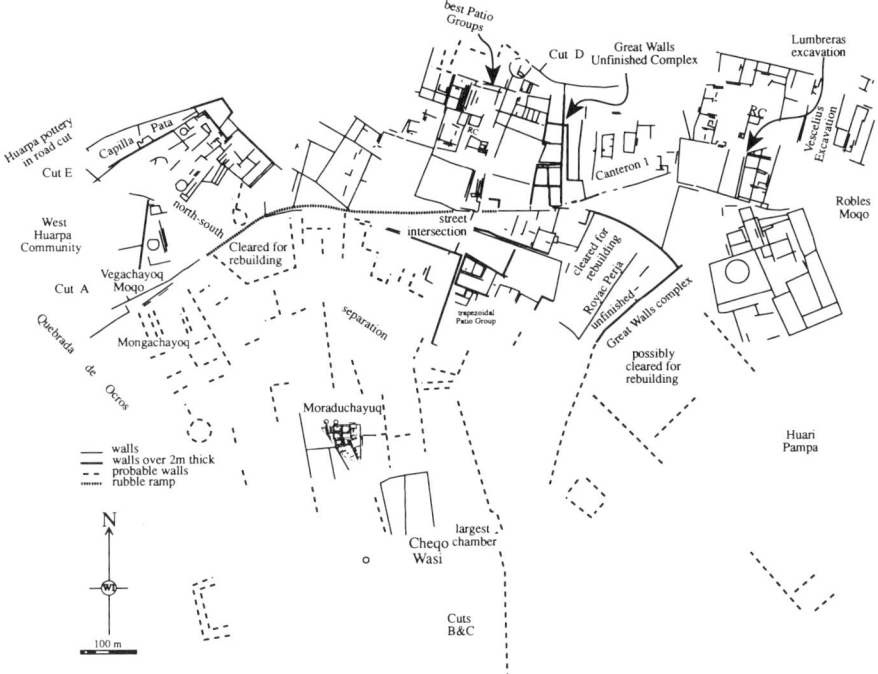

Figure 4. Huari architectural core.

to Tiwanaku. However, I want to follow Burger's lead at Chavín and tease apart monolithic constructions of the past, to ask different questions of different data sets, and to use different data sets in comparison with one another in order to construct richer and more interesting pasts. Like Burger, I will employ phase names that are neutral to avoid the creation of one big, assumption-laden concept. I will use the names Churucana, Vista Alegre, Quebrada de Ocros, Moraduchayuq, and Royac Perja, for the architectural/cultural phases at Huari (Figure 1).

Churucana Phase

Early Horizon (about 1200-200 B.C.)

The Huari city did not exist, but the zone was inhabited by people making Wichqana-like pottery. There was some permanent architecture where residential and/or ceremonial activities are indicated but information is very limited. The phase is named for the Churucana Hill at the east edge of Huari where we found a single construction, accompanied by some

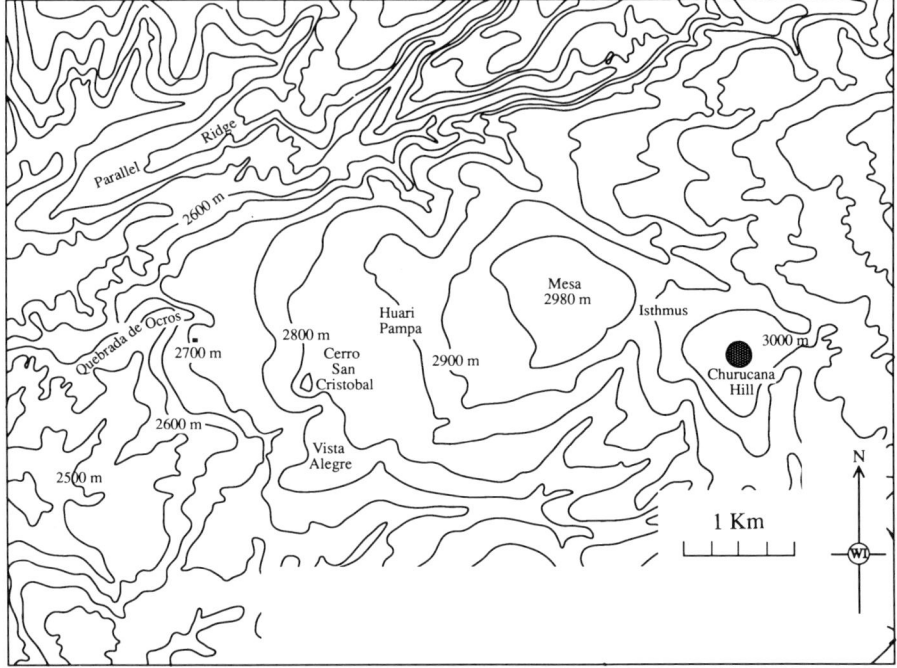

Figure 5. Huari archaeological zone. Churucana Phase occupation, 1200-200 B.C.

refuse that includes a small sample of sherds, at the bottom of a deep 2 × 2 m excavation pit. Figure 5 depicts my spatial construction of this occupation, although I have no real information about its spatial extent as there were no surface remains and we made only one excavation on the hill.

The Churucana building is a thick, clay walled structure with white plaster floor. The wall is about 50 cm thick, and straight, showing that the building was probably square or rectangular, but the full form and size were not revealed in the tiny exposure. The foundation, built on bedrock, consisted of large clay chunks, most likely reused pieces of an older wall. Pottery in and around the building relates to the local Wichqana style, part of the larger Chavín horizon of Peru's north and central coast, suggesting a date near the middle of the first millennium BC. Since no other remains of this period have been found in other excavations, and no more Early Horizon pottery has been collected on the surface it seems that during the Churucana Phase, occupation of the Huari zone was sparse. However, relatively sparse occupation is easily obliterated by later urban construction, and perhaps it is only because the Churucana Hill was not significantly

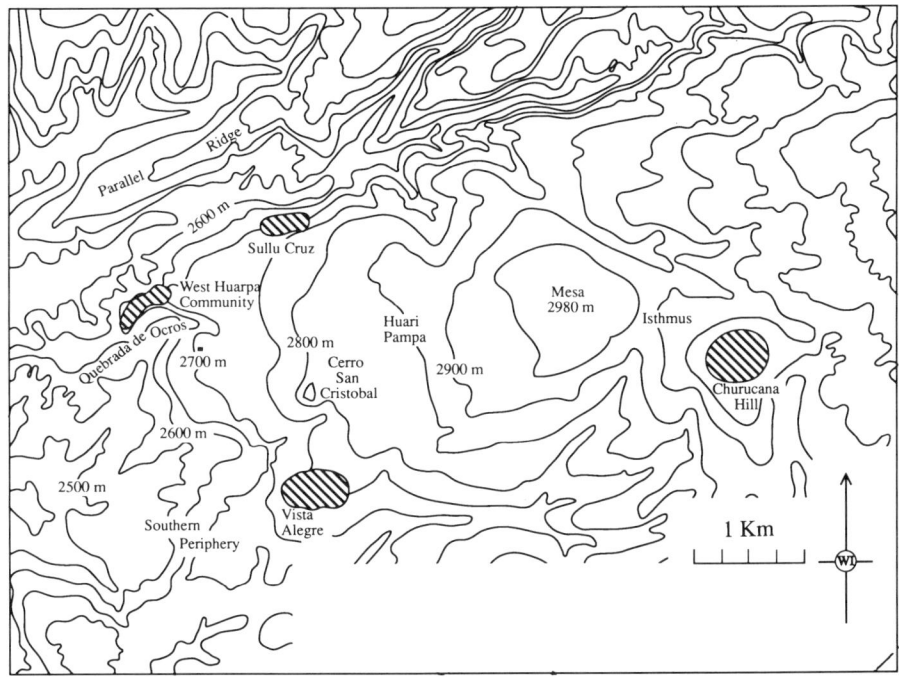

Figure 6. Huari archaeological zone. Vista Alegre occupation, 200 B.C.-A.D. 400.

occupied during the urban phases of Huari that Early Horizon architecture and refuse have survived.

Without more research it is impossible to determine whether the single Churucana Phase building was domestic, representing a rather massive and sophisticated residence, or perhaps public/ceremonial. The thickness of the wall and the white plaster floor suggest the latter, and possibly even some sort of ceremonial building relating to the wide spread tradition of prepared floors surrounding incinerators for ritual offerings that have been named after the archaeological site of Kotosh (Burger and Salazar Burger 1980; Terada 1985).

Vista Alegre Phase

Early Intermediate Period (about 200 B.C.-400 A.D.)

The Huari that I construct during the Vista Alegre Phase is illustrated in Figure 6. It consisted of several small settlements, probably farming hamlets located a couple of kilometers from one another, that interacted intensively. They probably shared water by cooperating in its distribution and constituted something of a local enclave. By the end of the phase (or early in the following phase), one of the hamlets was developing into a sizable village and the others were experiencing abandonment. I infer a long history of cooperation and competition among separate settlements, but eventual immigration into a principal community. New mechanisms of social and political integration must have been required to promote the coalescence of the entire population into one center.

The Vista Alegre Phase is named for a modern community of dispersed houses on the southeast edge of Huari. Much of the surface of the modern Vista Alegre community is littered with Huarpa-style pottery. The large area covered by this refuse may signal a big community, but it might also indicate a long occupation of dispersed huts, similar to today's settlement, and perhaps even the movement of houses about the site during several centuries of residence. There are no traces of architecture from the old Vista Alegre Community. Perhaps houses were of perishable materials, or stones from old walls have been reused, or cleared away for farming. The modern surface has been severely deflated by the wind and eroded by rain water. It is dry and barren, with little soil for dry farming. An irrigation canal does reach Vista Alegre, but the water it occasionally brings suffices only for drinking, and for watering the goats and sheep herded by its inhabitants among the ruins of Huari.

Stone buildings of the Vista Alegre phase have been found about 2 km to the northwest, on the steep edge of the Huari ridge above the Quebrada de Ocros. Modest stone walls are exposed in the road cut, often buried by three meters of later refuse. Toward the western edge of the half kilometer where these walls are found, charcoal was recovered from a buried trash pile containing black on white Huarpa pottery. It yielded a radiocarbon date of AD 285 ± 120. I consider this refuse and architecture to belong to a single Vista Alegre Phase settlement that I call the West Huarpa Community.

Vista Alegre Phase buildings of the West Huarpa Community have walls fashioned of rough stonework, consisting of irregular pieces of dark gray igneous rock, chunks of light colored tuff and rounded river cobbles, all apparently from the general area of construction. These stones were laid side by side in clay mortar to produce reasonably smooth walls, two or three stones thick, that average 40 cm in width. There is no evidence that the steep hill side was systematically terraced by the people of this West Huarpa Community before constructing their buildings and while the rooms are more or less rectangular, walls seem to have been oriented according to convenience. Rooms are frequently composed of unbonded sides or wall segments and they give the appearance of having been constructed in a series of small additions, one room added to the side of another. There is no evidence for streets, block organization, or an urban grid. At least some of the walls are plastered with clay. Floors are primarily of tamped earth, although a few are coated with white plaster. Stone-lined cysts and smaller clay-lined pits were occasionally placed beneath the floors. Stone-lined canals exist, although it is not clear whether they were subterranean or on the surface. The foundations of the buildings rest on bedrock. The road cut shows the West Huarpa Community to have been at least half a kilometer long but its full size is obscured by later refuse.

Sherds of Huarpa-style pottery have been found in abundance at two other locations within the Huari archaeological zone. One is at the extreme east of the archaeological zone, on the Churucana hill, where slightly more than 2 m of strata containing Huarpa pottery occur above the Churucana Phase building. The second find of Huarpa pottery came in a deep excavation on Huari's steep north slope (Bennett 1953; Menzel 1964), more or less in the Sullu Cruz region, where it is buried by more than a meter or Middle Horizon refuse. Consequently, I construct a Churucana Community and a Sullu Cruz Community, in addition to the Old Vista Alegre Community and the West Huarpa Community. The Churucana sherd scatter is extensive and often dense, suggesting a big settlement. On the other hand, the Sullu Cruz settlement size can only be guessed at. Architectural remains have not been found associated with the Huarpa pottery in either Churucana or Sullu Cruz.

Only two of the four Vista Alegre Phase, Huarpa pottery using communities were detectable from surface remains. The other two came to light as a result of excavations. This leads me to believe that there may be more Vista Alegre Phase communities yet to find, and a history and chronology for them is critical for understanding the rise of Huari. What is apparent is that during the Vista Alegre Phase a number of settlements, probably farming hamlets and villages separated from one another by no more than two or three kilometers, were all located within the area that was to become the city of Huari. Today all the communities in the archaeological zone, as well as settlements immediately above and below the zone share limited and interconnected water sources and constitute something of an irrigation community. I suspect that similar pottery, short distances between hamlets, common concerns for water, and the geomorphological configurations of the Huari ridge all mean that the Vista Alegre communities interacted a great deal, and were probably mutually interdependent. What brought them together into a single settlement?

The evidence now available indicates that the West Huarpa Community was sizable, and probably a dense agglutination of permanent, stone buildings. Was it unique in its stone architecture? Was it the largest of the communities? Was it in some way the nucleus of the cluster? If it was a

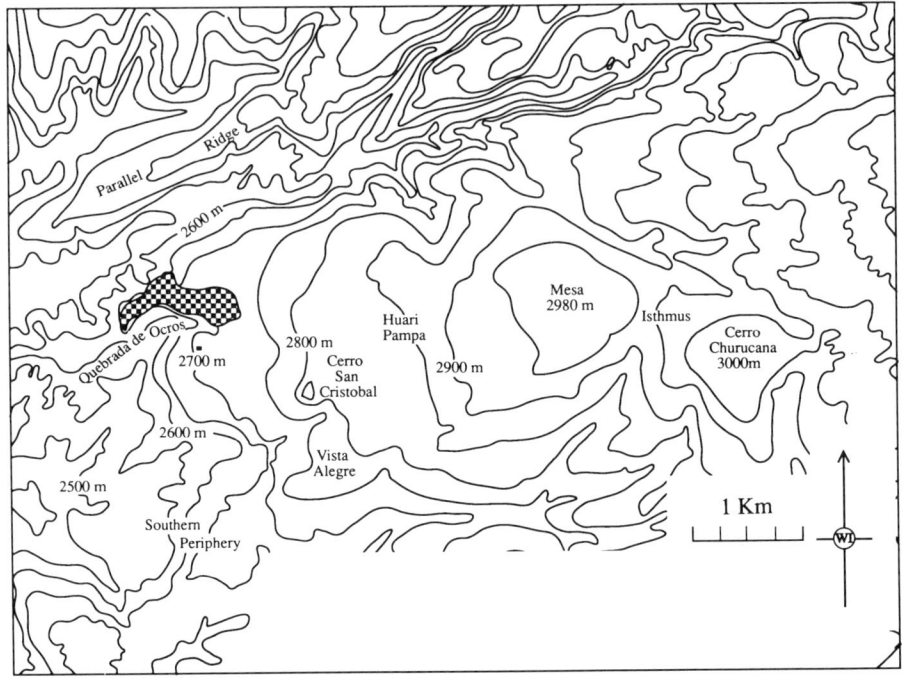

Figure 7. Huari archaeological zone. Quebrada de Ocros occupation, A.D. 400-600.

center, how was this centrality created, and reproduced socially, spatially and architecturally? What kinds of social groups resided in the communities, and how did life change during more than half a millennium of occupation within the Huari archaeological zone? Some of the answers to these questions may be implied by the importance and prominence of large ceremonial monuments in the succeeding Quebrada de Ocros phase. Somehow, the West Huarpa Community was growing into a core settlement around which Huari was to develop.

Quebrada de Ocros Phase

Terminal Early Intermediate–Middle Horizon 1A (A.D. 400–600)

Quebrada de Ocros Phase Huari appears to have begun with the abandonment of all the Vista Alegre settlements except for the West Huarpa Community (Figure 7). The timing and dynamics of this requires more study, but the West Huarpa Community became the proto-city of Huari and for the first time we can speak of Huari. I infer that the proto-city grew by attracting the inhabitants of the former settlements into the growing core. However this was achieved, the process probably continued beyond the bounds of the local cluster, affecting first the communities of the southern Ayacucho Valley, and subsequently the entire valley.

The southern Huamanga Basin site of Conchopata seems to have experienced a similar history (Figure 3) (see Lumbreras 1974, 1981). It was also located on the edge of a steep-sided canyon, at the center of a cluster of settlements. Like Huari it experienced considerable growth that seems to relate to the abandonment of its neighboring hamlets, and more or less at the same time built new temples and engaged in impressive ceremonial activities. Conchopata was probably a competitor of Huari during Quebrada de Ocros time, one that eventually lost to Huari for it was depopulated in the succeeding Moraduchayuq Phase, when Huari's growth seems so phenomenal that it must have involved massive immigration.

During the Quebrada de Ocros Phase, the West Huarpa Community grew at least half a kilometer to the east of its former extension and ceremonial architecture became a prominent feature of the emerging city. I suspect that temples played key roles in building new social relations required for urban residence, and perhaps they were mechanisms for attracting followers to resettle from communities of origin into the growing city.

The phase name "Quebrada de Ocros" comes from to a long dry canyon, or *quebrada*, that cuts a deep gash into the southeast edge of Huari. It furnishes the easiest ascent from the river bottom to the ridge top, and even today contains a foot trail communicating with the upper lip of the valley to the east. Chronicler Cieza de León reported visiting the ruins of Huari, probably following the Inca road before the Ayacucho Valley highway was shifted to accommodate the new location of the colonial town of Huamanga. I suspect that the old road either passed through the Quebrada de Ocros itself, or that the Quebrada was an important western branch of a north-south route located slightly higher on the valley side. At any rate I believe that this communication route gained importance in this phase when Huari's regional influence was expanding. It is no accident that early urban growth was along the north side of the narrow canyon, the steeper side where defense would be easy without removing the population from the important thoroughfare.

The Quebrada de Ocros Phase probably began in the fifth century, or perhaps a bit earlier, when Huarpa ceramic decoration was being transformed by the progressive addition of new decorative colors as well as new designs that included both abstract shapes and highly idealized representational figures. The coastal Nazca style probably had some role in this change (Menzel 1964; Paulsen 1983). The eventual outcome was the Ocros and Chakipampa styles. Tentatively, I would include Middle Horizon 1A, with its Ocros A and Chakipampa A pottery in the Quebrada de Ocros Phase, and assign Epoch 1B to the succeeding Moraduchayuq Phase, suggesting that the Quebrada de Ocros Phase ended by the beginning of the 7th century.

The place called Moraduchayuq is located about half a km to the east of the original West Huarpa Community (Figures 4 and 10). Excavations reveal late Quebrada de Ocros Phase buildings, apparently the first constructions at this part of the site. There are straight wall segments indicating rectangular rooms but also some circular buildings. This is the first documentation of circular structures in the Huari study sample but since circular and oval buildings occur on other Ayacucho Valley settlements where Huarpa pottery is found, the form must have greater antiquity. On the other hand, important technological innovations are documented that were lacking in the West Huarpa Community of Vista Alegre times.

Walls are much thicker, in one case, 80 cm thick. Foundation trenches were excavated into bedrock, and walls were constructed as two carefully assembled stone faces with a clay and rubble core between. This technology implies much more durable and probably taller walls. I suspect that the foundations represent tower-like structures as well as buildings with several floor levels.

Red or pink plaster was used on one of the circular towers. Traces of white plaster are found on other buildings.

The existence of rectangular structures alongside of circular buildings implies that building form was diversifying, creating differentiated and specialized activity areas within the emerging urban settlement. Indeed, refuse from one of the circular buildings, the one that may have been white, indicates a workshop where exotic raw materials were transformed into ornaments.

When the circular buildings were constructed at Moraduchayuq, a natural hole in the ground, at least 25 m across, was located only a few meters to their south. An impressive sunken court of cut stone was built inside this hole. This building is square, about 24 m on each side, and its orientation between 4° and 5° west of magnetic north is so close to true north that careful astronomical observations must have been required.

Sunken courtyards, sometimes called semisubterranean temples, are especially associated with the Tiwanaku cultural sphere of the south *altiplano*. However, they are also an old and popular form for Andean religious buildings with a long and broadly diffused history. The sunken courtyard form integrates inside and outside space, permitting a view of both from a high position, in a way impossible for any other volume-based architecture. I believe that the sunken court at Moraduchayuq was a temple.

When first constructed the sunken court had walls at least 3.8 meters high of perfectly fitted polygonal stone blocks. The blocks were bonded into a fill of large fieldstones and clay behind the wall, filling the area between it and the edge of the hole. The construction of the court must have occurred fairly late in the Quebrada de Ocros phase, for charcoal from the fill associated with the initial construction yielded the date of AD 560 ± 60.

The sunken court, or semisubterranean temple at Moraduchayuq was contained within a walled compound. The eastern perimeter wall, with the same north-south orientation as the temple, is preserved 20 m from the edge of the sunken, polygonal block court. This compound perimeter consists of two massive walls about 1.5 m apart, forming a narrow street. I suspect that enclosed compounds surrounded by walled streets originated at Huari in the Quebrada de Ocros Phase with the construction of temples, whose sacred precincts had to be separated from surrounding profane space. The ideas were new in the early 6th century but they became standard for subsequent architectural forms, both sacred and secular.

The Quebrada de Ocros Phase temple was renewed frequently by the addition of new floors, one on top of the other. The first floor was of white plaster laid only a few cm above the base of the polygonal block wall. Later, fills and new floors were added. A very well preserved white plaster floor was identified 1.43 m above the foundation. A third was detected 1.6 m above the base of the wall. This floor was paved with similar plaster but it had been painted red. Charcoal from the fill between the 1.43 m and 1.6 m floor indicates that the remodeling associated with the red floor can be dated about AD 720 ± 60, implying that the final transformations of the Semisubterranean Temple took place during the subsequent Moraduchayuq Phase.

Traces of red paint were identified on some of the cut stone blocks from the temple walls and it seems likely that at the beginning of the 8th century the semisubterranean temple was painted red. Since one of the circular buildings a few meters north of the temple also had traces of red paint it may have been part of the semisubterranean temple complex.

Another walled compound that was certainly a temple is located at Vegachayoq Moqo, closer to the old West Huarpa Community than Moraduchayuq (Figure 4) (Bragayrac 1991). It too was enclosed by large perimeter walls, including a walled street bordering the compound on the south side. Unlike the semisubterranean temple compound where walls were neatly parallel and perpendicular to one another, the Vegachayoq Mogo complex consists of a deep trapezoidal court flanked on the east by a series of high terraces, and even the walls of the bordering street are not parallel to one another. In the trapezoidal depression is a large, thick walled, "D"-shaped building with a doorway in the flattened, northern side. Large niches line the inner wall of the "D" and great quantities of ash suggest ceremonial burning.

In terms of urban architectural development, the irregularity of Vegachayoq Moqo suggests an early date in the history of the city. Furthermore, one of Vegachayoq Moqo's upper terraces has a retaining wall with megalithic cut stone ashlars, stonework of the same general type as the cut stone blocks of Moraduchayuq's semisubterranean temple. Finally, pottery in a trash pile on the floor of Vegachayoq Moqo's courtyard, between the "D"-shaped building and the eastern terraces, contains Chakipampa B pottery, contemporary with ceramics overlying the Moraduchayuq temple. I doubt that this trash accumulated until the temple was in decline, suggesting construction and use in Middle Horizon 1A or earlier times.

Adjacent to Vegachayoq Moqo, and between it and Moraduchayuq is another architectural complex with megalithic cut stone construction. Named Mongachayoq, and now severely looted, it too was probably enclosed by a compound wall (Figure 4). There is a helter-skelter of shaped stones but the best preserved buildings are two long halls with rough stone walls and massive cut stone roofs. When recorded in 1977, one of the halls had small rough stone walls dividing it into segments, and it contained great numbers of human bones.

Sector A is a triangular zone with a group of buildings within the Moraduchayuq area that was partially exposed while archaeologists were seeking to completely define at least one Huari compound. I now believe that it belongs to a separate architectural group that was nearly destroyed by the highway that traverses Huari. Most importantly, Sector A is transitional in time and form between Quebrada de Ocros and the Moraduchayuq Phases.

Sector A is nestled against the south side of the walled street that defined the Moraduchayuq semisubterranean temple, where it was built long after the temple was in service. Like the earlier architecture of the West Huarpa Community, it is composed of unbonded segments of rough stone walls. Unlike the West Huarpa Community, its walls are relatively thick, have two faces with clay and rubble cores, and all the walls are more or less parallel and perpendicular to one another—except for the walled street that predates the complex. Another feature that differentiates Sector A from the West Huarpa Community is a narrow walled street that borders the complex on the north.

I doubt that unbonded wall segments are temporal markers in Huari architecture. Rather, they are part of a system of construction based on a low rate of labor input over a long time. Large, integrated complexes with bonded walls were produced by high labor investment over a short time. This bonded architecture required activity differentiation, including supervisors who planned and oversaw the construction. At the risk of oversimplifying, integrated architectural complexes represent community projects while rooms of unbonded wall segments represent domestic efforts.

Segmented buildings show that Sector A was not a community undertaking but it was nonetheless an architectural block bounded on the east and north by parallel walled streets. On the basis of Ocros B and Chakipampa B ceramic associations, I believe that Sector A was constructed about A.D. 700, in radiocarbon time. Its interpretation is confused by the fact that its bigger rooms contained large pits under the floors, mostly circular but some rectangular, that were generally capped by megalithic stone lids. They contained luxury artifacts, as well as human bones, and included large quantities of fine pottery. The subfloor pits or cysts were all looted, and vast numbers of sherds from fine ceramics were scattered about the rooms. We suspect that these ceramics were broken when deposited in the cysts, representing some sort of ritual activity, but the looting has confused the context and made it almost impossible to securely identify domestic activities and refuse in these rooms. Domestic trash in one of the small rooms of Sector A suggests both ritual and residential functions for the compound.

Sector A does seem to show that compound organization, based on the earlier temple compounds, was reorganizing domestic architecture within the metropolis. A city block, defined by walled streets, and containing more or less consistently oriented buildings was appearing. By this time a continuous urban core was developing that included walls and streets that might be called an urban grid. I suspect that immigrant populations were filling in areas between temple complexes by constructing new enclosures.

Moraduchayuq Phase

Middle Horizon 1B, 2A, and Early 2B (A.D. 700-900)

The semisubterranean temple at Moraduchayuq received its final remodelings early in the Moraduchayuq Phase. A new floor of cut stone blocks was laid 40 cm above the old red floor and the walls of the temple were refinished by grinding them smooth. Finally, a coating of plaster and several layers of clay were placed over the cut stone block floor. Soon the temple was leveled to make way for a completely new building. It is not clear whether several clay layers represent different kinds of floors or

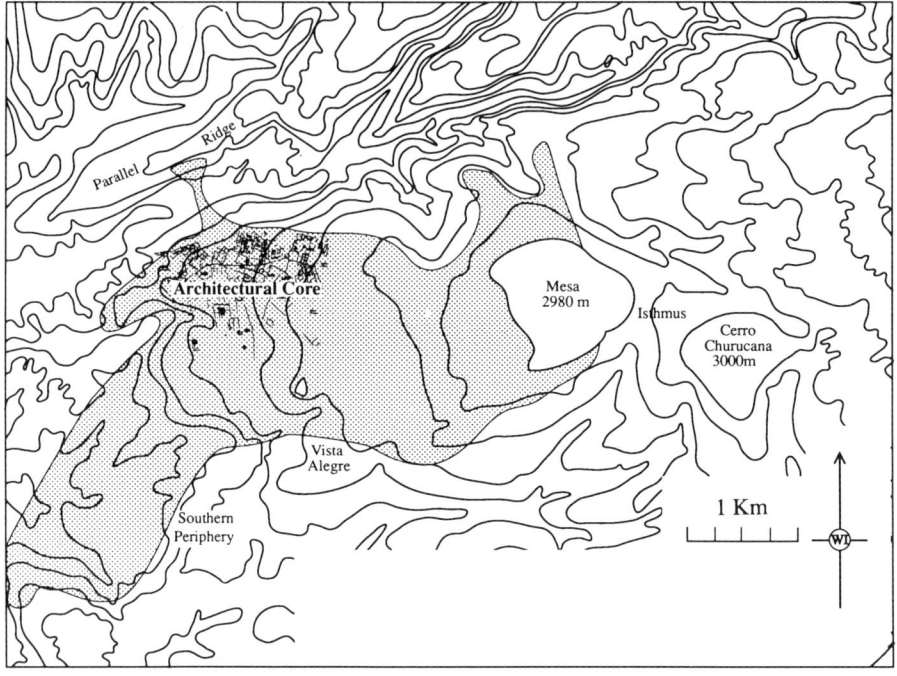

Figure 8. Huari archaeological zone. Moraduchayuq occupation, A.D. 600-800.

whether they were intended to seal the sacred building before reusing the site, but the fact that the clays were clean shows that they were placed there deliberately, and there was no dumping of trash into the semisubterranean temple during a period of abandonment. Clearly, a strong tradition of remodeling and rebuilding existed at Huari, and periodic renewal of ceremonial buildings may have been expected.

The new building form at Moraduchayuq represents a new Huari architecture (Figure 11) diagnostic of a successful and aggressive city devoting vast amounts of labor to enlarging a monumental architectural core, and expanding its residential area to unprecedented size. The civic core of big stone buildings was extended, especially to the north of the old Quebrada de Ocros community (see Figure 4). Residential area increased greatly. Surface sherd scatter, sometimes very dense, sometimes very sparse, extends far to the east, to the south and to the southwest of the expanded architectural core (Figure 8). Unfortunately coarse ware pottery characteristic of most of the peripheral scatters is not temporally sensitive, so it is possible that some of the occupation began, or continued into the succeeding and subsequent phase, but it is clear that the Moraduchayuq

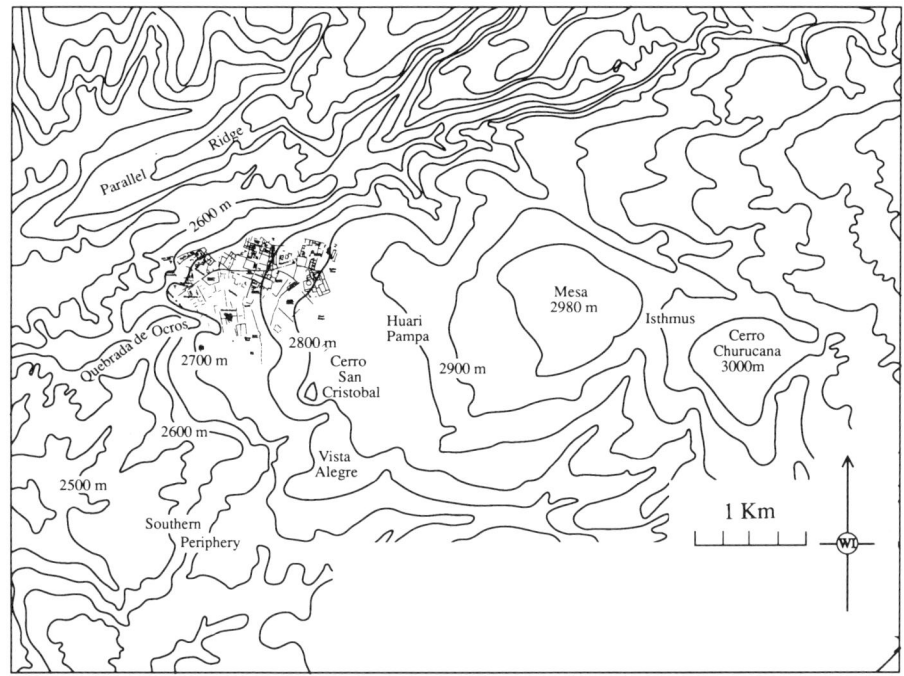

Figure 9. Huari archaeological zone. Royac Perja occupation, A.D. 800-900.

Phase was a time of great growth at Huari, reaching a size that was indeed impressive.

The new architectural style probably relates to Quebrada de Ocros Phase urban planning experiences in the capital, as well as to interactions with north highlanders, especially the peoples of Huamachuco and the Callejón de Huaylas where a long and vibrant tradition of stone architecture flourished (J. Topic 1991; T. Topic 1991; Topic and Topic 1985; Isbell 1989, 1991a). Most significantly, I believe that the newly popular Moraduchayuq Phase buildings were initially realized in provincial architecture by an emerging military elite that was experimenting with the control of soldiers and the administration of new territories on the frontier of an expanding state. Presented with the requirement of constructing forts, garrisons, and/or administrative centers on untouched ground, and having a vast surplus of labor at hand, Huari's field commanders let their imaginations run wild, and designed incredibly rigid orthogonal cellular compounds.

Diagnostic Moraduchayuq Phase architecture, based on the Moraduchayuq sector of Huari as well as provincial sites, is characterized by

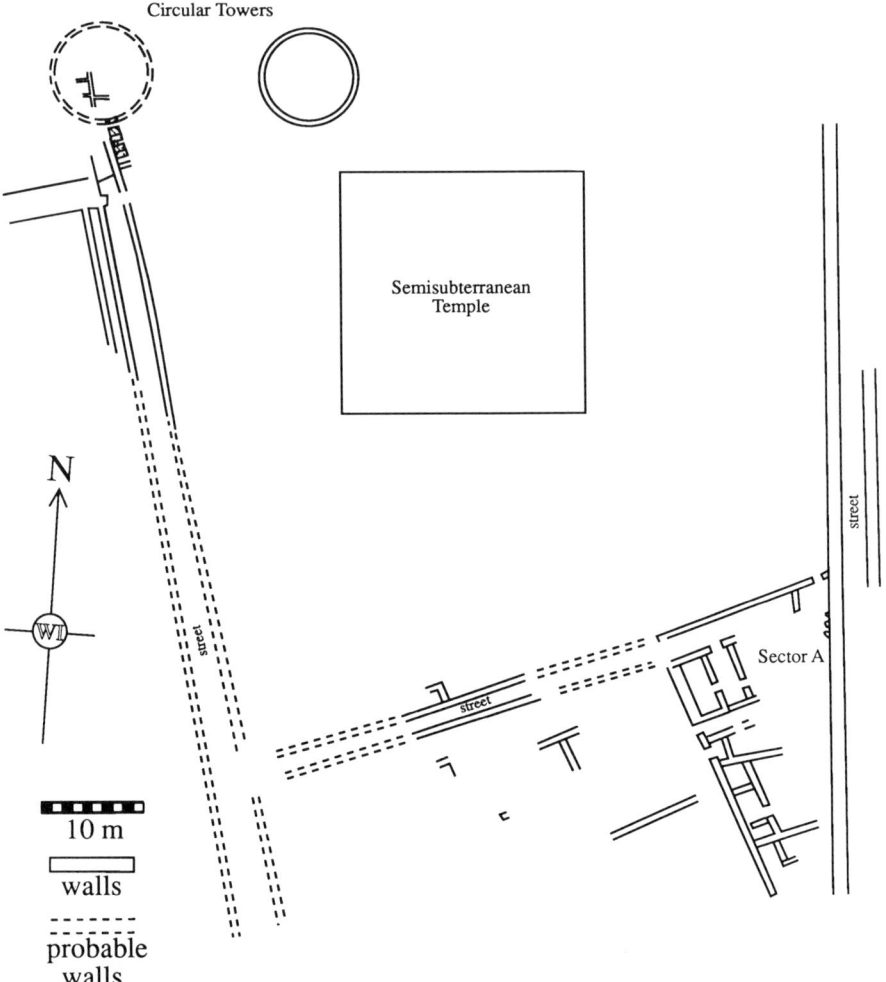

Figure 10. Moraduchayuq compound. Quebrada de Ocros Phase architecture.

compound enclosures composed of parallel and perpendicular walls (Figure 11). The basic unit or cell is a square or rectangular enclosure that created an open patio in which other buildings could be constructed. Most popular was to construct elongated halls around three or four sides of the patio, with low benches along the front of each of the halls. These patio units could be repeated side by side to construct a giant enclosure, but in fact the Huari architects built the giant enclosure first and then divided it

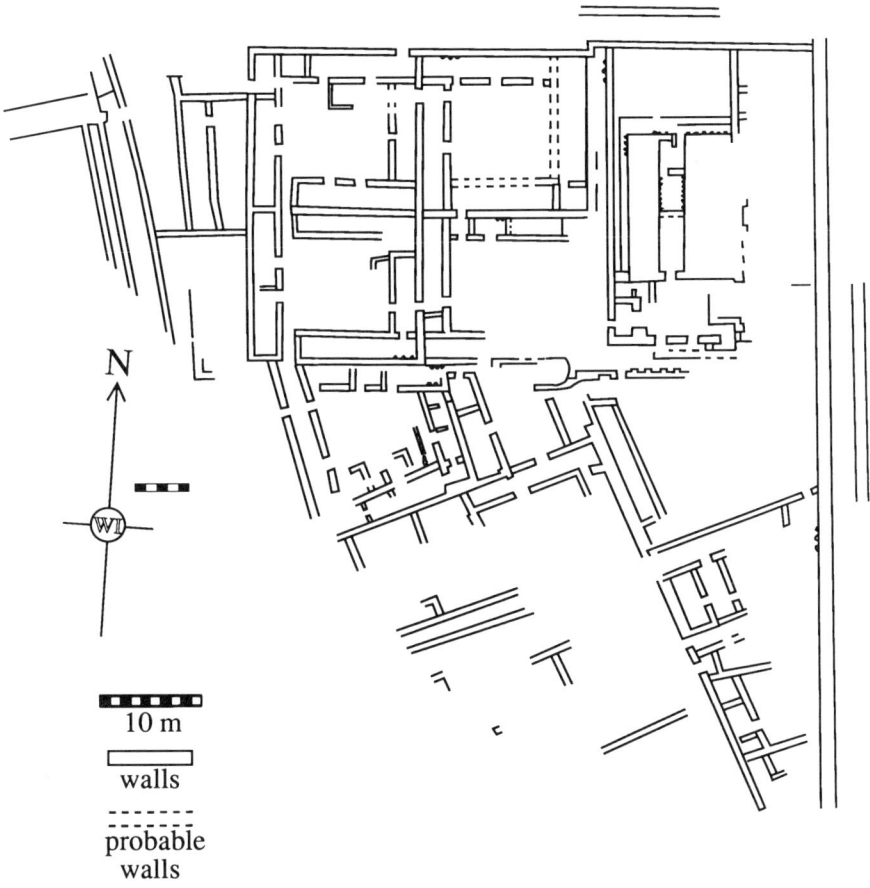

Figure 11. Moraduchayuq compound. Moraduchayuq Phase architecture.

into the patio cells. The dominant idea seems to have been the unity of a whole that could be subdivided into equivalent parts, not the construction of an assemblage from independent but similar components.

The semisubterranean temple at Moraduchayuq was abandoned and leveled shortly after A.D. 700, sometime in Middle Horizon 1B according to ceramic associations. A new architectural complex was built that was a self-contained, walled compound with only a few entrances. It was divided into interior units that replicate one another, almost like the modular units of a modern apartment building. Construction followed a hierarchical sequence, beginning with the perimeter walls, then the walls that define major interior patios, and then walls that created long lateral rooms along the edges of each patio, and finally some subdivisions in the lateral rooms. Where it was not necessary to accommodate to irregularly shaped space, the building is strictly orthogonal—parallel and perpendicular walls. This orthogonal character, and the regularity of the modular units of which each building inspired the name "orthogonal cellular architecture style."

The orthogonal cellular architecture of the Moraduchayuq Phase Moraduchayuq Compound has a walled street on its east and south sides, and probably another on the north. It was built in two construction epochs. The first, the northern part of the compound, overlies the destroyed semisubterranean temple, and some walls of the compound used the megalithic temple as foundation. The square semisubterranean temple surely served as a template for the rigid orthogonal orientation of the rough stone walls of the early Moraduchayuq Compound, but I doubt that this played a deterministic role in architectural evolution for the trend toward orthogonality was already well established in Huari's provincial architecture, as we shall see below. The second epoch of construction is trapezoidal in outline. Apparently, it was accommodated to the trapezoidal space that remained between the early Compound and Sector A.

The early and late parts of the Moraduchayuq Compound are divided into the same kind of modular units, the patio group. The ideal patio group is a square or slightly rectangular enclosure with a patio of the same shape at its center. The patio is surrounded on all four sides by long, narrow rooms called lateral halls. In turn, lateral halls may be divided into smaller rooms. Entrances into the lateral halls are from the central patio. A stone faced terrace of earth, or bench, rings the patio, providing a raised porch in front of each lateral hall. In the Moraduchayuq compound the lateral halls have a row of corbels on the inside walls about 2 m above the floors showing that they were two (or possibly more) stories tall. The lateral halls were apparently roofed, and I suspect that the roof covered the benches as well, providing a protected but well lighted work place. Direct communication between lateral halls of a single patio group is fairly rare, but there is usually a door between the lateral halls of adjacent patio groups. In fact, these doors between lateral halls of adjacent patio groups are often the only apparent means of entering the patio group at the level of the ground floor. In other cases patio groups connect to one another by a corridor created by leaving a gap at the end of the wall between two patio groups and making the lateral halls next to that wall less than the full length of the patio side.

The patio group is an excellent module for highly compact, rigidly orthogonal urban architecture. It was easy to lay out and build, there was no wasted space, and it was general enough to meet diverse needs. There is also open area for future additions, and small rooms were built in several of Moraduchayuq's patio groups. But what was life in such a compound like? How was human waste disposed of? Where did children play? Did residents wander from one compound to another, and if so, what of privacy, and how did one avoid getting lost? Or did residents live out much of their lives in one tiny patio-world?

At Moraduchayuq it is clear that patio group architecture was not a casual decision, but one carefully planned. With one patio group built next to another, roofs had to drain rain water into the patios themselves. Excavations indicate that each patio has a drain in its floor connected to an underground canal. Apparently the raised bench around the edge of the patio protected lateral halls from water while furnishing a convenient work area. Since drainage canals were incorporated into the foundations, they had to be part of the original plan for the Moraduchayuq Compound, being built first. This shows that Huari architects were already well experienced with orthogonal cellular patio group architecture by the early eighth century.

In the Moraduchayuq compound there were at least 6 and possibly as many as 9 patio groups. All are of similar size and form, and differences seem to have resulted form the irregular area bordering Sector A. Only the architecture of the eastern part of the Moraduchayuq Compound lacks patio groups, although even here there are elongated halls divided into smaller rooms, and rows of corbels for second floors. It appears that the eastern part of the Moraduchayuq Compound contained some sort of platform. However, it is in especially poor condition and more research will be required to determine its age, form and functions.

Formal repetition in the patio groups of the Moraduchayuq Compound suggests that they served similar rather than different functions. That is, rather than the Moraduchayuq Compound having been a building where different activities were carried out in different spaces, like a palace, industrial complex, or temple community, the Moraduchayuq Compound was like an apartment building or office building with more or less identical suites of rooms intended for more or less identical activities. This inference is born out by similar trash from one patio group to another, including comparable relative frequencies of ceramic vessel shapes.

While all the patio groups seem to have served similar functions, there is a suggestion of differentiation among lateral halls within a patio group. Several lateral halls lacked distinguishing features while others contained built in furnishings of stone and clay, a hearth area, and clay lined pits below a plaster floor. More research will be required to prove that the variation is not a produce of preservation, and to refine a typology but I suspect that each patio group contained several types of lateral halls and that the types reoccur throughout the patio groups.

Trash excavated in the patio groups is the product of daily life, including food preparation and consumption. Consequently the Moraduchayuq Compound patio groups were residential, being occupied by domestic social units. Some of the shallow pits under the plaster floors of the lateral halls contained caches of luxury goods indicating that the residents were permanent, not transients who could have made off with the valuables, although severely looted, luxury goods—including fine pottery, *Spondylus* shell ornaments, lapis lazuli beads, and other exotic materials—are common enough to suggest that the residents of Moraduchayuq Compound were comfortable, if not rich. Animal bones show that only choice cuts of meat were brought into the compound, the animals having apparently been butchered elsewhere. Stone flakes are consistent with the resharpening of tools, not with their manufacture. No *agricultural* implements or weapons were found in residential strata. Few weaving tools were identified. While it is possible that the residents were engaged in productive activities in other buildings within the city, the relative frequency of ceramic vessel shapes reveals the possibility of a different kind of activity. Serving bowls (and/or cups) are unusually common in comparison with food preparation and storage vessels. This reveals a disproportionately large amount of serving food and drink—community dining or feasting. While a restaurant or inn would produce the disproportionately large number of serving vessels, one would also expect some very large food preparation vessels, not adequately represented at Moraduchayuq. Consequently, much of the food and drink served at Moraduchayuq seems to have been prepared elsewhere.

The Moraduchayuq Compound residents were permanent, well off, and not apparently engaged in farming, fighting, or craft production. They lived in buildings constructed with corporate labor and they served a great deal of food and drink apparently prepared elsewhere. Who were they? I believe that they were middle level administrators of a growing state government. It is well known that in the Inca state, and indeed in other archaic states and chiefdoms, community leaders were obliged to confirm their authority by conspicuous displays of generosity usually involving feasts and drinking boughts. While the Moraduchayuq residents probably prepared food and drink for their own consumption, what they served to retainers was prepared elsewhere, perhaps by other servants of the central government, and perhaps from state stores.

While no other examples of orthogonal cellular architecture have been excavated at Huari, standing ruins on the north side have the characteristic parallel and perpendicular wall patterns. In fact, there is so much orthogonal cellular architecture that there must have been a major phase of construction at Huari while this architecture was popular. The confusion of architecture along a rough line through the middle of Huari may reveal a demarcation between an area of orthogonal cellular urban expansion and the older, less planned city bordering the Quebrada de Ocros canyon, where Moraduchayuq is located, that developed around more or less independent ceremonial compounds.

Several lines of evidence suggest that Huari's Moraduchayuq Phase orthogonal cellular patio group architecture is best dated to the two centuries between A.D. 600 and 800, although it almost certainly endured longer in some places. First, it bases itself on innovations that occurred during the Quebrada de Ocros Phase, temple compound stage of architectural development, from double-faced and rubble-filled walls to grid organization based on walled compounds surrounded by streets. Second, at Moraduchayuq, orthogonal cellular architecture overlies the semisubterranean temple compound and a radiocarbon date of A.D. 720 ± 60. Third, trash in the Moraduchayuq Compound patio groups includes pottery of the Chakipampa B and Ocros B styles that belong to the last part of Middle Horizon 1B, and also Vinaque pottery of Middle Horizon 2A and 2B. Finally, my small excavation in the northern half of Huari, where orthogonal cellular architecture abounds, revealed Ocros B and Chakipampa B pottery in occupation layers immediately overlying bedrock, and Vinaque pottery in strata above.

Following the construction of the orthogonal cellular patio group architecture, the Moraduchayuq Compound experienced heavy occupation, minor modifications, and finally gradual disoccupation until, along with the rest of Huari, it was abandoned, probably about the beginning of the 10th century. But that occurred in another, albeit short, phase I call Royac Perja.

Before going on to the final phase of Huari's existence as a capital city I want to mention the Cheqo Wasi area of the site, excavated by Mario Benavides (1991). Cheqo Wasi is southeast of Moraduchayuq, and separated from it by a rectangular compound consistent with Moraduchayuq Phase orthogonal cellular architecture. In fact, Chego Wasi lies in a hollow at the head of the Quebrada de Ocros, and the modern trail that ascends the canyon passes a few meters north of the complex. It may be that it was deliberately constructed at the head of the early road, perhaps even by filling and leveling, to give it locational importance in the early portion of the city almost entirely occupied by old temples and residential compounds.

The Cheqo Wasi complex includes a number of dressed stone chambers, crypt-like megalithic stone chambers that were originally wholly or partially underground. Some contain two or even three levels. Most are surrounded by rough stone walls organized into rectangular enclosures with more or less orthogonal orientations, but not patio groups. Groups of 5 chambers occur within some enclosures, and one such group is enclosed by a "D"-shaped building with a doorway in the flattened side, similar to that of the Vegachayoq Moqo temple. The Cheqo Wasi complex may have been enclosed by a perimeter wall, or perhaps it consisted of several large compounds.

Cheqo Wasi is now terribly looted but the chambers obviously contained luxury goods and human remains. The destruction has created a jumble of everything, confusing interpretations and preventing secure dating. However, the majority of the ceramics described by Benavides (1984, 1991) appears to belong to the Vinaque and the Ocros B and Chakipampa B styles. In view of the orthogonality of the walls, I suggest that Cheqo Wasi was in use during the Moraduchayuq Phase of Huari's history. It probably represents some sort of high status burial complex, perhaps replacing or supplementing tunnel-like, communal tombs of the Quebrada de Ocros phase found at Mongachayuq, and the ridded, under floor cysts like those of Sector A.

Royac Perja Phase

Late Middle Horizon 2B and Early Middle Horizon 3 (A.D. 800-900)

Before Huari was abandoned another major phase of construction was begun, but this was less an effort at expanding the city than one of remodeling, or of urban renewal according to a new ideal. This final construction episode is revealed by its being unfinished (see Figures 9 and 4). Areas were cleared of architecture but nothing was built on them. A huge cache of building stone crosses the site, and some giant walls disappear without a trace, implying that they were still under construction. Some big building complexes also appear unfinished, albeit complete in outline, and these are not inconsistent with orthogonal cellular canons. I call this the Royac Perja Phase after a named sector on Wendell Bennett's (1953:19) map of Huari, that is empty of constructions, even though it is located near the middle of Huari.

As with orthogonal cellular architecture, the focus of Royac Perja Phase construction was the north half of the Huari city. Several areas in the core were cleared of architecture. A long pile of stone and rubble, probably a cache of construction materials that may also have served as a causeway for transporting workmen and materials within the heavily built up urban area, dominates the city plan as we see it today. This feature would surely have been removed had Huari continued to prosper.

The most prominent Royac Perja architecture was neither orthogonal nor cellular. Patio groups, with narrow lateral halls and rows of corbels for upper floors seem to have been discarded all together. The new buildings were very large. Their unusually thick and high walls are slightly curved, and form elongated compounds intended to be trapezoidal and irregular. The lack of repetitive cellular forms so basic to the Moraduchayuq Phase suggests not only new architectural canons, but the triumph of new forms of sociopolitical organization. The unfinished trapezoidal buildings appear to be limited to the northern side of Huari, and southern Huari, the old city may have been little affected. Unfortunately, the ceramics of late Huari are not easily differentiated from earlier Epoch 2 Middle Horizon pottery, making it at present impossible to describe the spatial contraction of the city. However, if the Moraduchayuq compound is a meaningful indicator, the Royac Perja Phase did not last long and the city was soon experiencing depopulation. At Moraduchayuq, occupied patio groups were those closest to doorways through the exterior perimeter wall. Inner patio groups were being used for dumping trash so I infer that they were no longer seriously occupied. Since the late residents preferred housing close to compound doorways, it seems unlikely that they lived in fear of military attack.

PROVINCIAL HUARI ARCHITECTURE

I doubt that orthogonal cellular architecture originated in the Huari metropole. Rather, it developed in the administered periphery where a rising military elite was supreme. It came from field campaigns, established itself in provincial administrative centers first, and eventually overcame the metropole.

The earliest Huari provincial center may be Huaca del Loro in the Nazca Valley of Peru's south coast. Clearly, the distinctive Nazca pottery of this site is stylistically and iconographically mixed with features of Huari's Huarpa and early Ocros and Chakipampa ceramics (Paulsen 1983). There are no radiocarbon dates for Huaca del Loro but these stylistic relationships suggest that the occupation was contemporary with the transformation of Huari's West Huarpa Community, by the early temple compounds and therefore probably early to middle Quebrada de Ocros Phase in the architectural chronology, dating around A.D. 400 and 500.

The architecture of Huaca del Loro consists of a thick-walled circular building surrounded by concentric rooms. Its identification as a temple was based more on ceremonial artifacts than on building form. While Schreiber (1989) has found circular buildings to have existed in Nazca before the construction of Huaca del Loro, we know that thick-walled circular and "D"-shaped buildings were being constructed at Huari as parts of temple compounds during the Quebrada de Ocros Phase.

Farther south on Peru's coast is the Moquegua Valley and the fortress of Cerro Baúl (Moseley *et al.* 1991). The archaeological record indicates that during most of its history, this Valley was allied, culturally and perhaps politically, with Tiwanaku, a great highland city at the southern end of Lake Titicaca. Huari made a successful military intrusion into the Valley early in the Middle Horizon, an intrusion that must have been very violent for all the earlier architectural monuments were reduced to rubble. This implies a policy of dramatic reprisalsú against any who would resist Huari expansion, not unlike policies of the later Inca state. Huari commanders also built a fortress capital on the flat-topped mountain called Cerro Baúl.

Ceramics show that Huari activities in the Moquegua Valley continued into Epoch 2 of the Middle Horizon, but began earlier (Knobloch 1991), perhaps during Middle Horizon 1A, in late Quebrada de Ocros Phase times, between A.D. 500 and 600. Cerro Baúl's architecture includes circular buildings, and has numerous walled rectangular complexes with perpendicular walls and elongated rooms around central areas. But the walled compounds are not one single and consistently oriented unit across the 700 x 150 m area of mountain top and nothing that is a true patio group has been identified. Cerro Baúl's buildings do not appear to be fully blown orthogonal cellular architecture, but they represent a clear step in that direction. Perhaps Cerro Baúl is close in form and organization to Sector A at Moraduchayuq, representing the end of the Quebrada de Ocros Phase. However, it was this sort of building experience that created orthogonal cellular architecture.

Honcopampa is another important center, but located in the north highlands. It helps reveal Huari's expansionist strategy. Cerro Baúl represents an advance against Tiwanaku, probably the largest competitive highland capital in Huari's world of the late sixth century. After Tiwanaku, there can be little doubt that Marca Huamachuco was Huari's next largest potential rival. Honcopampa is located in the Callejón de Huaylas, one basin south of the Huamachuco Valley, and its inhabitants were culturally if not politically allied with Marca Huamachuco. The architecture of Honcopampa is not true orthogonal cellular in form either (Isbell 1989, 1991a, 1991b). But many of the buildings are orthogonal, there are obvious patio groups, and some parts of the site were probably constructed as large units to be subsequently divided. On the other hand, other buildings are obviously independent compounds abutted against one another. There are two "D"-shaped buildings.

Huari-style pottery is too scarce at Honcopampa to do more than confirm its presence, but if "D"-shaped buildings appeared in the Quebrada de Ocros phase, and orthogonal cellular architecture in the Moraduchayuq Phase, Honcopampa lies at the boundary between the two. Radiocarbon dates for Honcopampa confirm the probability that construction was initiated by or slightly before AD 600, and continued at least through 700 AD, the early part of the Moraduchayuq Phase.

In addition to Huaca del Loro and the two proto-orthogonal cellular sites, at least five orthogonal cellular sites are known outside Huari. They define what I am calling the Orthogonal Cellular Architecture Horizon (Isbell 1991b). Radiocarbon dates place the horizon between AD 550 and 900. I believe that this shows that orthogonal cellular architecture had its origin in provincial locations far from the capital, where it was under way by the end of the Quebrada de Ocros Phase and very early Moraduchayuq Phase. The three orthogonal cellular provincial centers relate to the same strategy observable in the locations selected for the proto-orthogonal cellular installations, intrusion into the south coast, and aggressive defense toward Tiwanaku in the south, and Huamachuco in the north. I suspect that Huari military leaders were aware that simultaneous and coordinated action by the northern and the southern power blocks could have very serious consequences, rather like Germany with its position between the Russians and the Franco-British during the First and Second World Wars. Significantly, the latest orthogonal cellular complexes are the ones in the Huari urban hinterland, and I suspect the ones at Huari probably represent a late Moraduchayuq Phase expansive reconstruction of the city. I infer the rise of a military elite, with profound power, first in battlefield and provincial contexts, but progressively their power of command and of wealth extended back to the capital until they replaced the old elite who had emerged in relation to the temple compounds constructed during Quebrada de Ocros times.

Jincamocco is 150 km south of Huari, in the Carhuarazo Valley (Schreiber 1978, 1987a, 1987b, 1991, 1992), on an important Middle Horizon road that connected Huari with the Nazca Valley. Measuring approximately 136 × 260 m, the walled compound was vacant in the north but the southern portion is divided into cells of patio groups and modified patio groups. There is some architecture of unbonded wall segments in the northern part of the enclosure as well as outside the perimeter wall. Katharina Schreiber (1991) has revealed the impact of Huari's administrators on local culture by showing how economics and settlement throughout the Carhuarazo Valley were transformed following the construction of the walled compound. Vinaque pottery is common at Jincamocco, although late Ocros and Chakipampa styles occur and radiocarbon affirms construction and occupation between A.D. 600 and 800 beginning very early in the Moraduchayuq Phase.

The largest provincial center of the Orthogonal Cellular Architecture Horizon is Pikillacta, 300 km from Huari and 20 km south of modern Cuzco (McEwan 1985, 1991). This archaeological complex consists of many constructions spread over much of the Lucre Basin, including defensive walls, roads, terraces and seemingly vacant enclosures, but the principal orthogonal cellular compound alone is approximately 745 × 630 m. Patio groups, and variations on the patio group form with lateral rooms that have corbels for second floors, are the most common cellular units. There are parallel walled streets, walled areas lacking interior constructions, and several areas filled with parallel rows of small, conjoined rooms. Ceramic refuse includes Ocros B and Chakipampa B as well as Vinaque style pottery. Radiocarbon dates suggest that some construction may have been underway before A.D. 600, but most building and occupation occurred between 600 and 800, beginning very early in the Moraduchayuq Phase (Knobloch 1991).

Pikillacta is close to the boundary between the distributions of Huari style objects and those in the Tiwanaku style (Rowe 1956). Along with Cerro Baúl it surely contributed to Huari's strong military posture along a southern frontier with Tiwanaku.

Viracochapampa is located 750 km north of Huari, in the Huamachuco Valley and within sight of the local capital of Marca Huamachuco (Topic and Topic 1985; J. Topic 1991). The great enclosure measures approximately 570 m square, and is part of a complex of structures that includes a north-south road, a canal, and other buildings. A parallel walled street passes through Viracochapampa, and it has patio groups and lateral rooms with rows of corbels.

Viracochapampa implies a Huari militarily intrusion into the Huamachuco Valley, but Canadian archaeologists John and Theresa Topic have shown that construction of the great compound was never completed. This may demonstrate that Huari did not consolidate power after initial incursion, but more probably, unlike the relatively static and fortified frontier established with Tiwanaku in the south, Huari's northern frontier involved alliances and leap-frogged forward from one highland valley to the next with little resistance. Small orthogonal cellular compounds at Ichabamba and Yamobamba, in the Cajamarca Valley 75 km north of Huamachuco (Williams and Pineda 1985), probably took over frontier functions for which Viracochapampa had been intended, but without the garrison potential so emphasized at Pikillacta.

The fact that Viracochapampa was never completed means that it has little or no occupation that can be dated. Huari-style pottery has not been found and two radiocarbon dates appear to come from an earlier and a later occupation rather than workmen involved in construction. On the basis of the archaeological chronology for the Huamachuco Valley, that includes a local ceramic sequence as well as numerous radiocarbon dates, Theresa and John Topic (Topic and Topic 1985; J. Topic 1991) propose that the construction of Viracochapampa dates between AD 500 and 700. If correct, the building began in late Quebrada de Ocros times, and this may be the earliest of the Huari's orthogonal cellular provincial centers. Clearly, more research is needed in and around Huamachuco for I suspect that Huari's relations with the north highlands shaped much of its subsequent architecture, administration, and religious ideology.

The orthogonal cellular centers close to Huari, that I take to be something similar to the rural estates of Inca kings, are Azángaro and Jargampata. Radiocarbon dates for both suggest that they were not established before the beginning of A.D. 700, contemporary with the late Moraduchayuq Phase in the metropole.

Azángaro is located in the Ayacucho Valley itself, 17 km to the north of Huari (Anders 1991). It is a walled rectangular compound 447 × 175 m divided into 3 large sections. The northern section includes patio groups, modified patio groups, several vacant rectangles and a walled street. The central section contains a walled street down the middle, with 20 rows of small, conjoined rooms on each side accessible only via streets branching at right angles from the medial one. The southern section contains irregularly distributed rooms of short, unbonded wall segments reminiscent of the architecture from Moraduchayuq's Sector A. Some Chakipampa B and Ocros B but considerable Vinaque-style pottery support radiocarbon dates between A.D. 700 and 950 for the construction and occupation of Azángaro, placing it in the late Moraduchayuq to Royac Perja Phases.

The next closest Orthogonal Cellular complex is Jargampata, located in the San Miguel Valley only 20 km to the east of Huari (Isbell 1977). It consists of a square enclosure 25 × 25 m, to which a rectangle 25 × 15 m was added later. The square is a modified patio group, with lateral rooms along the north and south sides of its patio but a distinct room complex on the west. The east side was vacant. A bench rings the patio, and rows of corbels for second floors were used in the room complex on the west side of the patio. Outside the compound a short distance to the south is a domestic residential complex with rooms composed of short unbonded wall segments, like Sector A at Moraduchayuq, and the south section of Azángaro.

Primarily Vinaque sherds and radiocarbon dates in the 700's imply late Moraduchayuq Phase construction, although occupation may have continued for there is a date in the twelfth century from the uppermost occupation stratum. Like the Moraduchayuq Compound, the square enclosure at Jargampata has been shown to have a higher frequency of serving vessels than expected in domestic trash. In fact, it was the first Huari compound for which administrative activities were inferred on the basis of such ceramic evidence for feasting (Isbell 1977, 1978).

CONCLUSION

Huari's architectural chronology reveals the development of the city in a less politicized fashion, and one in which we can begin to recognize Huari people acting in their prehistoric context, responding to pressures and desires with innovative solutions that fostered change. We witness a sparse occupation on a valley-side ridge growing into a cluster of neighboring communities that interacted with one another. This cluster of hamlets or villages surely shared common origins and interests, as well as competitive desires and traditions of independence. Temple compounds seem to have been instrumental innovations in the transformation of the West Huarpa Community into Huari, and from a village within the cluster of communities into an urban center and state capital. The diversity of the village cluster was perhaps represented by multiple temple compounds but architectural order grew around them, contributing to the formation of a consistent whole. I infer a fragmented society with an emerging theocratic leadership that was striving to create ideological unity as well as spatial unity and boundedness. Curiously, we do not see individual elites, either in the art or the architecture. Is this due to sample error or to Huari's true situation? Religious iconography seems to have been simplified and standardized, as documented by Cook (1987), and architectural changes seem to have been in the direction of unity and interchangability, to the degree of individual anonymity.

Orthogonal cellular architecture of the Moraduchayuq Phase reveals that the social whole was viewed as a precondition of existence, and subordination of the parts was clearly stated. It is apparent that the orthogonal cellular compound was conceptualized, and constructed, as a rigidly bounded unit that was then subdivided in terms of a sequence mandated by strict hierarchy. Orthogonal form and order were imposed upon the environment as well as the occupants, overpowering variation with repetition and exclusion. From the outside the orthogonal cellular city must have looked like a solid block. Its doorways were small and (as indicated by Pikillacta and Viracochapampa) approaching avenues were probably walled. Internally the complex was orderly, subordinated to the grand plan, homogeneous, and extremely disciplined. Walled streets and small doorways emphasized static closure rather than transformation or flow. Cellular subdivisions are repetitive and undifferentiated modules focused internally on their own patios. Hierarchy and centrality are emphasized only in the order of the form and plan, for there is an obvious lack of central public space designed for assembly and ritual.

These final features of orthogonal cellular architecture are surprising. While the temple compounds of the Quebrada de Ocros phase are certainly more enclosed and internally focused than the ceremonial complexes of some of Peru's prehistoric centers, they were organized around a central court appropriate for public ritual. De-emphasis of a central public area, in favor of repetitive units with their own patios leaves little opportunity for theocrats to construct power in theatrical public ritual and for that reason I doubt that patio group architecture expresses the needs of theocratic administrators. Rather, I believe that Huari's orthogonal cellular architecture was conceived by military commanders turned architects and administrators, whose power was based on repetitive regimentation and strong nationalist ideology rather than public performance. Designers of orthogonal cellular architecture were stating the priority of a rigid social order, the composition of the community in homogeneous and replicated units, and the subordination of individualism and variation.

The architectural chronology for Huari, and the Orthogonal Cellular Architecture Horizon document the growth of a metropolitan capital and its imposition of control in provincial territories far from the heartland. But power and interest groups within Huari have been revealed as well. Temple compounds of the Quebrada de Ocros Phase correspond with early development of ceremonial power, and a group of priestly administrators, in the capital. At almost the same time, military campaigns at the frontiers encouraged the emergence of a military elite with a different power base, different ideology and interests, and its own administrative architecture. The shift from the Quebrada de Ocros to the Moraduchayuq Phase in the capital records the marginalization of ceremonial interests and the ascension of a military elite. Soon this new elite set about rebuilding the city in its own image. The megalithic chambers I have tentatively placed in the Moraduchayuq phase are especially interesting in this light. If I am correct that they represent elite tombs, they seem to contradict orthogonal cellular architecture, expressing individuality and difference. Chamber tombs associated with offering rituals seem to glorify prominent ancestors and to distinguish descendants as separate and non-interchangeable kin groups.

The Royac Perja Phase clearly represents a different interest group, and one that seems to have deliberately rejected the orthogonal cellular buildings of the military elite in favor of huge, irregular compounds and great walls dividing the city into sections. Far too little is known of this phase, but the great compounds may have based themselves in archaizing return to the past, although they seem not to have the same religious functions. They look more like palaces, or some kind of aristocratic family halls, and some of the huge walls may have defined walled quarters of the city occupied by localized kin organizations. At any rate, it seems likely that the orthogonal cellular attempt to obliterate variability gave way to a new tolerance, perhaps even promotion, of difference. Separation of architectural cells was maintained but their equivalence and subordination to a general plan were not. The unity of the Huari state expressed in orthogonal cellular architecture was fragmenting into smaller and repetitive power centers. But the late attempt to rebuild Huari in a new image failed. Many of the buildings remained incomplete and the city's prosperity came to an end. Within a few decades the metropole was abandoned.

POSTSCRIPT

I have constructed an alternative past for Huari. I use the term "construct" because all pasts are socially constructed. But I have deemphasized the context of social critique within which much of the earlier construction of the Huari past took place, and I have sought to present prehistoric people as actors within a cultural context of their own. I admit to having been creative in my interpretation of the limited archaeological data. For example, I have placed settlements of unknown size on maps, I have inferred street patterns from unfortunately incomplete architectural data, I have inferred that different architectural forms preserved at the surface probably represent different building phases, and I have inferred that vacant areas of the city in combination with partial buildings and caches of stones represent an unfinished construction phase. These bold decisions have been made because the opportunity for ongoing research have been curtailed, because the inferences are consistent with the data as I know them, and because my interpretation provides a plausible account that can establish constructive dialogue with the negaters of Huari as well as the investigators of other early cities, whether Tiwanaku, Teotihuacan, or Uruk.

I hope to see an era in Andean archaeology when archaeologists and others can discuss and evaluate alternative pasts, recognizing that the contexts in which the alternative pasts have been constructed, and the contexts in which they will perform, are different. We need not insist on only one past, or perhaps more correctly, on a single "right" past. But we must also remember that while alternative pasts are intended to perform in different arenas, we as archaeologists should not accept or reject them on the basis of how well they promote or fail to promote our theoretical and political convictions. They should be evaluated in terms of "fit" with the actual archaeological record. And we must take care to recognize the political and theoretical biases underlying particular pasts, not allowing any single construct to overtake, dominate, and control investigation of the archaeological record, as well as the questions we ask of the archaeological record. If one past is allowed to eclipse all alternative pasts because it conforms with politico-economic needs and if this past becomes the "true" past, we may find ourselves constructing the archaeological *record* in terms of this "true" past, rather than the reverse.

APPENDIX: OUTLINE OF ARCHITECTURAL CHANGES AT HUARI, BY PHASE

Churucana Phase Architecture

Technical

- A. *Thick, straight wall of puddled adobe or tapia.*
- B. The base of the wall is a double line of clay lumps placed on bedrock, and covered with clay plaster.
- C. *Floor of layers of white lime plaster* covering a fill of clay lumps and trash placed on bedrock.

Formal

- A. A rather massive *rectangular or square building* of sonably large size is implied.

Organizational/Conceptual

- A. Orientation was not to cardinal directions.

Inferences

- A. This structure was *probably ceremonial* in nature and may have resembled clay buildings of Early Huacaloma in Cajamarca. *Occupation of the Huari ridge was probably sparse.*

Vista Alegre Phase Architecture

Technical

- A. *Rough stone walls about 40-cm thick* appear not to have been battered. Construction employs field stones and river cobbles set in clay to create a homogeneous and well bonded unit.

B. *Rooms are small and generally composed of unbonded sides or wall segments* that give the impression of having been constructed in a series of small additions.
C. There is no evidence for deep foundations, or for terracing the surface before constructing walls and rooms.
D. Floors are primarily of tamped earth, although a few are coated with white plaster.
E. Stone lined cysts and possibly clay lined pits were occasionally placed beneath the floors.
F. Stone lined canals exist, although it is not clear whether they were subterranean or at the surface.
G. Some walls are plastered with clay.

Formal

A. *Agglutinated rooms with straight walls and angular corners.* (No doorways were observed.)
B. Walls are oriented between the cardinal directions, although orientation seems to have been a matter of convenience.

Organizational/Conceptual

A. *Heavily built up residential area of durable housing that appears to have developed through progressive additions.*

Inferences

A. This was a high density residential area appearing to *lack an explicit urban grid, well defined streets,* or clearly established formal building categories.

Quebrada de Ocros Phase Architecture

Technical

A. *Thick walls*, sometimes measuring almost a meter, *with well fitted faces of rough stone and a clay and rubble core. Foundations were laid in trenches cut into bedrock.* In addition to *white lime plaster, pink or red plaster* is indicated. Plaster was used on floors but also to cover rough stone walls.
B. *Polygonal, dressed stone masonry* walls and floors. Dressed stone constructions may have been painted red. Notches and grooves are

found in some dressed stone blocks. Tenoned projections were used in dressed stone walls.
C. *Stone lined, subterranean canal systems,* sometimes with capped shafts to floors of rooms and streets.
D. Steps in floors of rooms, and in corridors, forming stairs between occupation levels.
E. Wall niches.
F. Doorways with well constructed, vertical jambs.

Formal

A. *Round buildings,* perhaps evenly spaced in a line.
B. *Deep, sunken court or semisubterranean temple of square outline, oriented to astronomical north.*
C. *Agglutinated, interconnected, rectangular rooms with consistent orientations.*
D. *Streets formed by long, high, parallel walls.* They tend to isolate architectural blocks with limited access.
E. Stone walled and plastered cysts with megalithic lids under floors. Often the lids have one or two circular holes. Cyst lids were covered by floor plaster.

Organizational/Conceptual

A. Superimposed floors and probable renewal of buildings. Possible ritual interment of architecture.
B. Monumental constructions.
C. *Ceremonial compounds.*
D. *Formal urban grid* making appearance.

Inferences

A. Several ceremonial compounds were constructed on the east side of the old population nucleus, along the Quebrada de Ocros. Ceremonial buildings, especially compounds, were the source of architectural innovation. Construction between ceremonial compounds was creating a city with explicit urban grid.
A. Tall, possibly multi-storied constructions.
B. *"D" shaped buildings were popular.*
E. Vegachayoq Moqo and Mongachayoq date to this time.

Moraduchayuq Phase Architecture

Technical

   A. *Construction of bonded complexes in a sequence that appears to express a functional hierarchy among the walls.*
   B. *Rows of stone corbels for upper floor supports.*
   C. Low benches surrounding patio areas.
   D. Small, lined "burial" cysts and unlined cache cavities under floors.
   E. Construction of thin walls with little or no foundation rooms and patios to individualize space. (This may date to Royac Perja Phase.)

Formal

   A. *Rigidly orthogonal layout.*
   B. *High walled, rectangular compounds that were internally subdivided. They had strictly limited access and internal circulation controlled by walled streets and doorways.*
   C. *Patio group complexes.*
   D. *Long narrow rooms with several stories.*
   E. Mound in an isolated section of an enclosure.

Organizational/Conceptual

   A. *Orthogonal cellular architecture composed of large rectangular enclosures subdivided into modular, cell-like units.*
   B. Emphasis on order, repetition and comparability in form and spatial arrangement. Spatial organization seems to minimize hierarchy, to the point of avoiding the use of floor level to state relevant difference.
   C. *Deliberate destruction of older buildings and their replacement by new buildings.*

Inferences

   A. Major phase of urban renewal at Huari. This may have involved ritual interment of some buildings.
   B. Orthogonal cellular construction focused on the north side of the city, creating an old and new section of the city.
   C. Thick walled rooms with niches and rounded corners.
   D. Provincial architecture may be the inspiration for innovation in this phase.
   E. Megalithic chambers of Cheqo Wasi date to this time. Significant new emphasis on burial of elites.

Royac Perja Phase Architecture

Technical

A. *Very large and massive walls that often are not straight.*
B. Small niches scattered randomly about a wall.

Formal

A. *Use of trapezoidal and irregular building plans.* Avoidance of orthogonal layout, patio groups, lateral rooms, rows of corbels, and other features of orthogonal cellular architecture.

Organizational/Conceptual

A. *Very large complexes that avoid repetition and duplication.* Space seems to be highly individualized and possibly hierarchical.

Inferences

A. The new buildings are extremely large, but unfinished. Several areas, especially along the dividing line between the old and new city, seem to have been cleared of architecture but no new building was constructed.
B. A great rubble ramp that was probably a temporary facility for moving construction materials was abandoned in place.

REFERENCES

Arnold, D. E., 1975, Ceramic Ecology of the Ayacucho Basin, Peru: Implications for Prehistory, *Current Anthropology* 16, 2:183-205.

Bawden, G., and G. W. Conrad, 1982, *The Andean Heritage: An Exhibition at The Peabody Museum,* Harvard University, Peabody Museum, Cambridge.

Benavides, M., 1964, Estudio de la cerámica decorada de Qonchopata, B. A. Thesis in Anthropology, Universidad Nacional San Cristóbal de Huamanga, Ayacucho, Peru.

Benavides, M., 1984, *Carácter del Estado Wari,* Universidad Nacional de San Cristóbal de Huamanga, Ayacucho.

Benavides, M., 1991, Cheqo Wasi, Huari, in: *Huari Administrative Structure: Prehistoric Monumental Architecture and State Government* (W. H. Isbell and G. McEwan, eds.), Dumbarton Oaks Research Library and Collection, Washington D.C., pp. 55-70.

Bennett, W. C., 1944, *The North Highlands of Peru: Excavations in the Callejón de Huaylas and at Chavin de Huántar,* Anthropological Papers 39, 1, American Museum of Natural History, New York.

Bennett, W. C., 1953, *Excavations at Wari, Ayacácho, Peru,* Yale University Publications in Anthropology 49, New Haven.

Bragayrac D., E., 1991, Archaeological Excavations in the Vegachayoq Moqo Sector of Huari, in: *Huari Administrative Structure: Prehistoric Monumental Architecture and State Government* (W. H. Isbell and G. McEwan, eds.), Dumbarton Oaks Research Library and Collection, Washington D.C., pp. 71-80.

Brewster-Wray, C. C., 1983, Spatial Patterning and the Function of a Huari Architectural Compound, in: *Investigations of the Andean Past* (D. H. Sandweiss, ed.), Latin American Studies Program, Cornell University, Ithaca, pp. 122-135.

Brewster-Wray, C. C., 1990, *Moraduchayuq: An Administrative Compound at the Site of Huari, Peru,* Ph. D. Dissertation, State University of New York at Binghamton.

Bueno, A., 1982, *El antiguo valle de Pachacamac: Espacio, tiempo y culture,* Editorial Los Pinos, Lima.

Burger, R., 1992, *Chavin and the Origins of Andean Civilization,* Thames and Hudson, London.

Burger, R. L., and L. Salazar-Burger, 1980, Ritual and Religion at Huaricoto, *Archaeology* 33, 1:26-32.

Cook, A. G., 1979, The Iconography of Empire: Symbolic Communication in Seventh-Century Peru, MA thesis, Department of Anthropology, State University of New York at Binghamton.

Cook, A. G., 1983, Aspects of State Ideology in Huari and Tiwanaku Iconography: the Central Deity and the Sacrificer, in: *Investigations of the Andean Past* (D. Sandweiss, ed.), Latin American Studies Program, Cornell University, Ithaca, pp. 161-185.

Cook, A. G., 1987, The Middle Horizon Ceramic Offerings from Conchapata, *Ñawpa Pacha* 22-23:49-90.

González Carre, E., 1982, *Historia prehispánica de Ayacucho,* Universidad Nacional de San Cristóbal de Huamanga, Ayacucho.

Isbell, W. H., 1977, *The Rural Foundation for Urbanism: Economic and Stylistic Interaction Between Rural and Urban Communities in Eighth-Century Peru,* Illinois Studies in Anthropology 10, University of Illinois, Urbana, Chicago, and London.

Isbell, W. H., 1978, El Imperio Huari: ¿Estado o Ciudad? *Revista del Museo Nacional* 43:227-241.

Isbell, W. H., 1983, Shared Ideology and Parallel Political Development: Huari and Tiwanaku, in: *Investigations of the Andean Past,* Papers of the First Annual Northeast Conference on Andean Archaeology and Ethnohistory (D. H. Sandweiss, ed.), Latin American Studies Program, Cornell University, Ithaca, pp. 186-208.

Isbell, W. H., 1984, Huari Urban Prehistory, in: *Current Archaeological Projects in the Central Andes* (A. Kendall, ed. and N. Hammond, gent ed.), Proceedings of the 44th International Congress of Americanists, BAR International Series 210, Oxford, pp. 95-131.

Isbell, W. H., 1985, El origen del Estado en el Valle de Ayacucho, *Revista Andina* Año 3, 1:57-106.

Isbell, W. H., 1986, Emergence of City and State at Wari, Ayacucho, Peru, during the Middle Horizon, in: *Andean Archaeology: Papers in Memory of Clifford Evans* (R. Matos M., S. A. Turpin, and H. H. Eling, eds.), Monograph XXVII, Institute of Archaeology, University of California, Los Angeles, pp. 189-200.

Isbell, W. H., 1987, Conchopata, Ideological Innovator in Middle Horizon 1A, *Ñawpa Pacha* 22-23:91-134.

Isbell, W. H., 1989, Honcopampa: Was it a Huari Administrative Center?, in: *The Nature of Wari: A Reappraisal of the Middle Horizon in Peru* (R. M. Czwarno, F. M. Meddens, and A. Morgan, eds.), British Archaeological Reports, International Series 525, Oxford, pp. 98-115.

Isbell, W. H., 1991a, Honcopampa: Monumental Ruines in Peru's North Highlands, *Expedition* 33, 3:27-36.
Isbell, W. H., 1991b, Huari Administration and the Orthogonal Cellular Architecture Horizon, in: *Huari Administrative Structure: Prehistoric Monumental Architecture and State Government* (W. H. Isbell and G. McEwan, eds.), Dumbarton Oaks Research Library and Collection, Washington D.C., pp. 293-315.
Isbell, W. H., and A. G. Cook, 1987, Ideological Origins of an Andean Conquest State, *Archaeology* 40, 4:26-33.
Isbell, W. H., and K. J. Schreiber, 1978, Was Huari a State?, *American Antiquity* 43, 3:372-389.
Isbell, W. H., C. Brewster-Wray, and L. Spickard, 1991, Architecture and Spatial Organization at Huari, in: *Huari Administrative Structure: Prehistoric Monumental Architecture and State Government* (W. H. Isbell and G. McEwan, eds.), Dumbarton Oaks Research Library and Collection, Washington D.C., pp. 19-54.
Kolata, A., 1983, The South Andes, in: *Ancient South Americans* (J. Jennings, ed.), W. H. Freeman and Co., San Francisco, pp. 241-285.
Kolata, A., 1983, Chan Chan and Cuzco: On the Nature of the Andean City, in: *Civilization in the Ancient Americas: Essays in Honor of Gordon Willey* (R. M. Leventhal and A. L. Kolata, eds.), University of New Mexico Press and Peabody Museum of Archaeology and Ethnology, Harvard University, Cambridge, pp. 345-371.
Kolata, A., 1985, El papel de la agricultura intensiva en la economáa política del estado Tiwanaku, *Diálogo Andino* 4:1138.
Kolata, A., 1986, The Agricultural Foundation of the Tiwanaku State: A View from the Heartland, *American Antiquity* 51, 4:748-762.
Kolata, A., 1987, Tiwanaku and its Hinterland, *Archaeology* 40, 1:36-41.
Kolata, A., 1993, *The Tiwanaku: Portrait of an Andean Civilization,* Blackwell, Cambridge.
Knobloch, P. J., 1976, A Study of the Huarpa Ceramic Style of the Andean Early Intermediate Period, MA thesis, Department of Anthropology, State University of New York at Binghamton, New York.
Knobloch, P. J., 1983, *A Study of the Andean Huari Ceramics of Middle Horizon 1,* Ph. D. Dissertation, Department of Anthropology, State University of New York at Binghamton, New York.
Knobloch, P. J., 1991, Stylistic Date of Ceramics from the Huari Centers, in: *Huari Administrative Structure: Prehistoric Monumental Architecture and State Government* (W. H. Isbell and G. McEwan, eds.), Dumbarton Oaks Research Library and Collection, Washington D.C., pp. 247-258.
Lanning, E. P., 1967, *Peru Before the Incas,* Prentice Hall, Englewood Cliffs, N.J.
Lumbreras, L. G., 1959, Esquema Arqueológico de la Sierra Central del Peru, *Revista del Museo Nacional* 28:63-116.
Lumbreras, L. G., 1960, La Cultura Wari, *Etnología y Arqueologia 1, 1,* Universidad Nacional de San Marcos, Lima.
Lumbreras, L. G., 1969, *De los pueblos, las culturas y las artes del antiguo Perú,* Moncloa, Lima.
Lumbreras, L. G., 1974, *Las fundaciones de Huamanga,* Editorial Nueva Edición, Lima.
Lumbreras, L. G., 1981, The Strategy of the Open Sites, in: *Prehistory of the Ayacucho Basin II* (R. MacNeish *et al.,* eds.), University of Michigan Press, Ann Arbor, pp. 169-198.
McEwan, G. F., 1984, *The Middle Horizon in the Valley of Cusco, Peru: The Impact of the Wari Occupation of Pikillacta in the Lucre Basin,* Ph. D. dissertation, Department of Anthropology, University of Texas at Austin.
McEwan, G. F., 1991, Investigations at the Pikillacta Site: A Provincial Huari Center in the Valley of Cuzco, in: *Huari Administrative Structure: Prehistoric Monumental Architecture*

and *State Government* (W. H. Isbell and G. McEwan, eds.), Dumbarton Oaks Research Library and Collection, Washington D.C., pp. 93-120.

Menzel, D., 1964, Style and Time in the Middle Horizon, *Ñawpa Pacha* 2:1-105.

Menzel, D., 1968, New Data on the Huari Empire in Middle Horizon Epoch 2A, *Ñawpa Pacha* 6:47-114.

Menzel, D., 1977, *The Archaeology of Ancient Peru and the Work of Max Uhle*, R. H. Lowie Museum, Berkeley.

Morris, C., 1971, The Identification of Function in Inca Architecture and Ceramics, *Revista del Museo Nacional* 37:135-144.

Morris, C., 1979, Maize Beer in the Economics, Politics, and Religion of the Inca Empire, in: *Fermented Food Beverages in Nutrition* (C. F. Gastineau, W. J. Darby, and T. B. Turner, eds.), Academic Press, New York, pp. 21-34.

Morris, C., 1982, The Infrastructure of Inka Control in the Peruvian Central Highlands, in: *The Inca and Aztec States, 1400-1800* (G. A. Collier *et al.*, eds.), Academic Press, New York and London, pp. 153-171.

Moseley, M. E., 1978, The Evolution of Andean Civilization, in: *Ancient Native Americans* (J. D. Jennings, ed.), W. H. Freeman and Co., San Francisco, pp. 491-542.

Moseley, M. E., 1983, Central Andean Civilization, in: *Ancient South Americans* (J. D. Jennings, ed.), W. H. Freeman and Co., San Francisco, pp. 179-240.

Moseley, M. E, R. A. Feldman, P. S. Goldstein, and L. Watanabe, 1991, Colonies and Conquest: Tiahuanaco and Huari in Moquegua, in: *Huari Administrative Structure: Prehistoric Monumental Architecture and State Government* (W. H. Isbell and G. McEwan, eds.), Dumbarton Oaks Research Library and Collection, Washington D.C., pp. 121-140.

Paulsen, A., 1983, Huaca del Loro Revisited: the Nasca-Huarpa Connection, in: *Investigations of the Andean Past* (D. Sandweiss, ed.), Latin American Studies Program, Cornell University, Ithaca, pp. 98-121.

Ponce Sanginés, C., 1969, La ciudad de Tiwanaku, *Arte y Arqueología* 1:5-32.

Ponce Sanginés, C., 1976, *Tiwanaku: espacio, tiempo y culture,* Ediciones Pumapuncu, Editorial Los Amigos del Libro, La Paz and Cochabamba.

Ponce Sanginés, C., 1980, *Panorama de la Arqueología boliviana,* Librería y Editorial Juventud, La Paz.

Posnansky, A., 1945, *Tihuanacu, the Cradle of American Man* I-II. J. Augustin and Ministerio de Educación de Bolivia, New York and La Paz.

Ravines, R., 1968, Un depósito del Horizonte Medio en la Sierra Central del Perú, *Ñawpa Pacha* 6:19-45.

Ravines, R., 1977, Excavaciones en Ayapata, Huancavelica, Perú, *Ñawpa Pacha* 15:49-100.

Rowe, J. H., 1956, Archaeological Explorations in Southern Peru, 1954-55, *American Antiquity* 22, 2:120-137.

Rowe, J. H., 1962, Stages and Periods in Archaeological Interpretation, in: *Southwestern Journal of Anthropology*, 18:40-54.

Rowe, J. H., 1963, Urban Settlements in Ancient Peru, *Ñawpa Pacha* 1:28.

Rowe, J. H., 1967, An Interpretation of Radiocarbon Measurements from Archaeological Samples from Peru, in: *Peruvian Archaeology: Selected Readings* (J. H. Rowe and D. Menzel, eds.), Peek Publications, Palo Alto, pp. 16-30.

Rowe, J. H., and C. T. Brandel, 1971, Pucara Style Pottery Designs, *Ñawpa Pacha* 7-8:1-16.

Rowe, J. H., D. Collier, and G. R. Willey, 1950, Reconnaissance Notes on the Site of Huari, near Ayacucho, Peru, *American Antiquity* 16, 2:120-137.

Ruiz Estrada, A., 1969, Alfarería del estilo Huari en Cuelap, *Boletín del Semanario de Arqueología* 4, Pontífica Universidad Católica, Lima:60-64.

Schaedel, R., 1948, Monolithic Sculpture of the Southern Andes, *Archaeology* 1, 2:66-73.

Schaedel, R., 1948b, Stone Sculpture in the Callejón de Huaylas, in: *A Reappraisal of Peruvian Archaeology* (W. C. Bennett, ed.), Society for American Archaeology Memoir 4, Menasha, pp. 66-79.
Schaedel, R., 1951, Major Ceremonial and Population Centers in Northern Peru, in: *Civilizations of Ancient America: Selected Papers of the 29th International Congress of Americanists,* University of Chicago Press, Chicago, pp. 232-243.
Schaedel, R., 1952, *An Analysis of Central Andean Stone Sculpture,* Ph. D. Dissertation, Department of Anthropology, Yale University, University Microfilms, Ann Arbor.
Schaedel, R., 1966a, Incipient Urbanization and Secularization in Tiahuanacoid Peru, *American Antiquity* 31, 2:338-344.
Schaedel, R., 1966b, Urban Growth and Ekistics on the Peruvian Coast, *Proceedings of the 36th International Congress of Americanists* 1: 531-539.
Schaedel, R., 1985a, The Transition from Chiefdom to State in Northern Peru, in: *Development and Decline: The Evolution of Sociopolitical Organization* (H. J. M. Claessen, P. van de Valde, and M. Estelle Smith, eds.), Bergin and Garvey Publishers, South Hadley, pp. 156-170.
Schaedel, R., 1985b, Coast-Highland Interactions and Ethnic Groups in Northern Peru (500 B.C.-A.D. 1980), in: *Andean Ecology and Civilization: An Interdisciplinary Perspective on Andean Complimentarity* (S. Masuda, I. Shimada, and C. Morris, eds.), University of Tokyo Press, Tokyo, pp. 443-473.
Schacdel, R., 1985c, Discussion: An Interdisciplinary Perspective on Andean Ecological Complementarity, in: *Andean Ecology and Civilization: An Interdisciplinary Perspective on Andean Complimentarity* (S. Masuda, I. Shimada, and C. Morris, eds.), University of Tokyo Press, Tokyo, pp. 505-509.
Schreiber, K. J., 1978, *Planned Architecture of Middle Horizon Peru: Implications for Social and Political Organization,* Ph.D. Dissertation, State University of New York at Binghamton.
Schreiber, K. J., 1987a, Conquest and Consolidation: A Comparison of the Wari and Inka Occupations of a Highland Peruvian Valley, *American Antiquity* 52, 2:266-284.
Schreiber, K. J., 1987b, From State to Empire: The Expansion of Huari Outside the Ayacucho Basin, in: *The Origins and Development of the State in the Andes* (J. Haas, S. Pozorski, and T. Pozorski, eds.), Cambridge, pp. 91-96.
Schreiber, K. J., 1989, On Revisiting Huaca del Loro: A Cautionary Note, *Andean Past* 2:69-79.
Schreiber, K. J., 1991, Jincamocco: A Huari Administrative Center in the South Highlands of Peru, in: *Huari Administrative Structure: Prehistoric Monumental Architecture and State Government* (W. H. Isbell and G. McEwan, eds.), Dumbarton Oaks Research Library and Collection, Washington D.C., pp. 199-214.
Schreiber, K. J., 1992, Wari Imperialism in Middle Horizon Peru, *Anthropological Papers* 87, Museum of Anthropology, Univeristy of Michigan, Ann Arbor.
Shady Solís, R., 1982, La culture Nievería y la interacción social en el mundo andino en la época Huari, *Arqueológicas* 19, Museo Nacional de Antropología y Arqueología, Lima:5-108.
Shady Solís, R., 1988, La época Huari como interacción de las sociedades regionales, *Revista Andina* 6, 1, Cuzco:67-99.
Shady Solís, R., 1989, Cambios significativos occurridos en el mundo andino, in: *The Nature of Wari: A Reappraisal of the Middle Horizon Period in Peru* (R. M. Czwarno, F. M. Meddens, and A. Morgan, eds.), BAR International Series 525, Oxford, pp. 1-22.
Shady Solís, R., and A. Ruiz, 1979, Evidence for Interregional Relationships During the Middle Horizon on the North-Central Coast of Peru, *American Antiquity* 44, 4:676-684.

Spickard, L. E., 1983, The Development of Huari Administrative Architecture, in: *Investigations of the Andean Past* (D. Sandweiss, ed.), Cornell University, Latin American Studies Program, Ithaca, pp. 136-160.

Spinden, H. J., 1928, *Ancient Civilizations of Mexico and Central America*, American Museum of Natural History Handbook Series 3, 3rd edition, New York.

Tello, J. C., 1942, Origen y desarrollo de las civilizaciones prehistóricas andinas, in: *Actas y Trabajos Científicos, 27° Congreso Internacional de Americanistas* 1, 1939, Lima, pp. 589-720.

Tello, J. C., 1943, Discovery of the Chavin Culture in Peru, *American Antiquity* 9:135-150.

Terada, K., 1985, Early Ceremonial Architecture in the Cajamarca Valley, in: *Early Ceremonial Architecture in the Andes* (M. E. Moseley, ed.), Dumbarton Oaks, Washington D.C., pp. 191-208.

Thatcher, J. P., 1972, *Continuity and Change in the Ceramics of Huamachuco, North Highlands, Peru*, Ph. D. Dissertation, Department of Anthropology, University of Pennsylvania.

Thatcher, J. P., 1975, Early Intermediate Period and Middle Horizon 1B Ceramic Assemblages of Huamachuco, North Highlands, Peru, *Ñawpa Pacha* 10-12:109-128.

Thatcher, J. P., 1977, A Middle Horizon 1B Cache from Huamachuco, North Highlands, Peru, *Ñawpa Pacha* 15:101-110.

Topic, J. R., 1986, A Sequence of Monumental Architecture from Huamachuco, in: *Perspectives on Andean Prehistory and Protohistory: Papers from the Third Northeastern Conference on Andean Archaeology and Ethnohistory* (D. H. Sandweiss and D. P. Kvietok, eds.), Latin American Studies Program, Cornell University, Ithaca, pp. 63-83.

Topic, J. R., 1991, Huari and Huamachuco, in: *Huari Administrative Structure: Prehistoric Monumental Architecture and State Government* (W. H. Isbell and G. McEwan, eds.), Dumbarton Oaks Research Library and Collection, Washington D.C., pp. 233-246.

Topic, J. R. and T. Lange Topic, 1978, Prehistoric Fortification Systems in Northern Peru, *Current Anthropology* 19, 3:618-619.

Topic, J. R., and T. Lange Topic, 1982, The Huamachuco Archaeological Project: Preliminary Report of the First Season, July-August 1981, Department of Anthropology, Trent University, Peterborough, Ontario

Topic, J. R., and T. Lange Topic, 1983a, North Highland Political Geography: Some Observations on Routes, Networks, and Scale, in: *Civilization in the Ancient Andes* (R. Leventhal and A. Kolata, eds.), Peabody Museum of Archaeology and Ethnology, Cambridge, pp. 237-260.

Topic, J. R., and T. Lange Topic, 1983b, The Huamachuco Archaeological Project: Preliminary Report of the Second Season, June-August, 1982, Department of Anthropology, Trent University, Peterborough.

Topic, J. R., and T. Lange Topic, 1985, El Horizonte Medio en Huamachuco, *Revista del Museo Nacional* 47, Lima:13-52.

Topic, J. R., and T. Lange Topic, 1987, The Archaeological Investigation of Militarism: Some Cautionary Observations, in: *The Origins and Development of the Andean State* (J. Haas, S. Pozorski, and T. Pozorski, eds.), Cambridge University Press, Cambridge, pp. 47-55.

Topic, T. L., 1982, The Early Intermediate Period and its Legacy, in: *Chan Chan: Andean Desert City* (M. E. Moseley and K. C. Day, eds.), University of New Mexico Press, Albuquerque, pp. 255-284.

Topic, T. L., 1991, The Middle Horizon in Northern Peru, in: *Huari Administrative Structure: Prehistoric Monumental Architecture and State Government* (W. H. Isbell and G. McEwan, eds.), Dumbarton Oaks Research Library and Collection, Washington D.C., pp. 233-246.

Topic, T. L. and J. R. Topic, 1982, Prehistoric Fortification Systems of Northern Peru: Preliminary Report of the Final Season, January-December, 1980, MS, Department of Anthropology, Trent University, Peterbourough.
Topic, T. L., and J. R. Topic, 1984, Huamachuco Archaeological Project: Prelimnary Report of the Third Field Season, June-August 1983, *Trent University Occasional Papers in Anthropology* 1, Peterborough.
Topic, T. L., and J. R. Topic, 1987, Huamachuco Archaeological Project: Preliminary Report of the 1986 Field Season, *Trent University Occasional Papers in Anthropology* 4, Peterborough.
Uhle, M., 1922, Influencias Mayas en al Alto Ecuador, *Boletín de la Academia Nacional de Historia de Ecuador* 4:108-114.
Wagner, L. J., 1981, *Information Exchange as Seen in Middle Horizon 2 Ceramics from the Site of Huari, Peru,* Ph.D. Dissertation, University of Wisconsin, Madison.
Watanabe, L., 1984, Cerro Baúl: Un santuario de filiación Wari en Moquegua, *Boletín de Lima* 32:40-49.
Williams, C., and J. Pineda, 1985, Desde Ayacucho hasta Cajamarca: formas arquitectónicas con filiación Wari, *Boletín de Lima* 40, Año 7:55-81.

Chapter 9

Political Institutional Factors Contributing to the Integration of the Tiwanaku State

DAVID L. BROWMAN

INTRODUCTION

A number of different hypotheses have been put forward to define the relationship of the Tiwanaku urban center to various areas under Tiwanaku influence in western Bolivia, Northern Chile, and Southern Peru. The nature of the city of Tiwanaku will be directly impacted by its political arena. For instance, there will be different implications with respect to urban functioning of Tiwanaku city if it is the chief amongst quasi-equals in a federation as contrasted to its being the capital city of a conquest state.

The dichotomy of territorial state vs. hegemonic state (D'Altroy 1992; Hassig 1992; Santley and Alexander 1992) provides a fruitful heuristic tool against which to display the archaeological data.

A territorial state is one which maintains direct control of its dependencies. The various hinterlands are incorporated into the state as prov-

---

DAVID L. BROWMAN • Department of Anthropology, Washington University, Campus Box 1114, One Brookings Drive, St. Louis, Missouri 63130-4899, U.S.A.

Emergence and Change in Early Urban Societies, edited by Linda Manzanilla, Plenum Press, New York, 1997.

inces. The state must provide the military power to maintain its borders and police its dependencies. State coffers must be used to finance the political and military power to enforce governmental decisions via troops, and administrative personnel who manage the province. Thus territorial or direct control is an expensive option of governance in terms of economic resources expended.

A hegemonic state relies on indirect control. Local level leaders are responsible for the day-to-day operations of the dependencies. In return for central government recognition of their legitimacy, these local polity authorities collect the tribute and taxes to be forwarded to the central government. Such an arrangement is much less expensive, economically, than the direct control mechanism, but involves a potentially higher political risk, because the local leadership has an established power base for any attempted rebellion.

There are three current models or explanations proposed to define the organization of the Tiwanaku state. Two of these may be subsumed under explanations involving direct control mechanisms. The first direct control model involves the outright complete colonization or seizure of territory by force. This model has been favored by Ponce Sanginés (1991) and Isbell (1991). The second direct control model identifies the Andean institution of *mitmaqkuna*—the sending of small groups of residents into desirable resource locations occupied by other ethnic groups, to secure direct control of the resources. In some instances, the *mitmaqkuna* are sufficiently numerous or are backed up by such evident political might from the home base that they are able to secure effective political and economic control. This is not always the case, however, so that in other instances *mitmaqkuna* may not constitute a means of direct political control of a region, but merely a means of direct economic access to resources of a region. The third model is one that emphasizes at best indirect control, through a loose alliance or federation of polities, and allows for even less evident political control by emphasizing the importance of securing access to resources through unhindered and free movement of goods by llama caravans. Although nothing precludes llama caravans being important mechanisms for territorial states as well, this latter model [one variant of which is called the *altiplano* model by Browman (1981)] highlights economic well-being over political agendas.

An essential argument of this paper is that all of these models are partly correct, but none of them is solely accurate. The Tiwanaku state appears to be characterized by a very pragmatic nature. For the six areas summarized below, empirical data supports different economic and political integration for each case. Because each of these six patterns will have a different potential set of implications for effective institutions in the core city of

Tiwanaku, we must first understand the nature of the patterns of governance and resource extraction at the broader level before we can adequately reconstruct institutional power in the core city.

COCHABAMBA VALLEY, BOLIVIA

Prior to the appearance of Tiwanaku influence in Cochabamba, the greater valley region is characterized by a fairly uniform ceramic style, Tupuraya, suggesting some kind of local political integration (Brockington and Pereira 1989:21, Brockington 1993). Tiwanaku influence is evident in three subsequent Cochabamba valley styles: Nazcoid or Nascoide (a.k.a. Mizque-Tiahuanaco), Mojocoya, and later, Yampara. It does not spread south of the Río Grande, although there are Tupuraya materials found south of the Río Grande (Byrne de Caballero 1984), suggesting Tiwanaku linkages were only to specific polities. Nazcoide materials are more frequently reported from the western portions of the Cochabamba region, Mojocoya from the eastern sectors, and Yampara from the southern zones (Branisa 1957; Knutson 1974; Ibarra Grasso and Querejazu Lewis 1986), probably reflecting different political groupings, although our current control of time-space systematics is insufficient to state this with certainty. The three radiocarbon assays available suggest late Tiwanaku V associations: A.D. 1050 ± 200 (M-509) at Omereque, associated with Nazcoide ceramics, Tiwanaku textiles, and snuff complex paraphernalia; and A.D. 950 ±170 (HV-115) and A.D. 1100 ± 90 (HV-114) at Icla-Chullpamoko, associated with Yampara wares.

Geraldine Byrne de Caballero (1984) suggested that the first influence into the Nazcoide complex might occur during Tiwanaku IV, based on a preliminary assessment of some ceramics from Cayacayani. She identified major continuing influence in Tiwanaku V, with up to 70% of the western Cochabamba ceramics showing Tiwanaku influence, but noted out (as is also mainly the case for the North Chile Azapa area) that the Tiwanaku materials she had located all came from cemeteries, and that at that point she had identified no Tiwanaku buildings or clear habitation sites. An inspection of the grave lots published from Cayacayani (Byrne de Caballero 1965:93) shows that the stratigraphically earliest grave had a mixture of Nazcoide and Tiwanaku V-like materials only. Thus while there is an unprovenienced sculpture piece that suggests Tiwanaku IV associations elsewhere in Cochabamba (Browman n.d.), all the ceramics identified to date only show Tiwanaku V relationships.

The pattern of evidence so far available from Cochabamba is one of trade, one of indirect influence through prestige, but no evidence of colonists and no evidence of conquest. Oakland (1986) investigated textiles from three sites in this region: Omereque, Mojocoya, and Pérez. Omereque and Perez had Nascoide (or Mizque-Tiahuanaco) style ceramics, and Mojocoya had Mojocoya and Nascoide ceramics. The textiles from all three of the site were clearly highland in construction and iconography, and are part of what Oakland (1986:233) defines as a unified Tiwanaku textile complex. She suggests (1986:246) that the textile complex should be added to the snuff paraphernalia complex, as defined by Browman (1981), as a set of goods spread by independent trading alliances.

Support for the separate trade alliance idea can be derived from the Tiwanaku heartland as well. Earlier only a few Nascoide ceramics were known from Tiwanaku, from unstratified contexts, as illustrated by Posnansky (1957) or general association with Tiwanaku V context (Cordero Miranda, cited by Ibarra Grasso and Querejazu Lewis 1986:210). But recently Janusek (1993:16) has identified Nascoide ceramics in a house compound complex at Lukurmata. Here he finds evidence of continued contact with Cochabamba, as evidenced by Nascoide sherds found in several chronological units from this compound of panpipe manufacturers, while the adjacent compounds lacked any Nascoide materials. He suggests independent continuing trade or long-distance linkages carried on by this compound with the Cochabamba area over decades, perhaps even centuries.

Tiwanaku relationships with the Cochabamba area seem to fall under the federation model. Tiwanaku influence on the local culture is substantial, in terms of local borrowing or copying of Tiwanaku decorative ideas, cosmological symbols and vessels inventories, but these are clearly local copies, in forms and techniques easily distinguishable from the highland center. Tiwanaku textiles and components of the Tiwanaku snuff complex appear to be secured through llama trade caravan mechanisms. Certainly Cochabamba sodalite is being transported back up to Tiwanaku, and no doubt certain perishables such as maize and perhaps *Anadenanthera* sp. hallucinogenic snuff are also going back up to Tiwanaku from the valley.

ORURO, CENTRAL ALTIPLANO, BOLIVIA

The pattern of evidence in Oruro is just beginning to emerge. Bermann (1992, 1993) has recently identified the Jachakala complex. In this area, local communities with no apparent connections to the Titicaca basin polities to the north display an apparent sharp shift to Tiwanaku V style ceramics. The assemblages I have observed in local collections mirror that reported in the field by Bermann; while there are *tazones* and other typical Tiwanaku V forms, there are no *incensarios*, incised wares, or black wares.

To me this suggests that the ideological component so important in the initial spread of Tiwanaku ideas in Tiwanaku Phase IV is lacking, and the Oruro complex thus represents the result of secular expansion. Tiwanaku wares, based on our very fragmentary control of the chronological sequence, disappear nearly as suddenly. This pattern would suggest a political power base, an expansion backed up by force or threat of military force, of the direct or territorial model.

SILLUMOCCO, SOUTH PUNO, PERU

Earlier work by Hyslop and Tschopik had indicated substantial Tiwanaku V presence in the southern part of Puno Department in Peru. The mechanism of Tiwanaku control over this area was not clear. However Stanish (1992) now identifies a regional polity called "Sillumocco", which retains political independence until Tiwanaku V. No Sillumocco sites were abandoned in the Tiwanaku expansion; rather existing Sillumocco sites continued to be occupied, and over time, with population growth (as well as an apparent shift in focus by Tiwanaku to lake-side agricultural fields), a few new sites, now with just Tiwanaku-related materials, are found. In Sillumocco area sites, some of the prestige cosmologically related ceramic materials have been recovered.

For the Sillumocco area, there is an apparently different pattern of integration than either Oruro or Cochabamba. Sillumocco is integrated into the Tiwanaku heartland, but by more co-optation of an equal. This is the sort of hegemonic pattern, where local lords provide the necessary political mechanisms and force to manage the political unit, the more indirect means of integrating a region into the expanding sphere of influence.

SAN PEDRO DE ATACAMA, NORTH CHILE REGION II

San Pedro has Tiwanaku trade items in terms of the snuff complex and the textile complex, plus a few ceramic and metal items as well. Particularly well known are the wooden snuff tablets, with images of the *sacrificador* or *degollador* figure, and the *personajes de perfil* (Berenguer 1987:44; Muñoz Ovalle 1989:125). *Anadenanthera* sp. snuff residues have been identified from Solcor 3 in San Pedro, dating to A.D. 780 (Torres *et al*. 1990:10). The textile complex includes Tiwanaku tapestry, rectangular mantles, transposed warps, and warp-faced plain weave (Oakland 1986; Oakland Rodman 1990).

There is no evidence of massive colonization, and no evidence of moving in of smaller colonial groups of the *mitmaqkuna* type. Tiwanaku contact appears during Tiwanaku IV, when it seems to be wholly trade caravan related. In Tiwanaku V, influence from the *altiplano* intensifies, to the point that some San Pedro settlements appear to represent multi-ethnic settlements. Oakland Rodman (1990) suggests the establishment of the "Señorío de Quitor," with an *altiplano*-based group securing control over the local population. Orellana Rodriguez (1986:253), and Thomas and colleagues (1986:269) see less direct Tiwanaku control, particularly based on the occurrence of Southern Bolivian altiplano ceramic styles such as Uruquilla and Dupont in Quitor, suggesting prestige goods reached San Pedro via intermediary polities in Lipez and Potosí.

Some of the burials that Oakland Rodman and various Chileans have investigated do contain very ethnic Tiwanaku-looking materials, but the region in general displays mainly indirect patterning. Are these ethnic *altiplano* types simply merchants, caravaneers, setting up a port-of-trade? This seems, based on current evidence, more likely than suggesting a handful of Tiwanaku elites have seized power, but have otherwise left the polity unchanged.

Tiwanaku V influence, at this point, seems to just gradually fade away, with no apparent dislocation of settlement patterns or trade networks. Northern altiplano influence is replaced by southern altiplano influence; Bolivian ceramic of Yura, Huruquilla, Chaqui, and Hedionda styles are found in the San Pedro oasis and other regional sites (Browman 1986:244, Orellana Rodriguez 1986:253, Schiappacasse *et al.* 1989:214-219, and many others). Tiwanaku people spoke Aymara; if there had been a colonization of San Pedro by the Tiwanaku 'state', we should expect still to find a few outliers of Aymara, but this is not the case. Thus the evidence at hand for San Pedro supports substantial contact via llama caravan trade, even to the point of the establishment of a small port of trade or outlying group of merchants, but no evidence that San Pedro de Atacama was ever integrated, politically, in any fashion with Tiwanaku.

AZAPA, NORTH CHILE REGION I

The Azapa valley Cabuza phase displays significant Tiwanaku influence. Most Chilean archaeologists interpret the available evidence as indicating some kind of colonizing movement from the Titicaca basin. In contrast to the San Pedro de Atacama region to the south, there are major cemeteries where the populations appear to be predominantly of highland origin. But in contrast to Moquegua to the north, there is no evidence of public or ceremonial architecture of highland origin, and reputed Tiwanaku sites are very small compared to the Alto Ramírez, Arica, or other locally based phases. Tiwanaku influence and control thus is much greater than in San Pedro, but also less than in Moquegua.

Tiwanaku influence seems to be exhibited in much the same fashion in several North Chilean valleys. In valleys just to the south of Azapa, such as Codpa and Camarones (Rivera 1991:36), significant highland presence is defined in the mid-valley areas, but the coastal zones retain essentially Chilean coastal manifestations, a pattern which continues on in the subsequent Late Prehistoric Period (Schiappacasse and Niemeyer 1992:75; Muñoz Ovalle *et al.* 1990). Santoro (1992:15) suggests that the coastal Chilean populations control resources in enclaves, and trade with the intrusive *altiplano* populations, resulting in gradual cultural changes, as various features of the intrusive *altiplano* mid-valley settlers are integrated into the coastal format.

The North Chilean scenario sounds much like the pattern that is much better documented on the Central Coast of Peru. Maria Rostworowski de Diez Canseco (1977, 1978, 1981, 1991) has reconstructed in great detail the shifting fortunes of various mid-valley areas in the Lima, Canta and Huarochiri areas, where mid-valley areas were controlled by highland polities when the highlands were in ascendancy, but where control was re-secured by coastal groups when highland political strength waned, a cyclical process that apparently recurred a number of times over the centuries. The data from Azapa and other Region I North Chilean valleys appear to document the same kind of shift from highland to coastal control as Tiwanaku influence grew and then later collapsed.

The Chilean coast was an important source of maritime resources for the Titicaca basin; trade caravans thus could collect both coastal maritime goods as well as returning to the highlands with maize grown in small enclaves in mid-valley locations. Berenguer and Dauelsberg (1989:163) see North Chile as an important source of arsenic copper ores for Tiwanaku arsenic bronzes. My own work from Chiripa, Bolivia, confirms extraction of Chilean coastal ores from as early as formative periods, supporting this argument. However Lechtman (1988:358) also notes important arsenic copper ores deposits in Northwest Argentina. Ores from Northwest Argentina would have been traded through San Pedro; thus the wealth and importance of San Pedro may also have been based on trade in metal resources.

The evidence from North Chile seems to support the presence of small enclaves of Titicaca basin peoples intrusive into the middle valley maize growing lands, but co-existing with communities of indigenous coastal peoples. During the peak of Tiwanaku economic and political power, the coastal groups are apparently nearly excluded from certain sections of the mid-valley lands, but they are never completely removed nor wholly acculturated. While Tiwanaku would seem to control much of the agricultural production of the mid-valley area on one hand, on the other hand the mid-valley areas do not seem to be incorporated as part of the actual territory of the state.

MOQUEGUA, PERU

The work in the last decade by the Programa Contisuyu staff makes it abundantly clear that a quite different pattern exists for the mid-valley area of the Ilo/Moquegua river area. There is a massive colonization of the maize-growing lands in the middle elevations of the valley by Tiwanaku ethnic groups. This colony is complete with its own local ceremonial center at Omo, which Goldstein (1992, 1993) sees as a replica of the temple precincts of sites in the Tiwanaku heartland. Most recent interpretations (Goldstein 1992, 1993; Stanish 1992) have a sequence of late Tiwanaku IV/early Tiwanaku V colonists arriving, with Tiwanaku ideology still a strong driving force, with items such as black ware, *huaco retratos*, and the like still in the ceramic inventory. A provincial capital is set up at Omo responsible for the management of the colony. Sandness (1992) reports that the local diet was one based to a large extent on maize, with limited access to coastal resources, as contrasted to periods before or after, where access to coastal resources via camelid caravans was in much greater evidence. Goldstein (1993:42) argues that by controlling religious practice, and access to cosmologically important information, the Tiwanaku provinicial elite in Moquegua solidified their position.

A rebellion, breaking the linkages to the highland center, occurred near the end of Tiwanaku V phase occupations. Political entities are dynamic, not stable, institutions; thus incorporation or disincorporation of peripheral areas, and re-organization of internal institutional structures are not uncommon events. Hinterland provinces located at a long distance from the heartland, such as Omo/Moquegua, are very expensive to maintain. In addition, local elites may opt to exert more independence, and escape core polity dominance. In the Omo case, the evidence reported by Goldstein, Moseley, Rice, Stanish, Watanabe and other staff from the Programa Contisuyu indicates an apparent internal revolt, with the public architecture and political center destroyed, but with the agricultural Tiwanaku population still resident. This kind of scenario seems to fit the model of excessive taxation, where local tax revolt is staged against the core polity, a situation which obtains frequently when bureaucratic costs and other center demands drive the amount of tribute required beyond the limits of benefits that the subject population feels they receive from continued association or allegiance to the core. Subsequently evidence is found in the Moquegua area for a refugee population (Tumilaca) and re-colonization from the coast (Chiribaya).

TIWANAKU CORE

Before Tiwanaku emerged as the dominant center in the region, there were a series of mini-polities, such as Pukara, Sillumocco, and Jachakala, which held sway in their own local regions, much as the Colla, Lupaca, Pacajes, Carangas, and Mallku *señoríos* did in the Late Prehistoric period. These *señoríos* (assumed to be kin- or *ayllu*-based) developed the raised field systems of the Titicaca basin (Graffam 1990; Erickson 1988), which were in place long before Tiwanaku emerged as the dominant polity. A shift occurs around A.D. 500, with Tiwanaku developing rapidly as a population and political center. Major population shifts are found in the immediate vicinity of Tiwanaku, with Albarracín-Jordán and Mathews (1990) seeing almost no sites relating to preceding Tiwanaku III groups in the local valley, and a massive growth of the Tiwanaku center by rural populations moving into the urban area (Albarracín-Jordán 1992). The population density of this zone is estimated minimally 10X greater than areas only 40 km or so away. Secondary centers such as Lukurmata also experience the same massive growth, expanding from 20 ha to 120 ha in a century or less (Graffam 1992:884). These new data suggest a possible hyper-urbanism during the initial phases of Tiwanaku growth.

Janusek (1993) argues that the initial center is characterized as having heterogeneous local groups but that by A.D. 800 there is a substantial growth of elites with their attached subsidiary servers. He sees the development of mercantile production, with redistribution via the organized state, and with specialization, as indications of profound divisions of labor at the major administrative centers such as Tiwanaku and Lukurmata. Tiwanaku city includes a public ceremonial core with monumental architecture; an area of elite residences; an area of artisanal activity, also apparently including the residences of the artisans; a series of residential terraces thought to be the locus of the lower classes; and also some enclosed agricultural zones with *qochas*, elaborate canals and other agricultural constructions.

In addition to the artisanal areas reported by Janusek (1993), other evidence suggests increased mercantile activity during the Tiwanaku IV and V period. Webster (1992, 1993) reports substantial increase of castrated llamas in Tiwanaku IV and V, in addition to the general increase of use of llamas for meat and other purposes. Castrated llamas are the principal caravan animals documented from Inca times to the present; the substantial increase that Webster identifies in castrated animals thus reflects the marked increase in importance of caravan trade. These shifts in camelid frequency Webster believes imply the increase of state bred herds, which would thus supply meat animals as well as caravan animals.

Thus we have evidence for industrial or artisanal activities fabricating manufactured goods, and the growth of the llama caravan infrastructure in the heartland center. The patterns identified for the various regions were predicated on significant increases in llama caravan trade, and significant movement of goods fabricated at Tiwanaku; identification of workshops and increase in castrated caravan llamas is compelling support for this argument.

Albarracín-Jordán (1992:27) and Bermann (1992:257) see a significant population relocation with decentralization and perhaps even fragmentation of administration in the Tiwanaku heartland, occurring in Tiwanaku V. If this pattern holds up, it presages the subsequent reappearance of the minipolities or *señoríos* in the Late Prehistoric Period.

The collapse of Tiwanaku cannot be fully discussed here, but identification of probable causes may help shed a bit of additional light on the means by which Tiwanaku was integrated with its hinterlands. Richerson (1991) suggests inspecting four sets of hypotheses: (1) exogenous environmental change, such as drought, or long term climatic shifts; (2) endogenous envrionmental change, such as anthropogenetically caused decreases in carrying capacity due to erosion or soil salinization; (3) exogenous political and economic factors, such as the loss of critical trade, or invasions; and (4) endogenous political and economic factors, such as new ideological systems or political reorganization.

(1) Kolata (1987; Ortloff and Kolata 1993) has championed the idea of Tiwanaku collapse from environmental deterioration. However Erickson (1988) and Graffam (1990) find no support for Kolata's proposed dramatic collapse of the agricultural system in a rapid fashion, and Browman (this volume) finds no support for deteriorating environmental conditions, until a point well after the decline of the polity.

(2) Anthropogenetic changes have resulted in erosion and salinization and abandonment of fields around Lake Titicaca; several systems of raised fields have been abandoned owing to excess salinization. While earlier Kolata suggested this as a factor in Tiwanaku's decline, more recently he has favored exogenous causes.

(3) Browman (1981) suggested the alienation of markets in Cochabamba and Moquegua as possibly contributing to the down-sizing of Tiwanaku. Berenguer and Dauelsberg (1989:180) see evidence for massive

destruction of all late Tiwanaku temples and centers in the hinterlands, and infer a serious of revolts and uprisings, fracturing linkages. To the extent that the functioning of Tiwanaku was predicated on securing raw materials from the hinterlands, and marketing manufactured items from the core, loss of markets owing to local revolts in the hinterlands or other factors removing the markets and resources would be a significant factor under the models suggested here.

(4) The fragmentation and decentralization of the Tiwanaku core noted by Albarracín-Jordán (1992) and Bermann (1992) may include the genesis for local heartland political and economic changes as well.

SUMMARY REMARKS

Areas seen as being under Tiwanaku influence display a varying set of relationships with the Tiwanaku heartland. There is a much richer inventory of mechanisms employed by Tiwanaku than we have previously appreciated, possibly helping to contribute to what Kolata (1992) has called its millennium of political importance.

Cochabamba seems to be an excellent example of economic linkages through trade. No political control from the *altiplano* can be identified. Ideological prestige properties, along with other Tiwanaku goods, are widely copied. While Tiwanaku prestige products, such as the textile complex and snuff complex, are evidence of direct imports, information on political organization suggest independence, or loose federation at most. San Pedro de Atacama displays another pattern of political independence but trade interdependence. Small numbers of Tiwanaku individuals have been tentatively identified, apparently operating out of a kind of 'port of trade' situation. Thus review of San Pedro and Cochabamba suggest support for the hegemonic or indirect model of political power, at most, and perhaps no more than economic linkages via trade caravans.

The Sillumocco polity evidence is in the process of being analyzed by Stanish. The current co-optation of Sillumocco centers by Tiwanaku phase groups would fit, at this point, either a territorial or a hegemonic model. If no evidence of physical or military force can be found in the Sillumocco polity, then unless other factors contra-indicate, it would be possible to see Sillumocco being integrated into the Tiwanaku heartland polity through a process of federation. Military bases, or other evidence of Tiwanaku peoples directly intrusive into the Sillumocco area would fit better with a territorial model. But in either case, the pattern of Tiwanaku presence is quite different than that of San Pedro or Cochabamba; Sillumocco seems likely to be a province of the Tiwanaku state.

Three of the areas provide support for direct or territorial power bases. At this juncture, the preliminary information from the Jachakala complex of Oruro suggests direct military conquest of the area by Tiwanaku forces moving south. No demographic movement or migration of the Oruro population is currently proposed; rather simple incorporation into the Tiwanaku state by force.

The other two examples of direct control involve migrations. The Moquegua area shows evidence of a massive migration of Tiwanaku people into mid-valley. The small population of the Trapiche phase disappears, either wholly engulfed in the Tiwanaku colony, or forced elsewhere as refugees. The Azapa and North Chilean areas reflect another sort of colonization approach. In these areas the coastal polities maintain a significant presence in the mid-valley regions. We have evidence of small groups of *altiplano mitmaqkuna* moving down to these same mid-valleys to secure access to resources, but current evidence suggests that the mid-valley areas retain a multi-ethnic composition. At the peak of Tiwanaku power in the highland, it may be that these *mitmaqkuna* effectively co-opted political power from the co-resident ethnic groups, and secured effective political control over the mid-valley areas, but at other times the Tiwanaku presence seems more directed at securing and maintaining direct access to the economic resources of the agricultural zone without insisting on enforcing complete political control of all inhabitants.

Tiwanaku core heartland information suggests economic organization there also along a number of alternative lines. Albarracín-Jordán and Mathews (1990) have identified agricultural production on hillslopes, on raised field complexes, in *qocha* depression management systems, and on agricultural terraces. Kolata (1992) has suggested that major state or 'corporate' farms were established for generation of agricultural surplus for trade and state projects. Significant state effort was directed at agricultural reclamation and management in the Pampa Koani and Tiwanaku drainages. Specialized artisanal workshops areas have been identified in Tiwanaku city by Janusek (1993). Increased numbers of caravan animals are documented not only for the Tiwanaku metropolitan area (Webster 1992, 1993), but Stanish (1992) also sees increased camelid usage in the Sillumocco province. The ultimate collapse of Tiwanaku appears, based on the evidence at hand, to be due mainly to an unraveling of the complex economic and political system involved. Alienation of markets and local political seizures of power have been suggested by various researchers for San Pedro de Atacama, Cochabamba, Azapa, and Moquegua. The *altiplano* polities of Sillumocco and Jachakala continue to share large numbers of cultural traits with Tiwanaku, but seem to exhibit gradual fragmentation and re-organization into smaller *señorío* style polities. While environmental factors have some undeniable impacts, the principal factors for cultural change appear to be more sociological than environmental for this specific event.

REFERENCES

Albarracín-Jordán, J. V., 1992, *Prehispanic and Early Colonial Settlement Patterns in the Lower Tiwanaku Valley, Bolivia*, Ph. D. Dissertation, Department of Anthropology, Southern Methodist University, Dallas.

Albarracín-Jordán, J. V., and J. E. Mathews, 1990, *Asentamientos prehispánicos del Valle de Tiwanaku*, Producciones Cima, La Paz.

Berenguer R., J., 1987, Consumo nasal de alucinógenos en Tiwanaku: una aproximación iconográfica, *Boletín del Museo Chileno de Arte Precolombino* 2:33-53.

Berenguer R., J., and P. Dauelsberg Hahmann, 1989, El norte grande en la órbita de Tiwanaku (4,000 a 1,200 d.C.), in: *Culturas de Chile: Prehistoria desde sus orígenes hasta los albores de la Conquista* (J. Hidalgo, V. Schiappacasse, H. Niemeyer, C. Aldunate, and I. Solimano, eds.), Editorial Andrés Bello, Santiago, pp. 129-180.

Bermann, M., 1992, The Southern Tiwanaku margin, a view from Oruro, Paper presented at the 57th Annual Meeting, Society for American Archaeology, Pittsburgh.

Bermann, M., 1993, Jachakala: a New Archaeological Complex in the Department of Oruro, Bolivia, manuscript, Carnegie Museum, University of Pittsburgh.

Branisa, L., 1957, Un nuevo estilo de cerámica precolombina de Chuquisaca: Mojocoya tricolor, in: *Arqueología Boliviana* (Primera Mesa Redonda) (C. Ponce Sanginés, ed.), Biblioteca Paceña, Alcaldía Municipal, La Paz, pp. 289-320.

Brockington, D. L., 1993, Recent Research in Central, Southern and Tropical Bolivia, Paper presented at the 58th Annual Meeting of the Society of American Archaeology, St. Louis.

Brockington, D. L., and D. M. Pereira Herrera, 1989, Archaeological Investigations into the Formative Period in Cochabamba Bolivia 1984-1988, Report submitted to the National Geographic Society, Washington D. C.

Browman, D., 1981, New Light on Andean Tiwanaku, *American Scientist* 69, 4:408-419.

Browman, D., 1986, Prehispanic Aymara Expansion, the Southern Altiplano, and San Pedro de Atacama, *Estudios Atacameños* 7:236-252.

Browman, D., n.d., Lithic Provenience Analysis and Emerging Material Complexity at Formative Period Chiripa, Bolivia, Manuscript submitted for publication review.

Byrne de Caballero, G., 1965, Cayacayani: a New Sequence in Andean Pottery, *Ethnos* 29, 1-2:87-96.

Byrne de Caballero, G, 1984, El Tiwanaku en Cochabamba, *Arqueología Boliviana* 1:67-71.

D'Altroy, T. N., 1992, *Provincial Power in the Inka Empire*, Smithsonian Institution Press, Washington D. C.

Erickson, C. L., 1988, *An Archaeological Investigation of Raised Field Agriculture in the Lake Titicaca Basin of Peru*. Ph. D. Dissertation, Department of Anthropology, University of Illinois, Urbana.

Goldstein, P., 1992, Tiwanaku State Settlement of the Azapa and Moquegua Valleys: a Preliminary Comparison, Paper presented at the 57th Annual Meeting, Society for American Archaeology, Pittsburgh.

Goldstein, P., 1993, Tiwanaku Temples and State Expansion: a Tiwanaku Sunken-Court Temple in Moquegua, Peru, *Latin American Antiquity* 4, 1:22-47.

Graffam, G., 1990, *Raised Fields without Bureaucracy: an Archaeological Examination of Intensive Wetland Cultivation in the Pampa Koani Zone, Lake Titicaca, Bolivia*, Ph. D. Dissertation, Department of Anthropology, University of Toronto.

Graffam, G., 1992, Beyond State Collapse: Rural History, Raised Fields, and Pastoralism in the South Andes, *American Anthropologist* 94, 4:882-904.

Hassig, R., 1992, *War and Society in Ancient Mesoamerica*, University of California Press, Berkeley.

Ibarra Grasso, D. E., and R. Querejazu Lewis, 1986, *30,000 años de prehistoria en Bolivia*, Los Amigos del Libro, Cochabamba.

Isbell, W. H., 1991, Huari Administration and the Orthogonal Cellular Architectural Horizon, in: *Huari Administrative Structure: Prehistoric Monumental Architecture and State Government* (W. H. Isbell and G. F. McEwan, eds.), Dumbarton Oaks Research Library and Collection, Washington D. C., pp. 293-315.

Janusek, J. W., 1993, Nuevos datos sobre el significado de la producción y uso de instrumentos musicales en el estado de Tiwanaku, *Pumapunku* n. s., 2, 4:9-47.

Knutson, J., 1974, Mojocoya Ceramics of Comarapa. Mimeographed report, Instituto de Investigaciones Antropológicas, Universidad Mayor de San Simón.

Kolata, A. L., 1987, Tiwanaku and its Hinterland, *Archaeology* 40, 1:36-41.

Kolata, A. L., 1992, Economy, Ideology and Imperialism in the South-Central Andes, in: *Ideology and Pre-Columbian Civilizations* (A. Demarest and G. W. Conrad, eds.), School of American Research Advanced Seminar Series, Santa Fe, pp. 65-85.

Lechtman, H., 1988, Traditions and Styles in Central Andean Metalworking, in: *The Beginning of the Use of Metals and Alloys* (R. Maddin, ed.), MIT Press, Cambridge, pp. 344-378.

Muñoz Ovalle, I., 1989, El periodo formativo en el norte grande, in: *Culturas de Chile: Prehistoria desde sus orígenes hasta los albores de la Conquista* (J. Hidalgo, V. Schiappacasse, H. Niemeyer, C. Aldunate, and I. Solimano, eds.), Editorial Andrés Bello, Santiago, pp. 107-128.

Muñoz Ovalle, I., J. M. Chacama R., and G. E. Espinosa V., 1990, El poblamiento prehispánico tardío en el valle de Codpa: una aproximación a la historia regional, *Revista Chungara* 19:7-61.

Oakland Rodman, A., 1986, *Tiwanaku textile style from the South Central Andes—Bolivia and North Chile*, Ph. D. Dissertation, Department of Art History, University of Texas at Austin.

Oakland Rodman, A., 1990, Textiles and Ethnicity: Tiwanaku in San Pedro de Atacama, North Chile, Report to the National Endowment for the Humanities.

Orellana Rodríguez, M., 1986, Relaciones culturales entre Tiwanaku y San Pedro de Atacama, *Diálogo Andino* 4:247-257.

Ortloff, C, R., and A. L. Kolata, 1993, Climate and Collapse: Agro-Ecological Perspectives on the Decline of the Tiwanaku State, *Journal of Archaeological Science* 20, 2:195-221.

Ponce Sanginés, C., 1991, El urbanismo de Tiwanaku, *Pumapunku* (n.s.) 1:7-27.

Posnansky, A., 1957, *Tihuanacu: La cuna del hombre americano* III y IV, Ministerio de Educación, La Paz.

Richerson, P. J., 1991, Humans as a Component of the Lake Titicaca Ecosystem: a Model System for the Study of Environmental Deterioration, Proceedings of the Cary Conference, May 1991.

Rivera Díaz, M. A., 1991, The Prehistory of Northern Chile: a Synthesis, *Journal of World Prehistory* 5, 1:1-48.

Rostworowski de Diez Canseco, M., 1977, *Etnía y sociedad: Costa peruana prehispánica*, Instituto de Estudios Peruanos, Lima.

Rostworowski de Diez Canseco, M., 1978, *Señoríos indígenas de Lima y Canta*, Instituto de Estudios Peruanos, Lima.
Rostworowski de Diez Canseco, M., 1981, *Recursos renovables naturales y pesca: siglos XVI y XVII*, Instituto de Estudios Peruanos, Lima.
Rostworowski de Diez Canseco, M., 1991, Las macroetnías en el ámbito andino, *Allpanchis* 35/36:3-28.
Sandness, K. L., 1992, Temporal and Spatial Dietary Variability in the Prehistoric Lower and Middle Osmore Drainage: the Carbon and Nitrogen Isotope Evidence, Master of Arts Thesis, Department of Anthropology, University of Nebraska, Lincoln.
Santley, R. S., and R. T. Alexander, 1992, The Political Economy of Core-Periphery Systems, in: *Resource, Power, and Interregional Interaction* (E. M. Schortman and P. A. Urban, eds.), Plenum Publishing Co., New York, pp. 23-49.
Santoro Vargas, C. M., 1992, Formativo en la región de valles occidentales del área centro sur andina (sur de Perú-norte de Chile), Paper presented at the Simposio Formativo en Sud-América, Cuenca, Ecuador.
Schiappacasee F., V., and H. Niemeyer Fernández, 1992, Avances y sugerencias para el conocimiento de la prehistoria tardía en la desembocadura del Valle de Camarones (Región de Tarapacá), *Chungara* 22:63-84.
Schiappacasse F., V., V. Castro R., and H. Niemeyer Fernández, 1989, Los desarrollos regionales en el Norte Grande (1000 a 1400 d.C.), in: *Culturas de Chile: Prehistoria desde sus orígenes hasta los albores de la Conquista* (J. Hidalgo, V. Schiappacasse, H. Niemeyer, C. Aldunate, and I. Solimano, eds.), Editorial Andrés Bello, Santiago, pp. 181-220.
Stanish, C., 1992, Track of the Puma: Regional Settlement and State Expansion North of Lake Titicaca, Paper presented at the 57th Annual Meetings Society for American Archaeology, Pittsburgh.
Thomas Winter, C., M. A. Benaventa Aninat, and C. Massone Messano, 1986, Zoomorphic Representations of the Snuff Trays and Rock Art in the Loa Medio Region, in: *Cultural Attitudes to Animals Including Birds, Fish and Invertebrates* (T. Ingold and M. Maltby, eds.) 3, World Archaeological Congress, Allen & Unwin, London, pp. 3-12.
Torres, C. M., D. B. Repke, K. Chan, D. McKenna, A. Llagostera, and R. E. Schultes, 1990, Botanical, Chemical and Contextual Analysis of Archaeological Snuff Powders from San Pedro de Atacama, Northern Chile, Mimeographed report.
Webster, A. D., 1992, Camelids before and during the Tiwanaku Hegemony, Paper presented at the 20th Midwest Conference on Andean and Amazonian Archaeology and Ethnohistory, Urbana.
Webster, A. D., 1993, Shifting species abundance patterns and the increased use of camelids in the Tiwanaku valley Bolivia: Formative period to Tiwanaku V. Paper presented at the 58th Annual Meeting, Society for American Archaeology, St. Louis, Mo.

Chapter **10**

Population and Agriculture in the Emergence of Complex Society in the Bolivian Altiplano
The Case of Tiwanaku

JAMES EDWARD MATHEWS

INTRODUCTION

Recent studies have advanced our understanding of the prehistoric culture-history, socio-political dynamics, and economic systems of the Middle Horizon Tiwanaku civilization (Kolata, i.p.; Kolata and Rivera 1989; Kolata, Stanish, and Rivera 1987). During the past two decades, three major models have been developed to explain Tiwanaku's evolution from incipient complex society to expansionist state in the southern Andean region (Figure 1). Two of these, John Murra's "vertical archipelago" (Murra 1975, 1980) and David Browman's "*altiplano* mode of production" are based on

---

JAMES EDWARD MATHEWS • Field Museum of Natural History, Roosevelt Road at Lake Shore Drive, Chicago, Illinois 60605, U.S.A.

Emergence and Change in Early Urban Societies, edited by Linda Manzanilla, Plenum Press, New York, 1997.

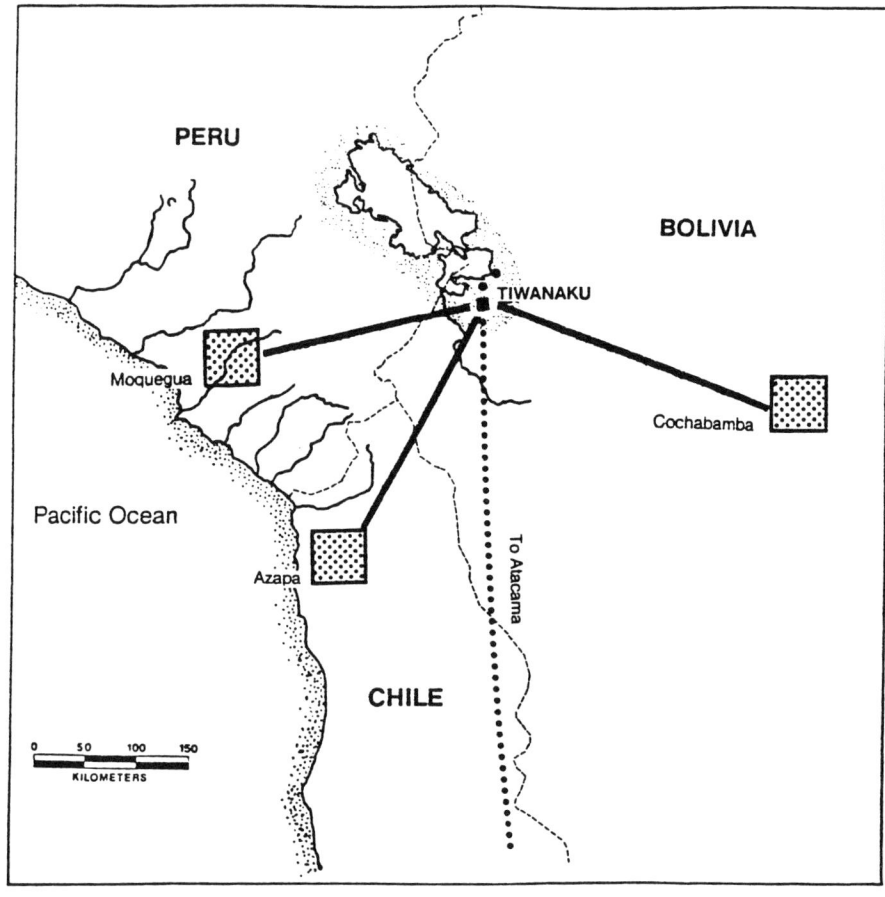

Figure 1. The south Andean region.

the premise that the Andean *altiplano* cannot support large, dense populations and complex societies. The third, Alan Kolata's agricultural production model, holds that using an indigenous agricultural technology, the *altiplano* near Lake Titicaca can be exploited in such a way as to sustain large populations.

The research reported here was designed to test these three models. At the core of this study was a systematic intensive archaeological survey of the Tiwanaku heartland. Prior to 1990, no such survey had been conducted. As part of the Proyecto Wila Jawira (Bolivia's *Instituto Nacional de Arqueología* and the University of Chicago), the valley was divided into

THE BOLIVIAN ALTIPLANO

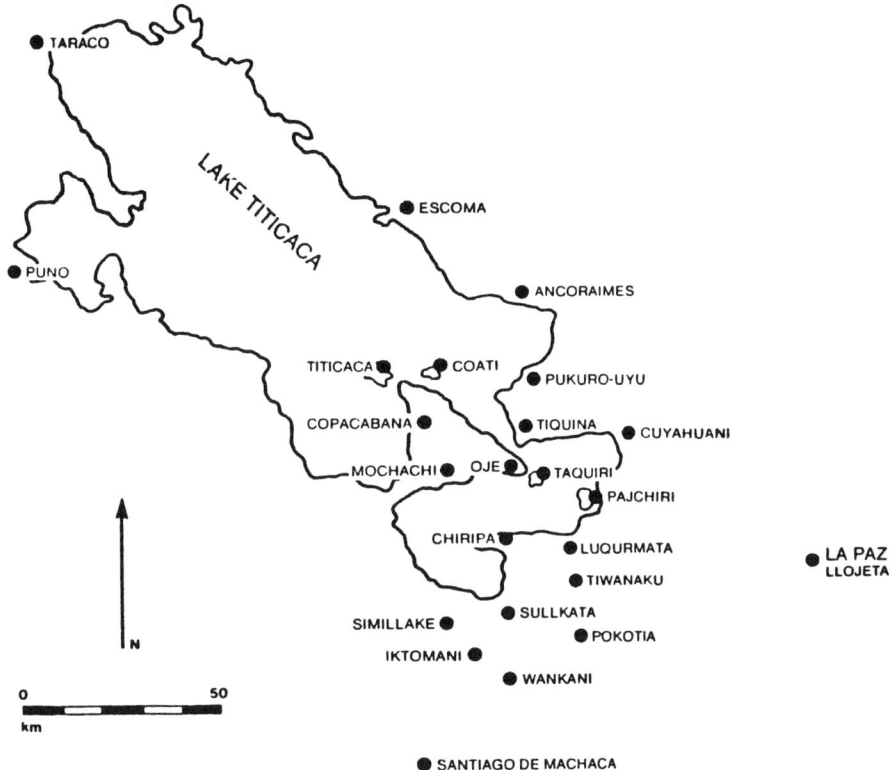

Figure 2. The Titicaca Basin.

three survey zones: the lower, middle, and upper sectors. This report presents the findings of the Middle Tiwanaku Valley Survey.

The Middle Tiwanaku Valley data demonstrate that Tiwanaku's development was initially founded on a tripartite economic base of lacustrine resources, camelid pastoralism, and agricultural production. By the latest stages of Tiwanaku's hegemony, agriculture has become the primary engine in driving Tiwanaku's economic expansion.

THE TIWANAKU VALLEY: ENVIRONMENT AND ECOLOGY

The Middle Tiwanaku Valley is situated in the northern Bolivian *altiplano*, at an elevation of 3800 meters above sea level (Figures 2 and 3). It is oriented roughly east-west, and covers an area of 180 square kilometers.

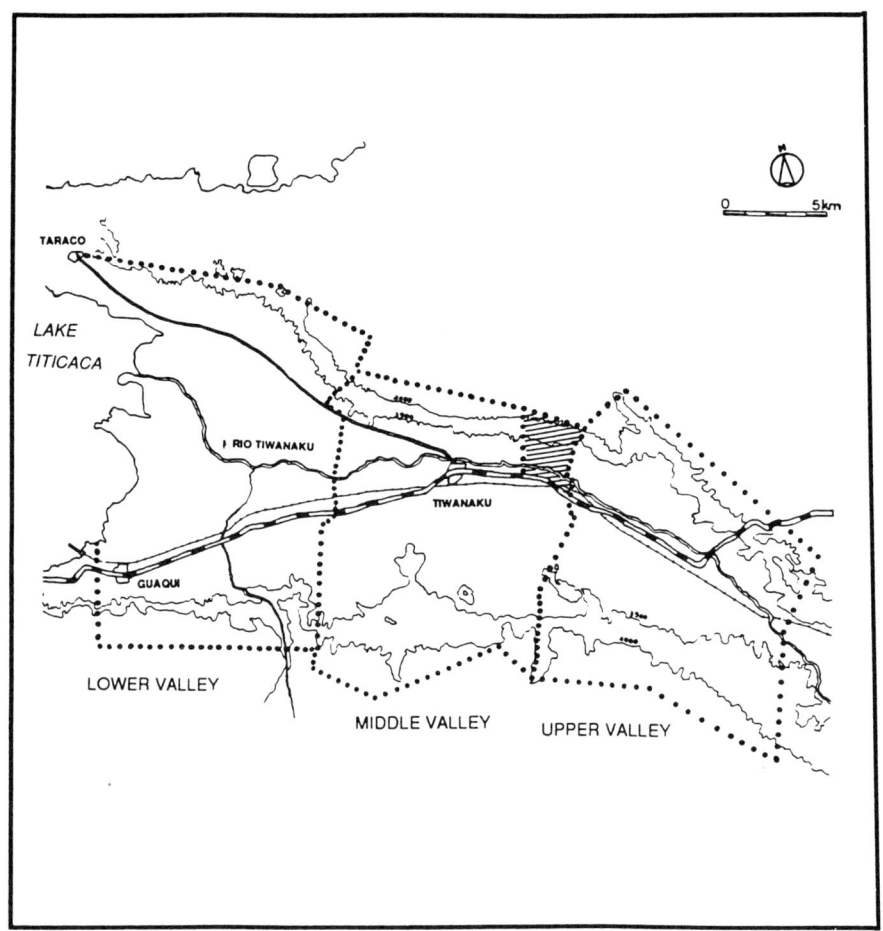

Figure 3. The Tiwanaku Valley.

The valley floor is a flat, relatively featureless alluvial plain bounded on the north and south by tertiary geological formations (Pérez Valencia 1984).

The *altiplano* is a difficult environment. Soils are poorly-suited for agriculture, being highly saline, with low nutrient content (ONERN 1965a, 1965b; Vacher *et al.* 1991). Climatic conditions are harsh, with irregular rainfall during the wet months of November to March. Low temperatures limit the growing season and contribute to the high risk endemic to subsistence agriculture in the region (Browman 1986; Pérez Valencia 1984).

These conditions, combined with the lack of domestic architecture visible on the surface at Tiwanaku, led early researchers to conclude that

Tiwanaku did not sustain a large resident population, but was a pilgrimage site or vacant ceremonial center (Bennett 1934, 1936; Squier 1877). Contemporary studies have disproved this hypothesis, supporting instead the perspective that Tiwanaku was a true urban site (Browman 1978; Kolata 1982, 1985, 1986, 1987; Parsons 1968; Ponce Sanginés 1969, 1981b; Stanish 1989). At present, there exists no direct data regarding developmental processes of Tiwanaku's urbanism.

RESULTS AND DISCUSSION

The Middle Tiwanaku Valley Survey was designed to obtain a 100 percent coverage of the region. Details on the methodology are available elsewhere (Mathews 1992a) and will not be reviewed here. It has been calculated that the survey results are accurate to within two percent in terms of surface remains (Mathews 1992a:36-37).

Nearly 600 archaeological sites were registered in the Middle Tiwanaku Valley, representing more than 3500 years of human occupation. The data bear directly on the problem of the formation of the Tiwanaku state; specifically, was Tiwanaku's development the result of endogenous factors afforded by the specific benefits of the lacustrine environmental niche, or was it a result of exogenous factors made necessary by the *altiplano* environment? The question will be addressed following a brief synopsis of field data from the Middle Tiwanaku Valley Survey.

SUMMARY OF FIELD DATA

The Formative Period: 1350 B.C.–A.D. 100

The earliest observable human occupation of the Middle Tiwanaku Valley is the Formative Period, from 1350 B.C. to A.D. 100. The Formative Period is far more complicated than previous research had suggested. It encompasses at least two, and possible four distinct cultural traditions (Mathews 1992a, 1992b, i.p.). The earliest ceramic producing cultures in the Middle Tiwanaku valley are represented by the lowest levels of the sites TMV-79 (*T'ijini Pata*) and TMV-101 (*Tilata*).

The most enigmatic material es that found beneath Tiwanaku I levels at Tilata, provisionally termed "Pre-Tiwanaku" (Figure 4). This crude ceramic comes from a single occupation level and an associated feature two-and-half meters below the surface. This ware bears little resemblance to later Tiwanaku tradition plainwares.

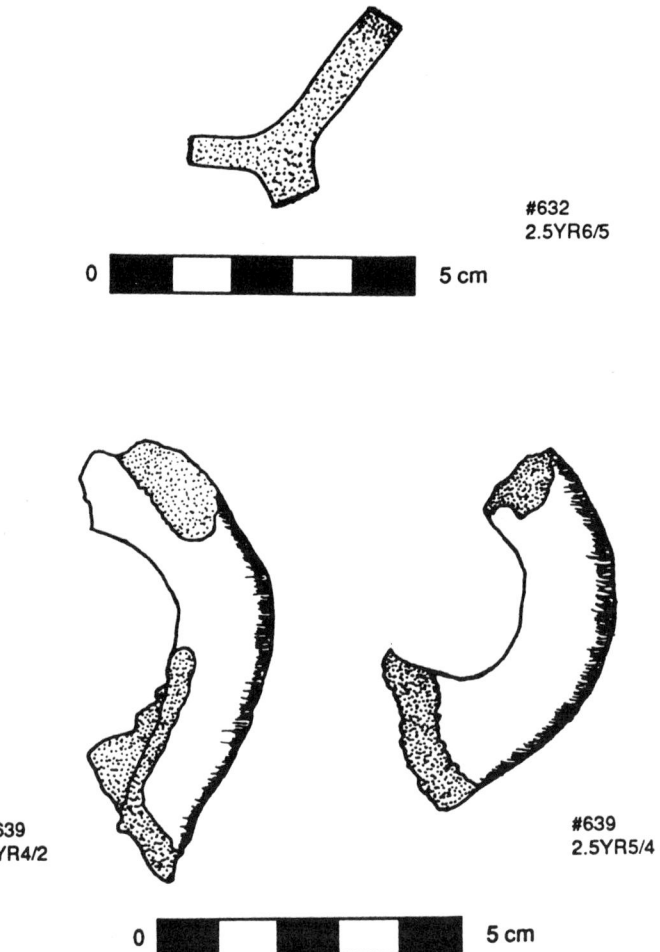

Figure 4. Pre-Tiwanaku ceramic material from TMV-101.

The second Early Formative culture identified in the Middle Tiwanaku Valley is better represented (Figure 5). This is the "Early Formative Lateral Banded/Incised (LBI)" material underlying Classic Chiripa levels at TMV-79 (Mathews 1992a), and dated by C-14 to 660±60 B.C. This culture appears to be similar to Chiripa in terms of subsistence systems and economy (*e.g.*, functional ceramic assemblages, and faunal and botanical remains), but the ceramic material is distinctive. This material is not found on the surface of TMV-79 or any of the other Chiripa sites in the valley, so its distribution remains poorly defined.

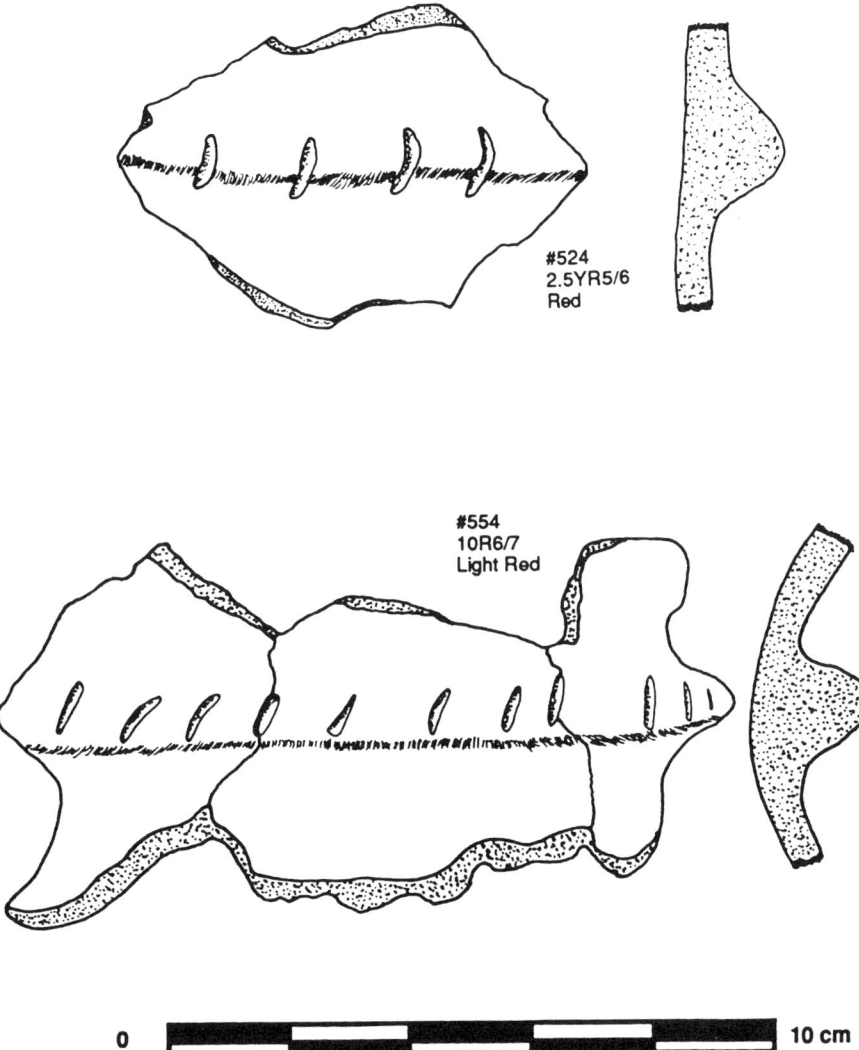

Figure 5. Early Formative LBI ceramic material from TMV-79.

The Chiripa sites in the middle valley correspond to the Classic Chiripa (Bennett 1936), or Mamani Phase (Browman 1980, 1981), dating from 600 B.C. to 100/200 A.D. (Figure 6). They are found exclusively in the foothills on the north and south sides of the valley, at elevations of 3850 to 4000 meters above sea level. The locations of these sites suggest that they are situated to exploit a variety of ecological zones (Albarracín-Jordán and

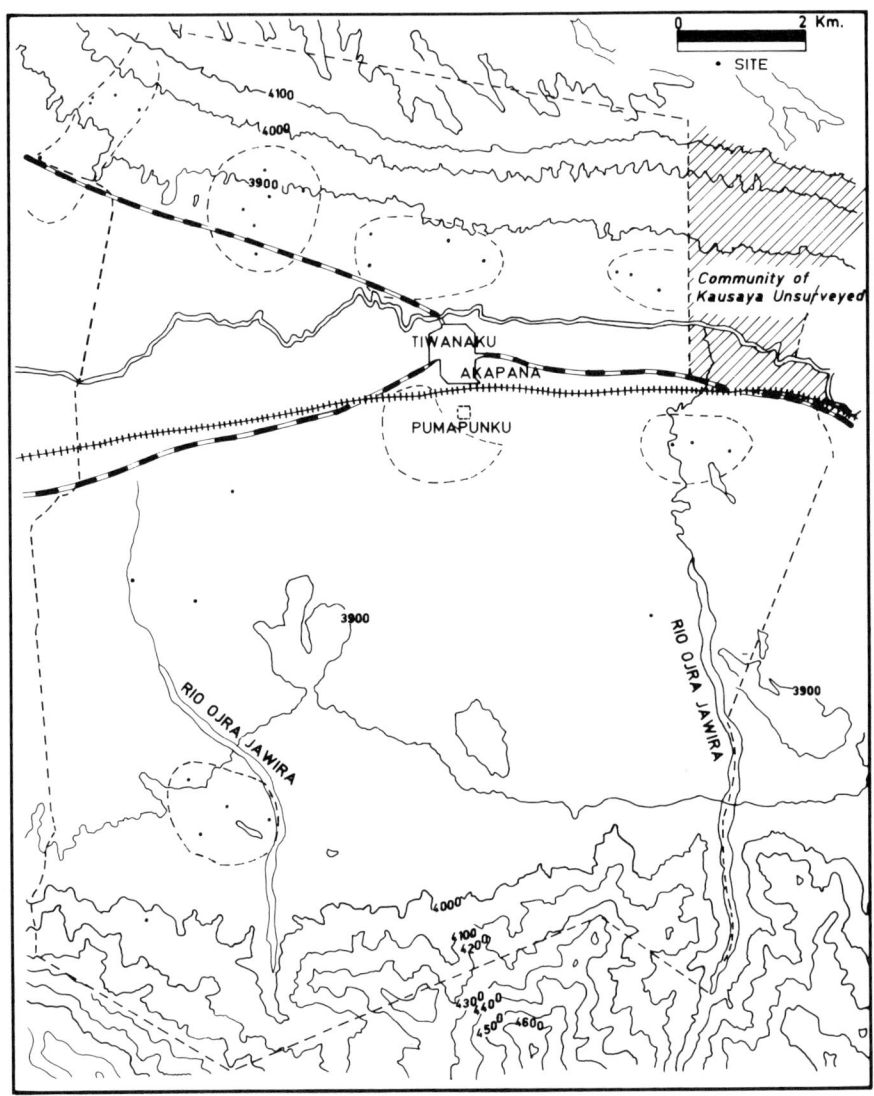

Figure 6. Chiripa settlement pattern, Middle Tiwanaku Valley.

Mathews 1990). Excavation data indicate a continuation of Early Formative economic patterns.

The sites exhibit a clustering pattern (Albarracín-Jordán and Mathews 1990), each cluster consisting of three to eight sites, with each discrete group separated by an average distance of three kilometers. The clusters are composed of a large, central site surrounded by several smaller ones. The large sites are situated on hills between deep *quebradas* with difficult access. All of the Chiripa-associated sites are abandoned with Tiwanaku control of the region.

The Chiripa sites in the Middle Tiwanaku Valley exhibit a high degree of settlement organization. However, the socio-political organization of the Chiripa culture is not well-defined. Its public architecture, and its central role in coordinating far-reaching exchange networks (Bermann 1990; Lanning 1967; Kolata 1983), suggest at least a chiefdom-level organization, a hypothesis suppported by the Middle Tiwanaku Valley settlement data.

Formative Tiwanaku

The earliest ceramic-producing cultures at Tiwanaku are poorly understood. The first three of Carlos Ponce Sanginés' (1981b) five-phase ceramic seriation have never been unambiguously described. Recent research (Arellano López 1991; Mathews 1992a) has offered evidence for the combination of Tiwanaku I and Tiwanaku III ceramic material, and it is widely accepted that Tiwanaku II material does not exist. This lack of description and definition creates certain difficulties for the investigation; however, it suffices at present to gloss this material as "Formative Tiwanaku," or Qeya (Wallace 1957).

Formative Tiwanaku sites are found exclusively on the alluvial plain below 3900 meters above sea level, and appear to be randomly distributed (Figure 7). Formative Tiwanaku sites do not exhibit earlier material on the surface. All of these sites are occupied during later Tiwanaku periods, contrasting with the abandonment of Chiripa sites at this time.

The significance of the seemingly random Formative Tiwanaku settlement pattern is unclear, but the distribution of these sites on the valley floor suggests a greater focus of Tiwanaku subsistence on floodplain agriculture (Albarracín-Jordán and Mathews 1990). However, the periodically inundated and saline soils of the Tiwanaku Valley would have made such cultivation a difficult undertaking, and available data are not adequate to test this hypothesis.

One gap in our knowledge of the Formative Tiwanaku Period is at Tiwanaku itself. It is possible that the valley population was concentrated in Tiwanaku and other proto-urban centers such as Lukurmata and Pajchiri (Ponce Sanginés 1979; Albarracín-Jordán and Mathews 1990). While data relevant to this question are limited, it is possible that during Formative Tiwanaku, the Tiwanaku Valley population was reorganized in a fashion similar to the concentration of population at other major prehispanic urban centers in the Americas such as Teotihuacán (Adams 1966; Cowgill

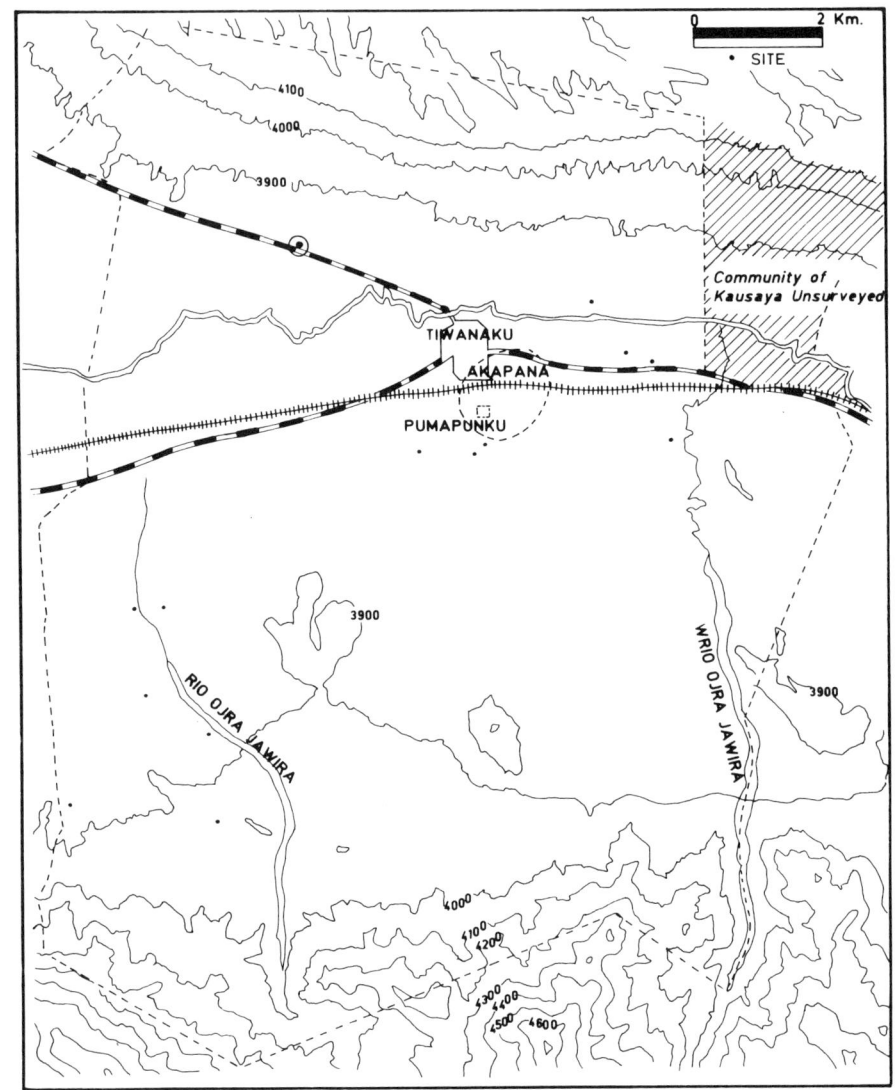

Figure 7. Formative Tiwanaku settlement pattern, Middle Tiwanaku Valley.

1975; Parsons 1971, 1974, 1976; Sanders 1965, 1972, 1976), and other chiefdom-level societies (*e.g.* Hasemann 1987; Flannery, Marcus, and Kowalewski 1981; Roosevelt 1987). If this hypothesis is correct, the Tiwanaku situation conforms to a model of urban genesis developed by Paul Wheatley (1967, 1971), which posits that the ceremonial center is the prototypical urban form *par excellence*.

The Formative Period is still poorly understood, and continued analysis of survey data and material recovered from test excavations at early sites in the Middle Tiwanaku Valley will be needed to refine our knowledge of this period of early cultural development in the region.

Tiwanaku IV: A.D. 375–750

The Tiwanaku IV, or Classic Tiahuanaco, Period has been defined by specific ceramic and architectural styles which characterized Tiwanaku from A.D. 375 to 750 (Albarracín-Jordán and Mathews 1990; Bennett 1934; Kolata 1983; Ponce Sanginés 1981b; Tapia Pineda 1978). This period corresponds to Tiwanaku's first pan-Titicaca Basin expansion and direct annexation (Kolata 1983; Ponce Sanginés 1979, 1981b; and others).

The settlement pattern in the Middle Tiwanaku Valley during Tiwanaku IV changes radically from that of Formative Tiwanaku. The most striking characteristic is the expansion of settlement beyond the perimeters of the urban core. There are several attributes of this pattern worthy of mention here.

There is a reappearance of large sites during this period, ranging 10 to 12 hectares (Figure 8). These sites again conform to a distinctive settlement pattern, spaced at intervals of one-and-a-half to three kilometers along the north and south sierras of the valley (Albarracín-Jordán 1990; Albarracín-Jordán and Mathews 1990). Some of these sites are connected to raised fields on the valley floor by causeways (Albarracín-Jordán and Mathews 1990). Unlike the Formative Period pattern, these sites do not form the core of site clusters. Smaller sites are not located according to an organized pattern, although it is likely that they had some relation to agricultural production.

There is a break in the pattern in the area near Tiwanaku, suggesting that many of the administrative functions carried out at the auxiliary nodes were handled at Tiwanaku in the central part of the valley. If the Tiwanaku IV settlement pattern represents control of agricultural production through directly subsidiary sites (Albarracín-Jordán and Mathews 1990), the fact that the pattern breaks down in the vicinity of Tiwanaku suggests that some urban residents were directly engaged in agricultural production on the outskirts of the city.

Not all of the Tiwanaku IV secondary sites were involved in agriculture, however. Agriculture does not appear to have been a viable proposition in the pampa to the south of Tiwanaku, which is higher, dryer, and characterized by different vegetation and hydrologic regimes. The area was not terraced, in contrast to the Lower Tiwanaku Valley (Albarracín-Jordán and Mathews 1990). The large site settlement pattern persists here nonetheless.

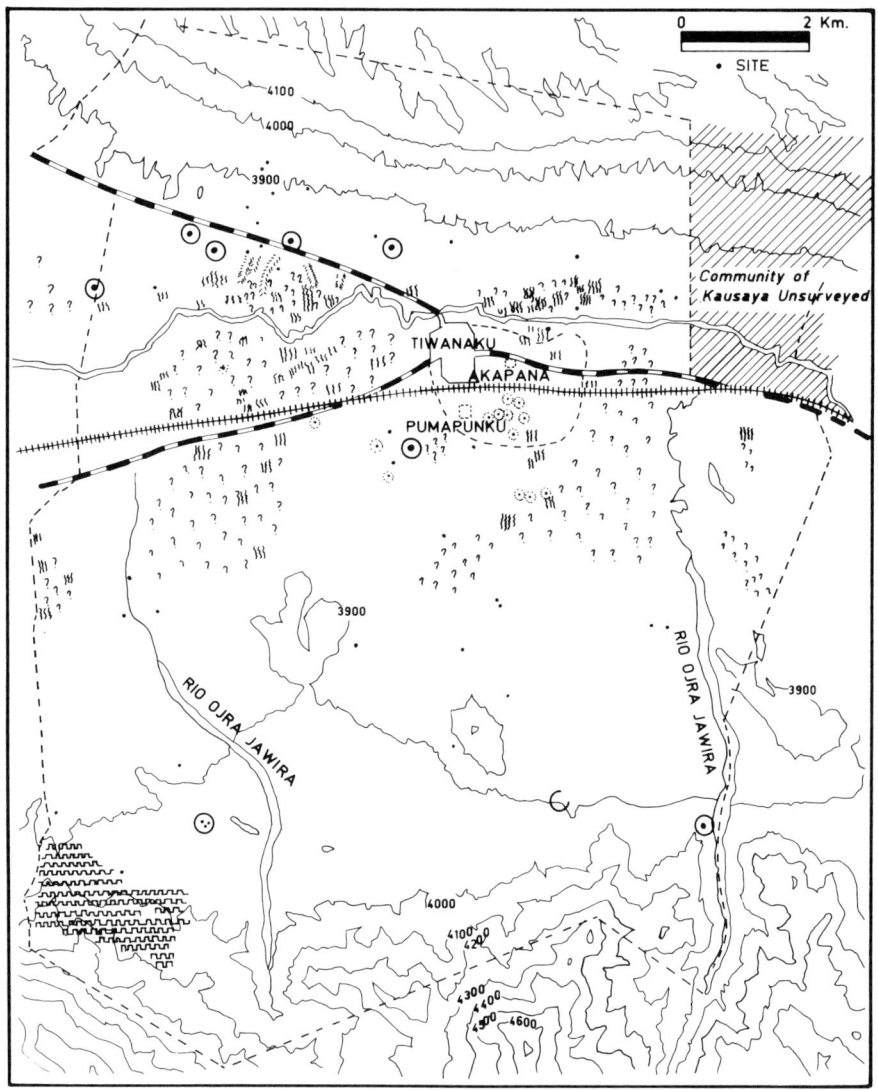

Figure 8. Tiwanaku IV settlement pattern, Middle Tiwanaku Valley.

It is likely that these sites fulfilled a role related to the transportation and distribution of resources to the growing urban core of Tiwanaku.

Analysis of excavated material from Tiwanaku IV sites in the Middle Tiwanaku Valley indicates a general reduction in species variability represented in domestic contexts, with camelids and fish being the major species represented. Another factor that distinguishes Tiwanaku IV from the earlier periods is a relative increase in ceremonial and storage vessels. These assemblage changes can be associated with increased social stratification and ascendency of elites, and the accentuation of redistributive aspects of the Tiwanaku economy.

Tiwanaku V: A.D. 750–1000

Tiwanaku V (Ponce Sanginés 1981a, 1981b), or Decadent Tiahuanaco (Bennett 1934) lasted from A.D. 750 to 1000. In terms of regional settlement systems, several phenomena distinguish the Tiwanaku V Period from Tiwanaku IV (Figure 9). First is an increase in the number of sites. Most of the new Tiwanaku V sites were small, and a large percentage of them were directly associated with agricultural fields. Second is an increase in the size of the large sites established in the Tiwanaku IV period. These facts indicate a population increase of the Tiwanaku Valley at this time. However, the distributions of sizes of sites abandoned at the end of Tiwanaku IV, Formative sites reoccupied during Tiwanaku V, and newly founded Tiwanaku V sites suggest that Tiwanaku's administrative structure did not expand with the increased population (Mathews 1992a).

The accentuation of the Tiwanaku IV pattern during Tiwanaku V indicates that several interrelated processes were taking place at this time. First, the increase in the number and size of sites (including Tiwanaku) represents an increasing total population in the valley. Second, the increased population required more intensive agricultural production, necessitating a more direct administration of the outlying areas. This scenario accounts for the larger sizes of the secondary sites, and the increased number of small sites associated with agricultural features.

These demographic changes and corresponding changes in the administrative structures of agricultural production and distribution may have contributed to the collapse of Tiwanaku. A larger population would have put increasing pressure on the biotic resources of the Tiwanaku Valley and its immediate environs, placing intense demands on an ever-decreasing environmental capacity to supply them. Further, more labor was required to maintain high levels of agricultural production. While the overall productive capacity of raised field systems has been amply demostrated (*e.g.*, Denevan 1982; Erickson 1985, 1988; Garaycochea 1986; Kolata 1986, 1991; and others), there are empirical pressures that affect and limit the productivity of *any* agricultural system. Over-exploitation of the complex raised field system, both in terms of natural resources and human labor, may have contributed to Tiwanaku's collapse.

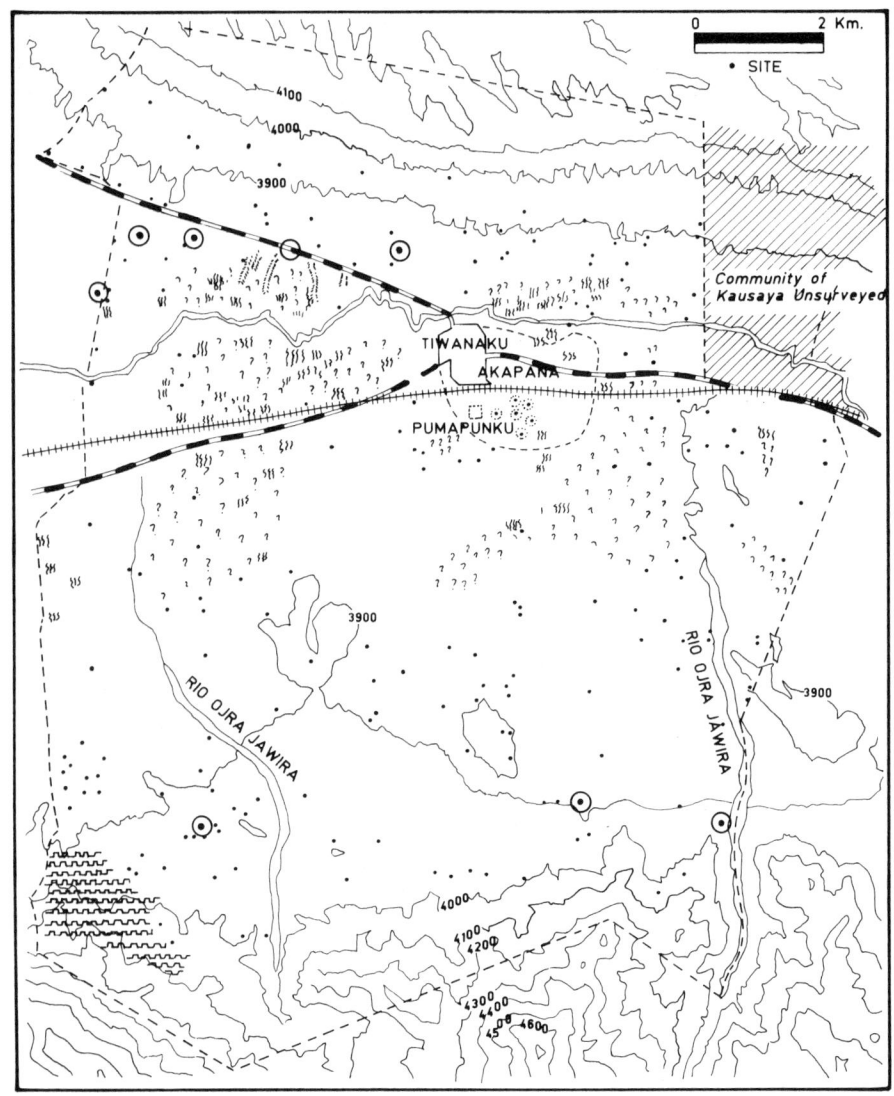

Figure 9. Tiwanaku V settlement pattern, Middle Tiwanaku Valley.

With increased population and more intensive agricultural production, the balance of Tiwanaku's power base may have shifted enough to create a condition of political instability in the context of ecological instability. The secondary centers such as TMV-101, TMV-149, TMC-558, *et cetera*, undoubtedly gained authority in the local administration of their own populations at this time. The greater demand for agricultural produce necessitated a relinquishing of control by Tiwanaku to the secondary centers and hence, an increasingly decentralized control of production. It is possible that the seeds of Tiwanaku's collapse were sown during the apogee of this hegemony in the south Andes.

The Post-Tiwanaku Period

Although the causes of the Tiwanaku collapse are still speculative, its results are vividly evident in the Post-Tiwanaku (A.D. 1000-1530) settlement patterns, in which the highly structured Tiwanaku organization disintegrates completely (Figure 10).

Three Post-Tiwanaku phases have been defined for the Tiwanaku Valley. The first of these, Early Pacajaes, is associated with the formation of the Aymara Kingdoms in the Titicaca Basin, from A.D. 1000 to 1470. This period reflects the complete collapse of the Tiwanaku state in the south Andes. In the Tiwanaku Valley, the large, evenly-spaced Tiwanaku V sites give way to a plethora of small sites, the majority less than one hectare in size. Early Pacajaes occupations were identified at some 526 sites. The large number of sites of this period may reflect differential preservation (Parsons 1976), but it is more likely that the Early Pacajaes settlement pattern is an accurate indication of the fractionation of Tiwanaku V nucleated settlements.

The second implication of the Early Pacajaes settlement pattern is the demographic change between Tiwanaku V and the immediately post-Tiwanaku period. The increase in number of sites by some 150 percent over the preceding Tiwanaku V period suggests not so much an overall population decrease in the valley with the collapse of Tiwanaku, but perhaps a population re-organization.

The Early Pacajaes sites are randomly scattered across the landscape, and are found in ecological zones that had not been settled previously (Albarracín-Jordán and Mathews 1990:141), suggesting that the collapse of the Tiwanaku administrative organization allowed or forced small social groups to seek individual habitation sites. There is some continuity with earlier Tiwanaku traditions, however, as manifested by settlement pattern and some continuation of decorated ceramic motifs and technology (Figure 11).

In the Middle Tiwanaku Valley, the Pacajaes Kingdom was impacted by the Inka expansion throughout the south Central Andes for a relatively brief period before the arrival of the Spanish *conquistadores*. No true purely Inka sites appear to have been settled at this time, but rather, the Inka "settlement pattern" more likely represents the diffusion of certain elements of Inka culture into the indigenous population. These charac-

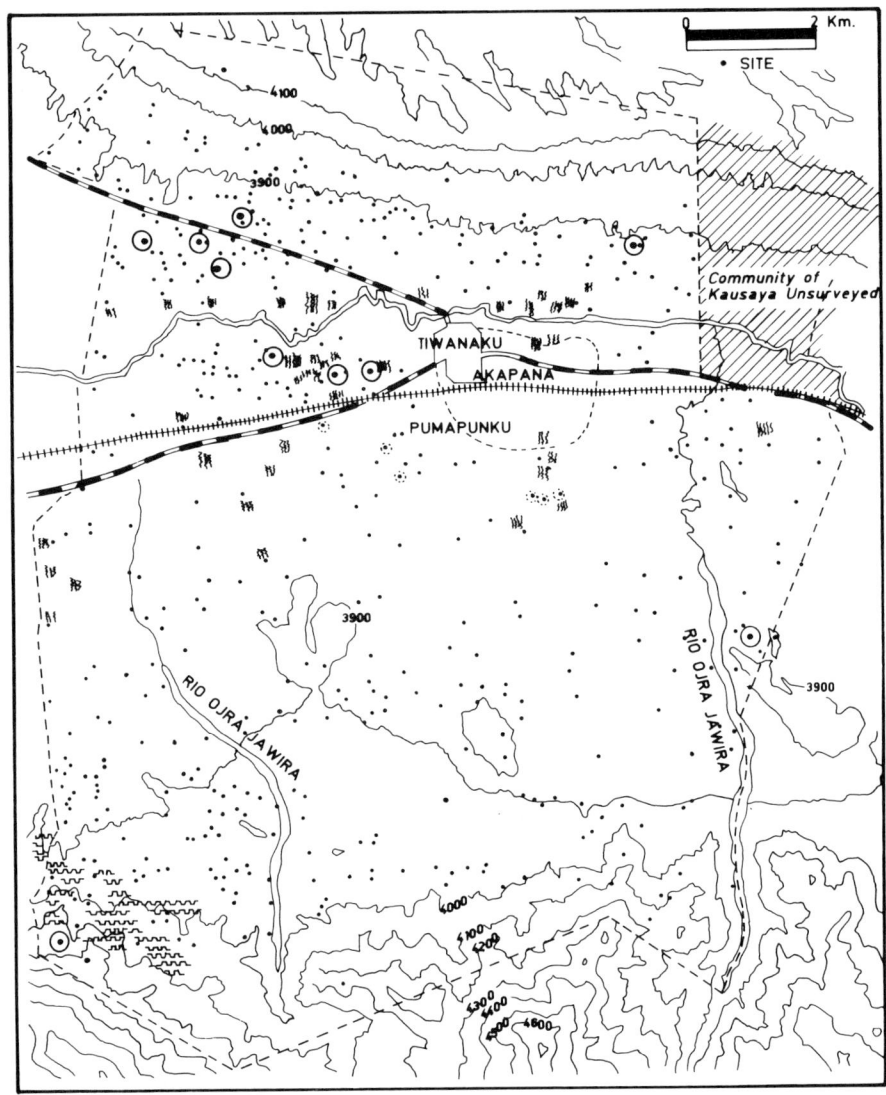

Figure 10. Early Pacajaes settlement pattern, Middle Tiwanaku Valley.

teristics are suggestive of Inka indirect rule. The Inka presence in the region did not necessarily completely undercut the indigenous cultural tradition, but rather existed over the matrix of local traditions of material culture.

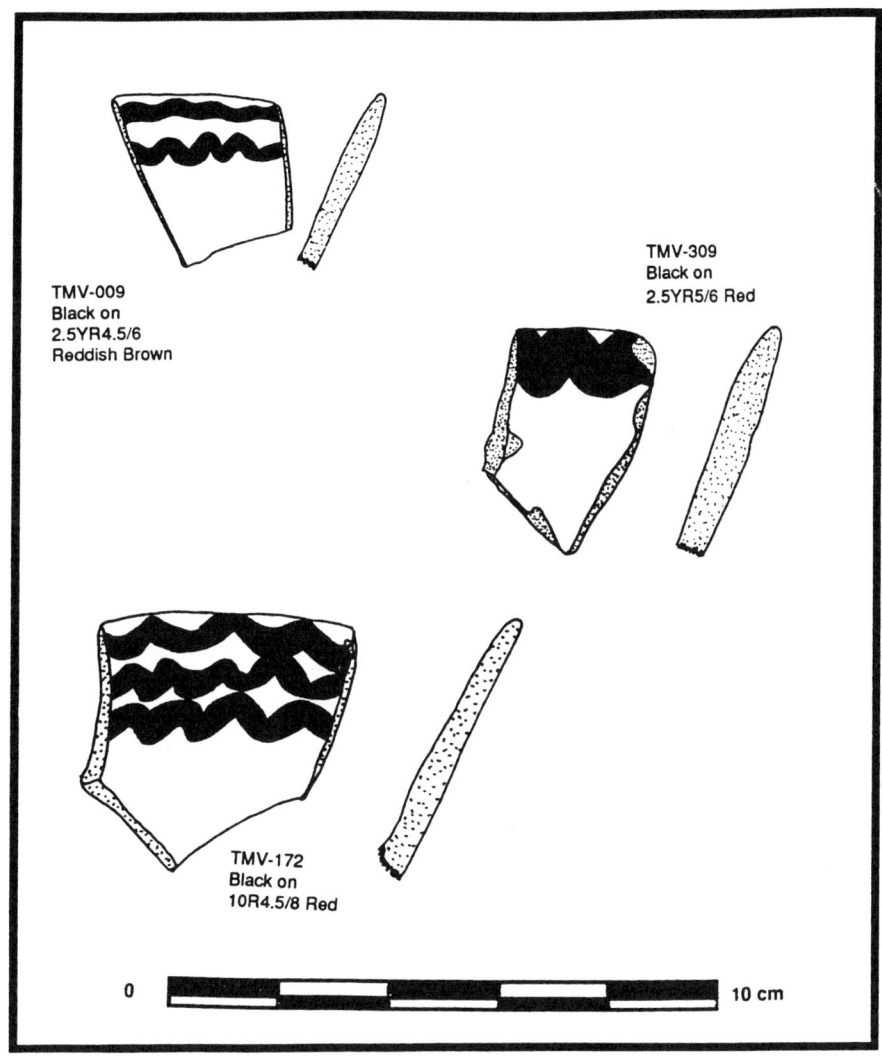

Figure 11. Early Pacajaes ceramic sherds with Tiwanaku V influence.

These survey data provide new insights into the diachronic development of the Tiwanaku state through an extrapolation of the regional, empirical, and systematic analysis of prehistoric settlement in the area. As a result, the results serve as a general framework within which to contextualize detailed, problem-specific investigations of still poorly-understood aspects of Tiwanaku's cultural and socio-political development (Figure 12).

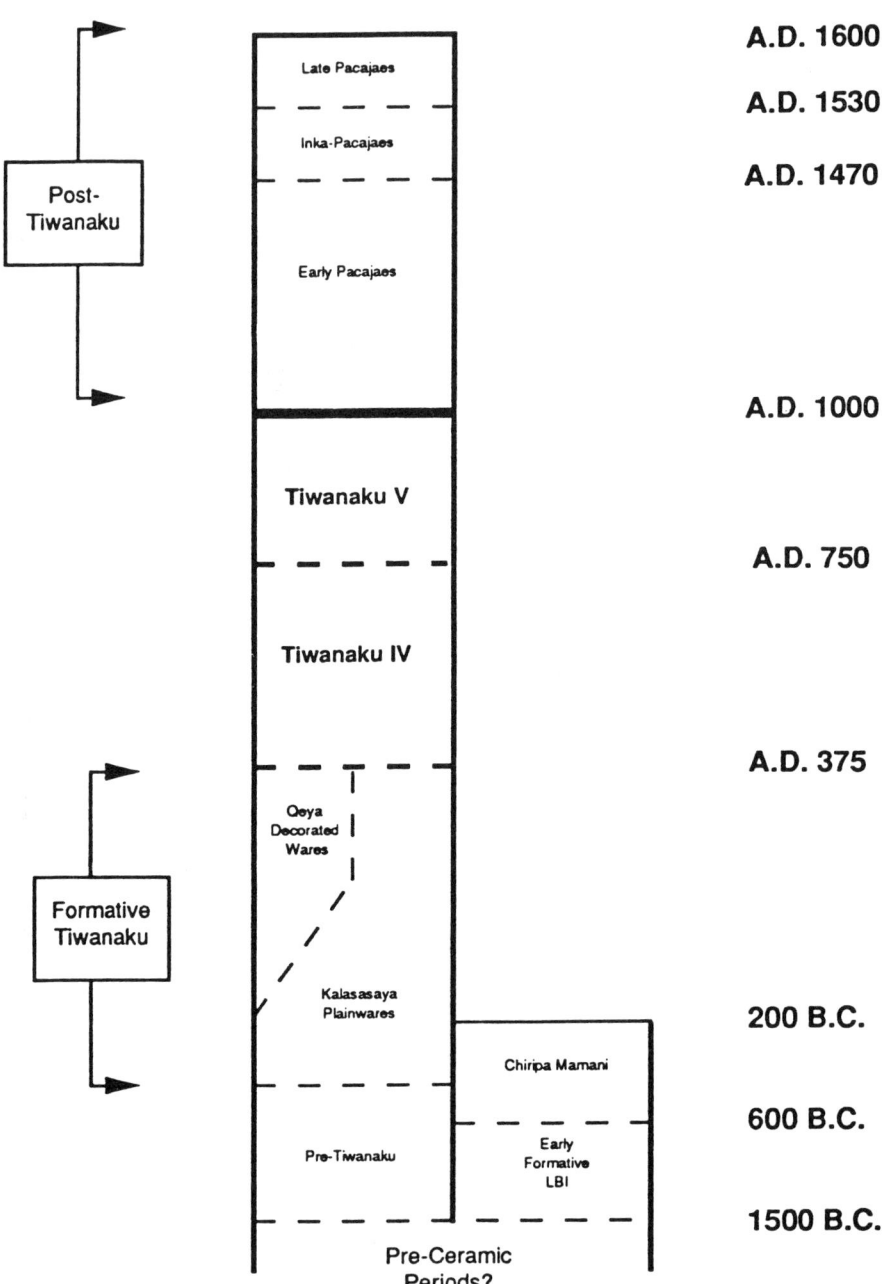

Figure 12. Proposed relative chronological sequence, Middle Tiwanaku Valley.

TESTING THE MODELS

We now have a considerable body of settlement data from the Middle Tiwanaku Valley, and limited (but systematic) excavation data with which to test the three major models of Tiwanaku's development enumerated above, the archipelago model, the "*altiplano*" model, and the autochthonous model. Briefly, the archaeological correlates of each model are:

The Vertical Archipelago

(1) Evidence for exchange in exotic (i.e., non-local) goods from an early stage of development. This may imply a number of means of procurement, but coupled with other evidence, supports a model of direct control, especially if access to these resource areas is stable through time.

(2)* Maintenance of ethnic identity between core and periphery regions. This criterion is difficult to prove except through comparative studies specifically designed to elucidate this type of data.

(3) Finally, the lack of strong evidence supporting an alternate model, such as trade or agricultural self-sufficiency, would lend support to an archipelago model of Tiwanaku's political and economic development.

The *Altiplano* Model of Production

(1) Evidence for exchange in exotic goods, but distinguished from the archipelago model by greater fluctuation in availability of goods from other resource zones. These non-local goods would include "long-distance, status-validating materials" (Browman 1980:108).

(2) Diversity of resources is maintained at constantly high levels through time, since the fundamental economic structures are established early in socio-political development.

(3) Factors related to utilization of camelids. Given importance of trade networks in the *altiplano* model, the archaeological record should demonstrate a change in patterns of animal husbandry from an emphasis on direct subsistence consumption to predominant use as pack animals and sources of wool.

(4) Regional specialization of craft production. This is a fundamental tenet of the *altiplano* model (Browman 1978, 1981, 1984). Accordingly, we should expect to see early accentuation of these patterns.

(5) As for the verticality model, the *altiplano* model could be refuted by negative evidence or overwhelming evidence in support of an alternate model of development.

Agricultural Production

(1) Large-scale water control projects including, but not limited to, raised fields, river canalizations, *et cetera* (Kolata 1986, 1991).

(2) Distinction between elite and "proletarian" material culture. This criteria holds for *any* complex society, not simply those based on agricultural production.

(3) Hierarchical settlement networks. Settlements may be expected in order to maximize efficiency of agricultural production.

(4) Evidence of intensive agricultural production, and botanical evidence of shifts from more to less diversity in cultivated species inventory (*e.g.* concentration on fewer crops).

It is now possible to systematically compare the survey and excavation data for best fit with one of the above models, or to determine if none of the above models apply and some other explanation is warranted.

The Archipelago Model

The archipelago model, or specifically, Mujica's (1985) variation of it based on research by Berenguer (1978; Berenguer *et al.* 1980; Berenguer and Dauelsberg 1988), Iván Muñoz (1983), Percy Dauelsberg, and others, posits a strong *altiplano* influence in the western slopes of the Andes to the Pacific coast from between 1500 B.C. and A.D. 500 (Mujica 1985:109). Following Núñez (1972), Mujica implicates Chiripa-related cultures as establishing direct control of the western valleys. These were independent corporate groups, rather that *altiplano* colonists. Therefore, Mujica (1985:120) suggests that the *altiplano* influence after the initial intrusion into the coastal valleys (500 B.C. and A.D. 300) is characteristic of trade; permanent Tiwanaku colonies do not appear until after A.D. 500.

Certain evidence supports the first part of Mujica's model, that the initial settlers of the western valleys from the *altiplano* did not act as economic colonists in the sense implied by verticality. However, while an *altiplano* influence can be substantiated on the southern Peruvian coast, there is little evidence from the *altiplano* for the reciprocal; *i.e.* coastal products making their way to the *altiplano*. No identifiable exotics were recovered from the two Formative sites tested in the Middle Tiwanaku Valley, with the exception of a single vessel recovered from TMV-79. Identifiable faunal species are all indigenous to the *altiplano*, and paleobotanical analysis did not identify any exotics. Mujica's (1985:11) scenario of *altiplano* immigrants breaking ties to the highlands in order to exploit coastal areas explains the *altiplano* influence in the valleys and the lack of corresponding coastal influence in the *altiplano*. However, these data do not support an archipelago model of Tiwanaku development.

Mujica's model is significant in that as early as 1500 B.C., socio-economic influences are directed *from* the *altiplano toward* the coast, an idea also used by Mario Rivera as evidence for the imposition of *altiplano* high cultures over less developed coastal societies (Rivera 1975, 1980). In essence, the model predicates a considerable degree of social and economic complexity in the *altiplano before* the establishment of peripheral settlements. Given this precondition, the vertical archipelago could have been an adaptive economic strategy put into practice by an already complex society, but was unlikely to have been instrumental in their early formation.

The *Altiplano* Model

Browman's *altiplano* model of Tiwanaku state development is subject to many of the same considerations as the verticality or archipelago model. Specifically, as in the archipelago model, there is little evidence from the Middle Tiwanaku Valley excavations for the procurement of exotic goods, in either constant or irregular supply. The single anomalous vessel noted above has yet to be *proven* an import, and even if so, hardly constitutes evidence for formal regional trade networks spanning thousands of square kilometers.

The second of the major tenets of the *altiplano* model, maintenance of a constant diversity of resources, is also unsupported by the present investigation. Archaeological data from all five sites tested in the Middle Tiwanaku Valley conclusively demonstrates a shift toward increasingly restricted resource bases (see Webster 1993). The diverse subsistence economies postulated by Browman (and corroborated by the present investigation) for the Formative Period are abandoned as the Tiwanaku economic system becomes more focused on pastoralism and intensive agriculture, most likely based on the production of a limited repertoire of crops.

The present investigation cannot adequately address the third element of the *altiplano* model, that related to changes in the dominant use of camelids. Recent research by Ann Webster (1993:151) has demonstrated a decreasingly intensive use of camelids for meat throughout the Tiwanaku sequence, but on the whole observes no major change in camelid utilization (Webster 1993:289). Webster's evidence thus tends to refute the *altiplano* model of Tiwanaku development.

Neither is the fourth aspect of the *altiplano* model, the development of regional craft specialization, supported by current data. While there is indeed a qualitative difference between Formative Tiwanaku and Chiripa ceramics and those of the preceding Lower Formative Period (e.g., Pre-Tiwanaku I and Early Formative LBI), this difference may be technical, and does not necessarily suggest "craft specialization" *per se*. Indeed, Chiripa and Formative Tiwanaku appear to have utilized similar ceramic assemblages and subsistence techniques, to the point that any "specialization" must be couched in terms of value rather than function. Craft specialization does occur during the Tiwanaku V Period (Mathews 1992a), but again, this would be much later than required by the *altiplano* model to have served as a stimulus to the formation of early exchange networks.

In short, the *altiplano* model is not supported by the Middle Tiwanaku Valley investigation. Having ruled out the two exogenous models of Tiwanaku state formation, we may now consider Kolata's agricultural production model.

The Autochthonous Model

In the agricultural production scenario, the Titicaca Basin's raised fields, especially those in the Tiwanaku heartland, were administered by "a classic agro-managerial bureaucracy" (Kolata 1987:40). Kolata (1987:41) suggests that agricultural production was the single most important *raison d'être* for the Tiwanaku administrative hierarchy, and speculates that raised fields were "chiefly responsible for supporting [Tiwanaku's] growing urban population" (Kolata 1979:24; see also Kolata 1986:748).

There is evidence in the Tiwanaku core area that supports Kolata's first criterion for an autochthonous development of the Tiwanaku state, that being a corporate focus on land reclamation projects and other types of water control. As reported elsewhere (Mathews 1989, 1991), the Tiwanaku Valley may have supported as many as 6,500 hectares of raised fields (Albarracín-Jordán and Mathews 1990:117). Large-scale river canalizations (Kolata 1986, 1991) have been documented in this region, and air photographs of the Tiwanaku Valley suggest that the length of the Río Tiwanaku near the prehistoric site itself may have been artificially straightened. The Middle Tiwanaku Valley evidences myriad smaller canals, dikes, and reservoirs such as *q'ochas* as well. While these projects are theoretically not beyond the capabilities of small (kin-based) corporate groups, in order to function as an integrated regional system, these works must have been coordinated by a supraregional organization with authority to direct labor, allocate resources, mediate disputes, *et cetera*.

The second of Kolata's criteria, the distinction between "elite" and "proletarian" material culture, is subject to a number of difficulties, stemming from the broad level of generalization implicit in the invocation of these terms. Here, it is sufficient to indicate that excavated materials in the

Middle Tiwanaku Valley suggest that these distinctions stem from local earlier traditions, rather than having been based on differential access to trade goods and other exotic materials.

Hierarchical settlement networks, the third element in Kolata's model, like differentiation between elite and common material culture, are characteristic of many complex societies, and need not specifically be associated with hydraulic bureaucracies. However, in the Middle Tiwanaku Valley, these hierarchical settlement patterns are directed towards agricultural production, with large sites connected to areas of raised fields and smaller sites via massive causeways.

Finally, evidence in the Middle Tiwanaku Valley suggests an increasingly intensive agricultural production and reduction in crop species inventory, to the point where the agricultural system and its corresponding administrative structure came under increasing stress. These interpretations are derived from an overall population increase in the valley, manifested by larger sites and greater numbers of them, and a decreased diversity of botanical species, with a notable emphasis on large chenopod grains (Lennstrom *et al.* 1991).

SUMMARY

The evidence in support of an autochthonous, agriculturally based model of Tiwanaku's state development is overwhelming. These data, coupled with a lack of corroborative data for alternative (exogenous) hypotheses, suggest that Kolata's formulations were fundamentally right in terms of theoretical orientation, although the present research demonstrates that a number of refinements in this model can be achieved through intensive and systematic field investigations.

It should also be noted that these data are presented as a developmental model; that is, they are meant to shed light on the primordial evolutionary processes of state formation in the Titicaca Basin. This exposition does not completely reject the analytic utility of the archipelago and *altiplano* models. For example, while Tiwanaku's early development may have stemmed largely from processes endemic to the Titicaca Basin, data from the Middle Tiwanaku Valley indicate considerable stress on the resulting structures by the Tiwanaku V Period. Coincidentally, this period corresponds to Tiwanaku's large-scale expansion outside the Titicaca Basin, and potentially also to the development of regional craft specialization, indicated by artifact assemblages at TMV-558. In this light, Tiwanaku expansion is not the result of an attempt to "complement" limited *altiplano* resources with goods from other ecological zones, but rather to procure basic foodstuffs given increasing pressures on the existing exploitative production system. The exact mechanism for this procurement could be either direct (colonization) or indirect (trade): further, either of these mechanisms could have been used exclusively depending on specific economic and socio-political considerations, or they may have been utilized in conjunction, as suggested by the data from southern Peru and the north coast of Chile. Final determination of the evolutionary culture-history of Tiwanaku must undoubtedly await many more years of research in the region.

REFERENCES

Adams, R. McC., 1966, *The Evolution of Urban Society: Early Mesopotamia and Prehispanic Mexico*, Aldine-Atherton, Chicago.

Albarracín-Jordán, J., 1990, Prehispanic Dynamics of Settlement in the Lower Tiwanaku Valley, Bolivia, Report submitted to the National Science Foundation and the National Endowment for the Humanities, Manuscript on file, University of Chicago, Department of Anthropology.

Albarracín-Jordán, J., and J. E. Mathews, 1990, *Asentamientos prehispánicos del Valle de Tiwanaku* 1, Producciones CIMA, La Paz.

Arellano López, J., 1991, The New Cultural Context of Tiahuanaco, in: *Wari Administrative Architecture* (W. H. Isbell and G. F. McEwan, eds.), Dumbarton Oaks, Washington, pp. 259-280.

Bennett, W. C., 1934, Excavations at Tiahuanaco, *Anthropological Papers of the American Museum of Natural History* 34, 3:359-491.

Bennett, W. C., 1936, Excavations in Bolivia, *Anthropological Papers of the American Museum of Natural History* 35, 4:329-507.

Berenguer, J., 1978, La problemática Tiwanaku en Chile: visión retrospectiva, *Revista Chilena de Arqueología* 1:17-40.

Berenguer, J., V. Castro, and O. Silva, 1980, Reflexiones acerca de la presencia de Tiwanaku en el norte de Chile, *Estudios Arqueológicos* 5, Antofagasta:81-93.

Berenguer, J., and P. Dauelsberg, 1988, El norte grande en la órbita de Tiwanaku (400 a 1200 d.C.), in: *Culturas de Chile: Prehistoria desde sus orígenes hasta los albores de la Conquista* (J. Hidalgo et al., eds.), Editorial Andrés Bello, Santiago, pp. 129-180.

Bermann, M. P., 1990, *Prehispanic Household and Empire at Lukurmata, Bolivia*, Unpublished Ph. D. Dissertation, University of Michigan, Ann Arbor.

Browman, D. L., 1978, Toward the Development of the Tiahuanaco (Tiwanaku) State, in: *Advances in Andean Archaeology* (D. L. Browman, ed.), Mouton, The Hague, pp. 327-349.

Browman, D. L., 1980, Tiwanaku Expansion and Altiplano Economic Patterns, *Estudios Arqueológicos* 5:107-120.

Browman, D. L., 1981, New Light on Andean Tiwanaku, *American Scientist* 69, 4:408-419.

Browman, D. L., 1984, Tiwanaku: Development of Interzonal Trade and Economic Expansion in the Altiplano, in: *Social and Economic Organization in the Prehispanic Andes* (D. L. Browman, R. L. Burger, and M. A. Rivera, eds.), International Series 194, British Archaeological Reports, Oxford, pp. 117-142.

Browman, D. L., 1986, Management of Agricultural Risk in the Titicaca Basin, Paper presented at the 51st Annual Meeting, Society for American Archaeology, New Orleans.

Cowgill, G. L., 1975, Population Pressure as a Non-Explanation, in: *Population Studies in Archaeology and Biological Anthropology: A Symposium* (A. C. Swedlund, ed.), *American Antiquity* 40, 2ii:127-131.
Denevan, W. M., 1982, Hydraulic Agriculture in the American Tropics: Forms, Measures, and Recent Research, in: *Maya Subsistence* (K. V. Flannery, ed.), Academic Press, New York, pp. 181-203.
Erickson, C. L., 1985, Applications of Prehistoric Andean Technology: Experiments in Raised Field Agriculture, Huatta, Lake Titicaca: 1981-2, in: *Prehistoric Intensive Agriculture in the Tropics* (I. S. Farrington, ed.), International Series 232(i), British Archaeological Reports, Oxford, pp. 209-232.
Erickson, C. L., 1988, *An Archaeological Investigation of Raised Field Agriculture in the Lake Titicaca Basin of Peru*, Ph. D. Dissertation, University of Illinois at Urbana-Champaign, University Microfilms, Ann Arbor.
Flannery, K. V., J. Marcus, and S. A. Kowalewski, 1981, The Preceramic and Formative of the Valley of Oaxaca, in: *Supplement to the Handbook of Middle American Indians* (V. Reifler Bricker, ed.), 1: *Archaeology* (J. A. Sabloff, ed.), University of Texas Press, Austin, pp. 48-93.
Garaycochea, I., 1986, Potencial agrícola de los camellones en el altiplano puneño, in: *Andenes y camellones en el Perú andino: historia, presente y futuro* (C. de la Torre and M. Burga, eds.), Consejo Nacional de Ciencia y Tecnología, Lima, pp. 241-251.
Hasemann, G., 1987, Late Classic Settlement on the Sulaco River, Central Honduras, in: *Chiefdoms in the Americas* (R. D. Drennan and C. A. Uribe), University Press of America, New York, pp. 85-102.
Kolata, A. L., 1979, Archaeology at the Top of the World, *Field Museum of Natural History Bulletin* 50, 9:16-24.
Kolata, A. L., 1982, Tiwanaku: Portrait of an Andean Civilization, *Field Museum of Natural History Bulletin* 53, 8:13-28.
Kolata, A. L., 1983, The South Andes, in: *Ancient South Americans* (J. D. Jennings, ed.), W. H. Freeman and Company, San Francisco, pp. 241-285.
Kolata, A. L., 1985, El papel de la agricultura intensiva en la economía del estado de Tiwanaku, *Diálogo Andino* 4:11-38.
Kolata, A. L., 1986, The Agricultural Foundations of the Tiwanaku State: a View from the Heartland, *American Antiquity* 51, 4:749-762.
Kolata, A. L., 1987, Tiwanaku and its Hinterland, *Archaeology* 40, 1:36-41.
Kolata, A. L., 1991, The Technology and Organization of Agricultural Production in the Tiwanaku State, *Latin American Antiquity* 2, 2:99-125.
Kolata, Alan L. (ed.), in press, *Tiwanaku and Its Hinterland: Archaeological and Paleoecological Investigations in the Lake Titicaca Basin of Bolivia*, Smithsonian Institution Press, Washington.
Kolata, A. L., C. Stanish, and O. Rivera S. (eds.), 1987, The Technology and Organization of Agricultural Production in the Tiwanaku State: First Preliminary Report of Proyecto Wila Jawira, Report submitted to the Instituto Nacional de Arqueología, La Paz; the National Science Foundation, and the National Endowment for the Humanities, Washington, D. C., and the Pittsburgh Foundation, Pittsburgh, Pennsylvania.
Kolata, A. L., and O. Rivera (eds.), 1989, The Archaeology and Paleoecology of Lukurmata, Bolivia: Second Preliminary Report of the Proyecto Wila Jawira, Manuscript submitted to the National Science Foundation, and National Endowment for the Humanities, Washington, D. C.
Lanning, E. P., 1967, *Peru Before the Incas*, Prentice-Hall, Englewood Cliffs, N. J.

Mathews, J. E., 1989, Preliminary Investigations of Prehistoric Raised Fields in the Tiwanaku Mid-Valley, Tiwanaku, Bolivia, Paper presented at the 17th Annual Midwest Conference on Andean and Amazonian Archaeology and Ethnohistory, Mount Pleasant, Michigan, February 25-26.

Mathews, J. E., 1991, Prehispanic Settlement and Agriculture in the Middle Tiwanaku Valley, Bolivia, Research report presented at the 56th Annual Meeting of the Society of American Archaeology, New Orleans, April 23-28.

Mathews, J. E., 1992a, *Prehispanic Settlement and Agriculture in the Middle Tiwanaku Valley, Bolivia*, Unpublished Ph. D. Dissertation, Department of Anthropology, University of Chicago, Chicago.

Mathews, J. E., 1992b, Some Notes on the Early Development of the Tiwanaku State, Paper presented at the 20th Annual Midwest Conference on Andean and Amazonian Archaeology and Ethnohistory, Urbana-Champaign, Illinois, February 29-March 1.

Mathews, J. E., in press, A Re-Evaluation of the Formative Period in the Southeast Titicaca Basin, Bolivia, *Journal of the Steward Anthropological Society* 21, 2.

Mujica, E., 1985, *Altiplano*-Coast Relationships in the South-Central Andes: from Indirect to Direct Complementarity, in: *Andean Ecology and Civilization* (S. Masuda, I. Shimada, and C. Morris, eds.), University of Tokyo Press, Tokyo, pp. 103-140.

Muñoz Ovalle, I., 1983, El poblamiento en el valle de Azapa y su vinculación con Tiwanaku, *Asentamientos aldeanos en los valles costeros de Arica*, Documento de Trabajo 3, Universidad de Tarapacá, Arica, pp. 43-93.

Murra, J. V., 1975, *Formaciones económicas y políticas del mundo andino*, Historia Andina 3, Instituto de Estudios Peruanos, Lima.

Murra, J. V., 1980 [1955], *The Economic Organization of the Inca State*, Supplement 1 to Research in Economic Anthropology, JAI Press, Greenwich.

Núñez A., L., 1972, Sobre el comienzo de la agricultura prehistórica en el norte de Chile, *Pumapunku* 4:25-48.

ONERN-CORPUNO, 1965a, *Programa de inventario y evaluación de los recursos naturales del Departamento de Puno* I, Capítulo II: Climatología, ONERN, Lima.

ONERN-CORPUNO, 1965b, *Programa de inventario y evaluación de los recursos naturales del Departamento de Puno* III, Capítulo V: Suelos, ONERN, Lima.

Parsons, J. R., 1968, An Estimate of Size and Population for Middle Horizon Tiahuanaco, Bolivia, *American Antiquity* 33, 2:243-245.

Parsons, J. R., 1971, *Prehistoric Settlement Patterns of the Texcoco Region, Mexico*, Memoirs 3, Museum of Anthropology, University of Michigan, Ann Arbor.

Parsons, J. R., 1974, The Development of Prehistoric Complex Society: a Regional Perspective from the Valley of Mexico, *Journal of Field Archaeology* 1:81-108.

Parsons, J. R., 1976, Settlement and Population History of the Basin of Mexico, in: *The Valley of Mexico: Studies in Prehistoric Ecology and Society* (E. R. Wolf, ed.), University of New Mexico Press, Albuquerque, pp. 69-100.

Pérez Valencia, A., 1984, *Estudio integrado de recursos naturales de la cuenca del Río Tiwanaku*, Escuela Militar de Ingeniería, Universidad Militar Mariscal Antonio José de Sucre, La Paz.

Ponce Sanginés, C., 1969, La ciudad de Tiwanaku: a propósito del último libro sobre planeamiento urbano precolombino de Jorge Hardoy, Supplement to *Arte y arqueología* 1, Universidad Mayor de San Andrés, La Paz:1-32.

Ponce Sanginés, C., 1979, *Nueva perspectiva para el estudio de la expansión de la cultura Tiwanaku*, Publication 29, Instituto Nacional de Arqueología, La Paz.

Ponce Sanginés, C., 1981a, *Descripción sumaria del Templete Semisubterráneo de Tiwanaku*, Fifth revised edition, Librería y Editorial Juventud, La Paz.

Ponce Sanginés, C., 1981b, *Tiwanaku: espacio, tiempo y cultura. Ensayo de síntesis arqueológica*, Fourth edition, Editorial Los Amigos del Libro, La Paz.
Rivera, M. A., 1975, Una hipótesis sobre movimientos poblacionales altiplánicos y transaltiplánicos en las costas del norte de Chile, *Chungará* 5:7-31.
Rivera, M. A., 1980, Algunos fenómenos de complementaridad económica a través de los datos arqueológicos en el área Centro Sur Andina: la fase Alto Ramírez reformulada, in: *Temas Antropológicos del Norte de Chile*, special edition of *Estudios Arqueológicos*, Universidad de Chile, Antofagasta, pp. 71-103.
Roosevelt, A. C., 1987, Chiefdoms in the Amazon and Orinoco, in: *Chiefdoms in the Americas* (R. D. Drennan and C. A. Uribe, eds.), University Press of America, New York, pp. 153-184.
Sanders, W. T., 1965, *Cultural Ecology of the Teotihuacan Valley*, Department of Sociology and Anthropology, Pennsylvania State University, University Park.
Sanders, W. T., 1972, Population, Agricultural History, and Societal Evolution in Mesoamerica, in: *Population Growth: Anthropological Implications* (B. Spooner, ed.), The Massachusetts Institute of Technology Press, Cambridge, pp. 101-153.
Sanders, W. T., 1976, The Agricultural History of the Valley of Mexico, in: *The Valley of Mexico: Studies in Prehispanic Ecology and Society* (E. R. Wolf, ed.), University of New Mexico Press, Albuquerque, pp. 101-159.
Squier, E. G., 1877, *Peru. Incidents of Travel and Exploration in the Land of the Incas*, Harper and Brothers, New York.
Stanish, C., 1989, Tamaño y complejidad de los asentamientos nucleares de Tiwanaku, in: *Arqueología de Lukurmata* 2: *La tecnología y organización de la producción agrícola en el Estado de Tiwanaku* (A. L. Kolata, ed.), Centro de Investigaciones Antropológicas Tiwanaku/Producciones Puma-Punku, La Paz, pp. 41-57.
Tapia Pineda, F. B., 1978, El fenómeno de la expansión tiwanakota, INAR Internal Documents 26-78, Paper presented at the Second Meeting of the Jornadas Peruano-Bolivianas de Estudio Científico del Altiplano Boliviano y Sur de Perú.
Vacher, J. J., E. Brasier de Thuy, and M. Liberman, 1991, Influencia del lago en la agricultura litoral, in: *El Lago Titicaca: síntesis del conocimiento limnológico actual* (C. Dejoux and A. Iltis, eds.), ORSTOM (Institut Français de Recherche Scientifique pour le Développement en Cooperation), Paris and La Paz, pp. 517-530.
Wallace, D. T., 1957, *The Tiahuanaco Horizon Styles in the Peruvian and Bolivian Highlands*, unpublished Ph. D. Dissertation, University of California, Berkeley.
Webster, A. D., 1993, *Camelids and the Rise of the Tiwanaku State*, unpublished Ph. D. Dissertation, Department of Anthropology, University of Chicago, Chicago.
Wheatley, P., 1967, Proleptic Observations on the Origins of Urbanism, in: *Liverpool Essays in Geography* (R. W. Steel and R. Lawton, eds.), Longmans, Green, and Company, London, pp. 315-345.
Wheatley, P., 1971, *The Pivot of the Four Quarters —A Preliminary Enquiry into the Origins and Character of the Ancient Chinese City*, Aldine Publishing Company, Chicago.

Part IV
Conclusion

Chapter **11**

Recapitulation and Concluding Remarks

LINDA MANZANILLA

In the chapters of this book, we have reviewed different aspects related to early urban societies. For Mesopotamia, we have stressed the importance of centralized storage embedded in village modes of life during the Hassuna period, and afterwards centered in the administrative organization of the temples during the Ubaid and Uruk periods, giving rise to the first urban developments of Lower Mesopotamia (Manzanilla 1983, 1986).

Eastern Anatolia, rich in raw materials (such as metals and obsidian) was a key region for Chalcolithic societies in the Mesopotamian lowlands, deprived of raw materials. In these northern regions, the emerging elite was linked more to the control of exchange of raw materials and crafts, that to the appropriation of staple goods, as Frangipane has stated.

At Arslantepé in Eastern Anatolia, the Italian Archaeological Mission has unearthed a superimposition of monumental buildings dating to the Late Chalcolithic and Early Bronze Age I. Late Chalcolithic monumental architecture in frontier sectors may indicate the development of a regionally strong elite. In the late fourth millennium, Arslantepé seems to have become an important regional administrative center.

Frangipane stated that the oldest of the three public buildings had a complex of adjacent storerooms, each with different functions. The north-

---

LINDA MANZANILLA • Instituto de Investigaciones Antropológicas, UNAM, Ciudad Universitaria, 04510 México D.F.

Emergence and Change in Early Urban Societies, edited by Linda Manzanilla. Plenum Press, New York, 1997.

ern ones had large containers for storage, to supply other rooms. The southern smaller ones had hundreds of mass-produced coarse bowls and numerous clay sealings, as discarded administrative material. These last bore the impression of 120 different seals and had been affixed on different containers including vessels and storeroom doors. Its function was intimately related to redistribution of foodstuff under administrative control. This evidence suggests that Arslantepé had an administrative system almost identical in its basic structure to the southern Mesopotamian one.

The core of the building was a very large temple. The concentrations of clay-sealings outside the cult area stress the connection of cult activities with administration and redistribution.

The organization of pottery production also appears to have changed with respect to the Late Chalcolithic period perhaps towards a greater centralization of artisanal activities, indicated by the disappearance of potters' marks. Another change related to the emergence of redistributive centralized institutions at Arslantepé was the greater increase in the number of sheep in detriment of pigs, that may suggest the centralized control of herds, a pattern also present in Late Uruk sites of the south.

Frangipane stresses the fact that in Eastern Anatolia there are evidences of an autochthonous process of formation of centralized power which nevertheless suffers change in the Late Uruk period. Only in the late IV millennium B.C., the local elite at Arslantepé takes charge of primary economic activities (staple finance) through the centralization of resources and labor-force and the complex redistribution system carried out under sophisticated administrative control. Perhaps this change is the result of the demand for raw materials from Mesopotamian centers which interact with northern communities more intensively than before.

The so-called "colonial sites" of the Middle and Upper Euphrates (Hassek Höyük, Jebel Aruda, Habuba Kabira) characterized by Mesopotamian traits, seem to be the result of the transfer of portions of communities to new lands.

After the Late Uruk period, the arrival of Transcaucasian groups provoked the final collapse of the Mesopotamian type of organization in this region.

With respect to Egypt, we lack settlement data for many regions and periods. There seem to be two models of mixed economy during the early Predynastic: a farmstead sedentary model in the north (with the raising of pigs, not compatible with transhumance) and a shepherding-hunting emphasis in the south. These two models offer two settlement types: the first is illustrated by Merimde and El-Omari A, and the second, by Locality 14 at Hieraconpolis and Hemamieh (Hoffman 1980:159; Manzanilla 1982, 1985:486-487).

During the Predynastic, there are also hints of a change from a relatively balanced mixed economy (hunting in the desert and Nile, fishing, gathering, cattle breeding, and agriculture) in the Badarian and Early Nagada to a predominance of agriculture during Nagada II, perhaps due to the gradual descent of the Nile level (Rizkana 1952:4; Hoffman 1980:154), a fact that stimuled a direct relationship of productive settlements to the flooded valley.

Clusters of sites, such as that centered in Hieraconpolis during Nagada II times, display manufacturing (pottery, basalt and diorite vases, bead-making) and burial activities, in a way that may be compared to the manufacturing and burial sites around Shang walled sites in China (Cheng Chou, An Yang, etc.)(Chang 1976). In parallelism with the Chinese examples, we should also remember that traces of fortified sites are found in Nubt (Nagada, southern town) and in depictions of early Nagada (a model found at Abadieh) and Protodynastic times (the different slate palettes)(Manzanilla 1985:488 *et seq.*).

Nagada II culture in Upper Egypt display rich grave goods and elites could have assumed greater control over economy. Bard states that Nagada II times (3600-3300 B.C.) witness the expansion of Upper Egyptian polities to the less-complex north, with the development of lucrative trade with regions in the eastern Mediterranean. Final unification was achieved through military conquest.

Thus there was a shift in settlement patterns with the emergence of the newly unified state: for example, in the Abydos and Hierakonpolis regions, scattered predynastic villages were replaced by a single town.

Bard (following Kemp 1977) mentions the fact that with the unification of the centralized state, town growth took place within the bureaucratic system, through the foundation of redistributive, administrative, and cult centers, as well as royal estates. The vast majority of the population were farmers, living in hamlets more or less homogenously dispersed throughout the valley. This linear, riverine pattern facilitated state control through taxation and conscription.

Even though Bard states that urbanization was unquestionably a part of the process of state formation and unification in Egypt, as the bureaucracy and mechanisms of state control were being established, we may ask how urban were the bureaucratic centers in the pharaonic state, when one of their hallmarks was the less nucleated character of their small living population.

During times of collapse of the centralized state, spatial organization was similar to the competing, fortified city-state pattern found elsewhere in the Near East. Thus, we may conclude that the Egyptian state lay down the guideline of the particular settlement pattern that characterized this region throughout most of its history.

With respect to China, Wiesheu stresses the appearance of early urban centers as walled secular settlements in a scenery of military conflict. One of the characteristics of these centers was the high degree of differentiation between distinct types of professionals, particularly craftsmen (potters, bone- or antler-workers, lapidaries, and finally bronze metallurgists). The presence of mutilated skeletons has been interpreted as an indicator of slave society since middle and late Longshan times (2400-2000 B.C.). And it is precisely in the Longshan culture where the transition to state society should be placed.

She discusses the possibility that Wangchenggang ("royal city mound") could have been the first capital of the legendary Xia dynasty of the Erlitou Culture (XXI to XVII centuries B.C.). It was a royal seat, and it consisted of two walled enclosures within which house foundations, ash pits, and remains of important buildings were found. Other walled centers were Pingliangtai, Hougang and Haojiatai, all located above the fertile alluvial plain of the tributaries of the Yellow River, in strategic protected sectors with respect to floods and enemies.

Thus, Wiesheu (*contra* Wheatley 1971) states that it is only in Han times (*c.* 200 B.C.) that the imperial ideology of the four quarters emerges.

In the Valley of Oaxaca, Mexico, Joyce sees a case for an actor-based theoretical perspective for state society emergence, where the development of an elite social identity and strategy through ideological change (involving increasing control of ritual and promotion of external conflict) takes place. Following Joyce, the state is viewed as a polity with variation in the administrative roles of political elites as well as great inequalities in statuses implying social stratification and political centralization.

Joyce states that power is generally derived through three overlapping types of social interactions:

1. Reciprocity, where low-status individuals provide material resources to high-status individuals in return for benefits in the form of information, when economic and political specializations, high risks from natural or human hazards, and heavy-investment technologies occur;
2. coercion, when physical harm or withholding of critical resources by the elite take place;
3. and deception, where elements of ideology are used to legitimate inequality and power relationships.

The formation of the first state polity in the Americas was centered at Monte Albán (500 B.C.-A.D. 200), on a previously unoccupied ridgetop where the three arms of the Valley of Oaxaca intersect. During Phases Ia through II, inequality is manifested in the difference in quality and quantity of burial offerings, the amount of energy expended in the preparation of graves, variations in spatial distribution of high-status markers (*i.e.,* prestige goods), individual control over resources (emergence of palaces at San José Mogote), rise in the monumentality of public buildings, greater power to mobilize material resources (pottery and obisidian) in the hands of the elite, increasing power over labor, etc.

By Period II, as the piedmont strategy of settlement location collapsed due to erosion and soil depletion, there was a drop in population, and the locations shifted away from Monte Albán and into the three arms of the valley. Rulers of Monte Albán had assured provisioning of the site by establishing connections with elites elsewhere in the valley (indicated by similarity in public buildings and ritual paraphernalia). Certain communities began to specialize productively, thus reducing local control from some types of craft production.

From Joyce's point of view, heterogeneity is seen in the emergence of craft and possibly military specialists. Household economic strategies as well as gender and elite roles may have been affected by social changes.

Joyce states that instead of reciprocity or coercion, elite power at Monte Albán resulted from social deception, that is, ideological change: the emergence of ritual specialists as mediators with the forces that controlled the cosmos. Non-elites provided productive tribute (foodstuff and labor) to the elite in ritualized contexts, rather that participating in a ritual redistributive network. Finally, the Monte Albán elite sponsored warfare as seen in the *Danzantes* stelae and conquest slabs, the construction of walls around Monte Albán, and the conquest of the Cuicatlán Cañada. Ideology was a driving force because it created and legitimated unequal social and economic relations.

By proposing that the state is present in Period II, due to the emergence of distinct social strata, political centralization, elite control of a centralized religion and of production in the form of tribute exaction, a four-tiered administrative hierarchy, as well as elite sponsoring of warfare, Joyce thus confirms Flannery and Marcus's interpretation (1983).

In the case of Teotihuacan and Oxkintok, an argument in favor of monumental sacred space construction for political and symbolic power concentration is given. In the first case, as Millon (1973:55) stated, "...there was a self-conscious attempt on the part of the architects of Teotihuacan's 'Street of the Dead' to overwhelm the viewer by the sheer size and monumentality of conception of both the avenue and of the pyramids and temples alond it...". I further argue that all the city was conceived as a model of the Mesoamerican cosmos, with a celestial, a four-course terrestrial, and an underworld spheres.

At the beginning, the huge demographic concentration at Teotihuacan was due to the population rearrangements when the Xitle and Popocatepetl volcanos erupted. Afterwards, rural-urban migration took place in part as a consequence of the attraction to craft production and of the services provided by the urban center. Teotihuacan was also a strategic site with respect to resources, when the southwestern sector of the Basin of Mexico was covered by the eruption of the Xitle volcano.

Urban planning is fully present from the Tlamimilolpa phase onwards (c. A.D. 250), eventhough the Street of the Dead was laid during the former Miccaotli phase (A.D. 150-200, Rattray 1993). It was a 20 square kilometer pluriethnic city, one of the vastest urban developments of preindustrial world, and perhaps the most planned example (orthogonal grid, presence of water supply and drainage systems, administrative and public buildings placed along the main axis, existence of craftsmen and foreign wards, multifamily corporate dwellings, etc.). Thus there was a sharp separation between the huge urban settlement and the vast rural environment around it. It was mainly a manufacturing and bureacratic site, as well as a pilgrimage center. One of its main characteristics stresses the construction of monumental sacred space as a means to convey political and symbolic power to its leaders.

We see Teotihuacan's history as the intersection of processes with diverse speeds of change (Manzanilla, in press b). The process of change in the natural environment witnesses dynamic erosion and flood events due to ashfalls in the Teotihuacan valley during the Classic horizon (McClung *et al.* 1993; McClung de Tapia in Manzanilla *et al.* 1994). The Teotihuacan society was thus in continuous environmental stress (Manzanilla, in press a).

The construction process of the city witnesses a climax of monumentality in the Tzacualli and Miccaotli phases (A.D. 1-200). The northwestern settlement attached to the main pyramids could have included clusters of houses around three-temple complexes near extraction locuses, more than a dense site, as Millon has suggested. Afterwards, with the laying of the Street of the Dead, some other three-temple plazas are constructed facing the Pyramid of the Moon or the main axis. The population will soon abandon the northwestern settlement and will locate itself around the Street of the Dead, in multifamily apartment compounds. This change in the organization of domestic life lies still uncomprehended, but certainly reflects a dramatic change in social and political organization. By the late Tlamimilolpa phase, parallel to a restructuring of the power spheres, the urban development of the city reaches its climax.

The processes of change involving craft production witnesses transformations in technological and stylistical spheres. Following Rattray (1993), in Tzacualli there is an abrupt ceasing of the Formative ceramic tradition; new elements appear, and in late Tlamimilolpa (A.D. 250-350, following Rattray 1993), particularly the most characteristic Teotihuacan pottery forms (Cowgill 1993).

Rattray (1993) underlines the high proportion of luxury items for the Tlamimilolpa phase. In mural painting, Magaloni (1993) describes changes in the technology and representations. Barbour (1993) points out the use of molds for figurine production in Tlamimilolpa (A.D. 200-350), and in the Xolalpan phase (A.D. 350-650), the beginnings of the second figurine production tradition, which could have been related to changes in the religious structure of the city. For this last phase, Rattray (1993) mentions the introduction of new and better manufactured wares, as well as a peak in foreign relations, that are retracted in late Xolalpan (A.D. 550-650), probably due to a time of reaction and reform.

With the end of the Classic horizon, portrait figurines and puppets cease to be made, a change that Barbour (1993) relates to a fracture between the domestic groups and the state hierarchy of the city.

The political process involving leadership in the city suggests changes in power spheres in specific moments of the history of Teotihuacan, particularly the Mythological Animals Mural, the dismantlement and covering of the Feathered Serpent Pyramid, as well as an iconographical change from serpents to jaguars in the Northwestern Compound of the Street of the Dead probably in Tlamimilolpa times (Manzanilla, in press b).

With the expansion of the orthogonal city to the alluvial plain, the strategy of the first settlement was drastically changed. We believe that increased deforestation, soil erosion, overexpoitation of the springs, loss of self-sufficiency, excessive rural-urban migration, increasing problems in food supply, and blocking of the exchange routes made the city a very vulnerable settlement, in a moment of increasing aridiy (Manzanilla, in press a).

The collapse of such a huge centralizing entity provoked a great void in the political setting of the late Classic, in a manner that can be paralleled to the collapse of the Tiwanaku polity and that of the Pharaonic state in the so-called Intermediate periods, having as a consequence a "balcanization" of power.

With respect to Mayan cities, such as Oxkintok, Rivera Dorado states that urban spaces were a materialization of apparent movements of the sun, and of the political power of the leader. The Mayan city was a representation of the heavens and the lower spaces, where gaps, axes and directions in the architecture related to the lord are planned around the model of the sun's behavior. Each building represents the reaffirmation of some lineage, the memory of its existence, and the justification of its power. Power relations are thus transmuted into cosmological symbols, with the sun-king as the polarizing element.

The relative importance of each group of buildings—particularly the temple—in the main settlement is the key to the real power of each family or corporate social unit. Rivera Dorado states that for this grammar, key issues are the dimensions, number of buildings, orientation, proximity or distance from the buildings belonging to the ruler, variety of sculptures and inscriptions, etc.

The subordinate centers (at average distances of 11 km from the main site) expand and contract, due to changes in their alliances and loyalties, thus modifying the overall territory. Rivera Dorado underlines the difficulty of widespread territorial control in the tropical rain forest, and stresses the strength of an organization based on kinship ties. War and marriage occur between sites at an average distance of 38 km.

Thus Oxkintok, as Teotihuacan, was built as a model of the cosmos, eventhough the former represents the center of a 40 km-diameter lineage-based polity, and the latter was the sacred city for all the central highlands of Mexico, the archetype of the civilized city, and this symbolic power was directed to underline its political and social preeminence.

The three last articles refer to the Andean Middle horizon, particularly the Huari and Tiwanaku politics. With respect to Huari, Isbell describes the growth of the city constructed on a ridge in the Huamanga Basin of the Ayacucho Valley of Peru, until it became the largest archaeological zone in South America. Its architectural core reached 2.5 km^2, but the 1500 years of occupational history covered 15 km^2.

From a previous phase of hamlets and villages with common concerns for water, separated by 2 or 3 km, a process of rural-urban migration took place in the Quebrada de Ocros Phase (A.D. 400-600), where temples could have played a key role in building new social relations. Walled sunken courts, such as the one in Moraduchayuq, constructed with polygonal stone blocks, make their appearance, separating sacred from profane spaces. There are also evidences of specialized activities, particularly the transformation of exotic raw materials at Moraduchayuq. In this phase, we also see the appearance of city blocks, defined by walled streets, as well as an urban grid.

A change occurs in the following Moraduchayuq Phase (A.D. 700-900), when a successful and aggressive city emerges, enlarging the former core and expanding its residential areas. The emergence of a military elite in the main settlement, after its first appearance in provincial locations, is related to an aggressive defense toward Tiwanaku in the south, and Huamachuco in the north. It is detected in the presence of rigid orthogonal cellular compounds, built around open patios. Serving bowls are unusually common, evidencing community dining or feasting. Isbell proposes that these compounds were occupied by middle-level administrators of a growing military state.

During the Royac Perja Phase (A.D. 800-900) a reaction to orthogonal and cellular architecture takes places perhaps when new forms of sociopolitical organization appear. In the tenth century A.D. there was a general abandonment of the region.

Isbell concludes that a de-emphasis of a central public area in favor of repetitive units leaves little opportunity for the former theocratic elite to construct power in theatrical public ritual. Huari's orthogonal cellular architecture was conceived by military commanders converted into administrators, imposing a rigid homogeneous social order, a new power base marginalizing ceremonial interests. A final rejection of this imposed order is observed before the final abandonment.

The two articles dealing with the Tiwanaku state focus on different problems: one related to its external relations, and the other to the model explaining its internal structure.

Browman establishes a contrast between territorial and hegemonic states. He defines the first as one with direct control of its dependencies, incorporating its hinterland as provinces, and with military power to maintain its borders. The hegemonic state has indirect control, through the recognition of the central government of local level chief legitimacy. Local polities collect the tribute and taxes to be forwarded to the central government.

With respect to the Tiwanaku state structure, Browman proposes different models of articulation with neighboring regions: the Cochabamba Valley in the southeast was integrated through a trade alliance (to obtain maize and hallucinogenic snuffs); San Pedro de Atacama in northern Chile, through trade interdependence where merchants and caravaneers established perhaps a port-of-trade; Oruro in southern Bolivia, integrated as part of a secular expansion in a territorial model; the Sillumocco polity in southern Puno, Peru, assumed as part of a hegemonic state; and Azapa (in northern Chile) and Moquegua (in Peru) colonized from the Titicaca Basin to obtain marine goods, arsenic copper ores, and maize.

Browman suggests that by A.D. 800 a substantial growth of elites and attached subsidiary servers occur, as well as mercantile production, with redistribution via the organized state, and with specialization at Tiwanaku and the secondary center of Lukurmata. Tiwanaku is a city with a public ceremonial core surrounded by areas of elite residences, of artisanal activity, of residential terraces, and of enclosed agricultural zones. The increase in caravan movements (and state bred herds) is attested by an increase of castrated llamas during Tiwanaku IV and V, a fact not taken into consideration by Mathews in his interpretation.

The collapse of the Tiwanaku polity is related to the allienation of markets and local political seizures of power, as well as the gradual fragmentation and reorganization of the state territory.

On the other hand, Mathews shares Kolata's "autochthonous model" of state formation (1986), where 6500 hectares of raised fields administered by an agro/managerial bureacracy produced hierarchical settlement networks, characteristic of many complex societies. Particularly in Tiwanaku V times (A.D. 750-1000) he observes increase in the number of sites as well as in the size of large former Tiwanaku IV settlements, and the appearance of new small sites associated with the agricultural fields. The intensive agricultural production and reduction in crop species inventory caused increasing stress in the system. Demographic and administrative changes in Tiwanaku V times (particularly decentralization of the control of production) contributed to its collapse. Mathews thus rejects that the distinction between "elite" and "proletarian" material cultures could have been based on differential access to trade or other exotic goods.

In general, we would like to stress the role of temple organizations in building new social relations, particularly through redistributive flows, giving rise to complex administrative systems and to nucleated settlements. This is seen in Mesopotamia and Eastern Anatolia, Teotihuacan, the first phases of the Huari polity, Tiwanaku, and perhaps also some Mayan cities.

In other cases of early urban developments, such as China, Egypt, and the Valley of Oaxaca in Mexico, political competition and defensive situations may account for demographic concentrations in walled and easily defensible settlements.

Urban grids—so characteristic of Teotihuacan in central Mexico, the Indus Valley cities in Pakistan, but also of Huari in Peru—are rare.

REFERENCES

Barbour, W. T. D., 1993, Hey figurine! Get back in line! Problems in the correlation of the figurine and ceramic chronologies, paper presented at the *Taller de Discusión de la Cronología de Teotihuacan*, Centro de Estudios Teotihuacanos, INAH, Teotihuacan, 24-27 de noviembre de 1993.

Chang, K. C., 1976, *Early Chinese Civilization: Anthropological Perspectives*, Harvard University Press, Cambridge.

Cowgill, G. J., 1993, Nuevos datos del proyecto Templo de Quetzalcoatl sobre la era Miccaotli-Tlamimilolpa, paper presented at the *Taller de Discusión de la Cronología de Teotihuacan*, Centro de Estudios Teotihuacanos, Teotihuacan, 24-27 de noviembre de 1993.

Flannery, K. V., and J. Marcus (eds.), 1983, *The Cloud People: Divergent Evolution of the Zapotec and Mixtec Civilizations*, Academic Press, New York.

Hoffman, M., 1980, *Egypt before the Pharaohs. The Prehistoric Foundation of Egyptian Civilization*, Routledge and Kegan Paul, London.
Kemp, B., 1977, The Early Development of Towns in Egypt, *Antiquity* 51, 203:185-200.
Kolata, A. L., 1986, The Agricultural Foundations of the Tiwanaku State: a View from the Heartland, *American Antiquity* 51, 4:748-762.
Magaloni, D., 1993, Secuencia evolutiva de la pintura mural en Teotihuacan, paper presented at the *Taller de Discusión de la Cronología de Teotihuacan*, Centro de Estudios Teotihuacanos, Teotihuacan, 24-27 de noviembre de 1993:279 *et seq.*
Manzanilla, L., 1982, *Hypothèses et indices du processus de formation de la civilisation égyptienne (cinquième et quatrième millénaires avant Jésus-Christ)*, PhD Dissertation, University of Paris IV (Sorbonne), Paris.
Manzanilla, L., 1983, La redistribución como proceso de centralización de la producción y circulación de bienes. Análisis de dos casos, *Boletín de Antropología Americana* 7, Instituto Panamericano de Geografía e Historia, México:5-18.
Manzanilla, L., 1985, Le développment des sociétés prédynastiques en Egypte: considérations méthodologiques, in: *Studi di Paletnologia in onore di Salvatore M. Puglisi* (M. Liverani, A. Palmieri, and R. Peroni, eds.), Universitá di Roma "La Sapienza", Roma, pp. 485-494.
Manzanilla, L., 1986, *La constitución de la sociedad urbana en Mesopotamia: Un proceso en la historia*, Serie Antropológica 80, Instituto de Investigaciones Antropológicas, UNAM, México.
Manzanilla, L., in press a, The Impact of Climatic Change on Past Civilizations. A Revisionist Agenda for Further Investigation", *Quaternary International*.
Manzanilla, L., in press b, Consideraciones finales, *Taller de Discusión de la Cronología de Teotihuacan*, Centro de Estudios Teotihuacanos, Teotihuacan (24-27 de noviembre de 1993).
Manzanilla, L., E. McClung de Tapia, and L. Barba Pingarrón, 1994, Informe técnico del segundo año del Proyecto "El cambio global en perspectiva histórica. El centro urbano preindustrial de Teotihuacan" (referencia 0060-H1906), CONACYT, México.
McClung de T., E., J. Zurita N., E. Ibarra, J. Cervantes B., and M. Meza S., 1993, Cronología de procesos geomorfológicos en el Valle de Teotihuacan, paper presented at the *Taller de Discusión de la Cronología de Teotihuacan*, Centro de Estudios Teotihuacanos, Teotihuacan, 24-27 de noviembre de 1993: 131 *et seq.*
Millon, R., 1973, *Urbanization at Teotihuacan, Mexico. v. I: The Teotihuacan map, part 1: Text*, University of Texas Press, Austin.
Rattray, E. C., 1993, Fechamientos por radiocarbono de Teotihuacan, paper presented at the *Taller de Discusión de la Cronología de Teotihuacan*, Centro de Estudios Teotihuacanos, Teotihuacan, 24-27 de noviembre de 1993: 137-166.
Rizkana, I., 1952, *Centres of Settlement in Prehistoric Egypt in the Area between Helwan and Heliopolis*, Cairo.
Wheatley, P., 1971, *The Pivot of the Four Quarters*, Aldine Publishing Co., Chicago.

Index

Abydos, Egypt, 65, 69-70, 77, 79, 277
Actor-based theory, of social change, 134, 135-138, 158, 278
Adaptive strategies, actor-based theory of, 136-137
Administrative role differentiation, 137-138
Agricultural production model, of state development, 246-247, 264, 265, 266, 276, 284
Aha, Pharaoah, 70
Akhenaten, Pharaoh, 62
Akhetaten (Tell el Amarna), Egypt, 62-63
Akkadian empire
  collapse of, 14
  as tributary state, 8
Alta Vista, Mexico, 25
Altiplano, Bolivia, as urban society development site, 18; *see also* Tiwanaku, Bolivia
Altiplano model, of state development, 107, 245-246, 263, 265-266, 267
Amorrites, 14
Amra, el-, Egypt, 69
Amratian Period, of Predynastic Egypt, 63, 69
'Amuq F period pottery, 76
Anatolia: *see* Eastern Anatolia
Andean Region
  Chavín Period, 19, 182, 185, 188
  El Niño events in, 17-18, 19

Andean Region (*Cont.*)
  Formative communities of, 14-15
  redistributive sphere size in, 11-12
  redistributive system, 20
  urban society development in, 18-21
  See also Huari, Peru; Tiwanaku, Bolivia
Aristoi, 4
Arslantepe-Malatya, Turkey, 43-58
  burials, 46
  centralized power development, 47-48, 49, 51-54, 55-57, 275-276
    as autochtonous process, 266-267, 276
  clay seals associated with, 51, 54, 276
  craft specialization, 46-47
  food redistribution system, 48, 49, 276
  ideological power basis of, 49, 56
  interregional exchange system, 49, 56-57
  labor force organization, 46-47, 55-56, 276
  during Late Uruk Period, 55-57
  livestock-raising system and, 54-55, 276
  Mesopotamian influence on, 54, 56-57
  Mesopotamian structure of, 54
Chalcolithic period, 43, 44
  Late, 46, 47-57
Neo-Hittite Period, 43

Arslantepe-Malatya, Turkey (*Cont.*)
  Chalcolithic period (*Cont.*)
    monumental architecture, 47-49, 50
      cella, 48, 49
      religious character of, 48-49
      store-room complex, 49, 51
      tell, 46, 48
      temple, 48-49
    pottery, 46-47, 49, 54-55
    Transcaucasian migration into, 276
    wall paintings, 49, 51
    weapons assemblage, 49
Assyrio, as tributary state, 8
Autochthonous model, of state development, 183, 266-267, 276, 284
Ayacucho Valley, Peru, 186, 187, 188, 282
Ayllu, 8
Aymara Kingdoms, of Titicaca Basin, 259
Aymara language, 234
Azapa Valley, Chile, influence of Tiwanaku on, 234-236, 240
Aztecs, redistribution system of, 15

Babylonia, as tributary state, 8
Badarian Period, of Predynastic Egypt, 63, 65, 70-71, 277
Balikh River, Turkey, 44
Bamboo Annals, 89
Basin of Mexico
  Central Mexican cities of, 109
  pochteca in, 8
  redistribution organization, 21
  as Teotihuacan food supply source, 22
  volcanic eruptions in, 110, 280
  See also Teotihuacan, Mexico
Batán Grande, Peru, 18
Beer, rationing of, 10
Bowls
  use in food redistribution, 7, 9, 10-11
  See also Pottery

Bronze Age sites
  Egyptian, 75
  of Yellow River Valley, China, 96, 98-99

Caballito Blanco, Oaxaca Valley, Mexico, 147
Cajamarca Valley, Peru, 212
Calendar, ritual, 124, 153
Callejón de Huaylas Basin, Peru, 201, 210
Calpulli, 8
Camarones Valley, Chile, 235
Canta, Peru, 235
Carangas *señorío*, 237
Carhuarazo Valley, Peru, 211
Cayacayani, Bolivia, 231
Ceramic ware: *see* Pottery
Cerro Baúl, Peru, 210
Cerro de la Campana, Mexico, 145
Cerro Gordo, Mexico, 122, 123, 126
Cerro Malinalco, Mexico, 123
Chalcolithic Period, at Arslantepe-Malatya, Turkey, 43, 44, 46, 47-57
Chalcolithic societies, corporate households of, 5
Chaqui-style ceramicware, 234
Chavín, 19, 182, 185, 188
Cheqo Wasi, Peru, 207-208
Chicha, 20
Chiefdoms
  group-oriented, 4
  corporate descent groups in, 5
  individualizing, 4
  religious-based power of, 151
Chimu state, 18
China
  early urban development in, 284
  Han dynasty of, 278
  See also Yellow River Valley, China, Henan Longshan Culture walled settlements
Chiribaya, re-colonization of Moquequa, Peru by, 237
Chiripa, Bolivia, ore trade with Tiwanaku, 235

INDEX

Chiripa Culture sites, 250-253, 262, 264, 265-266
Cholula, Mexico, 121
Chunchucmil, Yucatan, 177
Circular redistributional circuit, 6
Clans
  conical, 4
  corporate descent groups in, 5
Class societies, origin of, 8
Cochabama Valley, Bolivia
  influence of Tiwanaku on, 231-232, 238-239, 240, 283
  Tiwanaku-style ceramic assemblages, 231, 232
    Mojocoya, 231, 232
    Nazcoid (Nascoide), 231, 232
    Yampara, 231
  Tupuraya-style ceramic assemblages, 231
Cocijo (deity), 153
Codpa Valley, Chile, 235
Coercion, as power basis, 138, 139, 140
  at Monte Albán, Oaxaca Valley, Mexico, 149-150
Colla *señorío*, 237
Colonization model, of Tiwanaku's territorial influence, 230, 236-237
Communal meals, as food redistribution system, 9
Conchopata, Peru, 188, 195
Conquest slabs, 152, 154, 155, 156, 279
Craftsmen, in tributary states, 8
Craft specialization
  at Arslantepe-Malatya, Turkey, 46-47
  in Henan Longshan Culture, China, 98-99
  at Huari, Peru, 282
  at Oaxaca Valley, Mexico, 145, 146, 147, 149, 159
  in Predynastic Egypt, 77-78
  as social heterogeneity factor, 137-138
  at Teotihuacan, Mexico, 21, 114, 117-118, 120

Craft specialization (*Cont.*)
  at Tiwanaku, Bolivia, 237, 238, 240, 263, 265-266, 267
Cuanalan, Mexico, 22
Cuicatlán Cañada region, Mexico, 145-146, 156, 279
Cuicuilco, Mexico, 21
Cuilapan, Mexico, 145
Cultural ecology theory, of social change, 135-136, 148
Cupisnique Valley, Peru, El Niño events in, 17-18

Dainzú, Mexico, 145
Danzantes, 153-154, 155, 156, 157, 279
Deir el Medina, Egypt, 62
Deities
  as authority symbols, 139
  Mayan, 106, 174, 177-178, 281-282
  Zapotec, 153
Dengfeng County, China, 88-89
Desertification, of Sumer, 13
Diospolis Parva (Hu), Egypt, 65, 77, 68-69
Division of labor, relationship to redistributive organization, 12
Dominance/deference relations, 139
Drought
  in Andean Region, 17, 18-19
  in Basin of Mexico, 27
  El Niño-related, 17
  in Mesopotamia, 13
  at Tiwanaku, Bolivia, 18-19
Dupont-style ceramic ware, 234

Eastern Anatolia, 7, 41
  food redistribution patterns, 9
  interaction with Mesopotamia, 43-44, 56, 275
  social system development, 43-44, 44, 46
  temple organizations, 284
  See also Arslantepe-Malayta, Turkey
Ecological systems theory, of social change, 135-136, 148

Economic symbiosis model, of Formative communities, 14
Egypt
  Dynastic Period settlements, 61-63, 67
  Early Bronze Age settlements, 75
  Early Dynastic settlements, 59
    cemetery sites, 68, 70, 75
    Memphis site, 79
    Nagada site, 67
  First Dynasty, 59-60, 77
  food rationing measures used in, 11
  Lower Egyptian culture
    replacement by Upper Egyptian culture, 77-79, 277
    sites, 71-76
  Middle Kingdom settlements
    Deir el Medina site, 62
    el-Lahun site, 62
    settlement types, 62-63
  New Kingdom, 62
  Nile River Valley, 15-16, 17, 60
  Old Kingdom
    disintegration of, 17
    First Intermediate Period, 17
    rural population, 61
    settlement types, 62
  pharaonic, 16-17
  Predynastic Period settlements, 59-79, 284
    Abydos, 65, 69-70, 77, 277
    agricultural production, 277
    of Amratien Period, 63, 69
    of Badarian Period, 63, 65, 70-71, 277
    burial sites/grave goods, 66, 67, 68, 71, 73, 74, 75, 77
    centralized storage systems, 16-17, 61, 66
    craft specialization during, 77-78
    Diospolis Parva (Hu), 65, 68-69, 77
    early excavations of, 60
    Early Nagada Period, 277
    El-Amra, 69
    El-Khattara, 67

Egypt (*Cont.*)
  Predynastic Period settlements (*Cont.*)
    El-Mahasna, 69
    El-Omari site, 71-72
    Ezbet el-Qerdahi, 76
    of Fayum region, 71
    Gerza, 71
    of Gerzean Period, 63
    Hemamieh, 70
    Hierakonpolis (Nekhen), 61, 64, 65-67, 77-78, 276, 277
    kilns, 69-70
    Lower Egypt, Cairo region, 71-74
    Lower Egypt, the Delta, 74-76
    of Maadi culture, 17, 61, 71, 72-74, 76
    Matmar, 71
    Merimde Beni-salama site, 72, 74-75
    of Middle Egypt, 70-71
    Minshat Abu Omar, 75
    Minshat el Kom el Ahmar, 71
    Nagadan, 60, 63-70, 76-79
    of Nagada Ia-b Period, 65
    North Town, Nagada, 67
    pottery and ceramic ware, 72-73, 75, 76
    Qasr Qarun, 71
    Qau el Kebir, 71
    of Semainean Period, 68
    Sharqiya province, 74-75
    settlement types, 276, 277-278
    South Town, Nagada, 64, 67
    Tell el Fara'in/Buto, 75, 76
    Tell el-Farkha, 75
    Tell Ibrahim Awad site, 75
    temple sites, 65, 66-67, 69
    Umm el-Oa'ab, 70
    Upper Egypt (Nagadan Culture), 60, 63-70, 76-79
    Wadi Digla, 72
  Prehistoric, 15-16
  Protodynastic Period, 75
  state formation in, 76-79
  Upper/Lower Egypt unification, 77-79, 277

Ejutla region, Mexico, 156
El-Amra, Egypt, 69
Elders, in lineage societies, 4
El-Khattara, Egypt, 67
El-Lahun, Egypt, 62
El-Mahasna, Egypt, 69
El Mirador, Mexico, 172
El Niño, 17-18, 19
El-Omari, Egypt, 71-72, 73-74, 276
Erlitou Culture, 87, 90, 91n.
Euphrates River Valley, 44
  "colonial" sites, 46, 56, 276
  flooding of, 12
Exchange networks, relationship to redistributive organization, 12
Ezbet el-Qerdahi, Egypt, 76

Famine, in Mesopotamia, 13
Fayum, Egypt, 71
Fenitian food rationing system, 11
Floods
  in Andean Region, 17, 18
  El Niño-related, 17, 18
  effect on Henan Longshan Culture sites, 93-94, 102-103
  in Mesopotamia, 12
Food redistribution patterns: see Redistribution patterns
Formative communities, of Mesopotamian lowlands, 14-15

Gaocheng, China, 89, 91, 92
Gerza, Egypt, 71
Gonda, India, 4
Gouro, food redistribution system of, 4
Grain, redistribution of, 10
Gulf Coast, exchange network with Teotihuacan, 25
Gun, 104
Guti, 14

Habuba Kabira, Euphrates River Valley, 276
Hacinebi, Turkey, 44
Hamman et-Turkman, Turkey, 44
Harappan civilization, collapse of, 14

Hassek Höyük, Euphrates River Valley, 276
Hassuna, Mesopotamia, 6
Hawaii, redistributive hierarchies, 4-5
Hedionda-style ceramic ware, 234
Hegemonic state, definition of, 230
Hegemony model, of Tiwanaku territorial influence, 229-230, 239
Hemamieh, Egypt, 70, 276
Henan Longshan Culture, walled settlements of: see Yellow River Valley, China, Henan Longshan walled settlements
Hierakonpolis (Nekhen), Egypt, 61, 64, 65-67, 77-78, 276, 277
Hierarchical societies, chiefdoms in, 4
Hieroglyphics, 140, 147, 152, 153, 157, 176
Hierve el Agua, Mexico, 145
Honcopampa, Peru, 210
Hougang, China, 87-88, 89, 96, 278
Hoya de San Nicolás basin, Mexico, 26
Hu (Diospolis Parva), Egypt, 65, 68-69, 77
Huaca del Loro, Peru, 209-210
Huamachuco, Peru, 201, 211
Huananga Basin, Peru, 188, 195
Huangdi, 104
Huanta Basin, Peru, 188
Huánuco Pampa, Peru, 9, 15
  craft specialization, 20
  redistributional activities, 20, 23
  state-operated warehouses, 20
Huari, Peru, 181-227
  abandonment of, 207
  architectural styles, 282, 283
    chronological sequence of, 185-186
    relationship to administrative function, 181
  Churucana Phase, 185, 189-191, 217
  circular and "D"-shaped buildings, 197-198, 209-210, 219
  craft specialization, 282
  megalithic tombs, 215

Huari, Peru (Cont.)
　militarism and military elite, 106, 181, 183-184, 210, 211, 212, 215
　Moraduchayuq Phase, 185, 196, 220, 282-283
　　Cheqo Wasi site, 207-208
　　civic core, 200
　　food consumption patterns, 206
　　luxury goods assemblage, 206
　　new architectural complex, 203-204
　　orthogonal cellular architectural style, 201-205, 206-207, 214-215, 220
　　patio group architectural style, 202-206, 207
　　population growth, 195
　　pottery, 200, 207, 208
　　residential area expansion, 200
　　semisubterranean temple, 199-200, 202, 203-204
　　stone architecture, 198
　　sunken courtyards, 196-197
　orthogonal cellular architecture, 212
　　militaristic basis of, 106, 201, 212, 215
　　of Moraduchayuq Phase, 201-205, 206-207, 214-215, 220
　　of provincial administrative centers, 210, 212, 213-214
　Orthogonal Cellular Architecture Horizon, 211-214, 215
　patio group architectural style, 202-206, 207, 210
　political and nationalistic interpretations of, 182-185, 188
　provincial administrative centers
　　architectural styles, 209-214
　　Cerro Baul, 210
　　Honcopampa, 210
　　Huaca del Loro, 209-210
　　Jargampata, 213-214
　　Jincamocco, 212
　　of Moraduchayuq Phase, 213-214

Huari, Peru (Cont.)
　provincial administrative centers (Cont.)
　　Orthogonal Cellular Architecture Horizon, 211-214
　　Pikillacta, 212, 214
　　pottery, 210-211, 212, 213
　　Viracochapampa, 212-213, 214
　Quebrada de Ocros Phase, 185, 194-199, 201, 207, 282
　　architectural styles, 196-199
　　at Cerro Baul, 210
　　pottery, 195-196, 199
　　temples, 195, 197-198
　　Verachayoq Moqo walled compound, 197-198
　relationship with Huamachuco, 201, 211
　relationship with Moche, 182
　relationship with Pachacamac, 182
　relationship with Tiwanaku, 212
　Royac Perja Phase, 185, 221, 282
　　architectural styles, 208-209, 215-216
　　pottery, 209
　rural-urban migration into, 282
　site description, 186-188
　theocratic leadership of, 106, 215
　Vista Alegre Phase, 185, 191-194, 217
　　architectural styles, 192-194
　　pottery, 192, 193
　　settlement types, 191-192
　　Sullu Cruz Community, 193
　　West Huarpa Community, 192-194, 195, 196, 198, 209, 214
Huarochiri, Peru, 235
Huehuetéotl (deity), 119
Huitzo, Mexico, 142
Huruquilla-style ceramicware, 234

Ichabama, Peru, 212
Icla-Chullpamoko, Bolivia, 231
Ideological power, 106, 138, 139, 140
　at Arslantepe-Malatya, Turkey, 49, 56
　at Monte Albán, Oaxaca Valley, Mexico, 150-159

INDEX

Incas
  Peruvian nationalism and, 182
  redistribution system of, 10, 15
  storage facilities of, 20
  unification of Central Andes by, 19-20
India, Oudh society, 4
Indus Valley, 97, 284
Iraq, irrigation use in, 12-13
Iri-Hor, Pharaoah, 70
Irrigation, 6, 12-13, 149
Ix Chel, 178

Jachakala complex, Oruru, Bolivia, 232-233, 237, 240
Jargampata, Peru, 213-214
Jebel Aruba, Euphrates River Valley, 276
Jincamocco, Peru, 211
Jordan desert, 15

Ka, Pharaoh, 70
Kaminaljuyú, Mexico, 25
Khafajah, Mesopotamia, 9
Khattara, el-, Egypt, 67
Khuzistan, 10
Kinich Ahau, 178
Kinship ties
  in Andean Region exchange networks, 19
  architectural symbolization of, 178
  as territorial organization basis, 172-173

Lahun, el-, Egypt, 62
Lake Texcoco, Mexico, 26
Lake Titicaca, 18
Land acquisition, in territorial tribute states, 8
Léon, Cieza de, 195
Lerma Basin, Mexico, 26
Lima, Peru, 235
Lineage societies
  elders in, 4
  Mesopotamian, 6
Llamas, 230, 232, 237-238, 240, 283
Loma Torremote, Mexico, 21

Lukurmata, Bolivia, 232, 237, 283
Lupaca *señorío*, 237

Ma'adi, Egypt, 17, 60, 71, 72-74 76
Mahasna, el-, Egypt, 69
Mallku *señorío*, 237
Mamani phase sites, Bolivia, 251, 262
Marca Huamachuco, Peru, 210, 212
Markets, in territorial tribute states, 8
Marriage, 173
Matacapan, Mexico, 25
Matmar, Egypt, 71
Mayan cities
  as models of cosmos, 281-282
  temple organizations of, 284
Mayan culture
  Classic Period, 171, 172-173
  Late Pre-Classic Period, 172
  redistribution patterns of, 7
  religious beliefs and deities of, 106, 174, 177-178, 281-282
  territorial organization of, 172-173
Memphis, Egypt, 59, 79
Mengzhuang, China, 89, 96
Merchants, in territorial tribute states, 8
Mérida, Yucatan, 169-170
Merimde Beni-salama, Egypt, 72, 74-75, 276
Mesopotamia
  aridification in, 13-14
  centralized storage systems, 6, 275
  climatic change in, 12-14
  corporate households, 5
  Early Bronze Age, 11, 13
  Early Dynastic Period, 8, 9
  Formative communities, 14-15
  Hassuna Period, 275
  interaction with Anatolia, 41, 43-44, 56, 275
  Late Chalcolithic Period, 11
  lineage societies, 6
  metallurgy development, 7, 9
  proto-Sumerian cities, 12
  redistributive patterns, 5-15
    Neolithic, 6

Mesopotamia (Cont.)
  redistributive patterns (Cont.)
    temple organizations, 5-8, 9, 10, 22, 284
    territorial tributary state, 6, 8-15
    during Ubaid phase, 5-6
    during Uruk phase, 5-6, 7
    Third Dynasty of Ur, 13-14
    Ubaid phase, 5-6, 10, 275
    urban population densities, 97
    Uruk phase, 5-6, 7, 9, 10, 22, 275
Metallurgy, Mesopotamian, 7, 9
Mezquital Valley, Mexico, 27
Miahuatlan Valley, Mexico, 156
Minoan civilization, 14
Minshat Abu Omar, Egypt, 75
Minshat el Kom el Ahmar, Egypt, 71
Mirador, El, Mexico, 172
Mixteca Alta region, Mexico, 156
Mixteca Baja region, Mexico, 156
Moche state, relationship to Huari, Peru, 182
Moche Valley, Peru, 18
Mojocoya, Bolivia, 232
Mojocoya-style ceramic ware, 231, 232
Monte Albán: see Oxaca Valley, Mexico, Late/Terminal Formative Period Monte Albán site
Monumental architecture
  as political power symbol, 169-179, 279, 280
  See also under specific archaeological sites
Moquequa, Peru, influence of Tiwanaku on, 25, 234-240
Morelos Valley, Mexico, 111
Motecuhzoma (Aztec emperor), 15
Mount Tonalan, Mexico, 123

Nagadan Culture sites, Egypt, 60, 63-70, 76-79
Náhuat myths, 122, 123-124
Narmer, Pharaoah, 65, 70
Nazca Valley, Peru, 209-210, 211
Nazcoid (Nascoide)-style, of ceramic ware, 231, 232

Negev desert, 15
Nezahualcoyotl (Aztec emperor), 15
Nile River Valley, 15-16, 17, 60
Nome, 8
Nubia, 62, 77, 78
Nubt, Nagada, 277

Oaxaca Valley, Mexico, Late/Terminal Formative Period Monte Albán site, 133-168
  actor-based theory of, 134, 135-138, 158
  administrative hierarchy, 279
  agricultural practices, 142-143, 146, 159
    piedmont strategy, 143-144, 148-150, 159, 279
  ballcourt, 147, 154
  burials, 140-141
  Classic Period, 158
  coercive power base, 149-150, 278
  conquest slabs, 152, 154, 155, 156, 279
  corvée labor, 142, 144, 146, 152, 159
  craft specialization, 145, 146, 147, 149, 159
  Cuicatlán Cañada region conquest by, 145-146, 156, 279
  Cuilapan site, 145
  cultural ecology theory of, 135-136
  Dainzú site, 145
  danzantes, 153-154, 155, 156, 157, 279
  deities, 153
  ecological systems theory of, 135-136
  elite-administrative precincts, 142, 146-147
  Ejutla region, 156
  hieroglyphics, 140, 147, 152, 157
  Hierve el Agua site, 145
  household economic strategies, 146, 279
  Huitzo site, 142
  ideological and ritual power base, 150-159, 158-159, 278, 279
  irrigation system, 149

Oaxaca Valley, Mexico, Late/Terminal Formative Period Monte Albán (*Cont.*)
  Lambityeco site, 145
  markets, 146, 149
  Miahuatlán Valley site, 156
  military elite and militarism, 140, 145-146, 147, 153-158, 159, 279
  Mixteca Alta region, 156
  monumental architecture, 142, 143, 278-279
    Main Plaza, 144-145, 147, 153-156
    North Platform, 144
    palaces, 142
    South Platform, 144
    temples, 147
  population, 143, 146, 149
  population carrying capacity, 148
  pottery, 141, 145
  power consolidation, 148-159
  provisioning system, 149, 150
  reciprocal power base, 148-149
  religious beliefs and practices, 21
    human sacrifice, 150, 151, 157
  residential structures, 141-142
  ritual calendar, 153
  ritual paraphernalia, 145, 146, 147
  salt production, 145
  San Agustín de las Juntas site, 142
  San José Mogote site, 142, 145, 147
  social heterogeneity, 145-148, 279
  status inequality, 140-145, 278-279
  Tehuacan Valley site, 156
  Tierras Largas site, 141-142
  Tomaltepec site, 141-142
  tortilla development, 146
  tribute payments, 149-150, 154
Observatories, 19
Occupational specialization, 6; *see also* Craft specialization
Oil, rationing of, 10
Omari, el-, Egypt, 71-72, 73-74
Omereque, Bolivia, 231-232
Omo, Peru, colonization by Tiwanaku, 236

Oruro, Bolivia
  influence of Tiwanaku on, 232-233, 240
  Jachakala complex, 232-233, 237, 240
Oudh society, 4
Oxkintok, Yucatan, 174, 175-179
  ballcourt, 175-176, 177
  geographical location, 169-170
  governor, 176
  hieroglyphics, 176
  marriage patterns, 282
  militarism, 282
  as model of cosmos, 282
  monumental architecture, 174-177
    political power symbolism of, 279
    pyramids, 175, 176, 178
    religious symbolism of, 177-178
    Satunsat, 170, 176, 177-178
  political and territorial influence of, 282

Pacajes *señorío*, 237
Pachacamac, relationship to Huari, Peru, 181-182
Palace-based redistribution systems, 8, 9
  Aztec, 15
  Egyptian, 16-17
  Incan, 15
  Minoan, 14
Palenque, temples of, 174
Pátzcuaro basin, Mexico, 26
Pérez, Bolivia, 232
Pharaohs, 16, 177
  Aha, 70
  Akhenaten, 62
  Iri-Hor, 70
  Ka, 70
  Narmer, 65, 70
  redistribution role of, 16-17
  Tuthmose III, 65
Pikillacta, Peru, 212, 214
Pingliantai, China, 89, 96, 97, 98-99, 100, 278
Pochteca, 8

Political leadership, collective, 5
Popocatépetl volcano, Mexico, 110, 280
Popul Vuh, 175-176
Pottery
  'Amuq F Period, 76
  Badarian, 70
  Chakipampa-style, 195-196, 207, 209, 211, 213
  Chaqui-style, 234
  Dupont-style, 234
  Egyptian, of Predynastic Period, 70, 72-73
  fast-wheel-produced, 7, 9, 10-11
  Hedionda-style, 234
  Huruquilla-style, 234
  Mojocoya-style, 231, 232
  Nazca/Nazcoid-style, 195, 209, 231, 232
  Ocros-style, 195-196, 207, 208, 209, 213
  Tiwanaku-style, 231, 232
  Tupuraya-style, 231
  Uruquilla-style, 234
  Vinaque-style, 207, 208, 211, 213
  Yampara-style, 231
  Yura-style, 234
  See also under specific archaeological sites
Power
  coercive, 138, 139, 140, 149-150
  ideological, 138, 139, 140, 150-159
  monumental architecture as symbol of, 169-179
  reciprocal, 138-139, 140, 148-149
  as response to external threat, 156-158, 159
Prestige goods, as power basis, 151, 152
Profit, in redistributive organizations, 9
Proyecto Wila Jawira, 246-247
Puebla-Tlaxcala Region, Mexico, 121
Pukara, Bolivia, 237
"Pulsating galactic polities," 172
"Pyramidal system" of government, 172

Qasr Qarun, Egypt, 71
Qau el Kebir, Egypt, 71
Quelccaya ice cap, 18, 19
Quitor, "Señorío de," 234

Rajakhstan lake pollen sequences, 14
Rationing, as food redistribution system, 9-10
Reciprocal power, 138-139, 140, 148-149
Redistribution patterns
  archaeological indicators of, 8-10
  at Arslantepe-Malayta, Turkey, 48, 49, 276
  asymmetrical, 4
  circular, 9
  Mayan, 7
  Mesopotamian, 7
  Mesopotamian, 5-15
    temple organizations, 5-8, 9, 10
    territorial tributary state, 6, 8-15
    Ubaid phase, 5-6
    Uruk phase, 5-6,7
  Oudh, 4
  rationing, 9-10
  as reciprocal power basis, 148
  See also Storage, centralized
Religious ritual, as power base, 150-153, 158-159
Roots of the Generations, The, 89

Saharan desert, 15-16
San Agustín de las Juntas, 142
San José Mogote, Mexico, 145, 147
San Pedro de Atacama, Peru, influence of Tiwanaku on, 232-233, 235, 239, 240
Saqqara, Egypt, 59
Semainean Period, of Predynastic Egypt, 68
Sharqiya, Egypt, 74-75
Shining Path guerrillas, 184
Sierra de Puebla, *náhuat* myths of, 122, 123-124
Sillumocco, Peru, influence of Tiwanaku on, 232, 237, 239

Slavery, 99-100
Social change
  actor-based theory of, 134, 135-138, 158, 278
  cultural ecology theory of, 135-136, 148
  ecological systems theory of, 135-136, 148
Social complexity, relationship to social identity, 137-138
Social identity, actor-based theory of, 137-138
Social inequality
  definition of, 138
  relationship to social identity, 137, 138
Social organization, actor-based theory of, 136
Social status, power and wealth as determinants of, 137
Social stratification, relationship to redistributive organization, 12
Soil salinization, 12-13, 14
Sonjo, 4
Spondylus princeps, as climatic indicator, 19
State, definition of, 138
Storage, centralized, 12
  in Aztec society, 15
  in Mesopotamia, 6, 275
  in Predynastic Egypt, 16-17, 61, 11
  as redistributive society indicator, 9
  at Teotihuacan, Mexico, 22, 23
Subsistence activities
  actor-based theory of, 136
  occupational specialization in, 6
Sumer
  Akkadian Period, 8
  desertification of, 13
  Early Dynastic Period, 8
  food redistribution patterns in, 9-10
  territorial tribute state development in, 8
Sun-god (Mayan), 106, 177-178, 281-282

Surplus concentration, relationship to redistributive organization, 12
Susa, 53-54
Syro-Anatolia, 43
  Chalcolithic Period, 44
  interaction with Mesopotamia, 41, 43, 44
  Late Uruk Period, 44, 44, 45, 46
  Ubaid Period, 44
  See also Eastern Anatolia

Tayasal, Mexico, 171
Tehuacan Valley, Mexico, 156
Tell Brak, Turkey, 47
Tell el Amarna (Akhetaten), Egypt, 62-63
Tell el Fara'in/Buto, Egypt, 75, 76
Tell el-Farkha, Egypt, 75
Tell Ibrahim Awad, Egypt, 75
Temple-based redistribution systems, 5-8, 9, 10, 14
  Eastern Anatolian, 284
  influence on social relations, 284
  Mesopotamian, 6
Tenochtitlan, Mexico, 110, 171
Teotihuacan, Mexico, 21-27, 109-131
  administrative structure, clay seal use, 22
  apartment compounds, 23, 114, 115-116, 280
    Atetelco, 114, 122
    Bidasoa, 114
    Ciudadela, 23-24, 112, 120, 125
    El Cuartel, 114
    Las Ventilla, 114, 118, 119
    Oztoyahualco, 114-117, 118-119
    Oztoyahualco 15B:N6W3, 23, 114, 116-117, 118, 119
    San Antonio Las Palmas, 114, 116
    Teopancazo, 116
    Tepantitla, 114, 115, 116, 117
    Tetitla, 114, 115
    Tlajinga, 33, 114, 116, 117, 118, 119
    Tlamimilopa, 114, 118

Teotihuacan, Mexico (*Cont.*)
  apartment compounds (*Cont.*)
    Xolalpan, 114, 117, 118, 119
    Zacuala, 118-119, 124, 125
  burials, 118-119, 124, 125
  centralized storage, 22, 23
  Classic Period, 22
  collapse of, 26, 27, 126, 280, 281
  colonies, 25
  craft specialization, 21, 114, 117-118, 120
  Cuicuilco site, 21
  demographic concentration, 110-111
  diachronicity of, 125-126
  East-West Avenue, 113
  environmental impact of, 27
  exchange network, 22, 24-25, 120, 121
    colonies' involvement in, 25
    deterioration of, 26
  floral and faunal remains, 22, 116-117
  household organization, 114-116, 117-118, 119
  Loma Torremote site, 21
  as manufacturing center, 120, 280
  Merchants' *Barrios*, 25, 120
  Miccaotli phase, 280
  monumental architecture, 111-112, 125
    Great Compound, 23-24
    as political power symbol, 279, 280
    Pyramid of the Moon, 24, 111, 112, 120, 125, 126, 280
    Pyramid of the Sun, 111, 112, 113, 122, 123-124, 125, 126
    religious basis of, 279
    Temple of Agriculture, 22
    Temple of the Feathered Serpent, 26, 112, 113, 121-122, 126, 281
    temple plazas, 280
  Mythological Animals' Mural, 26, 121-122, 281

Teotihuacan, Mexico (*Cont.*)
  Oaxaca *Barrio*, 120
  obsidian industry, 24, 25, 116, 117, 120
  as pilgrimage site, 280
  as political center, 121-122
  population concentration, 253
  pottery, 117, 280-281
  as redistribution center, 121
  religious beliefs and practices, 119-120, 122-124, 125, 280
    deities, 22, 119-120, 122, 123, 126
    food redistribution, 23-24, 121
    priests, 21, 22, 23, 24, 25, 26
    ritual calendar, 124
    ritual meals, 23-24
    sacrificial consecrations, 121
  rural-urban migration into, 25-26, 279
  as sacred capital, 21, 122-124
  as strategic site, 110
  Street of the Dead, 111, 113, 120, 121-122, 123, 125, 126
  stucco use, 27
  Techinantitla military ward, 122
  Tlapacoya site, 21
  Tzacualli Period, 280-281
  volcanic eruptions, 110, 280
  Xolalpan Period, 22-23, 281
Tepe Gawra, 44, 53
Territorial model, of Tiwanaku territorial influence, 229-230
Territorial tributary state, 6,8-15
  definition of, 229-230
  Mesoamerican, 26
  origin of, 8
  Sumerian, 8
Texcoco, Lake, Mexico, 26
Tierras Largas, Mexico, 141-142
Tigris River, flooding by, 12
Tikal, Mexico, 172, 174
Titicaca, Lake, Bolivia, 18
Titicaca Basin, Bolivia, 247, 267
  Aymara Kingdoms of, 259
  See also Tiwanaku, Bolivia

INDEX

Tiwanaku, Bolivia
- administrative structure, 257, 258-259
- agricultural production, 237, 240, 257, 258, 259
  - deterioration of, 238
- agricultural production model of, 246-247, 264, 265, 266-267, 276, 284
- *altiplano* location of, 247-249
- *altiplano* model of, 107, 245-246, 263, 265-266, 267
- autochtonous model of, 183, 266-267, 276, 284
- as Bolivian national identity symbol, 182-183
- as ceremonial center, 254
- Classic Period, 255-257
- collapse of, 18-19, 238-239, 240-241, 284
- core region, 237-239
- craft specialization, 237, 238, 240, 263, 265-266, 267
- Decadent Tiahuanaco sites, 257-259, 266, 267
- elite residences, 237
- environment and ecology of, 247-249
- Formative Period sites, 249-252, 265-266
  - ceramic ware, 253
  - of Chiripa culture, 250-253, 262, 264, 265-266
  - Early Formative, 249-253, 262
  - Lukurmata proto-urban center, 253
  - Mamani phase sites, 251, 252
  - Pajchiri proto-urban center, 253
- ideological power base, 236
- Late Prehistoric Period, 238
- Lukurmata as secondary center of, 232, 237, 283
- mercantile production system, 237-238
- minipolities of, 237, 238
- monumental architecture, 20-21, 237

Tiwanaku, Bolivia (*Cont.*)
- political and territorial influence of, 229-243
  - on Azapa Valley, Chile, 234-236, 240
  - on Cerro Baúl, Peru, 210
  - on Cochabama Valley, Bolivia, 231-232, 238-239, 240, 283
  - colonization model of, 230, 236-237
  - direct control mechanism models of, 230, 236-237, 240
  - hegemony model of, 229-230, 239
  - indirect model of, 230
  - llama use and, 230, 232, 237-238, 240, 283
  - *mitmaqkuna* model of, 230
  - on Moquequa, Peru, 25, 234-235, 236-237, 238-239, 240
  - on Oruro, Bolivia, 232-233, 240, 283
  - on San Pedro de Atacama, Chile, 233-234, 235, 239, 240, 283
  - on Sillumocco, Peru, 232, 237, 239, 283
  - snuff paraphernalia complex and, 232, 233, 239
  - territorial versus hegemonic models of, 229-230, 239
  - textile complex and, 232, 233, 238
- population density, 237, 257, 258
- population re-organization, 259
- Post-Tiawanaku sites, 259-260, 262
- pottery, 231, 249, 250, 259, 264, 265-266
- Pre-Tiwanaku sites, 249, 250
- pyramid of Akapana, 18, 20-21
- rebellions against, 236-237, 238-239
- redistribution patterns, 257
- relationship to Huari, Peru, 181-182
- sacrificial offerings, 18
- social stratification, 257
- TM-558 site, 267
- unification of Central Andes by, 19-20

Tiwanaku, Bolivia (*Cont.*)
  vertical archipelago model of, 245-246, 263, 264-265, 267
Tlaloc (deity), 119, 122, 126
Tlapacoya, Mexico, 21
Tlatelolco, Mexico, 24
Tlaxcala Valley, Mexico, 111
Toluca Valley, Mexico, 111
Tomaltepec, Mexico, 141-142
Tonacatecuhtli (deity), 126
Tonalan, Mount, Mexico, 123
Tortilla, development of, 146
Totoquihuatzin (Aztec emperor), 15
Transcaucasian groups, migration into Arslantepe-Malatya, Turkey, 276
Tres Cerritos, Mexico, 25
Tula, Mexico, 121
Tumilaca, 237
Tuthmose III, Pharaoh, 65

Ubaid phase, 5-6, 10, 275
Umm Dabaghiyah, Mesopotamia, 6
Umm el-Oa'ab, Egypt, 70
Ur, Third Dynasty of, 13-14
Urban revolution, 6
Urban society, definition of, 5
Uruk, Turkey, 53-54
Uruk-Jemdet Nasr Period, 7
Uruk Phase, 5-6, 7, 9, 10, 22, 275
Uruk-Warka, 7
Uruquilla-style ceramic ware, 234
Uxmal, Yucatan, 169-170, 177

Venus (planet), 175-176
Vertical archipelago model, of state development, 14-15, 19, 245-246, 263, 264-265, 267
Viracochapampa, Peru, 212-213
Volcanic eruptions
  in Mesopotamia, 13
  Popocatépetl, Mexico, 110, 280
  Xitle, Mexico, 110, 280

Wadi Digla, Egypt, 72
Walas, 176

Wangchenggang, China, 41, 88-96
  Eastern City, 91, 93, 94
  exchange network, 99
  flood damage to, 93-94, 102-103
  geographical location, 89, 92
  hangtu construction technology of, 91, 94, 95, 94, 95, 100-101
  human skeletal remains, 95-96, 99-100, 103
  metal fragment remains, 96, 99
  military and political functions, 103-104
  as "palace-city," 102
  population density, 97-98
  pottery, 96
  slavery in, 99-100
  total area, 91, 93-94, 97
  Western City, 91, 93-96
  as Xia dynasty capital, 89, 91, 104, 278
Warfare
  as power basis, 156-158, 159
  relationship to religion, 157
Warka, 22
Wealth accumulation, through military conquest, 8
Wheat cultivation, in Iraq, 12-13
Wudu River, China, 89, 91

Xia dynasty, 87, 89, 91, 99-100, 104
Xitle volcano, Mexico, 110, 280

Yamobamba, Peru, 212
Yampara-style ceramicware, 231
Yangcheng, China, 89, 91, 104
Yangshao, China, 102, 103
Yanshi, China, 94
Yarim Tepé, 6
Yellow River Valley, China, Henan Longshan Culture walled settlements
  Bronze Age sites, 96, 98-99
  Chalcolithic sites, 99
  chronological sequence, 90
  craft specialization, 98-99

Yellow River Valley, China, Henan Longshan Culture walled settlements (*Cont.*)
  Erlitou Culture sites, 87, 90, 91n., 278
  hangtu construction technology of, 87, 93-96, 98, 100-103
  Haojiatia site, 89, 96, 278
  Hougang site, 87-88, 89, 96, 278
  Mengzhuang site, 89, 96
  as "palace-cities," 102
  Pingliangtai site, 89, 96, 97, 98-99, 100, 278
  population density, 97-98, 103
  secular versus religious origin of, 101, 102
  social stratification in, 99-102
  topography, 97
  total area, 97
  as urban centers, 102-104
  Wangchenggang site, 88-96
    ceramic ware, 96
    Eastern City, 91, 93, 94
    exchange network, 99
    flood damage to, 93-94, 102-103
    geographical location, 89, 92

Yellow River Valley, China, Henan Longshan Culture walled settlements (*Cont.*)
  Wangchenggang site (*Cont.*)
    hangtu construction technology of, 91, 94, 95, 100-102
    human skeletal remains, 95-96, 99-100, 103
    metal fragment remains, 96, 99
    military and political functions of, 103-104
    as "palace-city," 102
    population density, 97-98
    slavery in, 99-100
    total area, 91, 93-94, 97
    Western City, 91, 93-96
  Xia dynasty, 87, 89, 91, 99-100, 104, 278
  Yangcheng site, 91, 92, 104
  Yangshao sites, 102, 103
  Zhou Culture, 89, 90, 91
Ying River, China, 91
Yu, 89, 91, 104
Yura-style ceramic ware, 234

Zacapu basin, Mexico, 26
Zapotec, 152, 153
Zhou Culture, 89, 90, 91